Studies in Childhood and Youth

Series Editors
Afua Twum-Danso Imoh
University of Sheffield
Sheffield, UK

Nigel Thomas
University of Central Lancashire
Preston, UK

Spyros Spyrou
European University Cyprus
Nicosia, Cyprus

Penny Curtis
University of Sheffield
Sheffield, UK

This well-established series embraces global and multi-disciplinary scholarship on childhood and youth as social, historical, cultural and material phenomena. With the rapid expansion of childhood and youth studies in recent decades, the series encourages diverse and emerging theoretical and methodological approaches. We welcome proposals which explore the diversities and complexities of children's and young people's lives and which address gaps in the current literature relating to childhoods and youth in space, place and time.

Studies in Childhood and Youth will be of interest to students and scholars in a range of areas, including Childhood Studies, Youth Studies, Sociology, Anthropology, Geography, Politics, Psychology, Education, Health, Social Work and Social Policy.

More information about this series at
http://www.palgrave.com/gp/series/14474

Geetha Marcus

Gypsy and Traveller Girls

Silence, Agency and Power

Geetha Marcus
University of Glasgow
Glasgow, UK

Studies in Childhood and Youth
ISBN 978-3-030-03702-4   ISBN 978-3-030-03703-1   (eBook)
https://doi.org/10.1007/978-3-030-03703-1

Library of Congress Control Number: 2018961183

This Palgrave Macmillan imprint is published by the registered company Springer Nature Switzerland AG
The registered company address is: Gewerbestrasse 11, 6330 Cham, Switzerland

Preface

As an academic, former teacher and headteacher who has worked in the state and independent sectors in Scottish education, and as a British citizen of minority ethnic origin, I have developed a long-standing interest in circumstances that might adversely impact on the educational experiences of members of minority groups. It was initially through my work as a teacher engaging with Gypsy and Traveller children and their families in the north of Scotland, that I developed some first-hand knowledge of how their experiences in and out of school influences their education and social outlook.

Early in my teaching career, a young boy in my class announced that his grandfather was a storyteller and asked if he could come to tell the class his stories during Story Telling Festival Week. A dapper looking grandfather in a fine tweed jacket and cap, with gold rings on his fingers, walked in and introduced himself as Stanley Robertson. Little did I know then, what a famous storyteller and singer he was. Stanley entertained the children with his wild, wonderful tales and sang songs. He came to see us several times when I was a teacher in this private school. One day, at a School Assembly in which he was performing, a senior teacher took me aside and whispered, 'We don't have folk like him in our school'. At the time, I had no idea what she meant or why she would have said such a thing. He was a fantastic storyteller and the children loved him. She was being derogatory, and I sensed racist, but I could not understand why one white person had a problem with another white person. Stanley never returned to that school and it was the last time I saw him. It was in conducting my doctoral study that I learned that the Elphinstone Institute at the University of Aberdeen had archived work of Stanley Robertson, Scottish Traveller, storyteller, ballad singer and piper. I tried to make contact again, but discovered he passed away in 2009.

I also discovered that relatively little research has been undertaken on Scottish Gypsies and Travellers, who have lived in Scotland since the twelfth century, making them one of Britain's oldest nomadic communities. Sometimes referred to as the 'mist people' (Neat 1996: vii; Whyte 2001: 163; Smith 2002; Stewart 2008), Gypsy and Traveller lives are cloaked in invisibility. Although ostensibly 'white' and bearing little physical distinctiveness from the majority Scottish population, Gypsies and Travellers are often visibly absent while in plain sight, yet pathologically present in the Scottish imagination (Mirza 2015: 3). The indigenous perspective is captured through the rich oral tradition within Gypsy and Traveller communities, but this 'insider' worldview on the lives and experiences of Gypsies and Travellers in Scotland is not well recognised or appreciated in scholarly studies. The version of history we are taught is largely stories of heroes and villains, history that takes place in grand buildings and battlefields. It is often silent about our shared, inner and domestic histories, the narratives of the rest of us, the everyday battles of those who live quietly and privately in anonymous terraced houses, in caravans or on the margins. In addition, the veracity of what is written and said about minority groups by members of dominant groups ought to be questioned and tested against indigenous accounts (Schröter 2013; Mirza 2015; Surdu 2016; Matache 2017).

This book is important because it centres the voices of Gypsy and Traveller girls for the first time. There is currently no research that explores how girls and young women from Gypsy and Traveller communities fare in Scottish schools, and what they think of their experiences. The Scottish Government's Race Equality Statement (2009) accepts that Gypsies and Travellers are 'a particularly discriminated against and marginalised group'. Within education, research by Wilkin et al. (2009) indicates that Gypsy and Traveller children are the lowest achieving minority group in the United Kingdom.

It is against this backdrop that this book seeks to explore how Gypsy and Traveller girls frame their educational experiences, and to address a gap in the literature in which their experiences are misrecognised and erased through non-recognition. It offers space for their gendered voices to be heard, an 'oppositional gaze' (hooks 1992) to that of the dominant voices of politicians, policy makers, headteachers, teachers, activists, parents and families. It raises awareness of how these young people are caught at the harsh end and at times suffer or negotiate residual trauma associated with the endless cycle of cultural violence against a community marginalised for centuries. Crucially, the girls' stories also highlight their agency in the private spaces of home and the public spaces of education. Their coping strategies, including self-segregation, epitomise a gesture of resistance toward the oppression of minorities by the doubly intensive gendering and racialisation of women.

Their narratives contribute to our understanding of Gypsy and Traveller education in general, how their needs are not being met and why. Whilst in the spirit of inclusion, they are not formally segregated from State schools, the very nature of the education system and the people who work within it serve to physically and emotionally alienate and disempower through institutional and individual racism, ageism, gender and class discrimination. This book reveals that our education systems and their often laudable policies, which form the cradle of ideas, like inclusion, equity and excellence, can actually exacerbate exclusion, inequity and flawed deficiency.

I am not a Gypsy or Traveller and would be considered 'a gaujo' (outsider) by these communities. This book does not pretend to represent, replace or undermine the authenticity of the lives of Gypsies and Travellers. Following Spivak's (1988) advice, this book 'represents' the experiences and perspectives of the Gypsy and Traveller girls I met, their aspirations and the challenges they faced. It is a collection and exploration of the girls' accounts of their lives written from a gaujo's perspective, but as I explain later, I was also an empathetic observer, 'consciously partial' (Mies 1983: 126).

Our comprehension of Gypsies and Travellers in Scotland remains underdeveloped for several reasons. The hegemonic interpretations of Gypsies and Travellers are riddled with misperceptions and racialised assumptions that all Scottish Gypsies and Travellers are the same, that their experiences are largely negative, that they are poor and require access to benefits and that they are not a minority ethnic group, just a troublesome class of Scots (Clark 2001, 2006; Coxhead 2007). Given this complex background, the Economic and Social Research Council together with the Scottish Government provided joint funding that has culminated in this study to enhance understanding of Scottish Gypsy and Traveller lives. The book is therefore made possible by their generous funding, and for identifying the need to improve understanding of the lives of Travelling Peoples in Scotland. I was pleased to use my experience in education together with a longstanding interest in issues concerning marginalisation (my own included) to explore the voices of Gypsy and Traveller girls. This labyrinthine research journey first as a doctoral student at Edinburgh university, and then as a Lecturer at the University of Glasgow, continuing to develop my research and working with Gypsy and Traveller communities, has been both arduous and exciting.

This study presented real demands that I had never directly faced before in my professional life. Because of the mistrust which has grown up over generations between Gypsies, Travellers and the settled community, influenced by issues around rejection and cultural difference, it took twelve months to establish a dialogue with both parents and the girls, before permissions were granted to undertake 13 semi-structured interviews which form the heart of this research, and a focus group discussion with four other Gypsy and Traveller girls. I also conducted discussions and interviews with 30 stakeholders, including teachers and policy makers, who provided valuable background information. Gaining access via stakeholders in third sector organisations who worked with these communities was instructive. For many reasons which I will discuss in the book, there were walls of silence and barriers that were difficult to overcome.

The book is divided into eight chapters, the first of which introduces the subject and establishes the perimeters of the study. In Chapter 2, I offer a critical overview of the background historical knowledge and the main themes present in the literature on Gypsies and Travellers in the UK and in Scotland, and how both sit within the European context. I provide an account of the main groups and their identities and highlight how problematic this is for many concerned. Gypsies and Travellers are not one homogeneous entity, but rather different groups each with their own languages, lifestyles, cultures and ways of expressing their unique identities. I present a review of the minimal literature on Gypsy and Traveller women, which indicates the degree to which their perspectives are missing from the record. In Chapter 3, an explanation of the Scottish legal context for enrolment and attendance in school is established, and scholarly works and reports on the educational experiences of Gypsies and Travellers are examined.

Chapter 4 details decisions I made when conducting this research over a period of three years which clarify the complexities involved in working with communities that have been marginalised for centuries and to which the researcher does not belong. It represents the nested narrative of the research process itself that revealed the stories of the girls' lives and experiences. Beginning with a justification for the use of a black feminist intersectional framework in which to situate and analyse my findings, I highlight issues around sampling, strategies used to gain access to research participants and the ethical considerations and sensitivities surrounding research with children from minority ethnic backgrounds.

The findings that emerge from the research and the analysis of that data are presented and discussed in Chapter 5, using a typology of intersecting systems of structural/institutional (school), hegemonic (family and community culture) and interpersonal (family and personal) oppressions as advocated by Collins (2000: 276). I address how Gypsy and Traveller girls frame their educational experiences, foregrounding the girls' own definitions and understandings of education and learning, as it forms a useful backdrop upon which the tapestry of their lives is woven. An explanation of the types of educational establishments to which the Gypsy and Traveller girls have access, their positive experiences, and the difficulties and obstacles they face in the schools they attended are revealed. The narratives demonstrate that although their accounts are not homogenous, racism and bullying by non—Gypsy and Traveller peers, lack of respect or support and understanding from school staff alongside fear and lack of trust, account for reasons why most of the girls cite negative experiences at school and are deterred from attending mainstream educational settings. What emerges somewhat unexpectedly, are instances of gender discrimination by school staff. As revealed, by staying hidden, invisible and silent, or through self-exclusion from mainstream education, the girls and their families can exert a measure of control over their circumstances and perceived intrusions of the State.

Chapter 6 examines the girls' views and reflections on how family values, expectations and culture influence their educational experiences. I focus on the hegemonic inequalities reflected in family and community culture that also function as challenges and barriers to the girls' educational experiences. The positive influences of family and culture are highlighted, but the girls' own accounts reveal how these can be limiting or even obstructive. Their views are subdivided into three themes—love and care within family structures; freedom, control and honour; and gendered expectations. Juxtaposed against this segmented analysis, their interpretations of family expectations of education and school are challenged. This section underscores reasons the girls give for their families' decision not to enrol their daughters in secondary school. Their narratives reveal evidence of strict gender expectations and cultural taboos that can be restrictive. The evidence suggests that many of the girls appear to be caught betwixt and between structural inequalities in school and within their family and community structures. In the main, many lack options and the freedom to make informed choices.

In Chapter 7, the narrative focuses on interpersonal matters, including the girls' definitions of success, identity and aspirations. The chapter explores the complex ways in which the girls' identities as individuals are shaped, and at times restricted by family and cultural identity, traditions and values. Their personal definition of the word 'success' and their understanding of what it is to be a successful person are considered. Their aspirations are juxtaposed against the background of their experiences in school and at home, as detailed in the previous two chap-ters. A key finding in this chapter demonstrates how their goals resonate alongside the tension they negotiate between the love and respect they have for their families, and the restrictions imposed on them at home and at school, and the roles they perform.

Chapter 8 reflects on the salient outcomes and conclusions based on the girls' accounts of their lives, the arguments and debates raised and considers how Gypsy and Traveller girls and women can collectively imagine a new future, which subverts the patriarchal and hegemonic racial and gender order in their homes, schools and communities. It centres the voices of the girls representing the non-governmental organi-zation Article 12, who through interviews have posed recommendations for change and progressive dialogue on matters concerning the opportu-nities impacting Gypsy and Traveller girls within the wider community. Article 12 is a charity that works to empower the lives of young Gypsies and Travellers (YGTL) and other marginalized young people, encour-aging them to participate freely as equal citizens to help affect positive change in society.

All the girls and many of the stakeholders in the study have been anonymised for confidentiality within, or engagement with, the Gypsy and Traveller communities. In spite of this precaution, a censure on parts of the girls' narratives was encouraged by a gatekeeper and an aca-demic working in the field. Both highlighted the issues faced by Gypsy and Traveller girls within their families could further alienate the com-munity, could affirm calls for their assimilation into mainstream society, and seen as playing into the hands of racists. I was advised to delete anything that might be perceived as negative criticism of the commu-nity. Whilst I recognise their concerns, I have chosen not to modify the girls' stories, even if at times it makes for a more variegated interpre-tation. Instead I have tried to honour their narratives by sharing their accounts in this book. As a black feminist, and as my background will demonstrate, I have strong views about the overt and subtle oppression of girls and women, and will address these. Just because communities are marginalised and persecuted from outwith does not preclude them from introspection of within-group tensions and problems.

Because of the political, moral and ethical sensitivity of the research focus, and the power imbalance in the age and experiences of the researcher and research participants, as a feminist I thought it important to be open and honest about my personal background, assumptions and interest in the study, and my shared experiences with the girls I met, despite there also being distinct differences.

I am obliged here and throughout this book to use certain social categories, but I am fundamentally uncomfortable with the idea of categories and categorisation. I accept that within limits they are necessary to understand how the social world functions, particularly in signifying differences and relational power that can serve to subjugate some groups. Categories and categorisations are reductive, not wholly reliable and ought to be questioned to avoid the trap of essentialising and 'scientifically creating artificial groups on paper' (Inken 2014: 266). Terms like White/Black, native/immigrant, settled/Traveller, are dualistic and inadequately capture the complexity of life at the intersections 'where national boundaries, cultures, identities, and histories overlap, collide, and grind against each other to create new forms of consciousness' (Grzanka 2014: 35). Categories can be internalised as we rehearse stories of who we are. However, the re-telling can mask or induce confusion and tensions in the construction of our identities. Living amongst a population that is overwhelmingly white, as a person of colour, I am often asked, 'where are you from?'. If I reply, 'I live here in Scotland and have done so for a long time', the next question inevitably arises, 'But where are you *really* from?'. On the one hand, the inquisitor tries to make a connection, but then, seeks a definition, a category that reduces my identity and delineates my otherness.

Conducting this research has in itself compelled me to confront many established assumptions. I was raised in a pluralistic world where diversity and intercultural relations were the norm within a largely Chinese population. Although I am ethnically of Indian origin, I am third generation Singaporean, a product of two sets of aspiring diasporic families who escaped the British Raj in the late nineteenth century. I have lived in Scotland for over two decades. A diverse background is an advantage in today's distinctly globalised world. I do not belong anywhere and feel no strong attachment to a particular location or culture, a sort of world citizen. As a researcher, being a minority ethnic woman aids the oppositional gaze and sensitises me to the unconscious biases and discourses of the majority.

Having a good formal education has always been highly prized in my family, and many are educated professionals. I studied in a single sex Methodist missionary school, as had three generations of women in my family. In colonial Singapore, it was a way of bettering oneself and of assimilating into the gold standard of an 'English education'. However, the term 'educated' ought to be problematised. As a teacher, I value education but have come to recognise how it can also control and confine. As a 'non-white, colonial immigrant' doing intersectional research, I am equally aware of my potential to be 'ideologically co-opted' by the dominant systems of knowledge that have trained me to think and teach (Bilge 2014: 16). Pring (2004: 9) suggests 'there are different views as to what is to be counted as an "educated person", and there is no obvious way that these differences might be resolved'. The concept of the 'intellectual', what and whose knowledge counts can be used by dominant powers to restrict access to education, politics and other arenas of influence. Education can be used to maintain the status of the dominant, whilst prohibiting suppressed groups from improving their own (hooks 1994, 2003; Benjamin and Emejulu 2012). And yet, I value a formal education highly as I do the system I work within.

Encouraged by my parents since childhood, I also learned much from travelling. I travelled a lot as a young person and have moved regularly. Periodic migration or movement has its challenges, but I can appreciate the Gypsy and Traveller's love of travelling. This study recognises that crossing from one space to another has practical, political and social implications. Territories and borders may be socio-politically constructed, but they are not just a line on a map and migration is not just an arrow revealing direction of travel (Mekdjian 2015: 1). Some types of movement are permissible and deemed desirable, but other types disparaged or criminalised.

It surprised me to discover how much I had in common with the girls. Though set within a different cultural and geographical space, like them I too have experienced racialised and gendered discrimination. I too have attempted to self-exclude as a form of protective segregation.

Listening to their school experiences reminded me how tiring and debilitating it can be as a woman of colour to co-exist in spaces of whiteness (Ahmed 2012: 36). Not only did the research process and the girls' voices evoke the mental and emotional labour that comes from being different, but I recognise too the 'political labour that it takes to have spaces of relief from whiteness' (Ahmed 2012: 37).

The girls' lives within a traditional patriarchal family and community structure resonated with aspects of my own South Asian family life. Family honour was dependent on girls or young women 'preserving *their* honour' until they married, after which that responsibility was to be monitored by a husband. I empathised with and understood their accounts of their roles, identities and responsibilities within their families and communities. One of the girls said, 'you're Indian so you will know what I am talking about. Indian people are very strict too, aren't they?' Restrictions and obligations within the private world of family had either to be accepted or delicately negotiated in the public spaces of education and the workplace (Emejulu 2013: 59).

My 'social and economic locations' (Yuval-Davis 2006: 199)—in terms of gender, ethnicity, class, age group and profession—intersect with each other and with those of the girls I interviewed. To a certain extent, we exchanged parts of who we were and the relationship was reciprocal. The configuration of power and control between researcher and participant is not wholly one-sided throughout the research process. Though I used 'the interview' as the main tool of data collection, we were drawn into a relationship with each other. During our conversations, I was aware that the girls I met were curious about me, as much as I was curious about them. They were interested to know about my life as an Indian and as a woman of colour, and seemed less defensive about their encounters because they sensed I would understand. As an Indian woman, my 'racialised marking' was in fact an advantage. However, my research position, power and control of the interview process shifted. I might have seemed like the adult in charge at times, but the girls were in control of what they wanted to reveal.

As human beings our identities are multiple, socially constructed, not static and variable. It is not possible, as the philosopher Gadamer (1976) suggests, to be fully aware of this milieu of intersections and discipline one's prejudices. However, whilst there are many ways in which my identities differed from those of the young people I met, giving rise to instances of divergence of values and perspectives, there were several significant points of convergence and contradiction. Far from acting as points of bias, these aided my understanding of what I was about to discover about the lives of the girls and young women I met.

As a researcher, it was not possible to detach myself entirely. I did not hesitate to articulate my comprehension of their narratives, and as Mies (1983) would say, I was 'consciously partial'. Just as I could not remove the emotion from their experiences, neither could I remove the emotion from what I encountered in listening to them. In keeping with the feminist epistemology underpinning this research, I did not distance myself from participants during the interviews. Despite my ethnicity, age and professional status I was allowed access to information which I might not otherwise have gained. Yet, it could be argued that it is precisely because of these social locations that the girls took an interest in the research, connected with my identities as a 'coloured person', my ethnicity and gender, my previous job as a teacher, and my role as a parent. Following tradition in Gypsy and Traveller communities, the girls recognised that as an adult, mother, researcher, and teacher, I was in their eyes a person with experience and knowledge. In this sense, I was aware of their respect against the backdrop of my relative power and status. I was also deemed 'safe' to be with because their teachers and other contacts that they had come to trust introduced me to them.

The research was at times uncomfortable and emotionally challenging, particularly when presenting my work to largely white academic audiences where I was offering an inherently contrary worldview. On some of these occasions and particularly in Scotland, members of the audience were defensive or dismissive. Moments of hesitation and silences surrounding certain taboo topics exposed levels of discomfort. The research was not easy and it was not always comfortable for researcher and researched. There were no simple neat categories of truth and experience, and on occasion it was necessary to question just how effectively one can truly represent another person (Pillow 2003: 176). Following Haraway's (1988: 584) advice, 'the politics and epistemology of partial perspectives' undergirds this book. My personal experiences, assumptions and views on racism and gender bias, on education and travel, have impacted on the research process and in my interpretation of the complexities of the multiple realities involved. I am conscious of my status as a 'privileged interlocutor of the similitudes and differences that constitute post-Imperial Englishness', of which I am partially a product (Samantrai 2002: 2), challenging the racial and genderised undertones for minority ethnic women like myself. I acknowledge and use these to disrupt and problematise existing 'understandings of power, inequality and difference … firmly supported by the [decolonising] epistemological foundations of intersectionality' (Inken 2014: 266).

This research is careful in its use of pronouns like 'I', 'we', 'them', and 'us'. A change-oriented, transformative study (Cresswell 2007) that relies heavily on data from a set of interviews conducted and analysed by one researcher, necessitates the use of the first person to openly demonstrate the voice, interpretation, bias, and claims of the researcher. The 'them' and 'us' rhetoric is rejected, as are the patronisingly colonial 'we' and nosisms.

I owe heartfelt thanks to Dr. Akwugo Emejulu for her guidance and I treasure the bright moments of insight that developed from meaningful discussions and her courageous work on racial, gender and ethnic inequalities. Throughout this process, it has been a luxurious privilege to share and dwell upon ideas I might not otherwise have had time to, and I have learned much. Equally, Jess Smith, Traveller writer, storyteller and singer, has been inspirational and I value her wisdom and humanity. She has written inspiring stories and novels about her childhood and her community, and she laments the fact that her work has not been valued by academia.

In the context of the fieldwork, I owe especial thanks to the many stakeholders who shared their experience and knowledge of Gypsies and Travellers with me, with passionate enthusiasm and commitment to the work that they do. For reasons of confidentiality and due to the sensitivity of issues raised, it is with regret that I omit their names. I am grateful to my wonderful friends and family for their love, warmth and generosity. I owe much to my late father, a trade union activist exiled for his efforts. His invaluable insights and his outspoken courage inspire me to this day. Conducting fieldwork within Gypsy and Traveller communities and the interactions with the girls I met has been an immensely rewarding experience. Despite frustrations over the lengthy period of seeking access through numerous avenues to this understandably closed community, the realization of being able to do so and the opportunity of listening to the young women's views was humbling. A number of the individuals were intrigued by my interest in them and a few have requested a copy of 'the book' to read how their stories were re-presented. Thank you to the Gypsy and Traveller girls who welcomed me into their 'invisible' lives, at times risking their reputations. I acknowledge with deep respect their tenacity, their love of family and community, and their wisdom. This book is for them.

This work is supported by a joint grant from the ESRC and Scottish Government (No. ES/ J500136/1).

Glasgow, UK   Geetha Marcus

References

Ahmed, S. (2012) *On being included: Racism and diversity in institutional life.* Durham, NC: Duke University Press.

Benjamin, S., and Emejulu, A. (2012) Learning about concepts, terminology and theories. In: Arshad, R., Pratt, L., and Wrigley, T. (eds.) *Social justice re-examined.* Stoke-on-Trent: Trentham, pp. 33–48.

Bilge, S. (2014) Whitening intersectionality. *Racism and Sociology*, 5, p. 175.

Clark, C. (2001) 'Invisible lives': The Gypsies and Travellers of Britain.* Unpublished PhD thesis, Edinburgh: University of Edinburgh.

Clark, C. (2006) Defining ethnicity in a cultural and socio-legal context: The case of Scottish Gypsy-Travellers. *Scottish Affairs*, 54, pp. 39–67.

Collins. P. H. (2000) *Black feminist thought. Knowledge, consciousness and the politics of empowerment.* London: Routledge.

Coxhead, J. (2007) *The last bastion of racism: Gypsies, Travellers and policing.* Stoke on Trent: Trentham Books.

Cresswell, J. W. (2007) *Qualitative inquiry and research design: Choose among five approaches.* London: Sage.

Emejulu, A. (2013) Being and belonging in Scotland: Exploring the intersection of ethnicity, gender and national identity among Scottish Pakistani groups. *Scottish Affairs*, 84(1), pp. 41–64.

Gadamer, H. G. (1976) *Philosophical hermeneutics*. Berkeley: University of California Press.

Grzanka, P. (2014) *Intersectionality: A foundations and frontiers reader*. Boulder: Westview Press.

Haraway, D. (1988) Situated knowledges: The science question in feminism and the privilege of partial perspective. *Feminist Studies*, 14(3), pp. 575–599.

hooks, b. (1992) *Black looks: Race and representation*. Boston: South End Press.

hooks, b. (1994) Teaching to transgress: Education as the practice of freedom. *Journal of Engineering Education*, 1, pp. 126–138.

hooks, b. (2003) *Teaching community: A pedagogy of hope* (Vol. 36). London: Psychology Press.

Inken C. E. (2014) Connecting intersectionality and reflexivity: Methodological approaches to social positionalities. *Erkunde*, 68(4), pp. 265–276.

Matache, M. (2017) The legacy of Gypsy studies in modern Roma scholarship. Available at: https://fxb.harvard.edu/the-legacy-of-gypsy-studies-in-modern-romani-scholarship/. Accessed 23 August 2017.

Mekdjian, S. (2015) Mapping mobile borders: Critical cartographies of borders based on migration experiences. In: Szary, A. A., and Giraut, F. (eds.) *Borderities and the politics of contemporary mobile borders*. London: Palgrave Macmillan, pp. 204–223.

Mies, M. (1983) Towards a methodology for feminist research. In: Bowles, G., and Klein, R. (eds.) *Theories of women's studies*. London: Routledge and Kegan Paul, pp. 117–139.

Mirza, H. S. (2015) Harvesting our collective intelligence: Black British feminism in post-race times. *Women's Studies International Forum*, 51, pp. 1–9.

Neat, T. (1996) *The summer walkers: Travelling people and pearl-fishers in the highlands of Scotland*. Edinburgh: Canongate.

Pillow, W. (2003) Confession, catharsis, or cure? Rethinking the uses of reflexivity as methodological power in qualitative research. *International Journal of Qualitative Studies in Education*, 16(2), pp. 175–196.

Pring, R. (2004) *Philosophy of educational research*, 2nd ed. London: Continuum.

Samantrai, R. (2002) *AlterNatives: Black feminism in the postimperial nation.* Stanford: Stanford University Press.

Schröter, M. (2013) *Silence and concealment in political discourse* (Vol. 48). Amsterdam: John Benjamins Publishing.

Smith, J. (2002) *Jessie's journey: Autobiography of a Traveller girl* (Vol. 1). Edinburgh: Birlinn Ltd.

Spivak, G. (1988) Can the subaltern speak? In: Nelson, C., and Grossberg, L. (eds.) *Marxism and the interpretation of culture.* Urbana and Chicago: University of Illinois Press, pp. 271–316.

Stewart, S. (2008) *Pilgrims of the mist: The stories of Scotland's Travelling people.* Edinburgh: Birlinn Ltd.

Surdu, M. (2016) *Those who count: Expert practices of Roma classification.* Budapest: Central European University Press.

The Scottish Government. (2009) Race equality statement. Available at: http://www.scotland.gov.uk/Topics/People/Equality/18934/RaceEquality Statement. Accessed 2 April 2013.

Whyte, B. (2001) *The yellow on the broom: The early days of a Traveller woman.* Edinburgh: Birlinn Ltd.

Wilkin, A., Derrington, C., and Foster, B. (2009) *Improving the outcomes for Gypsy, Roma and Traveller pupils: Literature review.* London: DCSF.

Yuval-Davis, N. (2006) Belonging and the politics of belonging. *Patterns of Prejudice,* 40(3), pp. 197–214.

Contents

Abbreviations

BEMIS	Black and Ethnic Minorities Infrastructure in Scotland
CERES	Centre for Education for Racial Equality in Scotland
COE	Council of Europe
CRER	Coalition for Racial Equality and Rights
EBD	Emotional and Behavioural Disorder
EHE	Elective Home Education
EHRC	Equality and Human Rights Commission
EOC	Equal Opportunities Committee
MECOPP	Minority Ethnic Carers of Older People Project
MEPESS	Minority Ethnic Pupils' Experiences of Schools in Scotland
OECD	Organisation for Economic Cooperation and Development
SHRC	Scottish Human Rights Council
STEP	Scottish Traveller Education Programme
TENET	Traveller Education Network
UNCRC	United Nations Convention on the Rights of the Child

List of Figures

List of Tables

1

The Outsiders Within: Stereotypes, Definitions and Boundaries

This book explores the educational experiences of Scottish Gypsy and Traveller girls and seeks to centre the girls' voices and perspectives, initially considered through a series of papers and publications during the course of my research (Marcus 2013a, b, 2014a, b, 2015a, b, 2016). It offers space for their voices to be heard and features their agency in the private spaces of home and the public spaces of education. The girls' stories are highlighted and juxtaposed alongside the general problems encountered by Gypsies and Travellers and reveal a complex narrative that spans centuries.

This research builds on the limited literature on Gypsies and Travellers in Scotland (including Murray 1875; Wilson and Leighton 1885; Mackenzie 1883; MacRitchie 1894; McCormick 1907; Rehfisch and Rehfisch 1975; Williamson 1994; Neat 1996; Reid 1997; Kenrick 1998; Clark 2001, 2006, 2008, 2013; Clark and Taylor 2014; Shubin 2010, 2011). The relative paucity of scholarly literature on the experiences of those living in Scottish Gypsy and Traveller communities, in itself accentuates their invisibility and disguises the gravity of the discrimination and inequality that affect some Travelling peoples. Gypsies and Travellers are outliers within our society.

© The Author(s) 2019
G. Marcus, *Gypsy and Traveller Girls*, Studies in Childhood and Youth,
https://doi.org/10.1007/978-3-030-03703-1_1

Accounts of Scottish Gypsy and Traveller life also reflect an authored gender imbalance in being written largely by men. Existing studies thus risk further erasing or misrecognising the competing experiences of Gypsy and Traveller women. It demonstrates an essential gap in the literature in which Gypsy and Traveller girls' experiences are not represented. They are even more marginalised than the men and boys in their communities.

According to some studies, Gypsy and Traveller children have the lowest levels of educational achievement in the United Kingdom (Cemlyn et al. 2009; Wilkin et al. 2009). Organisations like the Scottish Traveller Education Programme (STEP), a national Knowledge Exchange and Information centre funded by the Scottish Government's Learning Directorate, have sought to investigate the reasons for this underachievement. Gypsy and Traveller children in Scotland often report negative social experiences in school and it is believed this factor is fuelled by poor communication, a lack of trust and a curriculum that can appear irrelevant to the travelling child and their family (STEP 2013). Gypsy and Traveller children are also outliers within our schools. None of these studies focus specifically on girls. There is currently no research that examines how girls and young women from Gypsy and Traveller communities fare in Scottish schools and what they think of their experiences. As the girls' voices are missing from the scholarly literature and policy documents, the critical exploration of their experiential accounts of education and schooling is timely and vital.

The Scottish Government and the UK government have yet to develop a comprehensive National Roma Integration Strategy, which includes education, but has relied on current equalities legislation, such as the EU Race Directive 2003 and the Equalities Act 2010, to promote the integration of all Roma people in the country (European Union Agency for Fundamental Rights 2015: 3). The EU has acknowledged that the improvements within its framework are still in its 'early phase and needs to be supported with sustainable funding' to translate national strategies into action at local level (European Union 2015: 14). There is insufficient involvement by local authorities and civil society, and the situation is not sufficiently monitored (European Union 2015: 14).

It should be noted that across Europe, Gypsies and Travellers are classified as Roma, however, there are distinct differences in these communities at many levels—origin, identity, ascription, nationality, language, culture. These distinctions are made clear in the next chapter. Scottish Gypsies and Travellers do not identify as European Roma. Whilst similar stories of persecution and discrimination pervade their lives as Gypsy/Roma/Travellers, the degree and manner to which this occurs differs, as do their needs.

In 2013, a Scottish mapping exercise was completed to 'ensure that Scotland is recognised at European levels for playing an active part in meeting the European Commission's Roma inclusion objectives, build an understanding of the Roma population living in Scotland and increase knowledge about the individual and institutional capacity that exists in Scotland to apply EU funds for the social and economic inclusion/integration of the Roma populations' (The Social Marketing Gateway 2013: 4).

Confusion exists about whether these strategies and funding should apply to Roma from Europe and/or indigenous Scottish Gypsies and Travellers. Organisations like Article 12, hitherto mentioned in the preface, for example, who obtain funding from the government, only support young people from Gypsy and Traveller communities and do not cater to the needs of European Roma youth. Whereas, the Roma Youth Project, amongst others, cater only to the needs of the latter.

In June 2016, the United Nations Committee on the Rights of the Child, stated under Section 20 (c) that 'many children in certain groups, including Roma, Gypsy and Traveller children… continue to experience discrimination and social stigmatization, including through the media' (UNCRC 2016: 5). It also notes in Section 47 (a) that 'bullying, including cyber bullying, remains a serious and widespread problem, particularly against…children belonging to minority groups, including Roma, Gypsy and Traveller children' (2016: 11). The committee expressed concern that in Scotland their health, accommodation and educational needs are not being adequately met. There is a disproportionate number of exclusions of Roma, Gypsy and Traveller children, including the use of informal exclusion practices like being 'taught off site', and isolation rooms to control behaviour (2016: 18). As the girls' accounts in this book attest, many experience being sent to these isolation rooms without clarification or work to occupy them.

My original proposal involved exploring educational data and guidelines, juxtaposing these materials and the voices of practitioners and that of the Gypsy and Traveller girls I interviewed. I also envisaged a study that balanced the views of practitioners and those of the girls. Over the course of my fieldwork, my research focus changed to take a more critical stance to question why so little is known about the lives of Gypsy and Traveller girls and why their experiences and perspectives have not significantly featured in academic and policy debates that concern these children.

An underlying question in the unfolding narrative relates to how history is represented given that 'a particular challenge in historiography arises when faced with two distinct cultural interpretations — one based on oral tradition and the other on written accounts' (Marcus 1995: 1). This query led me to consider a focus on what knowledge and whose knowledge counts in the research process and this provoked a different study than was originally envisaged.

Following arguments made by black feminist bell hooks (1994, 2003) that formal education systems maintain 'white supremacist patriarchy', I found her analysis resonated strongly with the girls' accounts of their lives in school. hooks (1992: 94) also states that there is 'power in looking', interrogating with a rebellious 'oppositional gaze', and in this context, at the education system that envelops these girls' lives. Benjamin and Emejulu (2012: 33) affirm that 'education is deeply political... at all levels it is shaped by relations of power'. Therefore, I felt I needed to undertake a process of 'decolonising' my study to disrupt how we think about education, the positive and negative power within it, and how to centre the views and experiences of Gypsy and Traveller girls, which seems to have been largely silenced.

While the original aims of my research would provide new data within a Scottish context, such a study was likely to have limited value in Scottish education and society unless I attempted to critically examine some of the structural, hegemonic and interpersonal practices (Collins 2000: 276) that surround Gypsy and Traveller girls in general. If the girls' voiced experiences were to be heard, my focus also had to include a deconstruction of the majority group's values and attitudes. Issues of identity, diversity, inclusion and their impact on achievement need to be confronted and contextualised.

I decided not to limit my investigation to racial discrimination, which from existing evidence seemed the most obvious inequality faced by the girls and their communities, but rather to enter the research process with an open mind to other inequalities that might arise. It was equally important to give space to discuss the girls' aspirations for themselves and focus on their agency at home and at school. Agency is a contested term, but I have chosen to define it broadly as the ability a person has to act in a given situation, however free and independent they may feel or actually are.

The image of Gypsy and Traveller women is plagued by stereotyped views and assumptions in the media, academia, third sector organisations and the general population. A common narrative is that all the girls want to do is get married and have children, and that they and their families are not interested in education or another career beyond being a homemaker. As I progressed through a comprehensive review of the literature, networked with stakeholders, conducted fieldwork and sought to establish a dialogue with the girls and their families, a different picture emerged out of the tapestry.

My work locates itself ethically within the growing respect and acknowledgement in academic literature that children and young people are active and knowledgeable agents (Davis et al. 2006; Konstantoni 2013). Given the low attendance and attainment figures of Gypsy and Traveller pupils, and that *Save the Children* (2005) highlight that 92% have reported being bullied in school, it is important that this study tries to foreground their views and accounts (Alanen 1994; Mayall 1994; James et al. 1998). What is the impact of bullying on young Gypsy and Travellers girls? Are these bullying incidents of a racist nature? Do they experience other forms of discrimination at school? If they are in school, why and if not, why not? Do they have aspirations, and if so, what shape might these take and what might enable or prevent them from realising their dreams?

I have also been challenged to justify why I chose to focus my study on Gypsy and Traveller girls and not boys, or indeed both. There is much evidence to suggest that girls do better in school compared to boys. Similarly, there is research that maintains girls are perceived to be doing well at the expense of boys, and that education systems tend to favour the way girls learn, but this is not always the case (Knowles and Lander 2011: 19). Girls are not a homogenous group, and they do not all have homogenous experiences in school. An OECD (2009) report suggests immigrant girls in Europe have higher educational attainment than their male counterparts. They may seem to do well in general when compared to immigrant boys, but when comparisons are made within the gender group itself, a different story emerges. Research findings, although still 'rare and limited', reveal that some girls enjoy less scholastic achievement (Farris and de Jong 2014: 1512). Second-generation immigrant girls in Europe perform considerably worse than their female non-immigrant peers (2014: 1512). Such anomalies inspired my curiosity about the heterogeneous educational experiences of minority ethnic girls in general, and the reasons why some do better in school than others.

Terminology

Gypsies and Travellers

As mentioned earlier, I am decidedly uncomfortable with categories and categorisations, and here lies a note of caution. Some of the terms used in this book are open to interpretation and are a fixture of decades of debate and will likely remain unresolved (Clark 2001). The term 'Gypsy and Traveller' as used throughout the book is not one that exactly captures or defines the mosaic of communities that may ascribe to common ancestry under this term. To have used one at the expense of the other would cause offense to one or more of these communities. I was advised by both Gypsies and Travellers that this umbrella term, for want of a better one, was possibly the most politic term in today's context. Liégeois (1998: 33) states that it is 'an imprecise concept' with no definite criteria for inclusion. However, he argues that 'these terms are relatively unstained by pejorative connotations … perhaps because to date they have not been in common use…It is convenient to use the term to describe the whole of the group, with the additional proviso that distinction between them is not always relevant nor indeed possible' (1998: 34).

In policy documents, guidelines and recommendations, the Scottish Government has chosen to use an oblique—'Gypsy/Traveller', instead of 'and'. This descriptor is the Scottish Government's official terminology and is also the preferred term used in some academic literature. The Equal Opportunities Committee believes 'using the term 'Gypsy/Traveller' acknowledges Gypsy/Travellers are not a homogenous group' (The Scottish Parliament 2013: 2). In Scotland, the term 'Travelling Communities' is also used. My research is primarily about Scottish Travellers or Scottish Gypsies and does not include Roma populations who have migrated recently to Scotland, therefore the broader term Gypsy/Roma/Traveller is not used in the title. At no point in the book are the terms 'Gypsy', 'Traveller' and 'Roma' used synonymously, and at no point are they viewed as one and the same peoples. In Chapter 2, the controversies over nomenclature, collective and individual ascription, exacerbated by government interventions, are made clear. The term Gypsy and Traveller is not water-tight, but then neither is identity (Acton 1974).

It is ethnicity and not nomadism that is in defining focus when we think about Gypsy and Traveller communities, as discussed at greater length in Chapter 2 (Morris 1998). The Scottish Government's (2018) most recent attempt to define who 'Gypsy/Travellers' are, states they are 'distinct groups – such as Roma, Romany Gypsies, Scottish and Irish Travellers – who consider *the travelling lifestyle* part of their ethnic identity'. This view echoes the Caravan Sites and Control of Development Act 1960 (Section 24), in which Gypsies and Travellers are defined as 'persons of nomadic habit of life' and confirms a longstanding misinterpretation that it is the act of travelling that defines who they are as an ethnic group. The nomadism of Gypsies and Travellers 'is neither irrational not unique'. Whilst not all Gypsies and Travellers are nomadic or semi-nomadic, they have over centuries been part of agricultural and industrial economies. It could even be argued that those who do move for employment are 'in advance of more general movements in society to claim freedom of movement, and freedom from the "alienating" effects of the traditional employer' (Acton 1974: 270).

The propagation of myths and assumptions contribute to neglect, inertia or interventionist policies that have largely sought to 'civilise' and assimilate Gypsies and Travellers within the majority settled population. Clark (2001: 24) contends that 'the overall picture which emerges from the research is that Gypsies and Travellers are misunderstood, unheard and subject to a type of discrimination and prejudice that could be termed, specifically, "anti-Gypsyism"'. Amnesty International (2013: 1) has accused the media and Scotland's 32 local authorities of perpetuating discrimination against Gypsies and Travellers, declaring that 'despite four inquiries by the Scottish Equal Opportunities Committee over the last 12 years, little or no progress has been made'. The Scottish Government's Race Equality Statement (2009) accepts that Gypsies and Travellers are 'a particularly discriminated against and marginalised group'. However, little progress has been made to address these inequalities. In December 2017, the government launched their *Race Equality Action Plan*, which includes a specific section on Gypsies and Travellers. They have also established a ministerial working group that aims to take action to improve the lives of Gypsy/Traveller communities in Scotland (The Scottish Government 2018).

The exact population of Gypsies and Travellers in Scotland is still unknown. Anything from around 684 families, to a possible population of 20,000 has been mooted (Scottish Traveller Education Programme 2013; Equality and Human Rights Commission 2013). In the 2011, Scottish Census approximately 4500 people self-identified as 'White Gypsy/Traveller'. Any available statistical data, including the Census, is not entirely representative. Given the differences between communities who fall within the category Gypsy and Traveller, it is not possible to make fixed generalisations, as their customs, language and practices are not universal.

Two men I met—one who self-identified as a 'Traveller' and the other as a 'Nacken' (see Chapter 2), could not agree if they each had 'Gypsy' ancestry from India, but agreed that as a community with many common characteristics, they were far from being a political collective representing a united front. Unlike the pan-European Roma movement, and arguably a growing united Gypsy/Roma/Traveller political voice in England, the situation in Scotland is more nuanced and complicated as they view themselves first and foremost as belonging to family groups, rather than communities in the ethnic, national or political sense. Upon first meeting a Gypsy or Traveller the question is more likely be '*who are you one of?*' rather than '*who are you?*' (Clark 2001: 397).

Just as there was no single narrative or single issue in the girls' accounts of their lives, so too is there no single established and agreed account of history and identity amongst Gypsies and Travellers in Scotland. Debate and discussion is ongoing and the temptation to essentialise, overgeneralise should be avoided in order that 'ethnic stereotypes are not formed to justify exploitative or oppressive relationships' (Acton 1974: 53). This book captures and presents a collection of narratives about a community of people within a specific timeframe, and acknowledges that perspectives and experiences are not rigid, fixed entities.

Girls or Young Women

Within Gypsy and Traveller cultures, I was initially uncertain if the term *girl* or *young woman* would be a more appropriate description of a young female over the age of 12. Gypsy and Traveller girls are often considered by their families and communities to be young women when they reach puberty. In the initial stages of this study, I took advice from an older Traveller woman who has spent many years as a liaison officer and consultant (Anon. Gypsy/Traveller Liaison Officer 1 2013, Personal communication). She said the former would be more accurate. However, most of the girls I interviewed thought of themselves as girls. Two in particular implied that they were girls because they are not married, and thus considered themselves to still be children. Therefore, they are all referred to as 'girls', as that is how they self-identify, but the term 'young woman' or 'young women' is used periodically to aid readability.

Cemlyn et al. (2009: 233–234) recommend that 'further research into gender inequalities experienced by Gypsy, Traveller and Show women' be undertaken. They state the importance of addressing 'education inequalities which have a disproportionate impact on women' and they state that there is a need to 'raise the profile of women' (Cemlyn et al. 2009: 233–234). Being a Gypsy and Traveller girl or woman does not automatically imply that she is oppressed or vulnerable. This book addresses a sensitive issue—gendered discrimination within communities facing racism. In the context of this racism, there is therefore significant potential for aspects of the content of the book to be misused to blame communities for the educational constraints faced by young Gypsy and Traveller women. This may in turn lead to further discrimination.

Not all Gypsy and Traveller women position themselves as victims of discrimination. Neither can it be assumed that all Gypsy and Traveller girls are unsuccessful at school or are uneducated in terms defined by the dominant majority. Some of the issues that affect them at school and at home are common to girls and women from other ethnicities and cultures and reflect practices in other communities. Differences in social locations may divide Gypsy and Traveller girls in distinct ways from other girls and women, and it might be appealing to assume that inequalities or unfair practices occur just within their ethnic group, but it is the racialised and gendered scourge within powerful patriarchal systems that binds us all together as women. In other words, the gendered discrimination is not unique to Gypsy and Traveller girls per se.

Against this background, the main research question seeks to discern how Gypsy and Traveller girls living in Scotland frame their educational experiences. This approach involves analysing how the girls themselves frame or explain these experiences and construct meaning from their individual perspectives.

Ethnicity and Race

In Scotland, 'ethnic minorities' is the traditional term used to refer to groups of people who are in the minority who have settled here from elsewhere, or who claim to be indigenous to Scotland, as some Scottish Gypsies and Travellers do. According to the 2011 Census, ethnic minority groups now account for 4% of the population in Scotland. The term 'ethnic minority' tends to imply a marginalised or powerless status in the face of the 'majority' ethnic or cultural milieu. This book prefers the term 'minority ethnic' (Arshad et al. 2005) to refer to people who are in the minority within a defined population on the grounds of 'race', colour, culture, language or nationality. Whilst we all have ethnicity; however, race is political. Ethnicity is not a fixed entity and ethnic groups are in themselves subject to change and modification.

Hawes and Perez (1996: 149) argue that 'if the concept of an ethnic minority is defined by its subordinate status within a wider society … and if its distinctive cementing features are to do with feelings of shared history, culture and tradition, there is no doubt that Gypsies and Travellers constitute a minority'. Even though Gypsies and Travellers have lived in the UK since the fifteenth century, and by some accounts as early as the twelfth century, in England they were only legally recognised as a minority ethnic group in 1989 and Irish Travellers in 2000. In Scotland, they were granted this recognition in 2008. As highlighted in Chapter 4, Gypsies and Travellers are entangled in a convoluted web of race, ethnicity and class, despite their 'whiteness'.

According to the Mandla Criteria (Mandla vs. Dowell-Lee, 1983), 'a group is identifiable in terms of its ethnic origins if it is a segment of the population distinguished from others by a sufficient combination of shared customs, beliefs, traditions and characteristics derived from a common or presumed common past, even if not drawn from what in biological terms is a common racial stock… [Gypsies and Travellers] have a distinct social identity based not simply on group cohesion and solidarity but also on their belief as to their historical antecedents'. Anthias and Yuval-Davis (1996: 19) contend that the 'race phenomena and the ethnic phenomena' are interconnected—ethnicity, racism, and racialisation are bound together in everyday social discourse and practice. They also highlight that 'race' involves the construction of boundaries between those who belong and those that do not belong in a particular population. These boundaries can be problematic and propagate various forms of discrimination (1996: 2). Throughout this book, the use of 'race' and 'racialisation' as key terms, rather than 'ethnicity', more accurately reflects the powerful and crippling discrimination faced by Gypsies and Travellers.

Racism as an ideology and racist discrimination as practice are relationships of power and involve processes 'whereby social groups categorize other groups as different or inferior on the basis of phenotypical characteristics, cultural markers or national origin' (Castles and Vasta 1996: 31). This study rejects the binary that a person is either 'racist' or 'not racist', as argued by Trepagnier (2006: 3), but rather that racism is on a continuum. One is 'more racist' or 'less racist', more racially aware or less racially aware (2006: 5). The continuum allows us to acknowledge that there are several forms of racism—'blatant and overt', 'silent', 'passive', 'everyday' and 'institutional' (Essed 1991; Anthias and Yuval-Davis 1996; Trepagnier 2006; Back and Solomos 2009; Garner 2010). Gypsies and Travellers report all these racisms.

The meaning of the term 'race' has changed over time. As race is increasingly being addressed in bureaucratic and political domains, 'it is not surprising that there is no agreement upon a clear definition of racism' (Banton 2009: 65). Old definitions continue to exist alongside newer explanations, which makes the concept of race all the more problematic (Gillborn 2008: 22). The Race Relations Act 1976 and later the Equality Act 2010, for example, do not define race as a concept. Both Acts do define racial groups as a group of persons defined by reference to 'color, race, nationality, ethnic or national origins' (Sections 3 (i), 1976 and Section 9 (i), 2000). This perhaps reflects the argument that concepts of race are not only context dependent, but will continue to change alongside political, social and cultural developments (Back and Solomos 2009). As mentioned above, understandings of race are related to issues of ethnicity, culture, gender and class (Back and Solomos 2009). In everyday popular discourse the term is still understood as 'meanings that people attach to colour or physical characteristics as they go about their everyday lives' (Walters, cited in Race and Lander 2014: 4).

Within the context of Gypsies and Travellers, their social construction as Other, and as inferior to the dominant White majority, is at the core of their racialisation and the racist discrimination they experience.

The term 'racialisation' is used to reflect the 'historical emergence of race [and its] reproduction and application over time' (Anthias and Yuval-Davis 1996: 11). Gypsies and Travellers experience all forms of racisms, however, the impact of this discrimination on girls and women in particular have yet to be explored from their perspective.

Educational Experience

The phrase 'educational experience' is not easy to interpret as it can involve a myriad of contributing factors and it is a term that is not readily defined in educational research. In this study, educational experience includes a student's experience of the curriculum, learning and teaching, relationships with teachers and extra-curricular activities (Thelen 1981). It also encompasses the hidden curriculum—the unintended or unrecognised culture, beliefs and values that the school as an institution may inadvertently impart to a pupil (Wren 1999). Educational experiences can be positive, negative or mixed. My study also acknowledges the external factors or structures that impact on educational experiences in formal school settings. Influences such as traditional cultural values, attitudes and behaviours, family expectations and dynamics, role models, and religious beliefs can either contribute to success or hamper progress in the education of a child (Schneider 1993; Gatto 2002; Knowles and Lander 2011). These external factors and relationships that impact on educational experiences, as viewed by Gypsy and Traveller girls, can yield considerable influence.

I was also interested to explore the challenges, barriers and successes the girls have encountered and the explanations they offered for any perceived challenges and barriers faced. Where there was perceived success, what explanations do the girls offer and why? The term 'challenge' is used to mean any test, problem, question or stimulant faced by the girls, but it does not imply that it is necessarily negative or that it precipitated a negative outcome. Rather the challenges may have been opportunities for change and improvement, for example, one can rise to a challenge. The word 'barrier' is used to highlight 'stumbling blocks' or obstacles that have hindered progress, or blocked their path to success.

I do not define the term 'success', as it is too subjective and personal, but it will be left open to interpretation by the girls. It could in one sense mean 'academic success', but the girls, by including achievements in other areas that have either impacted on their educational experiences or vice versa, could equally define it in a broader way. A search of the literature on the meaning of success identified one significant point—that definitions of success are a 'cross-cultural phenomenon' (Fan and Karnilowicz 1997; Mosconi and Emmett 2003). The use of the term is also dependent on the context in which it is used. As this book aims to centre the girls' views, it is in that spirit that the term success is left for them to interpret based on their own life experiences and culture, which might contrast and conflict with neo-liberal cultures of hyper-individualism that prioritise the advancement of self over and above family and community.

My study directly addresses this lacuna through presenting the girls' perspectives and my analysis to illuminate their multi-layered experiences of learning in institutional structures, as well as in the community and at home. Through this process, the naïve simplicity reflected in a received view of Gypsy and Traveller girls—that they do not value education, and only aspire to a traditional gender role of wife and mother—is undermined by the girls' accounts of their lives (Okely 1983; Lloyd et al. 1999; Lloyd 2005; Anon. Academic 1 2013, Personal communication; Anon. Academic 2 2013, Personal communication).

The girls' accounts of their experiences reflect institutional and everyday racism in the schools they attended, alongside gendered discrimination both in school and at home. Their age also places them at a disadvantage as they struggle to question and accept the discrimination they face in schools, and the pressure to conform to long held cultural values and expectations within their communities. Race, gender, age and class inequalities intersect to potentially limit the girls' capacity to fulfil their aspirations and ambitions as some of the participants confirmed. Yet, they are corseted within what may be viewed as caring and respectful family relationships that they value highly. Not unlike girls and young women from other cultures, the Gypsy and Traveller girls I met are loved but constrained at the same time, making it difficult, but not impossible, to negotiate competing expectations for their lives.

Thus, one of the key themes is the contradictory and complex situation that some Gypsy and Traveller girls must confront—trying to strike the balance between a safe, but restrictive life, in the private spaces of home and a hostile but potentially enriching life in the public spaces of education and work.

Another important point to emphasise is the way in which the girls use self-exclusion from school as a strategy for self-preservation and protection from institutionalised and everyday racism and sexism. Despite structural discrimination and deeply embedded cultural expectations, the girls shared their personal successes and aspirations for the future, with a few managing to carve out new paths and identities that visibly demonstrate a more overt exercising of agency and rejection of expected cultural conformities in both private and public life sectors.

Boundaries and Limitations

The book does not attempt to provide a detailed comparison of the educational experiences of Gypsy and Traveller girls between Scotland and other parts of the British Isles. It does however wherever relevant provide references to historical accounts of Gypsies and Travellers in Europe and recent developments in the European Union since the Decade of Roma Inclusion (2005–2015).

Historical, political and legal references and links pre-Scottish devolution with the rest of the UK were also necessary in helping to construct the background to the origin, history and identities of Gypsies and Travellers. A summary of the literature on the education of Gypsies and Travellers in England and Wales can be found in Chapter 3. I do not provide a comprehensive narrative history of the Scottish education system, but rather offer an overview for the reader, highlighting important developments and events especially since Scottish devolution in 1998. Even though the education system in Scotland, like other nations, has its own peculiarities, it has not developed in isolation as 'it shares many features in common with the growth of education systems throughout the developed world' (Paterson 2003: 9). In so far as the research explores definitions of education and learning, the analysis is situated within the changes and events in the Scottish education system in order to aid discussion and understanding of the context of the education of Gypsy and Traveller girls.

This study does not include the experiences of European Roma in Scotland, though on this topic there is much growing literature from the Scottish Universities Roma Network (Poole and Adamson 2008; Sime and Fox 2014; Clark and Taylor 2014; Clark 2014, 2015). There exists no similar Scottish Universities network devoted to the study of Scottish Gypsies and Travellers. There are various on-going research projects, though funded by the European Union that explore Roma issues (Sime and Fox 2014; Inserom Project, BEMIS 2011). As highlighted earlier and as will be discussed further in Chapter 2, little has been written about Scottish Gypsies and Travellers, compared with Gypsies, Roma and Travellers in the rest of the UK and Europe. This factor may reflect a general lack of interest in Gypsy and Traveller affairs as a whole, their invisibility within the larger society, and the challenges posed by attempting research with a closed community. Anecdotal evidence gathered from informal conversations and some formal reports suggest Gypsies and Travellers feel excluded by the attention focused on the newly arrived Roma groups from Eastern Europe (The Social Marketing Gateway 2013: 34). One Scottish Gypsy woman I met said she believed their history, heritage and issues were different to that of the Roma, and the latter were 'getting all the attention and becoming more important' (Anon. Gypsy Woman 2013, Personal communication).

The experiences of New Age Travellers are also not a focus of this study. These groups are recognised as communities who travel as a lifestyle choice, and have not been granted a separate ethnic status. This lifestyle definition is not supported by the Mandla Criteria (Mandla vs. Dowell-Lee 1983), which requires a minority, oppressed group to have a long-shared history and cultural tradition, including common language and literature, with a conscious sense of distinctness in order to be granted protected status under the Race Relations Act (1976, 2000).

Finally, this research does not consider the educational experiences of Gypsy and Traveller boys. My decision does not suggest that a focus on boys' experiences is not worthy of study, but following the reasons mentioned previously there is a critical need to focus on the margin-alised experiences of girls and, in this context, those from Travelling Communities in Scotland, of which little is known or understood exter-nal to the society.

The Collection of Data

As access to participants and time was limited, semi-structured inter-views were an efficient method of asking a set of questions about pre-vious events and provide valuable context on the Gypsy and Traveller girls' present understandings. Researching experiences and past events can be made easier by conducting interviews, than by trying to observe them first hand. Arksey and Knight (1999: 32) recommend that in general interviews are useful for 'uncovering and exploring the meanings that underpin people's lives'. It is also good way of 'giv-ing voice to sections of society who might otherwise be overlooked or excluded' (Greener 2011: 77; Romm 2014). The semi-structured interview method was also in keeping with the study's inductive, emic approach, which allowed for new information to emerge, rather than pre-conceived fixed ideas tested.

The interviews were recorded and transcribed verbatim, and these are used throughout the analysis chapters as they reflect upon the girls' culture, language, identity, thoughts and emotions. With 17 inter-views, the sample is grounded, though consequently this book makes no claims of generalisability. However, it serves as an initial portal on a closed community with members drawn from different parts of Scotland and sets the scene for future work in this area.

I also used focus group discussions with four Gypsy and Traveller girls who work for the non-governmental organisation called Article 12 as a means of validating the findings and to 'member check'. The Young Gypsy and Traveller or YGTL girls preferred not to be identified as individuals within the group, but wished to act and speak as represent-atives of the project. Their request was respectfully acknowledged and reflected in the consent forms they signed. Romm (2014: 1) argues that focus group discussions are particularly useful for engaging 'indigenous ways of knowing', which she defines as 'collectively constructing their understandings by experiencing their social being in relation to others'. The discussions provided rich data in addition to findings I gathered from the girls interviewed.

Participants

I did initially consider restricting the research to three local authorities in Scotland and delimit the sample within certain criteria—age, gender, accommodation type, and ethnicity. Locating the desired number of Gypsy and Traveller girls who fall into these age categories within the confines of three local authorities proved too ambitious. I would have liked to interview girls that moved all year in their trailers with their families, but could not find any who were willing to participate. The type of accommodation a girl lived in or how frequently she travelled proved to be unrealistic criteria. In studies such as this, where sections of a population are challenging to locate and 'categorise', a degree of flexibility from the outset seems necessary.

In researching Travellers, Judith Okely (1983: 48) revealed she 'could not select a single "village", nor was it feasible to restrict [herself] to one "group", even if it were possible to isolate such an entity... thus [she] only observed travellers when they entered [her] location'. She relied on the argument put forth by Dyson-Hudson that '[our] analytic units need not be population aggregates of some sort: they can as well (and sometimes more revealingly) be segments of time or action, points of contact or separation' (1972, cited in Okely 1983: 48).

I therefore widened my search to over a broader age range and more extensive geographical areas to include:

Gypsy and Traveller girls of Scottish or Celtic origin (not Roma or New Age Travellers)

- Aged 12 and above
- Living anywhere in Scotland

Focusing solely on Scottish Gypsies and Travellers, I had to rely on a non-probability based sampling technique like *snowball sampling* as it was initially difficult to meet Gypsy and Traveller girls. I discuss the reasons why in detail in Chapter 4. This kind of opportunistic sampling is arguably at a disadvantage as it is not a firm representative selection of Gypsy and Traveller girls in Scotland, but I believe it was the preferable method because of the challenges faced gaining access.

Gypsies and Travellers and those who work with them are a network of close-knit communities, as there are only a limited number of council and privately run Traveller sites. Table 1.1 summarises the girls' profiles, but for their protection I do not disclose names, places and schools, and have given the informants pseudonyms. A pen profile of each participant can be found in Appendix A.

Table 1.1 Profile of interviewed participants and school types attended

Name of participant	Age	Primary school	No. of primary schools attended	Secondary school	Local Authority (LA) mobile unit on site	Other LA provision for 12-16 year olds	Further Education (FE) college	Home or private tutor
May	12	✔	12			✔		
Cara	12	✔	5			✔		
Ailsa	13	✔	3			✔		
Islay	13	✔	8			✔		
Dana	13	✔	5			✔		
Fara	13	✔	13					
Skye	15	✔	1	✔				
Vaila	15	✔	3				✔	
Shona	16	✔	2	✔				
Iona	16	✔	13					
Kilda	18	✔	2[a]	✔				
Rona	19	✔	1	✔			✔	
Sandray	22	✔		✔			✔	
TOTAL		13		3	2	5	3	0

[a]Kilda spent only a few days in each of the two schools; mostly educated part time from the age of 5 by TENET teacher at mobile unit on site. Long periods of absences

Table 1.1 shows their age, whether they attended primary school and the number of schools they attended. Only three attended secondary school, and the others access a variety of educational establishments. Three girls attend further education colleges, and only two girls have had no access to any education from the age of 12 (see shaded box). Note that they are the same two who attended 13 primary schools, the most of any in the sample. None of the girls are home or privately tutored. The YGTL girls are not represented in this table as they chose to be represented as a group; their individual circumstances were not highlighted during the focus group discussions.

Given the lack of scholarly works in the field, I also conducted discussions and interviews with 30 stakeholders who provided valuable background information. In these personal communications conducted with teachers, social workers, health workers, planning officials, third sector organisations, policy makers, many requested anonymity. When audio recordings were not permitted, I took notes. Where there were several stakeholders from the same profession, these have been numbered accordingly (see Appendix B).

The book questions the status quo as represented by many of the stakeholders, gatekeepers and interested parties I met. I reject the notion that the researcher and the research are objective and welcome the multiple intersections of identities in both the girls I met and myself. The purpose of the study is not to discover the one reality or 'the truth' about the girls' educational experiences, but their dynamic, variable and multiple experiences within education. The emphasis was on listening and critically interpreting the girls' marginalised voices whose perspectives this research offers as 'better' claims to knowledge cradled by the pervasive structural and cultural influences that affect their lives. The research has produced findings that have answered some questions but generated more questions and dilemmas that I continue to grapple with.

References

Acton, T. (1974) *Gypsy politics and social change*. London: Routledge and Paul.
Alanen, L. (1994) Gender and generation: Feminism and the 'child question'. In: *Childhood matters: Social theory, practice and politics*, pp. 27–42.

Amnesty International (AIUK). (2013) *Scottish Gypsy Travellers, Amnesty International UK*. Available at: http://www.amnesty.org.uk/content.asp?categoryID=12418. Accessed 8 May 2013.

Anthias, F., and Yuval-Davis, N. (1996) *Racialized boundaries: Race, nation, gender, colour, and class and the anti-racist struggle*. London: Routledge.

Anon. Academic 1. (2013) Personal communication. Conversation and notes, 18 April.

Anon. Academic 2. (2013) Personal communication. Discussion, interview and notes, 15 April, 12 August.

Anon. Gypsy/Traveller Liaison Officer 1. (2013) Personal communication. Discussion and notes, 15 April.

Anon. Gypsy Woman (2013) Personal communication. Conversation at Roma Mapping Event, Glasgow, 4 October.

Arksey, H., and Knight, P. T. (1999) *Interviewing for social scientists: An introductory resource with examples*. London: Sage.

Arshad, R., Almeida Diniz, F., Kelly, E., O'Hara, P., Sharp, S., and Syed, R. (2005) *Minority Ethnic Pupils' Experiences of School in Scotland (MEPESS)*. Edinburgh: Scottish Executive.

Banton, M. (2009) The Idiom of race: A critique of presentism. In: Back, L., and Solomos, J. (eds.) *Theories of race and racism: A reader*. London: Routledge, pp. 55–67.

Back, L., and Solomos, J. (eds.). (2009) *Theories of race and racism: A reader*, 2nd ed. Abingdon: Routledge.

BEMIS. (2011) *Gypsy Travellers in contemporary Scotland: The 2001 'inquiry into Gypsy Travellers and public sector policies': Ten years on*. Glasgow: BEMIS.

Benjamin, S., and Emejulu, A. (2012) Social Justice: Learning about concepts, terminology and theories. In: Arshad, R., Pratt, L., and Wrigley, T. (eds.) *Social Justice re-examined*. Stoke-on-Trent: Trentham, pp. 33–48.

Caravan Sites and Control of Development Act. (1960) Available at: http://www.legislation.gov.uk/ukpga/Eliz2/8-9/62. Accessed 12 January 2013.

Castles, S., and Vasta, E. (1996) *The teeth are smiling: The persistence of racism in multicultural Australia*. Crows Nest: Allen and Unwin.

Cemlyn, S., Greenfields, M., Burnett, S., Matthews, Z., and Whitwell, C. (2009) *Inequalities experienced by Gypsy and Traveller communities: A review*. Research Report 12. Manchester: Equality and Human Rights Commission. Available at: https://dera.ioe.ac.uk/11129/1/12inequalities_experienced_by_gypsy_and_traveller_communities_a_review.pdf.

Clark, C. (2001) *'Invisible lives': The Gypsies and Travellers of Britain*. Unpublished PhD thesis, Edinburgh: University of Edinburgh.

Clark, C. (2006) Defining ethnicity in a cultural and socio-legal context: The case of Scottish Gypsy-Travellers. *Scottish Affairs*, 54, pp. 39–67.

Clark, C. (2008) Introduction themed section care or control? Gypsies, Travellers and the state. *Social Policy and Society*, 7(1), pp. 65–71.

Clark, C. (2013) Agency, empowerment and inclusion: The challenges facing Roma youth in Europe today. *Voice: A Global Youth Magazine*, 1(1), pp. 34–36.

Clark, C. (2014) 'Glasgow's Ellis Island? The integration and stigmatisation of Govanhill's Roma population'. *People, Place and Policy*, 8(1), pp. 34–50.

Clark, C. (2015) Integration, exclusion and the moral 'othering' of Roma migrant communities in Britain. In: Smith, M. (ed.) *Moral Regulation*. Bristol: Policy Press, pp. 43–56.

Clark, C., and Taylor, B. (2014) Is nomadism the 'problem'? The social construction of Gypsies and Travellers as perpetrators of 'anti-social' behaviour In Britain. In Pickard, S. (ed.) *Anti-social behaviour in Britain: Victorian and contemporary perspectives*, pp. 166–178.

Collins. P. H. (2000) *Black feminist thought. Knowledge, consciousness and the politics of empowerment.* London: Routledge.

Davis, J. M., Tisdall, K., Hill, M., and Prout, A. (2006) *Participation for what: Children young people and social inclusion.* Bristol: Policy Press.

EHRC. (2013) Gypsy Travellers in Scotland: A resource for the media. Available at: https://www.equalityhumanrights.com/sites/default/files/gt_media_guide_final.pdf. Accessed 15 March 2014.

Essed, P. (1991) *Understanding everyday racism: An interdisciplinary theory* (Vol. 2). London: Sage.

Equality Act. (2010). http://www.legislation.gov.uk/ukpga/2010/15/contents.

European Union. (2015) *Human rights of Roma and Travellers in Europe*. Brussels: Council of Europe.

European Union Agency for Fundamental Rights. (2015) Local Engagement for Roma Inclusion (LERI) project: Community summary. Available at: https://fra.europa.eu/sites/…/fra-2015-leri-community-summary-uk-glasgow_en.pdf. Accessed 16 July 2018.

Fan, C., and Karnilowicz, W. (1997) Measurement of definitions of success among Chinese and Australian girls. *Journal of Cross-Cultural Psychology*, 28(5), pp. 589–599.

Farris, S. R., and de Jong, S. (2014) Discontinuous intersections: Second-generation immigrant girls in transition from school to work. *Ethnic and Racial Studies*, 37(9), pp. 1505–1525.

Garner, S. (2010) *The entitled nation: How people make themselves white in contemporary England. Sens Public 2.* Available at: http://www.sens-public. org/article.php3?id_article=729andlang=fr. Accessed 24 July 2015.

Gatto, J. T. (2002) *Dumbing us down: The hidden curriculum of compulsory schooling.* Gabriola Island, BC: New Society Publishers.

Gillborn, D. (2008) *Racism and education: Coincidence or conspiracy?* London: Routledge.

Greener, I. (2011) *Designing social research: A guide for the bewildered.* London: Sage.

Hawes, D., and Perez, B. (1996) *The Gypsy and the state: The ethnic cleansing of British society,* 2nd ed. Bristol: Policy Press.

hooks, b. (1992) *Black looks: Race and representation.* Boston, MA: South End Press.

hooks, b. (1994) Teaching to transgress: Education as the practice of freedom. *Journal of Engineering Education,* 1, pp. 126–138.

hooks, b. (2003) *Teaching community: A pedagogy of hope* (Vol. 36). London: Psychology Press.

James, A., Jenks, C., and Prout, A. (1998) *Theorizing childhood.* Williston, VT: Teachers College Press.

Kenrick, D. (1998) *Historical dictionary of the Gypsies (Romanies).* Lanham: Scarecrow Press.

Knowles, G., and Lander, V. (2011) *Diversity, equality and achievement in education.* London: Sage.

Konstantoni, K. (2013) Children's rights-based approaches: The challenges of listening to 'taboo'/discriminatory issues and moving beyond children's participation. *International Journal of Early Years Education,* 21(4), pp. 362–374.

Liégeois, J. P. (1998) *School provision for ethnic minorities: The Gypsy paradigm* (Vol. 11). Hatfield: University of Hertfordshire Press.

Lloyd, G. (2005) *Problem girls: Understanding and supporting troubled and troublesome girls and young women.* London: Psychology Press.

Lloyd, G., Stead, J., Jordan, E., and Norris, C. (1999) Teachers and Gypsy Travellers. *Scottish Educational Review,* 31(1), pp. 48–65.

Mackenzie, A. (1883 [2012]) *The history of the highland clearances.* Lenox, MA: Hard Press Publishing.

MacRitchie, D. (1894) *Scottish Gypsies under the Stewarts.* Edinburgh: D. Douglas.

Mandla vs. Dowell-Lee [1983] UKHL 7, (1983) 2 AC 548.

Marcus, A. R. (1995) *Relocating Eden: The image and politics of Inuit exile in the Canadian Arctic*. Lebanon: Dartmouth College, University Press of New England.

Marcus, G. (2013a) The educational experiences of Gypsy and Traveller girls in Scottish schools. Paper presented at the interweaving: Connecting educational research within, across and between perspectives conference (21 August), Moray House School of Education, University of Edinburgh.

Marcus, G. (2013b) From the margins to the centre: The educational experiences of Gypsy and Traveller girls in Scottish schools. Paper presented at the British Educational Research Association (BERA) Postgraduate symposium (11 October), School of Education, University of Glasgow.

Marcus, G. (2014a) From the margins to the centre: The educational experiences of Gypsy/Traveller girls in Scotland. Paper presented at the *Kaleidoscope Conference: Opening Up the Ivory Tower* (29–30 May), Faculty of Education, University of Cambridge.

Marcus, G. (2014b) From the margins to the centre: The educational experiences of Gypsy/Traveller girls in Scotland. Paper presented at the *British Educational Research Association Annual Conference* (23–25 September), Institute of Education, London.

Marcus, G. (2015a) Marginalisation and the voices of Gypsy/Traveller girls. *Cambridge Open-Review Educational Research e-Journal (CORERJ)*, 1(2), pp. 55–77.

Marcus, G. (2015b) The intersecting invisible experiences of Gypsy/Traveller girls in Scotland. Paper presented at the *Childhood and Youth Studies Network Seminar* conference (25 November), School of Social and Political Science, University of Edinburgh.

Marcus, G. (2016) *Breaking the silence: The intersecting invisible experiences of Gypsy/Traveller girls in Scotland.* Unpublished PhD thesis, Edinburgh: University of Edinburgh.

Mayall, B. (1994) *Children's childhoods: Observed and experienced.* London: Psychology Press.

McCormick, A. (1907) *The Tinkler-Gypsies.* Dumfries: J. Maxwell and Son.

Morris, R. (1998) Gypsies and the planning system. *Journal of Planning and Environmental Law*, pp. 635–643.

Mosconi, J., and Emmett, J. (2003) Effects of a values clarification curriculum on high school students' definitions of success. *Professional School Counseling*, 7(2), pp. 68–78.

Murray, R. (1875, 1983) *The Gypsies of the border.* Galashiels: RC Hodges.

Neat, T. (1996) *The summer walkers: Travelling people and Pearl-Fishers in the highlands of Scotland.* Edinburgh: Canongate.

OECD. (2009) Annual Report 2009. Available at: https://www.oecd.org/newsroom/43125523.pdf. Accessed 13 February 2014.

Okely, J. (1983) *The Traveller-Gypsies.* Cambridge: Cambridge University Press.

Paterson, L. (2003) *Scottish education in the twentieth century.* Edinburgh: Edinburgh University Press.

Poole, L., and Adamson, K. (2008) *Report on the situation of the Roma community in Govanhill, Glasgow.* Oxfam.

Race, R., and Lander, V. (Eds.). (2014) *Advancing race and ethnicity in education.* Palgrave Macmillan.

Race Relations Act. (1976) Available at: http://www.legislation.gov.uk/ukpga/1976/74. Accessed 18 September 2014.

Race Relations (Amendment) Act. (2000). Available at http://www.homeofce.gov.uk/raceact/welcome.htm. Accessed 18 September 2014.

Rehfisch, A., and Rehfisch, F. (1975) Scottish Travellers or Tinkers. In: Rehfisch, F. (ed.) *Gypsies, Tinkers and other travellers.* London: Academic Press, pp. 271–283.

Reid, W. (1997) Scottish Gypsies/Travellers and the folklorists. *Romani Culture and Gypsy Identity*, pp. 29–37.

Romm, N. R. A. (2014) Conducting focus groups in terms of an appreciation of indigenous ways of knowing: Some examples from South Africa [62 paragraphs]. *Forum Qualitative Sozialforschung/Forum: Qualitative Social Research*, 16(1), Art. 2. http://nbn-resolving.de/urn:nbn:de:0114-fqs150120.

Save the Children Scotland. (2005) *Having our say.* Available at: http://www.gypsy-Traveller.org/your-family/young-people/educational-reports-and-resources. Accessed November 2012.

Schneider, B. H. (1993) *Children's social competence in context: The contributions of family, school and culture.* Oxford: Pergamon Press.

Shubin, S. (2010) "Where can a Gypsy stop?" Rethinking mobility in Scotland. *Antipode*, 43(2), pp. 494–524.

Shubin, S. (2011). Travelling as being: Understanding mobility amongst Scottish Gypsy Travellers. *Environment and Planning A*, 43(8), pp. 1930–1947.

Sime, D., and Fox, R. (2014) Home abroad: Eastern European children's family and peer relationships after migration. *Childhood*, 22(3), pp. 377–393.

STEP. (2013) Scottish Traveller education programme, The University of Edinburgh. Available at: http://www.step.education.ed.ac.uk/travelling-communities-in-scotland/. Accessed September 2012 to November 2014.

The Scottish Government. (2009) Race equality statement. Available at: http://
www.scotland.gov.uk/Topics/People/Equality/18934/RaceEqualityStatement.
Accessed 2 April 2013.

The Scottish Government. (2018) *Gypsy/Travellers*. Available at: https://beta.
gov.scot/policies/gypsy-travellers/. Accessed 15 March 2018.

The Scottish Parliament. (2013) *Equal opportunities committee 1st report 2013
(Session 4): Where Gypsy/Travellers live.* Available at: http://www.scottish.par-
liament.uk/S4_EqualOpportunitiesCommittee/Reports/eor-13-01w.pdf.
Accessed 10 May 2013.

The Social Marketing Gateway. (2013) Mapping the Roma Community in
Scotland: Final Report, 26 September 2013. Available at: www.gov.scot/
resource/0043/00434972.pdf. Accessed 16 July 2017.

Thelen, H. A. (1981) *The classroom society: The construction of educational experience.* London: Taylor and Francis.

Trepagnier, B. (2006) *Silent racism: How well-meaning white people perpetuate
the racial divide.* Boulder: Paradigm Publishing.

UNCRC. (2016) Concluding observations on the fifth periodic report of
the United Kingdom of Great Britain and Northern Ireland: Committee
on The Rights of the Child. Available at: http://www.ohchr.org/EN/
NewsEvents/Pages/DisplayNews.aspx?NewsID=19952&LangID=E.
Accessed 2 March 2017.

Wilkin, A., Derrington, C., and Foster, B. (2009) *Improving the outcomes for
Gypsy, Roma and Traveller pupils: Literature review.* London: DCSF.

Williamson, D. (1994) *The Horsieman: Memories of a Traveller 1928–1958.*
Edinburgh: Canongate Press.

Wilson, J. M., and Leighton, A. (1885) *Wilson's tales of the borders and of
Scotland: Historical, traditionary, and imaginative, with a glossary* (Vol. 2).
Glasgow: William MacKenzie.

Wren, D. J. (1999) School culture: Exploring the hidden curriculum.
Adolescence, 34(135), pp. 593–596.

2

Power and Silence: The Social Construction of Gypsies and Travellers

The purpose of this chapter is to outline my central argument that 'the Gypsy and Traveller', as a racialised minority community, is normatively absent yet pathologically present in the Scottish imagination (Mirza 2015: 3). Schröter (2013: 4) reminds us 'it is typical for societies to have discourses about minorities in which the minorities themselves are hardly ever heard'. This running theme, I argue, lies at the heart of much that is understood or misunderstood about Gypsies and Travellers. From the manipulation of the history and identity of the Gypsy and Traveller in Scottish culture, the lacuna in the existing literature on Gypsy and Traveller women, the suppression of alternative knowledge and modes of thinking, to the silences encountered within academia, policy documents, administrative data and Gypsies and Travellers themselves—the complexity of censorship and absence is problematised in this review of literature.

This chapter sets out arguments to demonstrate Gypsies and Travellers are ignored, erased or demonised as a central 'Other' in the European imagination. Gypsies and Travellers are simultaneously absent in terms of their views and experiences, and present in terms of serving as the disparaged Other in the Scottish and European mindsets.

© The Author(s) 2019
G. Marcus, *Gypsy and Traveller Girls*, Studies in Childhood and Youth,
https://doi.org/10.1007/978-3-030-03703-1_2

Mirza (2015: 1) echoes Schröter's (2013) view above and argues that the history and experiences of minority cultures are subject to manipulation by the dominant culture. Hence, the veracity of what is written and said about minorities ought to be questioned. I explain the 'problem' of trying to categorise, define and name Gypsies and Travellers. In Scotland, they constitute a heterogeneous group with different languages, cultures and ethnic identities. The contested origins and history of Gypsies and Travellers are discussed and I show how this serves to further marginalise, pathologise and erase them in the present.

The Scope of This Work: A Disclaimer

Given the relatively limited and nebulous foundation of current research and knowledge within Scotland on Gypsies and Travellers (Cemlyn et al. 2009; BEMIS 2011), the misrecognition and silencing of Gypsy and Traveller experiences and perspectives required me to undertake a wide-ranging review beyond the borders of Scotland. By misrecognition, I mean that Gypsies and Travellers are 'prevented from interacting on terms of parity by institutionalized hierarchies of cultural value that deny them the requisite standing; in that sense they suffer from status inequality or misrecognition' (Fraser 2007: 20).

Like other nomadic or semi-nomadic communities, many of the Gypsies and Travellers I met and interviewed travelled periodically, but some did not travel at all. Those that have family in England and Wales, for example, travel to visit or reside with them for extended periods of time. Physical space, laws, rules and regulations of the borders between the four nations of the United Kingdom do not seem to mentally and emotionally confine them. They are 'border crossers' (Anzaldúa 1987). The tensions and contradictions that accompany their lives as they move or travel across boundaries reflect the tensions and contradictions in deciding the national boundaries of the scholarly works I reviewed.

Academic literature before devolution continues to shed some light on the lives of Gypsies and Travellers in Scotland, just as much as the literature post-devolution attempts to build on current understandings.

Some issues of equality (and inequality) are not devolved to the Scottish Parliament. Legislation on human rights and equality, many of which stem from the United Nations and the European Union, are Acts of Parliament of the United Kingdom, necessitating Scotland's compliance. Cemlyn et al. (2009: 211) make a useful observation that 'since 1999, key legislation in Scotland has often been the subject of mirror enactment, with legislation in England and Wales simultaneously or subsequently passed in Edinburgh with only minor amendments reflecting the Scottish situation'. It was not possible to exclude material pre-devolution, just as it is necessary to include relevant academic material from England and Wales.

This account of the history and origins of Gypsies and Travellers warrants focus on relevant articles and monographs within the British Isles. The lack of literature on the gendered experiences and viewpoints of Gypsy and Traveller women and girls in Scotland necessitated a wider search and review of whatever was relevant in England and Wales. Later in this chapter I demonstrate the paucity of literature on women from Gypsy and Traveller communities.

The history of Gypsies and Travellers is discussed in three parts, highlighting heterogeneity and diversity of identity and perspectives. The first section in this chapter attempts to explain who 'Gypsies and Travellers' are, the history of how the 'communities' have been defined and labelled, the identity imposed on them in contrast to their own sense of identity, charting the range of terminologies used, and considered acceptable, over time and to the present day. 'Identity' and 'community' as concepts are problematised.

The second section reviews the historical construction of Gypsies and Travellers in Scotland, collectively viewed within the European Union today as being part of the 'Roma'. Referring to key texts, I provide background information detailing what has been written about their origins. Finally, I consider the literature on charting and explaining the communities' experiences of discrimination—from institutionalised racism to control and punishment, through policies, legislation and discourse that marginalise, demonise and silence. Relevant scholarly works which help to explain how and why Gypsies and Travellers are 'othered' are reviewed, but at the crux I expose the fact that the views and experiences of Gypsy and Traveller women are ignored, erased and absent from historical accounts.

The Construction of 'Gypsies and Travellers' in Scotland

Definitions and Language

There are a range of terms used to describe, define and control the kaleidoscope of groups with intersecting histories and experiences in Europe that are aggregated under the terms Gypsies and Travellers. In analysing the situation, I am an observer and outsider presenting the variety of perspectives and understandings which have changed over time. I acknowledge the complexity of collective and self-ascription, whilst being wary as mentioned earlier of the limitations of categorisations, and especially those that have been carved out of two cultural traditions—oral and written.

'No part of Europe is without Gypsies' (Cressy 2018: 1). Historically, the most common term used by the general population (by that I mean non-Travellers) to refer to these European wanderers, is 'Gypsy' or 'Gipsy', and often not capitalised in writing. According to Acton (1974: 61) the word 'Gypsy' is derived from the word 'Egyptian', which itself has the same root as the word 'Coptic'. Across Europe there are groups that call themselves Gitanos, Gitanes, Magup, Kiptii, Yifti, Gyupsi. As a generic term, 'Gypsy' is considered derogatory by some, but is still widely used in the media and in popular discourse. The term 'Gypsy' is linked to the first historical accounts of their existence in Europe, which I will discuss later.

The word 'Travellers' refers to occupational nomads, but some who call themselves Gypsies (and a very small minority of Roma) are occupational nomads with specific skills as craftsmen and metal workers. Acton (1974: 61) explains that many would rather refer to themselves as Travellers, despite having some Romani heritage, given that at several points in history to be identified as Gypsy or Rom meant death or enslavement; and this is true across Europe, especially in Eastern Europe. There are Irish Travellers and Scottish Travellers, for example, who reject the term 'Gypsy' and have their own identity and dialects. Despite this, however, they too face anti-Gypsy prejudice and experiences of suppression as a people.

Acton clarifies that the term Gypsy is 'probably the most widely used and inclusive word of self- and group-identification...Previous writers have sometimes suggested that it is a word to be used in opposition to 'Gypsy' or 'Romani', but that is certainly not the case today (1974: 64). Most of the Gypsies and Travellers I met self-identified as 'Travellers' or 'Scottish Travellers' and were proud to be so.

The word 'Romani', 'Roma' or 'Rom' has been defined to mean 'human'. Its primary meaning is 'decent, honourable, humane' and it distinguishes Gypsies from their non-Gypsy persecutors. The word 'Rom' can also mean 'husband' and 'Romni', can mean woman or wife (Acton 1974: 62). Some English Gypsies call themselves 'Romanichals' in their own dialect, whilst others avoided stigmatisation by referring to themselves as Travellers.

Liégeois and Gheorghe (1995: 6) refer to a report by The Minority Rights Group on *Roma/Gypsies: A European Minority*, which provides a useful description of the three main groups in Europe and in the UK:

'Gypsy' - Term used to denote ethnic groups formed by the dispersal of commercial, nomadic and other groups from within India from the tenth century, and their mixing with European and other groups during their Diaspora.

'Traveller' - A member of any of the (predominantly) indigenous European ethnic groups (Woonwagenbewoners, Minceiri, Jenisch, Quinquis, Resende, etc.), whose culture [are] characterized, inter-alia, by self-employment, occupational fluidity, and nomadism. These groups have been influenced, to a greater or lesser degree by ethnic groups of (predominantly) Indian origin with a similar cultural base.

'Roma I Rom' - A broad term used in various ways, to signify: (a) Ethnic groups (e.g., Kalderash, Lovari etc.) who speak the 'Vlach', 'Xoraxane' or 'Rom' varieties of the Romani language. (b) Any person identified by others as 'Tsigane' in Central and Eastern Europe and Turkey, plus those outside the region of East European extraction. (c) Romani people in general.

The Council of Europe (CoE) acknowledges the complexities involved and their preferred terminology has changed over time. Today, the CoE uses the term 'Roma' and this includes Scottish Gypsies and Travellers (CoE, Glossary of Roma 2012: 1, 6). There are approximately 10 to 12 million Roma living in Europe and the term 'Roma' 'used by the Council of Europe refers to Roma, Sinti, Kale and related groups in Europe, including Travellers and the Eastern groups (Dom and Lom), and covers the wide diversity of the groups concerned, and persons who identify themselves as "Gypsies"' (Council of Europe 2012).

In Scotland, terms other than 'Gypsy' or 'gipsy' have been used. In the twelfth century, there was mention of 'tinklers' (Clark 2001: 160). In Gaelic, Scottish Travellers have been known as 'cairdean' (Porter and Glower 1995: xix)—reflecting their ancient occupational function as iron or metal workers—or 'luchd siubhail' (people of travel) for Travellers in general. The term based on the Gaelic 'tinceard', and, as stated earlier, in Scots 'tinkers' or tinsmith was also used. 'To be called a 'Tinker' was probably once prestigious' (Acton 1974: 76). Some Travellers in Scotland refer to themselves as 'Nachins' or 'Nawkens' in their native language Cant, believing their ancestry traceable to North–West India. According to Dawson (2007: 9), the term probably means 'no home'. Dawson (2007: 9) believes, perhaps inaccurately, 'they had no real name for themselves, referring to "our people" or "our folk"'. Others argue the term is more akin to the word 'nach' (or nose), reflecting their strong instinctive response (following one's nose) in identifying a fellow member of the community and in their resilient struggle for survival over centuries.

Like English, Cant borrows heavily from a variety of sources, but it has strong links to Romani, Arabic and Gaelic, alongside other languages like Latin and French (Acton 1974: 56). Some Travellers speak 'Beurla-reagaird' which is related to the Shelta that Irish Travellers use. The Irish Travellers speak a version of Irish using many words from vocabularies known as Gammon or Shelta. Clark (2001: 407) explains:

Most Scottish Travellers speak English, but again with many words that are not used by the general population. Some of these words are of Romani origin, bearing out the theory that the Scottish Travellers have intermarried with *Romanichals* over the years. The dialect of the Borders is closer to that of the English *Romanichals* while some of the Highland and Islands Scottish Travellers who travel in the Highlands and to the Western Isles speak a Cant based on Scottish Gaelic. The Romanies and some of the *Kale* still speak the Romani *(Romanes)* language, using its traditional grammar.

As is obvious in the description above, each of the groups of traditional Gypsies or Travellers has its own language and there is a rich variety. Acton (1974: 56) argues that when considered from a neutral perspective, the variation in language is 'probably the simplest and most objective indicator of the extent of ethnic variation among Gypsies and Travellers in this country'. Although as Okely (1983: 8) reminds us, language itself cannot be 'equated with race' or ethnic identities, as some Gypsiologists have tended to do. English is widely spoken, for example, but of course not all who speak it are of English heritage.

Other derogatory descriptions like 'pike' or 'pikie' were, and remain, commonly used. Acton (1974: 74) notes, and perhaps incorrectly:

Hotten's dictionary of slang [1887] gives *pike at* as *go away* and *Pikey* as *a tramp or a Gypsy*. He continues - a *pikey-cart* is, in various parts of the country, one of those habitable vehicles suggestive of country life. Possibly the term has some reference to those who continually use the *pike* or turnpike road.

The *Journal of the Gypsy Lore Society* (1912) defines the term *pikey* as a negative term of address for Gypsies. 'Tinks', 'tinkies', 'pike', 'pikeys' and 'gypo', are regarded as racial slurs, especially when used by the general population to denigrate and insult. In keeping with anti-Gypsy sentiments, the English dictionary defines Cant as a language used among thieves and beggars, a kind of non-standard speech (Oxford Dictionary 2015). The word 'Gyp' in the English language, for example, means to cheat or swindle and the Cockney slang 'a Gypsy's kiss' rhymes and refers to piss. Note how these terms are intrinsically bound with notions of immorality, disorder and threat. Such discourse continues to be used without due regard to their origin and offensive meaning to Gypsies and Travellers, just as the term 'Paki' is used to describe a shop that is opened all hours, and 'Chinky' a slang name for a Chinese takeaway restaurant. Over time, these terms denigrate, subvert and control, whilst instigating fear and hatred of the perceived outsider or migrant.

It is not uncommon for some Gypsies and Travellers in Scotland to refer to each other as 'pike' or 'tink', rather like the way in which it is deemed acceptable amongst some Black Americans to refer to each other as 'nigger' or 'nigga'—particularly in Hip Hop and Rap cultures (Spears 2006). Unlike the term 'nigga', the terms 'pike or tink' are not reclamations of the original term; nevertheless, this intragroup usage remains controversial and is not always welcomed. Each of these terms may denote positive, neutral or negative attitudes, depending on who is speaking and what is being said.

Acton (1997) notes in recent years in England, the word 'Gypsy' is being embraced in the name of the thousands who perished in the Porajmos (The Devouring), Roma word for the Holocaust. Many Roma from Europe, as do many in Scotland, reject the name because they view it as predominantly contemptuous. Scottish Highland Travellers and Show People do not refer to themselves as Romani, Rom or Roma. Neither do they consider themselves Gypsies (Kenrick and Clark 1999; Clark 2001; Acton 2004, 2007). Other Travelling peoples in Scotland, such as 'Border Gypsies', however, do identify themselves in this way. There is a movement now both in Ireland and Scotland amongst some Irish and Scottish Travellers respectively of indigenisation of their language and ancestry. There is a small but growing movement to reclaim the terminology related to Scottish Gypsies and Travellers—objecting to the umbrella term 'Traveller' to band their communities together. One man I spoke to said he was proud to be called Gypsy. He believed it was time to re-energise the term (along with Romany and Roma Romani) and recover its rich ancient culture and traditions; a process of decolonisation and indigenisation seeking respect for their worldview, knowledge and heritage.

The Myth of Nomadism as Defining Characteristic

According to the Caravan Sites and Control of Development Act 1960 (Section 24), Gypsies and Travellers are 'persons of nomadic habit of life, whatever their race or origin'. Gypsies and Travellers are often neither viewed nor acknowledged as a separate race (Clark 2006). Legislation, attitude surveys and comments on social media indicate the general population (non-Travellers) still believe Gypsies and Travellers are called as such simply because they lead a travelling lifestyle (Richardson 2006: 5).

Richardson (2006: 5) rightly problematises the above legal definition of Gypsy and Traveller ethnic identity because it 'refers to nomadism as the defining characteristic'; but not all Gypsies and Travellers are permanently nomadic and some are not nomadic at all. There are those that lead a semi-nomadic lifestyle, while most have been forced to assimilate or partially assimilate over time and are permanently settled under bricks and mortar. Since 1989 in England, Gypsies and Travellers have been legally defined as having separate ethnic status, whether they travel or not. There, the communities are referred to as Gypsy/Roma/Traveller or GRT. In Scotland, Gypsies and Travellers were recognised as having separate ethnic status in 2008, as defined by the Mandla criteria (Mandla vs. Dowell-Lee 1983). Whilst legal recognition does not stop the problems faced by Gypsies and Travellers in Scotland, it is a symbolic recognition of their identity, and provides a tool for challenging discrimination within the legal structure (Cemlyn et al. 2009).

In 2001, the Equal Opportunities Committee (EOC) recommended the term 'Gypsy and Traveller' be used based on the 'precedent set by voluntary organisations working with Gypsies and Travellers' (The Scottish Parliament 2013). This descriptor is the Scottish Government's official terminology and is the preferred term used in some academic literature. The EOC believes 'using the term 'Gypsy/Traveller' acknowledges Gypsies and Travellers are not a homogenous group' (The Scottish Parliament 2013: 2). The use of the oblique allows the government to avoid taking a stance in the debate over nomenclature. Other governments in similar naming disputes over ethnicity use this punctuation mark to indicate 'or', and to suggest there is no stated preference. The term is capitalised; failure to do so in newspaper reports and in some government papers, have caused upset amongst some in the Travelling community, as they believe it reinforces the lack of recognition of their ethnicity. This term is not accepted by all Gypsies and Travellers and it is controversial. There are misunderstandings over identity and nomenclature by the 'settled community' and within the groups in question (McKinney 2001: 21). Some choose to use 'Scottish Traveller' or just 'Traveller' instead.

The Scottish Traveller Education Programme (STEP) website recommends the heading 'Travelling Communities in Scotland', preferring to use 'the umbrella term 'Travellers' [because it is] traditionally accepted terminology among the different groups in Scotland' (STEP 2013). The website acknowledges 'official terms referring to the different groups living in Scotland have changed over time, from Scotland's Travelling People to Gypsies/Travellers, Showmen, Roma and New Travellers. These changes reflect Scottish society's changing perceptions of Travellers' (STEP 2013). Identity, how it is perceived, constructed and labelled is neither static nor impervious. The term recommended by STEP could perpetuate the myth that the ethnicity of Gypsies and Travellers is chiefly related to and defined by their nomadism, which is not the case.

Clark (2006) offers a useful typology, which acknowledges the diverse communities, which exist under the umbrella term 'Gypsy and Traveller', and that each has their own unique culture and language. Acton and Mundy (1997: 238) describe this diversity as 'polarised variations of a common structure'. At no point are the terms 'Gypsy', 'Traveller' and 'Roma' used synonymously in this book, and at no point are they viewed as one and the same peoples.

The terms, 'settled population', 'general population' or 'settled communities' are used interchangeably to refer in this book (and in many academic texts) to non-Travellers or non-Gypsies, also known as 'gaujo' or 'gorgio'—'an Anglo-Romani term meaning an 'outsider' or someone who is not a Gypsy, Traveller or Romani' (Clark 2001: 397). The terms Traveller and non-Traveller are deceptive because they suggest an artificial binary, which does not reflect the many different ethnicities that live in settled housing, including of course Gypsies and Travellers. However, to highlight a simplistic distinction this binary serves a limited but useful purpose.

Race and ethnic identity do need to be acknowledged and respected, and such categorisations have their use, but flexibility in the use of nomenclature does allow for a more extensive study, unhindered by notions of identity that is limiting or inaccurate. The porous boundary reflects the variety of communities that live, travel and have intermarried in Scotland—Highland Scottish Travellers, Lowland Scottish Travellers, Showmen or Showpeople, Romanichals or English Romanies, English Gypsies, Irish Travellers, Welsh Kale, and European Roma. Show People comprise cultural and business communities and do not wish to have a separate ethnic status (STEP 2013).

Problematising Identity and Community

Identity
Debating what Gypsy/Roma/Traveller peoples ought to be called, or telling them what to call themselves or how they ought to envisage their own identity, is at best intrusive and at worst an exercise in patriarchal control and domination through discourse (Ni Shuinear 1997; Richardson 2006). A historical or comprehensive analysis of the merits and demerits of the various terminologies and categories used to describe 'Travelling Communities' is beyond the scope of this study. This work accepts the fluidity of the terms, which have evolved over centuries, and recognises they will continue to change. As Clark (2001: 22) contends, debates over identity will remain an 'unresolved issue'. Yet, Travelling folk know who they are (and who they are not) and do not have a problem naming themselves and their communities.

Heaslip's (2015) phenomenological study of 20 Gypsies and Travellers in South West England, however, suggests a note of caution. Her findings reveal that the participants, male and female, and who come from a range of backgrounds, ages, and housing, feel vulnerable both outwith and within their communities for several reasons highlighted in Table 2.1.

Table 2.1 Experiences of vulnerability from a Gypsy and Travelling perspective (Heaslip 2015: 3–4)

Vulnerability outside community	Vulnerability within community
Being an outsider	Insider identity
How they are perceived by others outside the Gypsy and travelling community	A split in one's identity
Feeling homogenised	A threatened cultural identity and heritage
Having to conform to live a particular way of life	Having to conform to live a particular way of life
Ambiguities of their historical, cultural and geographical identity	
Feeling discriminated, persecuted and threatened	
Potential or actual lack of physical travelling experience	
Powerlessness	

Centuries of marginalisation and control reveal identities are not only unresolved, but damaging to an individual's core being. However, I am wary of the discourse of vulnerability as applied to Gypsies and Travellers or any minority ethnic group within the context of research. It could be argued that Gypsies and Travellers are vulnerable because of low levels of literacy and numeracy (Okely 1983; McCaffery 2009), or because of institutionalised discrimination and being caught in a cycle of oppression. Or that centuries of being persecuted and marginalised situates them in a power imbalance with the dominant culture, thus making them continually vulnerable (Heaslip 2015). As there are multiple experiences and multiple identities, the reality is more nuanced than the single narrative of vulnerability applied to an entire ethnic group. Heaslip (2015: 50) gives a clear account of the many forms of vulnerability on a continuum as described by Copp (1986). Vulnerability within an individual or community could be a paternalistic political term used by the coloniser to help and control the colonised. The term should be used with introspection and care, as does the term 'community'. Heaslip's findings reveal tensions and splits in identity within the community, especially as her participants feel the threat to their cultural identity and heritage. Some of the girls I interviewed talked about straddling two worlds, two identities and acknowledged the tensions living within two cultures—theirs and the outside world, with their personal identity liminally entangled betwixt and between.

Community

Belton notes that 'community appears almost universally to be accepted as a positive phenomenon—a warm...focus for unity, allegiance, support and hope' (Bauman 2001; Belton 2013: 289). Community is generally understood to be a good thing. Fernback (2007: 50) offers a deceptively simple definition of community as a 'symbolic process of collective experience and cultural meaning'. Delanty (2010) views it as a collective ethnic identity, or based on geographical location, or on a group's shared interests and values, or more recently as virtual communities. Duffee (1980), Cohen (1985), and Belton (2013) argue, however, that the concept of community is complicated, as Heaslip's (2015) recent study suggests. The terms can be defined in at least three ways. A group or community can be distinguished and based on shared locality, shared identity (Seagrave 1996) or as Cohen (1985) suggests, it can be based on an individual's sense of belonging or ascription to a group. Groups or communities are social constructs, defined by the persons they include, but also, the boundary markers of those who are excluded. The insiders share common values, interests and lifestyles. Boundaries are formed, but the extent of those boundaries can be difficult to measure or control.

Groups and communities are problematic because they can elide the heterogeneity of experiences and within-group diversity (Belton 2013). They will share commonalities, but are not immune to disruptions and variations from the norm. There can therefore be constant tension between asserting individual identities or interests and securing the benefits of community membership (Gutiérrez 2004; Gutiérrez and Arzubiaga 2012). Moreover, groups and communities are dynamic and not fixed in time—changing norms, values and rules allow for new participants to join—and for others to be excluded. Belton (2013: 282) argues 'the social construct that is community, while propagating solidarity and fraternity, promotes social insularity and forms of discrimination and prejudice'. It is both a social structure and as symbolic one. It involves social interaction, but it has meaning and identity.

'Community is ultimately what people think it is, [but] also culturally defined units of meaning' (Cohen, cited in Delanty 2010: 3).

Belton (2005), himself a Gypsy, questions the nature of Gypsy identity and suggests there is no consistent Gypsy lineage. Unlike many Gypsy/Roma/Traveller scholars, he argues for the social nature of the Gypsy population, rather than ethnicity based on biology, blood or breed (Belton 2005: 4). He highlights the constant growth and dynamism of Gypsy and Traveller history, identity, social groupings and lifestyles. Similarly, Acton argues, 'racial purity is as much a myth among Gypsies as among any people of the world' (1974: 19).

Belton's (2013: 295) position about defining 'Gypsies' is by far the most cogent, because it warns against the myth of the singularity of cultures:

> A non-intersectional view of Gypsies is inherently one-dimensional because people are viewed as representing just a single personal circumstance [or a single identity]; 'Gypsies (all of them) are (being Gypsies) like this'; 'Gypsies (all of them) do that (because they are Gypsies)'... We need to take a multifaceted social stance rather than restrict analysis to a purely community-oriented perspective, which effectively translates to 'ghetto thinking'.

Belton (2013: 282) raises several critical points about the experience of Gypsy and Traveller identity, mostly defined via ethnic, cultural and community narratives, where 'identity is mutually constituted within unequal relations of power'. He reminds us there can be 'tension between individual and community identity' which can impact on experiences of 'equality and freedom'. As human beings we want to carve out our own individuality and fulfil our potential, but also desire the 'refuge' of being part of a group, to belong and to 'commune with others' we see as sharing similar values and identities. Community helps delineate 'us' from 'them', but there is a psychological and emotional balance to be negotiated—how to be true to oneself and yet be loyal to the group. Okely (1975: 65) and Belton (2013: 285) maintain identity is not a one-way process, as it requires both social and self-ascription, making debates over origins, history and ancestry less important.

Belton (2013: 294) cites Crenshaw's (1991) intersectional argument that the politics of identity and identity formation can 'obscure and/or overlook differences between people who are socially categorized as broadly sharing similar experiences'. Definitions of Gypsy identity may only include the axes of race or ethnicity, as they have tended to do thus far, but Belton contends that looking at Gypsy or Traveller experiences through a single lens cannot provide an accurate comprehension of experience. Gender, age, disability, class, and sexuality matter in helping to create multiple identities, within prescribed community categorisations. Cultures, communities and identities are not fixed constructs, but are rhizomatic and volatile (Deleuze and Guattari 1977, 1987; Grosz 1994). This multiplicity casts a shadow over existing theories, texts and research that hold focus on singularities, or dualisms (Grosz 1994).

Clark's (2001) summation that debates over the correct terminology will 'remain unresolved', applies to debates about origins, identity, belonging, and community. A way forward when conducting research of this kind, is to accept and acknowledge self-identification and self-ascription as Okely (1983), Nemeth (2002), Belton (2013) and others suggest, whilst being cautiously aware of the constructive (and destructive) role played by dominant systems and structures within institutions, communities and families.

History and Origins of Gypsies and Travellers in Scotland

The ancestors of the Romani-speaking peoples are thought to have left India some one thousand years ago, moving along trade routes trodden over the centuries by countless other migratory peoples (Kenrick 1993, 1998; Clark 2001; GRTPA 2014). Theories linking their origins to Egypt and India abound, but are debated and disputed (Thompson 1928; Okely 1983; Belton 2005). While Gypsies and Travellers continue to 'live throughout the world, sometimes intermarrying, sometimes not, disunited politically, heterogeneous culturally, and with the most diverse aspirations' (Acton 1974: 1). Apart from a few common cultural and linguistic links, Travelling Communities in Scotland have a separate history to European Roma (Okely 1983; Liégeois and Gheorghe 1995;

Clark 2001; Whyte 2001). Exploring the detailed history and origins of European Roma, and highlighting connections with Scottish Gypsies and Travellers though is beyond the scope of this study. However, it must be stated that both have similar experiences in that they have suffered persecution that dates back several hundred years.

According to Okely (1983), Gypsies and Travellers have lived in the British Isles since the fifteenth century, but their complex history is not fully understood. Rehfisch and Rehfisch (1975: 272) argues that trying to piece together the puzzle of Gypsy and Traveller identity is almost futile, because 'their origin is lost in the far past and can hardly be reconstructed'. However, the issue is not that their origin is 'lost' but that the political project of erasing Gypsy and Traveller history has over time largely succeeded. Moreover, their history and origins are not entirely 'lost' to Gypsy and Traveller families.

Within a rich and ancient oral tradition, families have passed down folk tales and stories through the generations. Famous storytellers— Duncan Williamson, Jimmy McBeath, Jeannie Robertson and her nephew Stanley Robertson, William McPhee, Belle Stewart, Betsy Whyte, and Jess Smith—have kept history and cultural traditions alive through ballads and songs (Hood 1960; Tong 1998; Neat 1999; Tobler 2012; Green 2013). These indigenous accounts have been recorded and archived, such as at the Elphinstone Institute at the University of Aberdeen and archives at the University of Liverpool. Some Traveller women have written novels, autobiographies and short stories (Smith 2006, 2008, 2012; Stewart 2006, 2008; Whyte 2000, 2001).

The term 'indigenous' is used informally to refer to communities with longstanding cultural and historical ties to a particular place. I recognise that the use of the term can be open to interpretation, depending on the context in which it is used. In the 1970s, the term was popularised when aboriginal groups throughout the world campaigned for greater presence in the United Nations. In the UN (2009), the term 'indigenous' is used to refer to people who have long established links to specific lands and whose lives have been disrupted by colonisation, industrialisation, displacement, and settlement of their traditional territories by others. Scottish Gypsies and Travellers have not been officially recognised as indigenous, although they were awarded separate ethnic status in 2008 and are considered to be vulnerable to exploitation, marginalisation and oppression by the dominant Scottish population. The term as used in this book distances itself from colonial theories that suggest indigenous communities ought to be civilised or made to conform to dominant ways of life and value systems.

Green (2013) advocates that the oral traditions of Scottish Gypsy Travellers have contributed to Scotland's national identity and its legacy; and that the history of Gypsies and Travellers is part of Scottish heritage, tradition, culture, and language: 'They are a Scotland in miniature' (Dawson 2007: 10). There are similarities and differences between the history of Gypsies and Travellers and mainstream Scottish heritage, and the two have been necessarily and inextricably linked for centuries (Neat 1996; Kenrick and Clark 1999). Whilst there is much value in these views, Belton (2013: 286) almost apologetically questions the strength and veracity of oral and literary accounts of history and tradition because:

> Narratives of this sort are hardly ever repeated verbatim; they shift, alter, transmute and adapt according to mood, time, audience, situation and a range of contextual considerations.

So, I would argue, are all other forms of histories. Belton (2013: 287) highlights that Gypsies and Travellers' accounts are 'a response ... at least in part, to their marginality'.

Scotland's Travelling people or 'the mist people' are thought to be a nomadic group, 'formed in Scotland in the period 1500–1800 from intermarriage between local nomadic craftsmen and immigrant Romanies from France and Spain in particular' (Clark 2001: 112). Some sources contend they are not Gypsies and may even have existed from the twelfth century, possibly making them Britain's oldest community of Travellers (Whyte 2001; Clark and Greenfields 2006, Clark and Taylor 2014). Records suggest a group known as 'tinklers' were identified in the Farandman Laws (Grampian Regional Council Social Strategy Unit 1994: 6). These laws permitted them to 'to go about their business' and they were viewed as skilled craftsmen and artisans (Gmelch 1975; Clark 2001: 160). Williamson (1994) argues they could possibly have even been hunter-gatherers from the Mesolithic period, and many Scottish Travellers believe this to be the foundation of their ancestry. Kenrick (1998) maintains today's Travellers in Scotland are a product of years of inter-marriage between pre-Celtic or Celtic and Romanies. As there was, and continues to be, 'both short and long term movement' of all Gypsies and Travellers and 'considerable inter-marriage between groups', it is difficult to ascertain how 'Romany' or 'Indian' or Celtic one group is compared to another (Okely 1983: 18). Neat (1996: 65) suggests that Scotland's Travelling Peoples are the nation's 'most substantially ancient culture… lying totally unregarded and essentially unknown'.

There is very little new or recent research on the history and origins of Gypsies and Travellers in Scotland. For example, out of a list of abstracts accepted for the annual meeting and conference of the Gypsy Lore Society held in Moldova in September 2015 (Gypsy Lore Society 2015) only five out of 80 abstracts were about Gypsy/Roma/Traveller communities in the UK, focusing mainly on the experiences of European Roma communities in England. This situation has been a growing trend since the arrival of Eastern European Roma around 2004 in the UK. None were on Gypsy/Roma/Traveller women in the UK, and none were on Gypsies and Travellers in Scotland.

Prior to Scottish devolution in 1998, most academic works tended to focus on the Gypsy/Roma/Travelling communities in England and Wales or Ireland. A review of this material indicates studies are predominantly from a historical perspective—exploring origins, language, culture, and ethnicity of Gypsy/Roma/Travellers. In Britain, Acton (1974, 1994, 1997, 2000, 2004, 2007) has written extensively on Romani culture. Kenrick (1993) charts the migration of the Gypsies, explores the possibilities of 'gaining ground through law reform' (Kenrick and Clark 1999) and has written extensively on the Romani language across Europe. Others like Mayall (1997) and Hancock (1987) present accounts of Gypsy slavery and persecution, and their demonisation (Hancock 2010) and struggle for control of their identity (Hancock 1997). Similarly, Mayall (2004) and Rehfisch and Rehfisch (1975) write about Gypsy and Traveller history from the 1500s onwards, and Mayall (1995) notably questions the stereotyped images presented in works of fiction and early nineteenth-century gypsiologists. He charts the history of anti-Gypsy legislation from the sixteenth century onwards, criticising the use of state power to criminalise their nomadism. Hawes and Perez (1996) examine public policy and planning issues, legislation and policing, arguing the Gypsy is subject to ethnic cleansing in Britain.

Along with Acton's recognised works on Gypsy/Roma/Travellers in the UK and in Europe, three other scholars have produced work that is of significant relevance to my study. Okely's (1983) monograph on *The Traveller-Gypsies* is the first account of British Gypsy life from a social anthropological perspective. Through extensive fieldwork conducted in England and Europe, she explores their history, economy and cultural practices, and their resilience in the face of centuries of persecution. Okely questions their Indian origins and offers relatively modern explanations for their lifestyle and practices. She writes about marriage and touches on the image of women within their communities and as perceived by Gorgio (non-Traveller) men. Clark's work on the Travelling Communities in Scotland (1999, 2001, 2006) has been crucial in laying the foundations for my understanding of Scottish Traveller history and culture. Clark is himself a Traveller and as there is a paucity of academic representation from the Travelling community itself, Clark's research is especially compelling. Belton (2005, 2013), also a Gypsy, questions Gypsy history and identity along distinct racial lines and argues instead for their dynamic social construction over time. However, there are no specific studies that focus entirely on the experiences and perspectives of Gypsy and Traveller women or girls.

Some scholarly works include ethnographic and case studies of various groups within the diverse community living in the UK, including Irish and Welsh Travellers, and New Forest Gypsies (Okely 1975; Jarman and Jarman 1991; Reynolds et al. 2003; Smith 2002; Griffin 2008). In Scotland, case studies on specific groups include, *The Gypsies of the Border* (Murray 1875 [1983]), *Tales of the Border* (Wilson and Leighton c. 1885), *Exploits and Anecdotes of the Scottish Gypsies* (Chambers, c. 1886), *Gypsies of Yetholm* (Brockie 1884), MacRitchie's (1894) *Scottish Gypsies Under the Stewarts, The Tinker-Gypsies of Galloway* (McCormick 1907), and *The Tinkers of Arran* (Dawson 1971).

A number of the above-mentioned texts were written by men in the late nineteenth century, and arguably reflect a 'colonial' or paternalistic 'male, imperial gaze' (Kaplan 1997, 2005; Mulvey 1975, 1989). As previously mentioned, Mayall (2004) highlights the tendency in these studies to propagate stereotyped images—criminalised or romanticised. Acton and Mundy (1997: 238) caution that researchers conducting specific case studies of particular groups ought to ensure their work is placed in a 'broader historical and structural context'. Extrapolations can only be limited, as there are a diverse range of groups with varied customs, rules and lifestyles. There is no caution, however, to highlight how such 'diversity' or 'broader historical and structural context' ought to include the perspectives of women in these communities, their accounts of history, origins and culture.

Key scholarly texts that examine the origins of Gypsies and Travellers in Scotland include Rehfisch and Rehfisch (1975), Williamson (1994), Reid (1997), Kenrick (1998), Clark (2001), Whyte (2001), McKinney (2003), and Shubin (2010, 2011). Since devolution several have focused on the inequalities experienced by Scottish Gypsies and Travellers, and most of these tend to be document-based enquiries (Clark 2001, 2006, 2008, 2013, 2014; Dawson 2005, 2007; Shubin 2010). Current literature on Gypsies and Travellers which focus on specific issues, such as education, health and employment, necessarily provide a short historical background, summarising and repeating much of the information provided in the works cited above, but the history of the Gypsy and Traveller and its construction is not critiqued or problematised in these texts.

The Demonised Other: Past and Present

The disputed history and origins of Gypsies and Travellers have powerfully framed how they are conceived in the minds of settled communities, consciously or subconsciously, for centuries. Gypsies and Travellers have traditionally often been viewed as 'rogues, vagabonds and vagrants' (Mayall 1995: 40), and in Scotland have experienced various forms of persecution or remedies for combating nomadism through deportation to the colonies, ethnic cleansing, removal of children from their parents to be sent to Australia and Canada and forced assimilation and 'extirpation' (extermination) as evidenced in *The 1895 Scottish Traveller Report* (Groome 1890–1891; Dawson 2005). Cases of forced adoptions reportedly take place today and social workers are still referred to by Gypsies and Travellers as 'The Cruelty' (*Traveller Times* 2018). In forcibly removing children from their families, they were also removed from their history and place of belonging. Reid's (2008) account of his experiences in *Never to Return* is a 'harrowing story of [his] stolen childhood'.

Genocidal laws against Gypsies and Travellers or 'Egyptians' were commonly enacted in many countries across Christian Europe (Acton 1974: 103). Cressy's (2018) account of their origins, history and 'proscriptions' provides comprehensive and informative reading. They were banned from the Holy Roman Empire in 1501 and could be caught and executed. By royal decree, in seventeenth century France, Gypsy women were sterilised, men condemned into forced labour and children separated from their parents. The same occurred in Spain, the Austro-Hungarian empire, Romania. Between 1530 and 1580, several laws were passed forbidding Gypsies from entering England, and those already living in the country were at risk of deportation. *The Egyptians Act* (1530) subjected Gypsies to the death penalty. In 1541, the first wave of anti-Gypsy laws was introduced in Scotland, and in the 1570s Scottish Gypsies and Travellers were ordered to stop travelling, leave Scotland or face the death penalty. A few decades later in 1609, a further law in Scotland declared that since all Gypsies were thieves by habit or repute they should be put to death or transported to the Americas. Staying hidden and invisible kept Gypsies and Travellers safe (Grönfors 1982), but their visible absence further corrupted their image in popular discourse and marginalised them. Even so, staying hidden could not protect them from major national events, such as famine and war.

There were other reasons why some Gypsy and Traveller families became economic nomads. The famine of 1623 saw many families made homeless. During the Jacobite Uprising at Culloden in 1745, 'families thought to have supported Charles were ruthlessly evicted and their homes destroyed… and so some found themselves on the road' (Dawson 2007: 17). Later, forced displacement during the Highland

Clearances had a major impact on Travellers (Mackenzie 1883 [2012]; Prebble 1971).

Gypsies, Roma and Travellers continued to be persecuted into the twentieth century. In Italy and Germany in the 1940s many were massacred in the Porajmos (Holocaust), reportedly wiping out around 25% of all European Roma, and over 90% in several European countries (Council of Europe 2018).

They remain segregated in schools across Slovakia, the Czech Republic and Hungary, and in some countries (like Italy and Sweden) the collection of databases and profiles of Roma families and communities are still mooted as acceptable forms of monitoring, control, forced assimilation and eradication. In Scotland, a twice-yearly count (undertaken in January and July) was introduced in 1998 to 'better understand the characteristics of this population and to assist and inform the development of public policies and services for Gypsies/Travellers, both nationally and locally' (The Scottish Government 2010). In 2011, this practice ceased, but was replaced by the inclusion of Gypsies and Travellers as an ethnic category in the national census.

The carefully crafted image in the Scottish mainstream still associates Gypsies and Travellers with being thieves, wild and dirty. They are accused of avoiding 'gainful employment' or paying taxes; their children do not go to school; they are cunning, involved in the mystical arts, witchcraft and magic spells. Their girls only want to get married and have children. They are all poor and they all live in caravans. The symbolic public perception reflects Gypsies and Travellers as a demonised Other (Okely 1994; Coxhead 2007; Richardson and Ryder 2012).

The 1895 Scottish Traveller Report was originally commissioned and produced by the Departmental Committee for the Secretary of State for Scotland, and presented to Parliament. The report gathered evidence:

> To call attention to habitual offenders, vagrants, beggars and inebriates in Scotland… to enquire **whether the numbers of such persons is increasing** and into the causes of such increase and to suggest such **remedies** as may, while deterrent, be likely to bring about **their reformation** and *to* **prevent further additions** to their numbers, due regard being had to **the cost**. (Dawson 2005: 9, my emphasis)

The troubles caused by 'Gipsies and tinkers' form a section of this extensive report, with witnesses and representatives from the Church, Police and Inspector of Prisons, in what would be the equivalent of a modern day parliamentary inquiry. Notably, the Church (not confined to any one denomination) had a long history of Gypsy persecution in Europe. Martin Luther, in his work entitled *Liber Vagatorium* (Book of Vagabonds, 1528), called them 'fake friars, wandering Jews and rogues' (The Encyclopaedia Britannica 1974: 852–853). The Church rejected Gypsies, and according to Greenfeld (1977: 22), abused, exhausted and took advantage of them as if they were indentured labourers or slaves.

Gypsies and Travellers were not called upon to testify at hearings and their voices were missing. The report is a crucial document that reveals the searing patriarchal mindset, which confuses care with cleansing and control (Clark 2008). The cost of carrying out all three was a primary concern of the State (Richardson 2006: 4). The discourse is patronising or disparaging, as every aspect of Gypsy and Traveller life is scrutinised against the white male, colonial, hegemonic standards of the time.

The Encyclopaedia Britannica (1954: 852) defines 'the Gypsy' as follows:

> The mental age of the average adult Gypsy is thought to be about that of a child of ten. Gypsies have never accomplished anything of great significance in writing, painting, musical composition, science or social organisation. Quarrelsome, quick to anger or laughter, they are unthinkingly but not deliberately cruel. Loving bright colours, they are ostentatious and boastful, but lack bravery.

This description was written only a decade after thousands of Gypsy and Traveller men sacrificed their lives for Britain in the Second World War (National Association of Teachers of Travellers 2015).

Sections of Gypsy and Traveller communities in Scotland, as yet undefined, and throughout the United Kingdom, continue to encounter grave problems in having their needs and rights met in ways that do not compromise their ancient traditions and culture. Today the situation for Scottish Gypsies and Travellers raises 'fundamental human rights concerns—particularly the rights to health, education, housing, family life and cultural life and the requirement to be free from discrimination in the realisation of these rights' (Amnesty International Letter 2010: 1).

In 2001, Clark's doctoral thesis gives a description of the issues facing Gypsies and Travellers in Scotland. Since then, in 2005 a survey conducted by Save The Children revealed 92% of young Gypsies and Travellers in Scotland stated they had been bullied or called names because of their ethnic identity. A doctor's surgery can still refuse to accept Gypsies and Travellers onto their patients list despite there being vacancies. Over 50% of Gypsies and Travellers in Scotland will have spent at least part of their lives without access to running water (MECOPP 2012). Numbers in prisons are disproportionately high and many report being 'victims of violence, bullying and racism…and are at risk of suicide' (Bhopal 2018: 33) The Scottish Social Attitudes Survey (Scottish Centre for Social Research 2010, 2015) confirmed there are negative and racist views towards Gypsies and Travellers. Scottish local authorities currently do not have a legal duty to provide caravan site accommodation for Gypsies and Travellers. 'The term caravan (as defined by the 1960 Caravan Sites Act) includes a mobile home comprising a maximum of two units, which despite the name, is not mobile. It is brought on to a site in two parts on a lorry and put together on site. A lorry cannot tow it and for practical purposes (as opposed to legal niceties) is the same as a chalet' (Clark 2001: 397). However, Gypsies and Travellers refer to caravans as 'trailers' whether fixed or mobile.

Accommodation is a major concern for some Gypsies and Travellers, affecting their physical, emotional and mental wellbeing (MECOPP 2012). Whilst the issue of housing is not a focus of this study, it should be acknowledged that it can bear a significant schooling impact on the lives of some children and young people:

> It is now well established that addressing the accommodation needs of Gypsy and Traveller communities is the shortest and quickest route to ensuring positive outcomes and good relations. Research has shown that a lack of suitable accommodation and poor conditions is related to poor education. (EHRC 2015: 30)

According to the Scottish Housing Regulator (Scottish Housing Charter Data 2013/2014), the number of Gypsy and Traveller pitches since 2009 has decreased or stayed the same in the 23 Local Authorities that provide sites. Many parts of Scotland have no provision (EHRC 2015). Most are in South Lanarkshire and Fife, and only Perth and Kinross increased their pitches, as seen in Table 2.2. This is the same progressive council that developed a policy on Gypsy and Traveller education, as opposed to just guidelines.

Stopping and camping sites, authorised or unauthorised, do not fit into traditional concepts of 'home' held by settled populations and policy makers, and are viewed instead as squatting, invasions upon space as real estate. The settled community sees itself as host and Gypsies and

Table 2.2   Change in the number of Gypsy and Traveller pitches since 2009

Local authority	Scottish Government twice yearly Gypsy and Traveller count	Scottish housing regulator housing charter	Change
	2009	2013/2014	
Aberdeen city	21	17	−4
Aberdeenshire	20	20	0
Angus	18	18	0
Argyll and Bute	32	30	−2
Clackmannanshire	16	16	0
Dumfries and Galloway	32	30	−2
Dundee city	20	20	0
East Dunbartonshire (1)	15	0	−15
East/Midlothian	20	16	−4
Edinburgh (city of)	20	20	0
Falkirk	15	15	0
Fife	50	50	0
Glasgow city (2)	10	0	−10
Highland	48	47	−1
North Ayrshire	16	16	0
Perth and Kinross	20	26	6
Scottish borders	10	10	0
South Ayrshire	8	8	0
South Lanarkshire	28	28	0
Stirling	18	18	0
West Dunbartonshire	20	20	0
West Lothian (3)	21	0	−21
Scotland	**478**	**425**	**−53**

Travellers as unwanted guests. 'Whilst the law has not outlawed the nomadic way of life it has served to restrict it' (Knowles and Lander 2011: 105).

In her work on *Race Space and the Law*, Razack (2002: 1) argues, 'spaces [can be] organised to sustain unequal social relations and... these relations [in turn] shape spaces'. Institutional spaces, according to Ahmed (2012), can be equally powerful in acts of inclusion or exclusion. Institutions such as schools that presumably aspire to create a shared social space, can by this very aim 'restrict to whom an institutional space is open' by creating a space that is 'not actually open to everyone' (Ahmed 2012: 39). Some are enabled to share in that social space, and find it easier to do so, but others may not. Spaces—both home and institutional—can be used to empower some and disempower others, and in the process a child's educational experiences can be adversely affected.

As increasing numbers are forced to 'settle' and assimilate by obtaining permanent addresses, either in houses or on designated caravan sites, they are beginning to exercise their right to live without the State interfering in their culture and traditional lifestyle, most often by not self-identifying. The effect of this 'passing' or hiding one's true ethnic identity presents complex challenges to Gypsies and Travellers, but manifests itself in the difficulties faced by statisticians and policymakers to 'count' and collate numbers and information about Gypsies and Travellers in Scotland (EHRC 2015). Surdu (2016) asserts that state-led population census, policy related surveys, as well as academic and scientific research, together craft an essentialised [Gypsy/Roma/Traveller] identity that categorises and fuses different ethnic communities into one deterministic entity, most often negatively perceived, in the public consciousness.

The exact number of Gypsies and Travellers in Scotland, as in the rest of the UK, can be difficult to establish, but it remains undisputed that the life experiences of some Gypsies and Travellers in all the key areas—accommodation, health, education and employment—reflect an unacceptable level of gross mistreatment and marginalisation

(Clark 2001, 2006; Coxhead 2007). There is the view that Gypsy and Traveller cultures 'expose and provoke the pathologies of European culture' (Heuss 2000: 52); and this condition is especially powerful in the face of economic expansion and rapid technological advances since the late nineteenth century. Cressy (2018: ix) also states that 'by considering Gypsies, as a people whose history deserves analysis, rather than a pathology to be examined, we may also learn something about ourselves'. The lifestyles and socio-economic needs of Gypsies and Travellers in Europe and Scotland, like all other ethnic groups, have changed with these developments. Whyte's (2001) account of Scottish Traveller history lists many occupations within a tradition of hard labour, strong work ethic, self-employment and self-reliance, based on the need to survive. Despite their resilience, unlike some groups, their historical contributions as skilled craftsmen, blacksmiths, fairground entertainers or seasonal workers on agricultural land, have been systematically minimised or expunged. This erasure has been more acutely felt in the last 50 years because Gypsy and Traveller communities have experienced new forms of restrictive legislation, particularly to do with accommodation and camping sites, which have undermined the communities' traditionally nomadic way of life.

Stewart (1997: 84) maintains that 'Gypsies all over Europe [including Scotland] have been remarkably successful in preserving their way of life, adapting to their changed conditions in order to remain the same'. Scrap metal work, landscaping, and second-hand car sales, have replaced traditional occupations. Even if Stewart's appraisal is reasoned, the preservation of the communities may have been achieved at a high cost to some members—especially girls and women—who strive for success at school and who attempt to enter other careers or professions.

Despite their diligence and self-sufficiency, Gypsies and Travellers continue to be demonised as being lazy, unemployed benefit scroungers or conniving rich tax dodgers. A survey of titles of academic literature on Gypsies and Travellers reveal a range of negative descriptors—'pariah' (Hancock 1987), 'menace' (Stewart 2012), 'Gypsy invasion' (Clark and Campbell 2000), 'invisible' (Morris 2000; Clark 2001), 'problem' (Fraser 1953; Gmelch 1982), 'itinerants' (Bell et al. 1983), 'folk devils' (Cohen 1972), and 'outsiders' (Bhopal and Myers 2008).

Richardson's (2006) *The Gypsy Debate: Can Discourse Control* provides a contemporary and incisive account of the social shaping of Gypsies and Travellers—what is said about the community and the effect this has on their daily, lived experiences—using theories on control and discourse (Cohen 1980; Foucault 1980; Bauman 1989). Although her work focuses on the situation in England, there are striking similarities with that in Scotland. In her review of recent literature, she compiles and highlights several major themes in published research: political prejudice (Hawes and Perez 1996); the invisibility of Gypsies and Travellers in policy (Morris 2003); the cost of providing for these communities (Morris and Clements 2002); neighbour's views (Duncan 1996; Holloway 2003); problems with planning and accommodation; and recommendations for the future. She asserts that for centuries there has been a 'spectrum of discrimination from negative discourse to execution'. As in *The 1895 Scottish Traveller Report* (Dawson 2005), the negative language of cost with regard to provision, 'not paying taxes' and 'cleaning up the mess' are identified as an ongoing significant feature (Richardson 2006: 27).

Academic literature (Williamson 1994; Reid 1997; Kenrick 1998; Clark 2001, 2006, 2008, 2013, 2014; Clark and Taylor 2014; McKinney 2003; Shubin 2010) points to the same recurring themes in Scotland, which is confirmed in many government policy documents and research done by the EOC, the Equality and Human Rights Council (EHRC), Scottish Human Rights Council (SHRC) and various charities.

This negative, controlling language, often 'racist and bigoted', is perpetuated and reinforced through legislation, government policy and the media (Richardson 2006: 34–35):

> It is important to remember that discourse is not just a matter of text and talk; it is not reactive but indeed productive and constructive. It is the translation of discourse into action that controls Gypsies and Travellers.

Clark (2008: 65) makes a relevant point that there is 'on the one hand, a desire to 'help' (*care*) for their well-being, safety and security as some texts maintain (Parry et al., 2004; Cemlyn 2006; Mason et al., 2006) whilst, on the other hand, there is a strong tendency to monitor, classify and regulate (*control*) their movement, accommodation, work practices, and cultural identity (Clark and Greenfields 2006; Richardson 2006; James 2007)'. State intervention, employing a discourse of care and control, is confusing and disconnected (Fig. 2.1).

> The permit to me is important because it shows how certain groups are targeted for removal. You become a leper colony (Shamus) (MECOPP et al. 2014: 19)

Belton (2013) provides an alternative and arguably more nuanced argument than that put forward by Richardson (2006). The idea that power and control only exist in the hands of governing institutions potentially denies the power of individual human agency. Citing Stuart Hall's writing on 'weak power', Belton (2013: 287) argues it might also be in the interest of the marginalised to maintain and take advantage of that marginality. Belton (2013: 287) further asserts that 'oppression can be a means to gain resources, [privileges and protection]' and suggests the 'socially excluded might exclude the included'. Hall's astute estimation of the nature of power and control is, I argue, more reflective of the reality of the existence of human agency. 'Paradoxically, marginality has become a powerful space. It is a space of weak power but it is a space of power nonetheless' (Hall, cited in Belton 2013: 287).

Gypsies and Travellers have, as Hawes and Perez (1996), Hancock (1997), and Stewart (1997) suggested, immense resilience and resourcefulness, which has enabled them to survive and oppose centuries of persecution. None of the above scholarly works explore in depth the experiences of Gypsy and Traveller women or provide the space for their voices to be heard. The community is still written about as a subjugated whole. Gender, age or class, do not as yet feature as defining inequalities to be analysed and understood.

Fig. 2.1 Pedlar's certificate (*Source* Courtesy of MECOPP/©Peter E. Ross)

Gendering the Gypsy and Traveller Experience

There is very little academic research into the lives of Gypsy and Traveller women in Scotland and none that solicit their views on their experiences. What little exists in the UK is dated (Okely 1983) and an extensive literature search reveals nothing new or substantial about women from Gypsy and Traveller communities. As stated earlier, the annual meeting and conference of the Gypsy Lore Society held in Moldova in September 2015 (Gypsy Lore Society 2015) featured no work on Gypsy and Traveller women in Scotland or in the rest of the UK.

In 2009, Cemlyn et al. conducted a comprehensive review of published research (since 2000) for the EHRC on the 'Inequalities Experienced by Gypsy and Traveller Communities'. In this report, several points were raised regarding gender. 'To date, there has been no policy drive to challenge or discuss the changing position of women in Gypsy and Traveller communities in Britain...Little research has been carried out into the role of women in Gypsy and Traveller communities' (2009: 225). The report recommends that work needs to be done to 'facilitate and support Gypsy, Traveller and Show-women to come together, to promote human rights for their communities and celebrate their cultures in a gender-positive manner'. It highlights in particular the importance of addressing 'education inequalities which have a disproportionate impact on women and negative consequences for Gypsies, Travellers and Showpeople of both genders' and recommends that 'further research into gender inequalities' should be undertaken (Cemlyn et al. 2009: 233–234).

Of the limited studies available, Gypsy and Traveller women are perceived as being a problem, having problems, being polluted and unclean or having the potential to pollute and dishonour their communities (Okely 1983; Dawson 2005; Lloyd 2005; Clavell-Bate 2012). Underlying the constructed image and discourse used about Gypsy and Traveller women is the language of sex and sensuality, pollution, shame and risk, and more recently their hypersexualisation through television programmes such as *My Big Fat Gypsy Wedding* (2010–2015).

The lack of contemporary research about Gypsy and Traveller women and girls follows a long tradition of women and girls either being erased from the Gypsy and Traveller experience or being discussed in sexist and racist ways. For instance, *The 1895 Scottish Traveller Report* (Dawson 2005: 19) hardly mentions the experiences of women and girls. The little that is written in this report is negative. Traveller women are described as 'drunken wives … a very difficult problem in connection with the School Board…[because] fathers frequently ascribe their incapacity to send their children to school owing to having drunken wives'. The Chairman gives testimony at the hearing saying of women, married or pregnant—'My experience is that directly they get money they go to drink, and when drunk they give way to disorder and brawling…[leaving] their children untended on the roadside during the night' (cited in Dawson 2005: 39). A Reverend Mackenzie complained that 'the mothers get drunk and fall over their children' (Dawson 2005: 46). A manager of a girls' industrial school in Perth reported to the committee: 'As these Tinker girls grow older they deteriorate in intelligence very much' (Dawson 2005: 45). The manager believes that Tinker girls do well when separated from their parents and sent abroad. Women are labelled 'immoral' because 'girls of 15, 16 and 17, and lads of the same age, and their parents all lodge and sleep' together (2005: 15).

Judith Okely's (1983: 204) chapter on '*Gypsy Women*' is more nuanced and clearly highlights the 'paradox embedded in the Gypsy woman's role' and image (not identity). She explores the contrast between the 'outsider's stereotyped perception of the Gypsy woman, and the ideal behaviours expected of her by the Gypsies themselves' (1983: 201). Okely uses the terms Gypsy and Traveller 'interchangeably' in her research, and the communities she observed were not in Scotland. There is such a paucity of information on Traveller women, aspects of Okely's analysis has bearing on the experiences of the girls I interviewed. Okely's work offers valuable insights into the lives of Gypsy and Traveller women and how they were regarded at the time. Okely acknowledges that there are aspects to their daily lives she was not permitted to observe or to seek explanation and this may be one reason for the gap in knowledge about Gypsy and Traveller women. Their lives are hidden from view and introspection reinforcing again their 'normative absence and pathological presence' (Mirza 2015: 3).

According to Okely (1983: 205), the Gypsy woman must strive to fulfil what is expected of her. Her honour and that of her family's are dependent on her actions and behaviour. In addition, a Gypsy or Traveller woman needs to manage the risk of being seen as potentially unclean because of her contact with the outside world, and gaujo men in particular. Based on her own extended fieldwork and case studies in England and on the continent, Okely explains that pollution, shame and risk are powerful themes inextricably tied to the image and role of the Gypsy woman. The Gypsy woman poses a threat, and she is a risk to Gypsy society. Pollution as a concept is both physical and symbolic, between the inner and outer body, the physical and the spiritual. Symbolically, Okely discovers that the outer body is seen as the public self by Gypsies and Travellers, that which is shared and visible to outsider communities. Okely argues that, based on her findings, this idea is central to how Gypsy women are defined, perceived, controlled and manipulated by Gypsy culture. Okely believes the patriarchal system that oppresses Gypsy women is ideological, rather than solely based on gender. Some women find ways to subtly circumvent rules and expectations within their communities, but other women are complicit in the patriarchal mindset. Both men and women have a vested interest in the preservation of their communities' culture and 'ethnic inheritance' and have a 'patriarchy has no gender' (Okely 1983: 207; hooks 2010: 170).

Okely (1983) suggests that in the case of a Gypsy woman, she can be perceived as weak and oppressed, but she is feared and thus ascribed the power to do much good for her community or much harm. The Gypsy women in Okely's study lead a restricted lifestyle and seem vulnerable, but I argue, they have the agency and the power to disrupt.

More recent academic studies focus on health issues and domestic violence experienced by Gypsy and Traveller women (Feder 1990; Lloyd 1996; Clarke 1998; Smart et al. 2003; Ridge and Yin-Har 2011). These studies concentrate on the *problems* faced by Gypsy and Traveller women, or that their lifestyle practices and habits are perceived as *problematic* when compared to the standards of the settled population. Heaslip (2015: 4) in her thesis on the *Experience of Vulnerability from a Gypsy and Travelling Perspective,* highlights the 'vulnerability of powerlessness' felt by some of her participants. As subsequent chapters reveal, the girls I interviewed simultaneously experience vulnerability, agency and the power to transform their lives.

As a dearth in the literature indicates, Gypsy and Traveller women have been erased from both the public and policy imagination (Cemlyn et al. 2009). The Gypsy and Traveller experience that has been written about is a male experience, and what little understanding there is currently is based on the male gaze. bell hooks (1981) argues, as many other Black feminists continue to do (Crenshaw 1991; Collins 2000; Lorde 2007; Davis and Evans 2011) that minority women must negotiate a complex terrain because of the inequalities that arise from the intersecting inequalities of race, class and gender. In Chapter 4, I discuss why an intersectional paradigm and approach is ideally suited for the study of the experiences of Gypsy and Traveller women and girls. Intersectional perspectives recognise the diversity of different groups and can critically explore how some groups are erased, silenced, and marginalised in such a way that their lives do not matter in dominant discourses.

As there is virtually no literature to draw upon about gendered experiences of Gypsy and Traveller girls in Scotland, there is a danger of pathologising or essentialising their experiences in schools and within their families and communities. For an effective and more nuanced analysis of my empirical data, I chose to draw on similarities and differences, where relevant, with other girls from minoritised (Basit 1996, 1997; Dwyer 2000; Talbani and Hasanali 2000; Archer 2002; Emejulu 2013; Farris and de Jong 2014) and white working class backgrounds (Walkerdine et al. 2001). Such comparisons reveal that some women are not just gendered agents of patriarchy, but racialised agents of patriarchy, both subtle and overt. Patricia Hill Collins (2000) points out that no one group has a monopoly over a type of oppression that is exclusive only to them. Under institutional and hegemonic patriarchy, women from a range of backgrounds share gendered and racialised experiences of exclusion and agency. There are ways in which the racialised and gendered experiences of Gypsy and Traveller girls are unique to their situated context (Mirza 2015: 4), but there are shared experiences that are in common with other, if not, most women. Society is not heterogeneous and neither is patriarchy.

Compounding problems of analysis is that when they are written about, Gypsy and Traveller girls are discussed in problematic terms, their competing experiences erased or misrecognised in such a way as fixes them in exclusion, pain and harm (Berlant 1997: 3). Taylor (1994: 75) argues that 'misrecognition can inflict harm, can be a form of oppression, imprisoning someone in a false, distorted and reduced mode of being'. None of the works cited seeks to examine the agency, aspirations and achievements of Gypsy and Traveller girls and young women. Gypsy and Traveller education in Scotland is predominantly and broadly viewed as a problem of interrupted learning and exclusion. Existing scholarly works tend to focus on pedagogy, advice for staff and solutions to help schools include Gypsy and Traveller pupils. Some studies, along with a plethora of reports and recommendations since devolution, do highlight underachievement linked to bullying, racist discrimination and lack of support for Gypsy and Traveller pupils and their culture.

Mirza's writing on the state of 'Black British feminism in post-race times' forms the foundation of my attempt to expose the predicament of Gypsy and Traveller girls and women. Mirza's (2015: 1) work inspires the need for this study to foreground the indigenous female voice, to follow the 'postcolonial impulse to chart counter-narratives and memories of racialised [as well as] gendered domination'. This book highlights the pernicious lack of recognition of the particular, yet diverse, accounts of the experiences of the Gypsy and Traveller girls I interviewed, especially their experiences of education in Scottish schools.

Gypsy and Traveller cultures 'expose and provoke the pathologies of European culture' (Heuss 2000: 52). However, I argue that looking at Gypsy or Traveller experiences through the single lens of ethnicity or race cannot provide a complete picture. Gender, age, and class matter in helping to create multiple identities within prescribed community categorisations. Gypsies and Travellers—their identities, communities, histories, and traditions—are not homogenous. Moreover, such debates over origins and nomenclature will 'remain unresolved' (Kohn, cited in Clark 2001: 64). Cultures, communities and identities are not fixed constructs, but are in fact rhizomatic and volatile. Cressy (2018: xv) argues that their ethnicity 'was inherited as well as constructed, fluid, flexible, and self-replicating'. Sections of Gypsy and Traveller communities, as yet undefined, continue to encounter grave problems having their needs and their rights met in a way that does not compromise their ancient traditions and culture. The situation for Scottish Gypsy and Travellers raises fundamental human rights concerns—particularly the rights to health, education, housing, family life and cultural life and the requirement to be free from discrimination in the realisation of these rights.

References

Acton, T. (1974) *Gypsy politics and social change*. London: Routledge and Paul.

Acton, T. (1994) Modernisation, moral panics and the Gypsies. *Sociology Review*, 4(1), pp. 24–28.

Acton, T. (ed.) (1997) *Gypsy politics and Traveller identity*. Hatfield: University of Hertfordshire Press.

Acton, T. A. (ed.) (2000) *Scholarship and the Gypsy Struggle: Commitment in Romani Studies: A Collection of Papers and Poems to Celebrate Donald Kenrick's Seventieth Year*. Hatfield: University of Hertfordshire Press.

Acton, T. (2004) Modernity, culture and 'Gypsies': Is there a meta-scientific method for understanding the representation of 'Gypsies'? And do Dutch really exist? In: Saul, N., and Tebbutt, S. *The role of the Romanies. Images and counter-images of 'Gypsies'/Romanies in European cultures*. Liverpool: Liverpool University Press.

Acton, T. (2007) Here to stay: The Gypsies and Travellers of Great Britain. *Ethnic and Racial Studies*, 30(2), pp. 1170–1171.

Acton, T., and Mundy, G. (eds.) (1997) *Romani culture and Gypsy identity*. Hatfield: University of Hertfordshire Press.

Ahmed, S. (2012) *On being included: Racism and diversity in institutional life*. Durham, NC: Duke University Press.

Amnesty International. (2010, June) Letter written by J. Watson to Aberdeen City Council Chief Executive.

Anzaldúa, G. (1987) *Borderlands/La frontera*. San Francisco: Aunt Lute.

Archer, L. (2002) Change, culture and tradition: British Muslim pupils talk about Muslim girls' post-16 'choices'. *Race, Ethnicity and Education*, 5(4), pp. 359–376.

Basit, T. N. (1996) 'I'd hate to be just a housewife': Career aspirations of British Muslim girls. *British Journal of Guidance and Counselling*, 24(2), pp. 227–242.

Basit, T. N. (1997) 'I want more freedom, but not too much': British Muslim girls and the dynamism of family values. *Gender and education*, 9(4), pp. 425–440.

Bauman, Z. (1989) *Modernity and the Holocaust*. Ithaca: Cornell University Press.

Bauman, Z. (2001) *Community*. Cambridge: Polity Press.

Bell, E. J., Riding, M. H., Collier, P. W., Wilson, N. C., and Reid, D. (1983) Susceptibility of itinerants ("travelling people") in Scotland to poliomyelitis. *Bulletin of the World Health Organization*, 61(5), p. 839.

Belton, B. (2005) *Questioning Gypsy identity: Ethnic narratives in Britain and America*. Walnut Creek, CA: Altamira.

Belton, B. A. (2013) 'Weak power': Community and identity. *Ethnic and Racial Studies*, 36(2), pp. 282–297.

BEMIS (2011) *Gypsy Travellers in contemporary Scotland: The 2001 'inquiry into Gypsy Travellers and public sector policies': Ten years on*. Glasgow: BEMIS.

Berlant, L. (1997) *The Queen of America Goes to Washington City: Essays on Sex and Citizenship*. Durham and London: Duke University Press.

Bhopal, K. (2018) *White privilege: The myth of a post-racial society*. Bristol: Policy Press.

Bhopal, K., and Myers, M. (2008) *Insiders, outsiders and others: Gypsies and identity*. Hatfield: University of Hertfordshire Press.

Brockie, W. (1884) *The Gypsies of Yetholm: Historical, traditional, philological and humorous*. Kelso: J. H. Rutherford.

Caravan Sites and Control of Development Act. (1960) Available at: http://www.legislation.gov.uk/ukpga/Eliz2/8-9/62. Accessed 12 January 2013.

Cemlyn, S. (2006) Human rights and Gypsies and Travellers: An exploration of the application of a human rights perspective to social work with a minority community in Britain. *British Journal of Social Work*, 38(1), pp. 153–173.

Cemlyn, S., Greenfields, M., Burnett, S., Matthews, Z., and Whitwell, C. (2009) *Inequalities experienced by Gypsy and Traveller communities: A review*. Research Report 12. Manchester: Equality and Human Rights Commission. Available at: https://dera.ioe.ac.uk/11129/1/12inequalities_experienced_by_gypsy_and_traveller_communities_a_review.pdf.

Chambers, W. (1886) *Exploits and anecdotes of the Scottish Gypsies: With traits of their origin, character, and manners*. Edinburgh: W. Brown.

Clarke, B. (1998) The Irish travelling community—Outcasts of the Celtic Tiger? Dilemmas for social work. *Social Work in Europe*, 5, pp. 28–34.

Clark, C. (2001) *'Invisible lives': The Gypsies and Travellers of Britain*. Unpublished PhD thesis, Edinburgh: University of Edinburgh.

Clark, C. (2006) Defining ethnicity in a cultural and socio-legal context: The case of Scottish Gypsy-Travellers. *Scottish Affairs*, 54, pp. 39–67.

Clark, C. (2008) Introduction themed section care or control? Gypsies, Travellers and the state. *Social Policy and Society*, 7(1), pp. 65–71.

Clark, C. (2013) Agency, empowerment and inclusion: The challenges facing Roma youth in Europe today. *Voice: A Global Youth Magazine*, 1(1), pp. 34–36.

Clark, C. (2014) 'Glasgow's Ellis Island? The integration and stigmatisation of Govanhill's Roma population'. *People, Place and Policy*, 8(1), pp. 34–50.

Clark, C., and Campbell E. (2000) "Gypsy Invasion": A critical analysis of newspaper reaction to Czech and Slovak Romani asylum-seekers in Britain, 1997. *Romani Studies (Continuing Journal of the Gypsy Lore Society)*, 10(1), pp. 23–47.

Clark, C., and Greenfields, M. (2006) *Here to stay: The Gypsies and Travellers of Britain*. Hatfield: University of Herfordshire Press.

Clark, C., and Taylor, B. (2014) Is nomadism the 'problem'? The social construction of Gypsies and Travellers as perpetrators of 'anti-social' behaviour in Britain. In: Pickard, S. (ed.) *Anti-social behaviour in Britain: Victorian and contemporary perspectives*. Basingstoke: Palgrave Macmillan, pp. 166–178.

Clavell-Bate, R. (2012) Elective home education: Supporting access to education for children and young people within the Gypsy, Roma and Traveller community. In: J. Visser, H. Daniels, and T. Cole (eds.) *Transforming troubled lives: Strategies and interventions for children with social, emotional and behavioural difficulties*. Bradford: Emerald Group Publishing, p.175–191.

Cohen, S. (1972) *Folk devils and moral panics*. Oxford: Blackwell.

Cohen, S. (1980) Symbols of trouble: Introduction to the new edition. In: S. Cohen (ed.) *Folk devils and moral panics: The creation of the mods and rockers*. London: Martin Robertson.

Cohen, S. (1985) *Visions of social control: Crime, punishment and classification*. Cambridge: Polity Press.

Collins. P. H. (2000) *Black feminist thought: Knowledge, consciousness and the politics of empowerment*. London: Routledge.

Copp, A. L. (1986) The nurse as advocate for vulnerable persons. *Journal of Advanced Nursing*, 11, pp. 255–263.

Council of Europe. (2012) Glossary on Roma (2006). Available at: http://hub.coe.int/what-we-do/human-rights/roma-and-travellers. Accessed 11 November 2013.

Council of Europe. (2018) Council of Europe honours Roma victims of the Holocaust: "Acknowledge the past and improve Roma rights today". Available at: https://www.coe.int/en/web/portal/-/council-of-europe-honours-roma-victims-of-the-holocaust-acknowledge-the-past-and-improve-roma-rights-today-. Accessed 16 August 2018.

Coxhead, J. (2007) *The last bastion of racism: Gypsies, Travellers and policing.* Stoke on Trent: Trentham Books.

Crenshaw, K. (1991) Mapping the margins: Intersectionality, identity politics, and violence against women of color. *Stanford Law Review*, 43(6), pp. 1241–1299.

Cressy, D. (2018) *Gypsies: An English history.* Oxford: Oxford University Press.

Davis, K., and Evans, M. (eds.) (2011) *Transatlantic conversations: Feminism as travelling theory.* Farnham: Ashgate Publishing.

Dawson, R. M. (1971) The Tinklers of Arran. *Romani Studies*, 50(65).

Dawson, R. (2005) *The 1895 Scottish Traveller Report.* Derbyshire: Dawson and Rackley.

Dawson, R. (2007) *Empty lands: Aspects of Scottish Traveller survival.* Derbyshire: Dawson Publishing.

Delanty, G. (2010) *Community.* London: Routledge.

Deleuze, G., and Guattari, F. (1977) *Rhizom* (Vol. 67). Berlin: Merve Verlag.

Deleuze, G., and Guattari, F. (1987) *A thousand plateaus: Capitalism and schizophrenia.* London: The Athlone Press, pp. 3–25.

Duffee, D. (1980) *Explaining criminal justice: Community theory and criminal justice reform.* Cambridge, MA: Oelgeschlager, Gunn and Hain.

Duncan, T. (1996) *Neighbour's views of official sites for Travelling people: A survey based on three case studies in Scotland.* Glasgow: The Planning Exchange, The Joseph Rowntree Foundation.

Dwyer, C. (2000) Negotiating diasporic identities: Young British South Asian Muslim women. *Women's Studies International Forum*, 23(4), pp. 475–486.

EHRC. (2015) Developing successful site provision for Scotland's Gypsy/Traveller communities. Available at: https://www.equalityhumanrights.com/sites/default/files/successful_site_provision_scotland.pdf. Accessed 21 April 2015.

Emejulu, A. (2013) Being and belonging in Scotland: Exploring the intersection of ethnicity, gender and national identity among Scottish Pakistani groups. *Scottish Affairs*, 84(1), pp. 41–64.

Equal Opportunities Committee. (2001) Inquiry into Gypsy Travellers and public sector policies. Available at: bemis.org.uk/docs/gypsy_travellers_in_contemporary_scotland.pdf. Accessed 6 March 2013.

Farris, S. R., and de Jong, S. (2014) Discontinuous intersections: Second-generation immigrant girls in transition from school to work. *Ethnic and Racial Studies*, 37(9), pp. 1505–1525.

Feder, G. (1990) The politics of Traveller health research. *Critical Public Health*, 1(3), pp. 10–14.

Fernback, J. (2007) Beyond the diluted community concept: A symbolic interactionist perspective on online social relations. *New Media & Society*, 9(1), pp. 49–69.

Foucault, M. (1980) *Power/knowledge: Selected interviews and other writings, 1972–1977*. New York: Pantheon.

Fraser, A. (1953) The Gypsy problem: A survey of post-war developments. *Journal of the Gypsy Lore Society*, 3(3–4), pp. 82–100.

Fraser, N. (2007) Re-framing justice in a globalizing world. In: T. Lovell (ed.) *(Mis)recognition, social inequality and social justice: Nancy Fraser and Pierre Bourdieu*. Abingdon: Routledge, pp. 17–35.

Gmelch, G. (1975) The effects of economic change on Irish Traveller sex roles and marriage patterns. In: Rehfisch, F. (ed.) *Gypsies, Tinkers and other Travellers*, London: Academic Press, pp. 257–269.

Gmelch, S. B. (1982) Gypsies in British cities: Problems and government response. *Urban Anthropology*, 11(3/4) pp. 347–376.

Grampian Regional Council Social Strategy Unit. (1994) *Movin' on: A staff development awareness training pack on Scotland's Travelling people*. Aberdeen: Grampian Regional Council.

Green, R. M. (2013) *Bearing memory: Re-visioning Scottish Traveller stories from 1950–2013*. Unpublished PhD thesis, Colchester: University of Essex.

Greenfeld, H. (1977) *Gypsies*. New York: Crown.

Griffin, C. (2008) *Nomads under the Westway: Irish Travellers, Gypsies and other traders in West London*. Hatfield: University of Hertfordshire Press.

Groome, F. H. (1890–1891) Transportation of Gypsies from Scotland to America. *Journal of the Gypsy Lore Society*, 2(1), pp. 60–62.

Grönfors, M. (1982) From scientific social science to responsible research: The lesson of the Finnish Gypsies. *Acta Sociologica*, 25(3), pp. 249–257.

Grosz, E. A. (1994) *Volatile bodies: Toward a corporeal feminism*. Bloomington: Indiana University Press.

GRTPA. (2014) Gypsy/Roma/Traveller police association. Available at: www. grtpa.com. Accessed 5 May 2014.

Gutiérrez, K. (2004) Rethinking community: Implications for research. In *The 17th Annual Conference on Interdisciplinary Qualitative Studies*. University of Georgia, Athens, GA, January, pp. 9–11.

Gutiérrez, K. D., and Arzubiaga, A. E. (2012) An ecological and activity theoretic approach to studying diasporic and nondominant communities. Research on schools, neighbourhoods, and communities: Toward civic responsibility, pp. 203–216.

Gypsy Lore Society. (1912) *Journal of the Gypsy lore society* (Vol. 6). Liverpool: The Gypsy Lore Society.

Gypsy Lore Society. (2015) Conference abstracts. Available at: http://www. gypsyloresociety.org/annual-meeting/2015-gypsy-lore-society-conference-abstracts. Accessed 5 August 2015.

Hancock, I. F. (1987) *The pariah syndrome: An account of Gypsy slavery and persecution*. Ann Arbor, MI: Karoma Publishers.

Hancock, I. (1997) The struggle for the control of identity. *The Patrin Web Journal*. Available at: www.geocities.com/Paris/5121/identity.htm.

Hancock, I. (2010) *Danger! educated Gypsy: Selected essays*. Hatfield: University of Hertfordshire Press.

Hawes, D., and Perez, B. (1996) *The Gypsy and the state: The ethnic cleansing of British society*, 2nd ed. Bristol: The Policy Press.

Heaslip, V. A. (2015) *Experience of vulnerability from a Gypsy/Travelling perspective: A phenomenological study.* Unpublished PhD thesis, Bournemouth: Bournemouth University.

Heuss, H. (2000) Anti-Gypsyism research: The creation of a new field of study. In: Acton, T. (ed.) *Scholarship and the Gypsy struggle: Commitment in Romani studies*. Hatfield: University of Hertfordshire Press, pp. 52–67.

Holloway, S. L. (2003) Outsiders in rural society? Constructions of rurality and nature-society relations in the racialisation of English Gypsy-Travellers, 1869–1934. *Environment and Planning D: Society and Space*, 21(6), pp. 695–716.

Hood, M. (1960) The challenge of "bi-musicality". *Ethnomusicology*, 4(2), pp. 55–59.

hooks, b. (1981) *Ain't I a woman: Black women and feminism*. Boston: South End Press.

hooks, b. (2010) *Teaching critical thinking: Practical wisdom.* London: Routledge.

James, Z. (2007) Policing marginal spaces: Controlling Gypsies and Travellers. *Criminology & Criminal Justice*, 7(4), pp. 367–389.

Jarman, E., and Jarman, A. O. H. (1991) *The Welsh Gypsies: Children of Abram Wood.* Cardiff: University of Wales Press.

Kaplan, A. (2005) *The anarchy of empire in the making of US culture.* Cambridge: Harvard University Press.

Kaplan, E. A. (1997) *Looking for the other: Feminism, film, and the imperial gaze.* New York: Routledge.

Kenrick, D. (1993) *From India to the Mediterranean: The migration of the Gypsies* (Vol. 3). Hatfield: University of Hertfordshire Press.

Kenrick, D. (1998) *Historical dictionary of the Gypsies (Romanies).* Lanham: Scarecrow Press.

Kenrick, D., and Clark, C. (1999) *Moving on: The Gypsies and Travellers of Britain.* Hatfield: University of Hertfordshire Press.

Knowles, G., and Lander, V. (2011) *Diversity, equality and achievement in education.* London: Sage.

Liégeois, J. P., and Gheorghe, N. (1995) *Roma/Gypsies.* London: Minority Rights Group.

Lloyd, S. (1996) Behind the picture postcard: Domestic violence in rural areas. *Women and access in rural areas*, pp. 82–95.

Lloyd, G. (2005) *Problem girls: Understanding and supporting troubled and troublesome girls and young women.* London: Psychology Press.

Lorde, A. (2007) *Sister outsider: Essays and speeches.* Berkeley: Crossing Press.

Mackenzie, A. (1883 [2012]) *The History of the Highland clearances,* Lenox, MA: Hard Press Publishing.

MacRitchie, D. (1894) *Scottish Gypsies under the Stewarts.* Edinburgh: D. Douglas.

Mandla vs. Dowell-Lee [1983] UKHL 7, (1983) 2 AC 548. Available at: http://www.bailii.org/uk/cases/UKHL/1982/7.html.

Mayall, D. (1995) *English Gypsies and state policy.* Hatfield: University of Hertfordshire Press.

Mayall, D. (1997) Egyptians and vagabonds: Representations of the Gypsy in early modern official and rogue literature. *Immigrants and Minorities*, 16(3), pp. 55–82.

Mayall, D. (2004) *History of Gypsy identities 1500–2000: From Egyptians and Moonmen to Ethnic Romany.* London: Routledge.

McCaffery, J. (2009) Gypsies and Travellers: Literacy, discourse and communicative practices. *Compare*, 39(5), pp. 643–657.

McCormick, A. (1907) *The Tinkler-Gypsies*. Dumfries: J. Maxwell and Son.

McKinney, R. (2001) *Different lessons: Scottish Gypsy/Travellers and the future of education*. Edinburgh: Scottish Travellers Consortium.

McKinney, R. (2003) Views from the margins: Gypsy/Travellers and the ethnicity debate in the new Scotland. *Scottish Affairs*, 42 (Winter), pp. 13–31.

MECOPP. (2012) *Hidden carers, unheard voices*. Edinburgh: Minority Ethnic Carers of People Project. Available at: http://www.mecopp.org.uk/files/documents/annual_reports/hidden_carers___unheard_voices_report.pdf. Accessed 21 November 2012.

MECOPP., Lloyd, M., and Ross, P. (eds.) (2014) *Moving Minds: Gypsy/Travellers in Scotland*. Edinburgh: MECOPP.

Mirza, H. S. (2015) Harvesting our collective intelligence: Black British feminism in post-race times. *Women's Studies International Forum*, 51, pp. 1–9.

Morris, R. (2000) The invisibility of Gypsies and other Travellers. *Journal of Social Welfare and Family Law*, 21(4), pp. 397–404.

Morris, R. (2003) *Romaphobia: Animosity, exclusion, invisibility and Travelling people in the UK*. Unpublished PhD thesis, Cardiff: Cardiff University.

Morris, R. C., and Clements, L. J. (2002) *At what cost?: The economics of Gypsy and Traveller encampments*. Bristol: Policy Press.

Mulvey, L. (1975) Visual pleasure and narrative cinema. *Screen*, 16(3), pp. 6–18.

Mulvey, L. (1989) British feminist film theory's female spectators: Presence and absence. *Camera Obscura: Feminism, Culture, and Media Studies*, 7(2–3 [20–21]), pp. 68–81.

Murray, R. (1875 [1983]) *The Gypsies of the border*. Galashiels: RC Hodges.

National Association of Teachers of Travellers (NATT). (2015) Gypsy Roma Traveller History Month: Myths and Truths. Available at: http://grthm.natt.org.uk/myths-and-truths.php. Accessed 3 September 2014.

Neat, T. (1996) *The summer walkers: Travelling people and pearl-fishers in the Highlands of Scotland*. Edinburgh: Canongate.

Neat, T. (1999) *The voice of the bard: Living poets and ancient tradition in the Highlands and Islands*. Edinburgh: Birlinn Limited.

Nemeth, D. (2002) *Gypsy-American: An ethnogeography*. Lewiston, NY: Edwin Mellen Press.

Ni Shuinear, S. (1997) Why do Gaujos hate Gypsies so much anyway? In: Acton, T. (ed.) *Gypsy politics and Traveller identity*, Hatfield: University of Hertfordshire Press, pp. 26–53.

Okely, J. (1975) Gypsies travelling in southern England. In: Rehfisch, F. (ed.) *Gypsies, Tinkers and other Travellers*, London: Academic Press, pp. 55–66.

Okely, J. (1983) *The Traveller-Gypsies*. Cambridge: Cambridge University Press.

Okely, J. (1994) Constructing difference: Gypsies as "other". *Anthropological Journal on European Cultures*, 3(2), pp. 55–73.

Oxford Dictionary. (2015) Oxford Dictionary Online. Cant [Def. 2]. Available at: http://www.oxforddictionaries.com/definition/english/cant. Accessed 13 September 2014.

Parry, G., Van Cleemput, P., Peters, J., and Moore, J. et al. (2004) *The Health Status of Gypsies and Travellers in England*. Sheffield: University of Sheffield.

Porter, J., and Gower, H. (1995) *Jeannie Robertson: Emergent singer, transformative voice*. Knoxville: University of Tennessee Press.

Prebble, J. (1971) *The lion in the north: A personal view of Scotland's history*. New York: Coward, McCann and Geoghegan.

Razack, S. (ed.). (2002) *Race, space, and the law: Unmapping a White Settler Society*. Toronto: Between the Lines.

Rehfisch, A., and Rehfisch, F. (1975) Scottish Travellers or Tinkers. In: Rehfisch, F. (ed.) *Gypsies, Tinkers and other Travellers*. London: Academic Press, pp. 271–283.

Reid, W. (1997) Scottish Gypsies/Travellers and the folklorists. *Romani culture and Gypsy identity*, pp. 29–37.

Reid, S. (2008) Never to return: The harrowing story of a stolen childhood. Edinburgh: Black and White Publishing.

Reynolds, M., McCartan, D., and Knipe, D. (2003) Traveller culture and lifestyle as factors influencing children's integration into mainstream secondary schools in West Belfast. *International Journal Inclusive Education*, 7(4), pp. 403–414.

Richardson, J. (2006) *The Gypsy debate: Can discourse control?* Exeter: Imprint Academic.

Richardson, J., and Ryder, A. (2012) *Gypsies and Travellers: Empowerment and inclusion in British society*. British: Policy Press.

Ridge, M., and Yin-Har Lau, A. (2011) Addressing the impact of social exclusion on mental health in Gypsy, Roma, and Traveller communities. *Mental Health and Social Inclusion*, 15(3), pp. 129–137.

Save the Children Scotland. (2005) *Having our say*. Available at: http://www.gypsy-Traveller.org/your-family/young-people/educational-reports-and-resources. Accessed November 2012.

Schröter, M. (2013) *Silence and concealment in political discourse* (Vol. 48). Amsterdam: John Benjamins Publishing.

Scottish Centre for Social Research. (2010) *Scottish Social Attitudes Survey 2010.* Available at: http://www.scotland.gov.uk/Resource/Doc/355763/0120175.pdf. Accessed 7 November 2012.

Scottish Centre for Social Research. (2015) Scottish Social Attitudes Survey 2015 [Online]. Available at: https://www.gov.scot/publications/scottish-social-attitudes-2015-attitudes-discrimination-positive-action/. Accessed 10 October 2016.

Seagrave, J. (1996) Defining community policing. *American Journal of Police*, 15(2), pp. 1–22.

Shubin, S. (2010) "Where can a Gypsy stop?" Rethinking mobility in Scotland. *Antipode*, 43(2), pp. 494–524.

Shubin, S. (2011) Travelling as being: Understanding mobility amongst Scottish Gypsy Travellers. *Environment and Planning A*, 43(8), pp. 1930–1947.

Smart, H., Titterton, M., and Clark, C. (2003) A literature review of the health of Gypsy/Traveller families in Scotland: The challenges for health promotion. *Health Education*, 103(3), pp. 156–165.

Smith, J. (2002) *Jessie's journey: Autobiography of a Traveller girl* (Vol. 1). Edinburgh: Birlinn Limited.

Smith, J. (2006) *Bruar's rest.* Edinburgh: Mercat Press.

Smith, J. (2008) *Tales from the tent.* Edinburgh: Birlinn Limited.

Smith, J. (2012) *Way of the wanderers: The story of Travellers in Scotland.* Edinburgh: Birlinn Limited.

Spears, A. K. (2006) "Perspectives: A view of the 'N-Word' from sociolinguistics". *Diverse Issues in Higher Education*, 12 July 2006. Retrieved October 2015: http://diverseeducation.com/article/6114/.

STEP. (2013) Scottish Traveller Education Programme, The University of Edinburgh. Available at: http://www.step.education.ed.ac.uk/travelling-communities-in-scotland/. Accessed September 2012 to November 2014.

Stewart, M. (1997) *The time of the Gypsies.* Oxford: Westview Press.

Stewart, S. (2006) *Queen amang the heather: The life of Belle Stewart.* Edinburgh: Birlinn Limited.

Stewart, S. (2008) *Pilgrims of the mist: The stories of Scotland's Travelling people.* Edinburgh: Birlinn Limited.

Stewart, M. (2012) *Gypsy 'menace'.* London: Hurst and Company.

Surdu, M. (2016) *Those who count*. Budapest: Central European University Press.

Talbani, A., and Hasanali, P. (2000) Adolescent females between tradition and modernity: Gender role socialization in South Asian immigrant culture. *Journal of Adolescence*, 23(5), pp. 615–627.

Taylor, Charles. (1994) The politics of recognition. In Goldberg D. T. (ed.) *Multiculturalism: A Critical Reader*. Oxford: Blackwell, pp. 75–106.

The Encyclopaedia Britannica. (1954) *Gypsy*, p. 852.

The Encyclopaedia Britannica. (1974) *Slang in European Languages*, pp. 852–853f.

The Scottish Government. (2010) Gypsies/Travellers in Scotland: The twice-yearly count. Available at: https://www.gov.scot/Publications/2010/08/18105029/3. Accessed 16 August 2018.

The Scottish Parliament. (2013) *Equal Opportunities Committee 1st Report 2013 (Session 4): Where Gypsy/Travellers live*. Available at: http://www.scottish.parliament.uk/S4_EqualOpportunitiesCommittee/Reports/eor-13-01w.pdf. Accessed 10 May 2013.

Thompson, T. W. (1928) Gleanings from constables' accounts and other sources. *Romani Studies*, 7(1), pp. 30–48.

Tobler, C. A. (2012) *Breathing it in: The musical identity of the Scottish Travellers*. Unpublished PhD thesis, Baltimore: University of Maryland Press.

Tong, D. (1998) *Gypsies: An interdisciplinary reader*. London: Taylor and Francis.

Traveller Times. (2018) Gypsy, Roma and Traveller children in care—A TT investigation. Available at: https://www.travellerstimes.org.uk/features/gypsy-roma-and-traveller-children-care-tt-investigation. Accessed 20 August 2018.

United Nations. (2009) Permanent forum in indigenous issues fact sheet. Available at: http://www.un.org/esa/socdev/unpfii/documents/5session_factsheet1.pdf. Accessed 8 March 2015.

Walkerdine, V., Lucey, H., and Melody, J. (2001) *Growing up girl: Psycho-social explorations of gender and class*. London: Palgrave Macmillan.

Whyte, B. (2000) *Red rowans and wild honey*. Edinburgh: Birlinn Limited.

Whyte, B. (2001) *The yellow on the broom: The early days of a Traveller woman*. Edinburgh: Birlinn Publishers.

Whyte, D. (2001) *Scottish Gypsies and other Travellers: A short history*. Alfreton: Robert Dawson.

Williamson, D. (1994) *The Horsieman: Memories of a Traveller 1928–1958*. Edinburgh: Canongate Press.

Wilson, J. M., and Leighton, A. (1885) *Wilson's Tales of the borders and of Scotland: Historical, traditionary, and imaginative, with a glossary* (Vol. 2). Glasgow: William MacKenzie.

Fig. 2.2 Three sisters (*Source* Courtesy of MECOPP/©McKenzie Family Archive)

3

Gypsies and Travellers in Education: Hidden, Deviant or Excluded

In the previous chapter, I stated that existing research on Gypsies and Travellers in the UK and in Scotland tends to focus on the experiences of the community as a whole. Specific research on education exists, and either explores the experiences of Gypsy and Traveller families in accessing education for their children, or the interrupted learning experienced by Gypsy and Traveller pupils viewed as being 'on the margins' or 'outside the mainstream' (Jordan 2000b; Jordan and Padfield 2003b; Padfield 2008); 'different', 'deviant' or 'excluded' (Lloyd and Norris 1998; Lloyd and Stead 2001). There is currently no research that gives voice to the gendered educational experiences of Gypsy and Traveller girls in Scotland, as seen from their perspective.

Neither are there studies that explore their educational experiences, in terms of their level of attainment and achievement, or their attendance in schools. The quality of schooling that they experience and how this relates to their ambitions and aspirations within school and beyond have not been considered or the external influences that might impact on their experiences at school. Their perspectives are missing.

Administrative data that focuses specifically on the education of Gypsies and Travellers does exist but is as yet not publically available.

© The Author(s) 2019
G. Marcus, *Gypsy and Traveller Girls*, Studies in Childhood and Youth,
https://doi.org/10.1007/978-3-030-03703-1_3

Continuing difficulties in identifying and 'counting' the Gypsy and Traveller population in Scotland, and pinpointing the number of Gypsy and Traveller children in the school system, means that they are quantitatively 'under-represented'. The educational experiences of Gypsy and Traveller girls are not even considered as a separate issue requiring contemplation and action.

Under Sections 28 and 29 of the United Nations Convention on the Rights of the Child (UNCRC), Gypsy and Traveller boys and girls have the same rights to appropriate education as all other children in Scotland. Article 12 in The European Framework Convention for the Protection of National Minorities (CoE 1995: 5) protects minority children's rights to an education, and this is binding on members of the CoE:

> Measures [have to be taken] in the fields of **education and research** to foster knowledge of the culture, history, language and religion of their national minorities and of the majority… provide adequate opportunities for teacher training…and equal opportunities for access to education at all levels for persons belonging to national minorities (my emphasis).

As suggested in the previous chapters, Gypsies and Travellers in Scotland are possibly the oldest minority ethnic group in the UK. The paucity of literature on the education of this minority group in Scotland and the rest of the UK ought to be addressed, and the issues faced by Gypsy and Traveller pupils needs to be respected and explored from their diverse perspectives.

There is a larger body of literature on the educational experiences of Gypsies and Travellers in England and Wales, than in Scotland. Whilst a few of these studies are relevant because they include analysis of the Scottish context, most are useful but not strictly relevant because they focus solely on educational matters south of the border. There is minimal analysis or comparisons with Scotland (Clark and Cemlyn 2005). In reviewing the educational experiences of Gypsy and Traveller pupils and girls in particular, I have focused largely on scholarly works about the Scottish educational context. Education is a devolved matter in Scotland and, as all the Gypsy and Traveller girls I interviewed were educated or are being educated within Scotland's distinctive education system. An overview of the Scottish system, its core emphasis on social justice and how this impacts on the experiences of Gypsy and Traveller girls is considered here. In addition, relevant Acts of Parliament, policy documents and reports on Gypsies and Travellers in Scotland are explored in this chapter.

Academic Literature in England and Wales

Many works explore the educational experiences of Gypsy and Traveller *pupils* around Britain—particularly in England and Wales—through case studies, highlighting both problems faced and examples of good practice (Bhopal 2000b, 2004, 2006; Deuchar and Bhopal 2017; Myers and Bhopal 2018; Tyler 2005). Binns (1990) offers a useful discussion of the history and growth of Traveller education. Diversity and strategies for inclusion, and how to maximise learning outcomes and achievement are major themes (O'Hanlon and Holmes 2004; Derrington and Kendall 2004; Danaher et al. 2007, 2009; Bhopal and Myers 2009a; Cemlyn and Greenfields 2012). The social exclusion of Gypsy and Traveller pupils, and the effects of racism and bullying are often discussed or alluded to, with several studies exploring teacher attitudes and bias to cultural diversity and inequalities (Bhopal 2000a, 2011a; Bhopal and Myers 2008; Duffy and Tomlinson 2009; Bhopal and Preston 2011). Studies reveal that as Gypsies and Travellers are considered 'white', teachers do not consider negative behaviour towards these pupils as racist (Bhopal 2011a, b).

Several studies consider the views and perspectives of Gypsies and Travellers. For example, there is research that explore reasons for Elective Home Education (EHE) from Gypsy and Traveller perspectives (Bhopal and Myers 2009b; D'Arcy 2014). Bhopal and Myers (2009a), Myers and Bhopal (2009, 2018), and Myers et al. (2010) explore Gypsy, Roma and Traveller understandings of safety, and Gypsy and Traveller parents' perceptions of education respectively. Derrington and Kendall (2003, 2004, 2007, 2008) expose findings on the challenges and barriers faced by Gypsy and Traveller pupils in secondary schools, and Derrington (2007) explores pupils' 'coping strategies'. In their edited volume, Allard and McLeod (2007) collate several works offering perspectives of young women 'routinely constructed as at risk', 'learning from the margins', but none of these explore the views of Scottish Gypsy and Traveller girls. Likewise, much of the research listed above is confined to England and Wales, with minimal analysis or comparisons with Scotland (Clark and Cemlyn 2005).

A full review of such studies from England and Wales is beyond the scope of this book, as they do not apply to the Scottish educational context, which is markedly different in several ways. Education is a devolved matter, meaning the Scottish Government has full political responsibility for education in Scotland. State schools are owned and operated by 32 local authorities, which act as Education authorities. The curriculum, school structure and examination systems are different (Humes and Bryce 2003). Furthermore, the education system in Scotland has traditionally emphasised greater breadth of learning with a wider and more flexible range of subjects particularly at secondary level, while the English system aims to provide more depth of education over a smaller subject range (Humes and Bryce 2003). Crucially, as all the Gypsy and Traveller girls I interviewed were educated or are being educated within the Scottish system, it makes sense to bind the scope of this study to just the Scottish context.

Two UK wide studies in particular are, however, significant. In 2009, Wilkin et al. produced a literature review for the Department of Children, Schools and Families. They listed ten common themes but, out of the 91 sources that were selected, there were no studies that focused specifically on gender-related issues. A report by Cemlyn et al. (2009) identified Gypsies and Travellers as one of the most socially marginalised and underachieving groups in the United Kingdom. The report asserts that 'the problems are immense' (Cemlyn et al. 2009: vii).

The Scottish Educational Context

Most of this section is devoted to a review of the literature on the educational experiences of Gypsy and Traveller pupils in Scotland, but crucially highlights the absence of gendered perspectives, particularly that of girls. First, I briefly situate my research within the context of the history and aims of Scottish education, stating what makes it distinctive. Then, with these aims in mind, I focus on what has been written about Gypsy and Traveller pupils in Scotland. The relatively few academic works that exist have been produced by STEP between 2000 and 2011, but there is a larger body of information found in local authority guidelines and recommendations, and reports from various government action groups, departments and agencies. A report by Black and Ethnic Minorities Infrastructure Scotland (BEMIS) (2011: 5) remarks, however, that 'little action has been advanced'.

The term 'education' is especially problematic and is an 'essentially contested concept' (Gallie 1956; Winch and Gingell 2008: 78). Pring (2004: 12) reminds us it is also a moral activity based on culture and values. Education is subjective, complex and difficult to measure. 'The relationship between theory and practice is often both complicated and subtle, and this is especially the case in an area like education which necessarily involves values as well as facts' (Winch and Gingell 2008: 212). These differences have a significant impact on classroom practice, educational debate and research, and public policy. Within the confines of this study, education is defined as the formal 'systems, structures and processes' of learning (Bartlett and Burton 2007: 59), which broadly includes education within council or privately run primary schools, secondary schools, community colleges, evening classes, apprenticeships and other organised learning initiatives where the girls may have participated. Informal learning experiences, for example, self-taught dressmaking, computer, or cooking skills, will be included in this research should they highlight these as valuable to them.

Educational practice and experiences, educational research and educational policy are interlinked (Bridges et al. 2009). Educational policy and its history in turn, as Ozga (2000: 114) advises, ought to be understood in the light of the grand narratives of 'political, social and economic contexts'. Pring (2004: 12) argues that at one level, there is generally broad consensus about what education is; 'at another it assumes different sets of values, different ways of seeing the world'. He reminds us of the 'moral character of education' (Pring 2004: 23). Education is an 'essentially contested' term because the concept of education implies a set of values, and there is disagreement over what these values are' (Pring 2004: 11). Values (morals and ethics) have an impact on policy, practice and educational experiences. There are different views about what or who an educated person is, and Pring believes that 'that there is no obvious way in which these differences might be resolved' (Pring 2004: 9).

hooks (1994, 2003), on the other hand, goes further and reminds us of education's power to emancipate. She asserts that education should in fact take place beyond the classroom into communities; beyond the didactic teacher-pupil power dynamic to one in which spaces are more democratic, equal and genuinely inclusive. She conceptualises a world in which difference is respected and enjoyed, but then moving beyond to value a shared humanity. hooks (1994: 2) explains that when she was at school some of her teachers 'were on a mission'; committed to nourishing the mind 'and by doing so uplift [her] race'.

Scotland's education system has a well-established tradition of providing public education and it is quite distinctive from the education systems in England, Wales and Northern Ireland. Scottish secondary education expanded to include all social classes, notably for girls too, in the early twentieth century. Uniquely, from 1889, with the introduction of the Universities (Scotland) Bill, reform of Scottish universities admitted women, many of whom became pioneers in their field (Rayner-Canham and Rayner-Canham 2008: 264). The nineteenth century arguably saw the rise of fundamental democratic principles and the opportunity for social advancement for those with ability, albeit for a minority (Anderson 2003). Universal access later became a major priority and the principles of egalitarianism and meritocracy seemingly formed the bedrock of the Scottish education system in the twentieth century (Devine 1999), and to this day remain embedded in the principles of the curriculum.

Since 2002, the Scottish education system has experienced a major overhaul of its aims, principles and curriculum. The Scottish Executive (2004) declared that it is their 'aspiration to enable all children to develop their capacities as successful learners, confident individuals, responsible citizens, and effective contributors to society'. They refer to these character traits or values as 'the four capacities' and are concerned primarily with the development of the child as citizen and economically productive. No child should be left behind and to the present day there are concerted efforts to reduce the impact of certain inequalities, particularly that of poverty and class, on the educational experiences and aspirations of pupils in Scotland.

It is stated that all children regardless of gender, class, ethnicity, ability, should have equal access to education and educational resources – a unifying nexus. Arshad (2008: v) states:

> Scots have long acknowledged that education has a central role in shaping a nation's identity, culture and economic prosperity. Education is a key area within which values and attitudes are formed and perpetuated. Scotland has also held sacrosanct the concept of 'education for all', viewing education as a democratic enterprise which can assist the reduction of privilege and contribute to the development of the collective democratic intellect.

'A recent National Literacy Trust (2007) report suggested that the Scottish Curriculum for Excellence (2008) may make schools more relevant for Gypsy [and] Traveller children' (Cemlyn et al. 2009). However, Arshad (2008: 8) argues that 'Scotland's [seemingly] natural commitment to issues of social justice and equality' should be problematised, and that 'Scottish confidence in meritocratic egalitarianism has impacted on how equity and anti-discrimination issues are being taken forward in Scottish education' (Arshad 2008: 37). She questions the 'naïve egalitarianism' (Causey et al. 2000: 34) that all people are equal, have equal ability and have an equal start in life that is so prevalent in the Scottish education system. The danger is that such ideas mask heterogeneous experiences of deep inequality and discrimination, because of the absence of recognition and discourse about race and racism (Arshad 2008: 37). Arshad (2008: 218) makes another important point about Scotland's Additional Support for Learning Act (2004). She claims that 'by focusing attention on individual pupil needs [the Act] has enabled Scottish education to disengage from considering institutional forms of discrimination as suggested by the Stephen Lawrence Inquiry report (Macpherson 1999)' (Arshad 2008: 218). The Act leans toward a deficit model of education, encouraging a focus on the individual pupil as having the problem or being problematic.

I prefer the use of the term anti-discrimination, as opposed to non-discrimination. The former is overtly proactive in challenging and reducing discriminatory practices instead of just not taking part in it (Arshad 2008: 225). It discounts the idea an individual can be 'unconscious' of discriminatory practices. King (2004, cited in Knowles and Lander 2011: 59) argues that one is instead 'dysconscious'—'having an uncritical habit of mind (including perceptions, attitudes, assumptions and beliefs) that justifies inequity by accepting the existing order of things as given'. A dysconcious person has impaired consciousness; a lack of knowledge is no excuse. I prefer the use of the term dysconscious. An individual is either consciously racist or dysconsciously racist.

The 2011 Census revealed that Scotland has a 96% white majority. Gypsies and Travellers have a particular problem in that they are visibly similar to the white Scottish majority, yet perceived as being different. Clark (2006: 7–8) describes this dilemma as an 'ethnicity conundrum' and this is explained in the next chapter. Dawson's (2007: 9) assertion reflects this tendency to avoid the pathologies of difference and the lack of recognition:

> No one wants to know about them [Gypsies and Travellers]. The prejudice is so deep rooted (and so undeserved) that almost no one is interested. Almost all universities ignore the subject. General publishers, almost entirely do the same... and yet Scotland's Travellers... are a Scotland in miniature.

Cressy (2018: xi) also argues that the social marginality of Gypsies, past and present, is matched by their marginality in modern scholarship'. The impact of race pales by comparison and whatever efforts made seem to have had minimal impact. Despite organisations like BEMIS, CRER, and CERES, Rowena Arshad, Head of the School of Education at the University of Edinburgh recently declared in a conference speech that 'there is still no national discussion about race in Scotland' (Arshad, Lecture, 18 November 2015). There is a lack of transparency as to what is actually happening in terms of race discrimination in our society and in our schools. At a macro level, in the name of egalitarianism, race has been squeezed out of the political process and indeed out of the Scottish education system, as is evidenced by the experiences of the girls I interviewed. At a micro level, teachers and other staff in the system, many of whom are white women, either reflect racist tendencies and attitudes, or are 'dysconsciously' so. This mindset impacts on practice in the classroom, and young Gypsy and Traveller girls report not only being racially discriminated against by their peers, but also by their teachers. As is highlighted by the girls' accounts, racist discrimination is then reflected in gender and age discrimination. The intersection of multiple discriminations and the ensuing inequalities are a core part of the girls' experiences highlighted in the book.

Evidence given at this recent conference, 'A Scottish Approach to Race Equality', by twelve representatives from academia, charities and other associations, paint a bleak picture. Policies are out of date, race equality legislation and strategies are not being consistently implemented, progress is glacial and they argue that there could be a normalization of low level racial discrimination. A question arose as to whether race has become lost in the Equality Act (2010), and that there is general suspicion that because of the policies and legislation in place we now live in post-racial times. A stakeholder I interviewed claimed that discrimination is high on the government's 'equalities agenda' but not on the government's 'education agenda', and in the interviewee's opinion, this is reflected in the way each department allocates its budget (Anon. Academic 1 (2014), Personal communication). This lends weight to the EU's assessment that the Framework for National Roma Integration which began in 2011, and which includes developments in education as a key area, has not produced sufficient progress (European Commission 2015: 14).

The rhetoric does not translate into meaningful social action that creates positive change. Interestingly, at this conference on Race Equality, the plight of Gypsies and Travellers in Scotland was not mentioned, except in a passing comment by one delegate in his speech. Even here, at a conference on race equality and discrimination, Gypsies and Travellers remain invisible, and do not merit discussion. Their experiences are consciously or dysconsciously still perceived as 'the last bastion of acceptable racism' (Coxhead 2007). And this remains a problem even in our schools and classrooms.

What Does 'Being in Education' Mean in Scotland?

All parents are legally expected to educate their children. However, the situation within the Scottish legal context for enrolment and attendance in school is not straightforward and I shed light on gaps and complications that make it possible for some travelling children and young people to legally miss out on an education, whether in school or at home.

I attended two Traveller Education Network (TENET) meetings and it was clear from the teachers' discussions and questions that there were discrepancies in understanding of what it means legally to 'be in education' in Scotland. Based on a talk at one TENET meeting (21 May 2014) given by Iain Nisbet, Head of Education Law Unit at the Govan Law Centre, and my subsequent interview with him, the following summary attempts to explain the position of the law regarding a child's right to an education and a parent's duty to enable that education to take place (Nisbet 2014a, b, Personal communication).

According to the Education (Scotland) Act 1980, a child is deemed to be in education when his/her parent (or carer) enrols him/her into a mainstream or independent primary school between the ages of 4½ and 5½ years, depending on when the child's birthday falls.

If a parent chooses not to enrol a child at this stage, the parent is not obliged, under the Education (Scotland) Act 1980 to declare or seek permission for their child to be educated at home (Section 35 (1)). The parent's right to choose *how* their child is educated takes precedence in the eyes of the law. But under Section 30 of the Act, the parent has a duty to provide 'efficient education…either by causing him [or her] to attend a public school regularly or by other means'. Once a child is officially enrolled, consent should be sought to remove a child from school to be home educated. Whilst the reason for doing so is immaterial, the local education authority in which the family resides is obliged under Section 37 of the Act, to carry out an annual check to evaluate that the child is being educated to a standard that befits that child's 'age, ability and aptitude' and that the parent is indeed providing an 'efficient education'.

Section 37 also requires an authority to act where they are not satisfied that an efficient and suitable education is being provided. The education authority is not responsible for undertaking the education of a child who is being home educated, but under Section 5 (4) and 29 (3) of the Education (Additional Support for Learning) (Scotland) 2004 and 2009, they do have certain discretionary powers to provide for additional support needs.

It becomes difficult to carry out these checks if a family has no fixed abode, moves sporadically between local authorities and does not remain in any given place for long periods of time. At the STEP meeting I attended, it was pointed out by some TENET teachers that local authorities can be reluctant to monitor a Travelling child's educational progress without formal records and well-defined boundaries as to which local area is actually responsible. Another teacher I met echoed this view and remarked, 'it feels like a complete waste of time to put in all that effort and then you turn up one day and they are gone…it's demoralising…you never see them again and you have no clue where they have gone next!' This situation is further compounded if a Traveller parent does not want or evades contact with education personnel from the local authority. It can be argued that a child in such a situation falls through the net.

I met one such very mobile family whose children, now teenagers, have never been enrolled in any school or received any formal education. Their mother admitted none of her daughters could read or write. She agreed to talk to me but only briefly because a trusted health visitor was present. She declined to be formally interviewed, suspicious that I might report her to the authorities. Legally, a parent does not need to have any teaching qualifications to home educate their child and it can be difficult to establish if a parent is fulfilling their duty and if so, how well this is being carried out. D'Arcy (2014) writes about a similar situation in England in which she acknowledges that 'statutory requirements for provision [of home education] are remarkably vague'. As highlighted in Chapter 4, Anthias (2013: 13) in discussing the prevention of intersecting inequalities reflects on the limits of legislation and public bodies to regulate experiences at home and in the private world of family.

When the child becomes eligible to attend a mainstream or independent secondary school, usually by the age of twelve years, the parent again has the right to choose if this should take place, and the education authority's duties to check on progress sets in if and when the child is declared to be 'home educated', as above. Only when a child is 16 years and is deemed a young person, does he/she have the right to choose how and when they are educated, or indeed may prefer to leave education and enter the world of work.

The right of a child to receive an education stems from and is enshrined in the European Convention on Human Rights (Article 2) and the UNCRC (Articles 12 and 28). The child's right to be educated or be in education is reflected within education authorities' attempts to provide formal structures—a physical space or school building, a curriculum and the professional relationship between a qualified teacher and pupil. Problems occur and choices become limited for Gypsy and Traveller families and their children when those very education spaces are viewed as unsafe and risky, particularly as a result of racism and bullying in schools (D'Arcy 2014). The young Gypsy and Traveller women I interviewed have a more flexible understanding of and approach to education.

Academic Literature in Scotland

Gypsy and Traveller education in Scotland is predominantly and broadly viewed as a problem of interrupted learning (Jordan 1998a, b, 2001a) and exclusion (Lloyd and Norris 1998; Lloyd et al. 1999; Jordan 1998a, 2000a, b, c, 2001b; Jordan and Padfield 2003b; McKinney 2003). In order to address the former problem, studies have been done on developing alternative and flexible methods to help improve access to the curriculum for Traveller children, chiefly through the use of information and communication technologies (ICT) to enable distance learning (Jordan and Padfield 2002, 2003a; Padfield 2006a). STEP (2013) continues to work towards developing use of e-learning or e-LATES, mobile and smartphones. The underlying implication stems from 'ambiguous understandings of their 'mobility'', which result in Gypsy and Traveller students in primary and secondary education in the UK being marginalised (Myers 2018). There remains a persistent misinterpretation that confuses and links their ethnicity to nomadism, which impacts on how they are perceived and supported in educational settings.

Their current ongoing research investigates 'young people's views on education, new media and digital technology' and the usefulness of 'family literacy programmes for Scottish Travelling communities'. In addition, STEP is working on a guide for 'digital learning resources' aimed at 13–16-year-old Gypsies and Travellers (STEP 2015). The organisation believes that the effectiveness of transitions between home and school, primary and secondary, is a crucial problem for Gypsy and Traveller families and their children, and is researching how to improve the situation (STEP 2015).

Alternative means of education through home schooling, or a combination of 'home and school learning' have also been explored. Jordan and Holmes (1997) and Jordan (2001c) analyse challenges and question whose responsibility it is to ensure that Gypsy and Traveller pupils have access to education. Home schooling can be viewed negatively, but they argue that for Gypsies and Travellers, this may be a sound alternative. Whilst enrolment attendance is a prime concern, Jordan and Padfield (2004) discuss attainment and support for learning, particularly for pupils that are educated on mobile learning centres on Traveller sites.

To address the problems of non-attendance, exclusion and exclusionary practices in schools, the existing research literature on Gypsy and Traveller education in Scotland investigates or evaluates pedagogical issues and inclusive approaches. Inclusive education is a strong theme in the Scottish research context. Jordan (1999, 2000d), Lloyd and Stead (2002), Padfield (2005, 2006b, 2008), and Padfield and Cameron (2009) provide information and advice to practitioners in schools and local authorities on how to cope with interrupted learning, the specific educational needs of Gypsy and Traveller pupils, and the issues facing the community; shedding light on the legal and social context around the education of Travelling children. There is guidance on Gypsy and Traveller terminology and how to keep records. STEP (n.d.) has written a pack of three pamphlets giving advice to Gypsy and Traveller parents on schooling, staying safe in school and additional support for learning.

Apart from its work on technological solutions for the education of Gypsy and Traveller pupils, STEP (2013, 2015) aims to '[encourage] positive approaches to diversity in education through supporting practitioners and families in challenging racism, harassment and bullying'. In 1998, Jordan argues for 'teacher training for inclusion', whilst Lloyd et al. (1999, 2010) 'raise issues about how teachers define discipline and good order in schools' and the impact of their response on Gypsy and Traveller pupils. They confirm that the behaviour of Gypsy and Traveller children is mainly constructed as 'problematic' by staff in schools that are keen to keep control of 'good' discipline. Lloyd and Stead (2001) again address the importance of teachers effectively handling reports of bullying and name-calling against Gypsy and Traveller pupils. They explore pupils' views on 'name-calling', and raise the issue that teachers do not 'believe' Gypsy and Traveller pupils when they report they have been bullied. However, McCluskey et al. (2011), and McCluskey and Watson (2012) make a powerful point about 'teachers making a difference', striving to move decidedly away from deficit modes of thinking.

As mentioned earlier, according to Save the Children (2005), which conducted extensive interviews with Gypsy and Traveller children, 92% reported bullying in schools. This mirrors a prior detailed study done a decade earlier, which provides a compelling account of Traveller opinions on various issues—health, education and accommodation. The study was carried out on behalf of Save The Children in Scotland (Bancroft et al. 1996), in which 114 (11–18 year olds) children were interviewed in groups or as individuals. The report covered reasons for attendance or non-attendance, accessibility, treatment at school, relations with non-travellers, bullying and preferences for education. Parents and stakeholders were also interviewed. Brief questions were raised about whether the educational experiences of girls and boys differed, but not much evidence was gathered about how they differed and why; other than that, girls possibly stayed on longer, boys having to work from the age of 12. Gendered division of labour was adhered to rigidly. Sex education was cited as a problem for girls' attendance, as was bullying. 41% of children interviewed said they attended primary school with some regularity, the figure dropping to only 20% for secondary. University or college attendance was very uncommon. However, when there have been positive experiences and integration at school, Gypsy and Traveller girls attended access courses and other adult learning opportunities mainly to manage their own businesses, or go to work (Bancroft et al. 1996). McKinney (2001: 21–23) argues that increasing numbers of Gypsy and Traveller parents think basic literacy and numeracy are important for their children. Attendance at primary school is seen as positive, useful, less threatening, and even safe.

Lloyd and Norris (1998) highlight the issue of 'disciplinary exclusion' at secondary level, investigating how school and teacher perceptions of Gypsy and Traveller pupils' culture, impact on their interaction with pupils. Interviews were conducted with staff, parents and young people. Just as Gypsies and Travellers are suspicious of mainstream education and cannot see its relevance to their lives, schools do not recognise and accommodate Gypsy and Traveller culture and lifestyle. The lack of genuine inclusion exacerbates conflict and further discourages Gypsy and Traveller pupils from secondary education. The study found that school staff tend to follow the deficit model—either expecting the individual to adapt to school practices and expectations, or trying to 'fix' the child and their family. Problems and solutions lie with the Gypsy and Traveller pupil and their family.

Inclusion is no longer just confined to students with special educational needs or defined by physical and cognitive disabilities, but embraces a broad range of needs with respect to ability, race, ethnicity, religion, gender, age, language, culture and other forms of differences. To be inclusive is to be 'culturally responsive' and to recognise how to tailor learning experiences on the cultural realities of the child, which includes home life, community experiences, language background, and belief systems (Cazdean and Leggett 1981, cited in Ladson-Billings 1992: 331). Wilkinson and Pickett (2010: 113) state that, 'student performance and behaviour in educational tasks can be profoundly affected by the way we feel, we are seen and judged by others. When we expect to be viewed as inferior, our abilities seem to diminish'. Education Scotland (2015) states 'an inclusive approach reflects a move away from a deficit model, which focuses on aspects of the learner as the problem, where the learner is viewed as deficient in some way'. This study questions if Gypsy/Traveller girls are included in the sense defined above.

Lloyd (2005) in her edited volume entitled, *'Problem' girls: understanding and supporting troubled and troublesome girls and young women*, focuses a chapter on young Gypsy and Traveller women. Within the context of emotional and behavioural disorder (EBD), the chapter called, *'EBD girls'—a critical view* discusses the experiences of Gypsy and Traveller girls (Lloyd 2005: 129–145). Bringing the Black and Gypsy female experience together, for example, she states:

> Black and Gypsy and Traveller girls may be name-called… in relation to both gender and ethnicity (Wright et al. 2000) and Scottish Gypsy Traveller girls in particular who got into trouble in school, negotiated and resisted labels of ethnicity and gender. (2005: 132)

She asserts that there are 'pressures on Gypsy and Traveller girls to defeat the prejudiced and stereotyped expectations of some teachers' (2005: 133). Teachers she interviewed in the study said they 'often valued' those girls who attempted to minimise difference and 'to produce themselves as like the settled pupils' (2005: 133). Gypsy and Traveller girls were defined as deviant and were subject to disciplinary exclusion. Lloyd (2005: 129) problematises the label 'EBD girls' and proposes that the voices of so-called 'problem' girls need to be heard, and that teachers need to 'recognise the individual complexity of their lives'.

Lloyd's (2005) book is not exclusively about educational experiences of Gypsy and Traveller girls, as it explores experiences of girls from a range of social and ethnic backgrounds. Nevertheless, it should be acknowledged that this is the only work that focuses on the experiences of Gypsy and Traveller girls in school, even if it is only about the 'EBD' ones.

Writing about Gypsy and Traveller women within the context of 'troubled lives', Clavell-Bate (2012) highlights concerns about the relationship between formal school education and young Gypsy and Traveller women. In her chapter, included in an edited volume entitled *Transforming troubled lives: Strategies and interventions for children with social, emotional and behavioural difficulties*, she confirms that 'the GRT community is considered a patriarchal society, with women having culturally defined roles from an early age'. Here too Gypsy and Traveller girls are written about in the context of EBD or 'troubled lives'.

Lloyd et al. (1999: 62) make a pertinent argument that 'by seeing issues [or problems] in individual terms, by not recognising difference, schools may continue merely to focus on behaviour, rather than explore the institutional response of the education system to a marginalised community'. Lloyd and McCluskey (2008: 335) write powerfully about 'contradictions and significant silences' in the education of Gypsies and Travellers, arguing that 'views of Gypsy/Travellers about education unveil an intensely complex and challenging set of relationships'. They raise several useful points for consideration:

- There is an increase in interest in formal mainstream education, but only enough to support their current lifestyle.
- Pupils wish to attend school, but fears of bullying and racist harassment mean they do not 'participate fully in state education, particularly at secondary level' (2008: 336).
- There is support for basic literacy and numeracy, but Gypsy and Traveller pupils and parents 'remain sceptical about much else that is on offer' (2008: 337).
- There is increased recognition of the problems faced by Gypsy and Traveller pupils and a range of initiatives have been introduced, but progress is 'slow' and 'patchy', some well-funded and others non-existent. There is still no 'integrated approach' (2008: 338).

Lloyd and McCluskey (2008: 341) acknowledge that despite the pressures faced by schools, many schools have made significant improvements in the service they offer to a diverse range of pupils. However, the inclusion agenda has only been partially successful. SEBD and those with 'little social and cultural capital' in particular, still face multifarious difficulties in schools (Lloyd and McCluskey 2008: 341).

From this, I make two observations. First, it is significant that after Lloyd and others point out the demerits of the deficit model, a decade later, Lloyd and McCluskey (2008) remind us again of the need to improve inclusion in schools. Arshad (2008) in her thesis on 'equity and anti-discrimination in Scotland' still felt compelled to put forward her argument about the myth of egalitarianism in Scottish education. In addition, Clark (2008) highlights the lack of sustained, concerted action—'non-performativity' (Ahmed 2004). Multiple reports and recommendations reflect this central theme of 'non-performativity' to this day for several reasons. Prejudice against Gypsies and Travellers is deep-seated and exists at every level. Politically, it is not a vote winner to be championing the cause of Gypsies and Travellers (Richardson 2006). Makers and writers of policy tend to see policy making as an act and an end (Ahmed 2004). In discussions with frontline service providers in social care, health and education whom I met, several highlighted that regular staff turnover led to a lack of sustained follow through of the guidance and recommendations. When these staff move on, so does their acquired knowledge and understanding of Gypsies and Travellers and the issues that affect their lives.

Gypsy and Traveller pupils continue to experience discrimination within the structures of education, one that reflects 'contradictions and significant silences' within the State's policies enacted to decrease social exclusion (Lloyd and McCluskey 2008).

Second, as a woman of colour, I find studying the lives of another minority ethnic group of women or girls as 'problems', 'deviant', 'on the margins', 'outsiders' and 'outside the mainstream', deeply problematic. Whilst these studies are arguably necessary and laudable, they perpetuate the othering of Gypsy and Traveller girls and young women. None of these works seeks to examine their agency, aspirations and achievements, and there is a danger that one might assume they simply do not exist in education, mainstream or otherwise. Similar to how researchers and policymakers overly focus on female genital mutilation in the lives of Muslim women or African women, and their 'subordination' in 'strong' patriarchal societies, there is a danger of presenting simplistic and patriarchal narratives—that of the vulnerable, helpless minority ethnic woman. Richardson's (2006) warning about the controlling power of discourse does not only apply to structures within politics, legislation, and the media, but also inadvertently in what researchers choose to research and write about. An interview with a government official revealed that the EHRC is aware of the racist bullying in schools and that:

> The Commission is currently engaged in a major improvement pro-gramme with Scottish schools on this issue. We will publish research shortly and then follow this with an intervention with selected schools to explore what steps need to be put in place to make a measurable reduc-tion in identity based bullying and harassment. (Oswald 2014, Personal communication)

Given that this issue is not a new one, there is a disconnect between the espoused rhetoric and what has actually been happening in our schools. There still remains little understanding of racism both as a structural issue and as an everyday occurrence in the lives of minority ethnic communities.

Reports, Recommendations and Guidelines

Since 1971, there have been many initiatives in Scotland to encour-age Gypsy and Traveller pupils to attend school and to do so regularly. However, these have been challenging to implement, as anecdotal evi-dence suggests that Gypsy and Traveller parents want flexibility and for their children to attend school only part-time, if and when they do so (Jordan and Padfield 2004). This section reviews relevant reports, rec-ommendations and guidelines in chronological order. A central fea-ture of these reports and recommendations, as previously mentioned, is the repetitiveness of concerns, explanations and guidance; the need to understand Gypsy and Traveller history, culture, terminology; the expectations of families for their children, and so on. The reports are usually divided into four separate problem areas—issues to do with accommodation, health, employment, and education. Sometimes, ref-erence is made to issues surrounding law and order, and policing. Not unlike *The 1895 Scottish Traveller Report* (Dawson 2005), many of the reports do not include direct evidence from Gypsies and Travellers themselves, with a few exceptions, and then often by the same few Travellers. Gypsies and Travellers are still generally discussed and written about by non-Travellers, albeit by those who work closely with Gypsy and Traveller communities. For the purposes of this book, I will only be focusing on the reports' guidance and recommendations about education.

In 1982, the third term report of the Secretary of State's Advisory Committee stressed the particular educational needs of Travellers (Scottish Office 1982). The report identified the need for 'urgent concerted action at local authority and national level, in order to redress the discriminatory situation' faced by Gypsy and Traveller pupils (Clark 2001: 178). This ultimately led in 1990 to the creation of a national agency to coordinate efforts to improve the educational experiences of Gypsy and Traveller pupils and their families—the Scottish Traveller Education Programme (STEP). The success of this project was noted in subsequent reports (Scottish Office 1992, 1995), but has been, from time to time, hampered by funding and other associated problems (Scottish Office, Eight Term Report 1998a). Nevertheless, STEP addresses a range of issues 'related to access, inclusion, innovation and flexibility, engagement with and active involvement of parents and the communities, anti-bullying strategies, ethnic monitoring and information systems, and adult learning' (Cemlyn et al. 2009: 9).

As in many of the scholarly works cited above, the 8th and 9th Term Reports of the Advisory Committee on Scotland's Travelling People (Scottish Office 1998b, 2000), and Race Equality Advisory Forum Report (The Scottish Executive 2001), advise and provide guidance to schools, teachers, local authorities, and other stakeholders on how to develop their practice with regard to supporting the needs of Gypsy and Traveller pupils and families. The same recommendations are essentially repeated in each of these reports—highlighting the pre-school needs of Gypsies and Travellers; suggesting that Colleges of Education should develop expertise on how to teach Traveller children; adoption of appropriate methods of educating; the importance of accessible and well-kept records of attendance and attainment; and adult literacy and numeracy programmes. In fact, in 2000 the 9th Term Report collated all of these recommendations spanning 28 years into an extensive table, which is available to view on the government's website (Scottish Executive 2007: Appendix C).

Since devolution, however, the Scottish Parliament has taken a renewed interest in the situation of Scottish Gypsies and Travellers. The 'Moving Targets' report (Lloyd et al. 1999), together with the pioneering EOC 'Inquiry into Gypsy Travellers and Public Sector Policies' (2001), found widespread evidence of discrimination, racism and social exclusion across a range of domains (EOC 2001). Within education there were 'difficulties experienced in accessing education services when travelling and managing interrupted learning'; bullying was reported as a 'common experience' for Gypsy and Traveller children; 'lack of support from some schools' 'resulting in parental reluctance to send children to school'; school policies, materials and teacher training reflect a lack of cultural awareness; and parents have difficulties in obtaining accurate information about access to education services and the educational attainment of Gypsy and Traveller children (EOC 2001).

The report was a crucial milestone in Gypsy and Traveller history in Scotland. With support and evidence from members of the Gypsy and Traveller community, the Scottish Executive made 37 recommendations, seven focusing on education. In 2005, a further inquiry reviewed the progress of the 2001 report and provided further recommendations (The Scottish Executive 2005). 'This highlighted that most of the 37 recommendations in the 2001 report had not been implemented; that very little progress had been made and that the general situation had not improved' (BEMIS 2011: 22). Again, this reflects the reasons for non-performativity mooted above.

In 2006, the Report of the Gypsies and Travellers Strategic Group (The Scottish Executive 2006: 9, 13) usefully identified several concerns in Scottish schools—inconsistencies in educational provision for Gypsy and Traveller children and young people across 32 local authorities; the lack of key liaison workers; and teachers being ill-equipped to recognise and handle racist bullying. The Report concludes that the education system as a whole is inflexible in its approach to facilitating access to the curriculum, as there is no national educational strategy specifically aimed at Gypsy and Traveller children. According to the report, bullying was still a major concern for Gypsy and Traveller pupils in Scottish schools. It reveals that teachers are seemingly unable to recognise, acknowledge and resolve racist bullying satisfactorily. This book explores some of these negative issues from the perspectives of Gypsy and Traveller girls.

A broad review of guidance and recommendations from all 32 Local Authorities in Scotland, elicited through the Freedom of Information (Scotland) Act (2002), revealed some of the inconsistencies and gaps in provision. Local Authority strategies ranged from a few examples of good practice, to one authority in particular referring Gypsy and Traveller parents wishing to make enquiries about their children's education to the authority's Child Protection Officer. At the time of the review conducted in late 2013, only one authority had a 'policy' on Gypsy and Traveller educational provision. A few authorities had no guidance for schools, staff or families on the education of Gypsy and Traveller pupils, because they decided they had no Gypsies and Travellers who had visibly self-identified. There is still no national policy specifically geared towards the education of Gypsy and Traveller pupils. A deeper review of the guidance and recommendations across the 32 Local Authorities is warranted.

The Report highlights the need for more teachers for Gypsies and Travellers, flexible access for young people to college courses, and for 'all authorities to accept Gypsies and Travellers and not to treat them differently to the rest of the community' (The Scottish Executive 2006: 13). It states that the challenge for the Scottish Executive, local authorities and all those involved in providing key services, is to learn to respect Gypsies and Travellers as different, but not to penalise them for it or force them to assimilate in ways that run contrary to their lifestyle and identity—valuing their humanity and their 'otherness'.

In the 2006 Report, a 'wish list of actions sought' was compiled in which young Gypsies and Travellers asked specifically to be respected by the authorities and the rest of the community. Crucially, the Report of the Gypsies and Travellers Strategic Group states that instances of good practice in schools do exist but are 'not being filtered through' (2006a: 9). A report in 2009 by Cemlyn et al. echoes this concern. As a contribution to existing literature in the field, and responding to the

2006 report in general and the 'wish list' of young Gypsies and Travellers in particular, my study aims to explore what is positive in the education of the girls, as perceived and articulated by the girls themselves. Their stories of achievement and success will be highlighted; the idea and meaning of success will be 'decolonised'; and the girls' *reasons* for their perceived success, as understood by the girls, will also be explored.

In 2009, after an extensive review of the *Inequalities Experienced by Gypsy and Traveller Communities in the UK* (including Scotland), Cemlyn et al. (2009: 108–110) make 17 recommendations for improving the educational experiences of Gypsy and Traveller children and young people, that mirror the recommendations made in all the reports above.

A decade since the EOC's report in 2001, which made 37 recommendations across all service areas, BEMIS (2011: 4) concluded that 'Scotland's Gypsy and Traveller community still faces numerous challenges'. Below is a summary of BEMIS' key areas of concern within the education sector:

Gypsy and Travellers' children remain at a disadvantage and are an underachieving group in the Scottish education system.

The interviews provide examples of bullying, harassment, racial incidence and discrimination against Gypsy and Traveller pupils. It was especially true in secondary schools.

Lack of recognition and acknowledgement of Gypsy/Travelling culture have an impact on inadequate provision of education service.

Lack of engagement of Gypsy and Traveller communities leads to confusion and miscommunication between schools and the Gypsy and Travellers community.

In light of the above summary, a recent report on behalf of the Jimmy Reid Foundation on *Social Justice, The Common Weal and Children and Young People in Scotland* (Davis et al. 2014), reveals yet again the myth of egalitarianism and meritocracy that Arshad (2008) maintains persists in Scottish consciousness.

Davis et al. (2014: 1) propose that 'Scotland should organise itself around social justice, which addresses entitlements, redistribution, recognition and respect'. They criticise as 'piecemeal' the passing-off of children's rights within an 'apolitical wellbeing framework' and argue that 'a lack of strong legislation to hold local authorities and other public services, private sector organisations and the third sector to account', gives rise to persistent everyday discrimination experienced by children and young people, including Gypsy and Traveller girls (2014: 1). Adults need to recognise and respect the voices, choices and contributions of children and young people. Crucially, Davis et al. (2014: 19) reason that 'wellbeing approaches to children's services' need to be disregarded, as these approaches are ineffective in addressing inequalities in childhood. 'Less GIRFEC-type professional interventions are required because children, young people and their families are better off, [when] more integrated into their communities' (2014: 19). GIRFEC or Getting It Right for Every Child is Scotland's approach to supporting the wellbeing of children and young people 'by offering the right help at the right time from the right people', working in partnership with families and communities. The authors call for 'a repositioning of the political debate… to analyse adult-child relations in Scotland in a way that recognises our collaborative strengths, abilities and potential' (2014: 19). There continues to be a disconnect between the espoused rhetoric in policy documents and reports, and what is actually happening.

References

Ahmed, S. (2004) Declarations of whiteness: The non-performativity of anti-racism. *Borderlands E-journal*, 3(2). Available at: http://borderlands. net.au/vol3no2_2004/ahmed_declarations.htm. Accessed 7 April 2016.

Allard, A., and Mcleod, J. (2007) *Learning from the margins: Young women, social exclusion and education*. London: Routledge.

Anderson, R. (2003) The history of Scottish education pre-1980. In: Bryce, T. G. K., and Humes, W. M. (eds.) *Scottish education: Post-devolution*, 2nd ed. Edinburgh: Edinburgh University Press, pp. 219–228.

Anon. Academic 1. (2014, May 15) Personal communication. Discussion, interview and notes.

Anthias, F. (2013) Intersectional what? Social divisions, intersectionality and levels of analysis. *Ethnicities*, 13(1), pp. 3–19.

Arshad, R. (2008) *Teacher activism in equity and anti-discrimination in Scotland: An interpretive study.* Unpublished PhD thesis, Edinburgh: University of Edinburgh.

Arshad, R. (2015, November 18) *Forging race equality policy in Scotland* [Lecture to Royal Society of Edinburgh], Edinburgh.

Bancroft, A., Lloyd, M., and Morran, R. (1996) *The right to roam: Travellers in Scotland 1995/96.* Dunfermline: Save the Children in Scotland.

Bartlett, S., and Burton, D. (2007) *Introduction to education studies.* 2nd ed. London: Sage.

BEMIS. (2011) *Gypsy Travellers in contemporary Scotland: The 2001 'Inquiry into Gypsy Travellers and public sector policies': Ten years on.* Glasgow: BEMIS.

Bhopal, K. (2000a) Gender, 'race' and power in the research process. In: *Research and inequality*, pp. 67–79.

Bhopal, K. (2000b) Working towards inclusive education: Aspects of good practice for Gypsy Traveller pupils. http://dera.ioe.ac.uk/4470/1/RR238.PDF.

Bhopal, K. (2004) Gypsy Travellers and education: Changing needs and changing perceptions. *British Journal of Educational Studies*, 52(1), pp. 47–64.

Bhopal, K. (2006) Issues of rurality and good practice: Gypsy Traveller pupils in schools.

Bhopal, K. (2011a) 'This is a school, it's not a site': Teachers' attitudes towards Gypsy and Traveller pupils in schools in England, UK. *British Educational Research Journal*, 37(3), pp. 465–483.

Bhopal, K. (2011b) 'What about us? 'Gypsies, Travellers and 'White racism' in secondary schools in England. *International Studies in Sociology of Education*, 21(4), pp. 315–329.

Bhopal, K., and Myers, M. (2008) *Insiders, outsiders and others: Gypsies and identity.* Hatfield: University of Hertfordshire Press.

Bhopal, K., and Myers, M. (2009a) Gypsy, Roma and Traveller pupils in schools in the UK: Inclusion and 'good practice'. *International Journal of Inclusive Education*, 13 (3), pp. 299–314.

Bhopal, K., and Myers, M. (2009b) *A pilot study to investigate reasons for elective home education for Gypsy/Traveller children in Hampshire.* Hampshire: Hampshire County Council.

Bhopal, K., and Preston, J. (eds.). (2011) *Intersectionality and 'race' in education.* London: Routledge Research in Education.

Binns, D. (1990) History and growth of Traveller education. *British Journal of Educational Studies*, 38(3), pp. 251–258.

Bridges, D., Smeyers, P., and Smith, R. (2009) *Evidence-based education policy: What evidence what basis whose policy* (Vol. 6). Chichester: Wiley.

Causey, V. E., Thomas, C. D., and Armento, B. J. (2000) Cultural diversity is basically a foreign term to me: The challenges of diversity for preservice teacher education. *Teaching and Teacher Education*, 16(1), pp. 33–45.

Cemlyn, S., and Greenfields, M. (2012) *Diversity, inclusion and social justice: Strategies for inclusion, promoting, redistribution, recognition and representation for Gypsies and Travellers*. Available at: dspace.bucks.ac.uk. Accessed 5 March 2013.

Cemlyn, S., Greenfields, M., Burnett, S., Matthews, Z., and Whitwell, C. (2009) *Inequalities experienced by Gypsy and Traveller communities: A review*. Research Report 12. Manchester: Equality and Human Rights Commission. Available at: https://dera.ioe.ac.uk/11129/1/12inequalities_experienced_by_gypsy_and_traveller_communities_a_review.pdf.

Clark, C. (2001) *'Invisible lives': The Gypsies and Travellers of Britain*. Unpublished PhD thesis, Edinburgh: University of Edinburgh.

Clark, C. (2006) Defining ethnicity in a cultural and socio-legal context: The case of Scottish Gypsy-Travellers. *Scottish Affairs*, 54(1), pp. 39–67.

Clark, C. (2008) Introduction themed section care or control? Gypsies, Travellers and the state. *Social Policy and Society*, 7(1), pp. 65–71.

Clark, C., and Cemlyn, S. (2005) The social exclusion of Gypsy and Traveller children. In: *At greatest risk*, 150–165. London: CPAG. Available at: http://strathprints.strath.ac.uk/id/eprint/835. Accessed 5 March 2013.

Clavell-Bate, R. (2012) Elective home education: Supporting access to education for children and young people within the Gypsy, Roma and Traveller community. In: Visser, J., Daniels, H., and Cole, T. (eds.) *Transforming troubled lives: Strategies and interventions for children with social, emotional and behavioural difficulties*. Bradford: Emerald Group Publishing, pp. 175–191.

Council of Europe. (1995) *Framework convention for the protection of national minorities and explanatory report*. Available at: https://www.coe.int/.../minorities/.../PDF_H(95)10_FCNM_ExplanReport_en.pdf. Accessed 30 April 2016.

Coxhead, J. (2007) *The last bastion of racism: Gypsies, Travellers and policing*. Stoke-on-Trent: Trentham Books.

Cressy, D. (2018) *Gypsies: An English History*. Oxford: Oxford University Press.

Danaher, P. A., Coombes, P. N., and Kiddle, C. (2007) *Teaching Traveller children: Maximising learning outcomes*. Stoke-on-Trent: Trentham Books.

Danaher, P. A., Kenny, M., and Leder, J. R. (eds.). (2009) *Traveller, nomadic and migrant education*. London: Routledge.

D'Arcy, K. W. (2014) *Travellers and home education: Safe spaces and inequality*. London: Institute of Education Press.

Davis, J., Hill, L., Tisdall, K., Cairns, L., and McCausland, S. (2014) *Social justice, the common weal and children and young people in Scotland*. Jimmy Reid Foundation. Edinburgh: University of Edinburgh.

Dawson, R. (2005) *The 1895 Scottish Traveller report*. Derbyshire: Dawson and Rackley.

Dawson, R. (2007) *Empty lands: Aspects of Scottish Traveller survival*. Derbyshire: Dawson Publishing.

Derrington, C. (2007) Fight, flight and playing white: An examination of coping strategies adopted by Gypsy Traveller Adolescents in English secondary schools. *International Journal of Educational Research*, 46(6), pp. 357–367.

Derrington, C., and Kendall, S. (2003) The experiences and perceptions of Gypsy Traveller pupils in English secondary schools. In: *Encouraging Voices*. Dublin: National Disability Authority.

Derrington, C., and Kendall, S. (2004) *Gypsy Traveller students in secondary schools: Culture, identity and achievement*. Stoke-on-Trent: Trentham Books.

Derrington, C., and Kendall, S. (2007) Still in school at 16? Conclusions from a longitudinal study of Gypsy Traveller students in English secondary schools. In: Bhatti, G., Gaine, C., Gobbo, F., and Leeman, Y. (eds.) *Social justice and intercultural education: An open ended dialogue*. Stoke-on-Trent: Trentham Books, pp. 17–31.

Derrington, C., and Kendall, S. (2008) Challenges and barriers to secondary education: The experiences of young Gypsy Traveller students in English secondary schools. *Social Policy and Society*, 7(1), pp. 119–128.

Deuchar, R., and Bhopal, K. (2017) *Young people and social control: Problems and prospects from the margins*. Basingstoke: Palgrave Macmillan.

Devine, T. M. (1999) *The Scottish Nation, 1700–2000*. London: Penguin.

Duffy, R., and Tomlinson, A. (2009) *Education on the Hoof*. Paper presented to First Centre for Education for Social Justice Seminar at Bishop Grosseteste University College Lincoln (19 January).

Education Scotland. (2015) *About inclusion and equalities*. Available at: http://www.educationscotland.gov.uk/inclusionandequalities/about/index.asp. Accessed 25 February 2016.

Education (Additional Support for Learning) (Scotland) Act. (2004) Available at: http://www.legislation.gov.uk/asp/2004/4/contents. Accessed 20 July 2013.

Equality Act. (2010) http://www.legislation.gov.uk/ukpga/2010/15/contents.

Equal Opportunities Committee. (2001) *Inquiry into Gypsy Travellers and public sector policies.* Available at: bemis.org.uk/docs/gypsy_travellers_in_contemporary_scotland.pdf. Accessed 6 March 2013.

European Commission. (2015) *Report on the implementation of the EU Framework for National Roma Integration Strategies: Communication from the Commission to the European Parliament, The Council, The European Economic and Social Committee and the Committee of the Regions.* Available at: https://eurlex.europa.eu/legal-content/EN/TXT/PDF/?uri=CELEX:52015DC0299&qid=1546026375643&from=EN.

Freedom of Information (Scotland) Act. (2002) Edinburgh: Scottish Parliament.

Gallie, W. B. (1956) Art as an essentially contested concept. *The Philosophical Quarterly (1950–),* 6(23), pp. 97–114.

Humes, W. M., and Bryce, T. G. K. (2003) The distinctiveness of Scottish education. In: *Scottish Education: Second edition post-devolution.* Edinburgh: Edinburgh University Press, pp. 108–118.

hooks, B. (1994) Teaching to Transgress: Education as the Practice of Freedom. *Journal of Engineering Education,* 1, pp. 126–138.

hooks, B. (2003) *Teaching community: A pedagogy of hope* (Vol. 36). London: Psychology Press.

Jordan, E. (1998a) *Travellers and Scottish schools* (Vol. 1 and 2). Unpublished PhD thesis, Edinburgh: Heriot Watt University.

Jordan, E. (1998b) The Interrupted Learner; the Traveller paradigm, paper for Association of Teachers of Travelling People, Dublin.

Jordan, E. (1999) Travelling towards inclusion. In *EFECOT Newsline,* 23.

Jordan, E. (2000a) *Traveller pupils and Scottish schools.* Scottish Council for Research in Education.

Jordan, E. (2000b) Outside the mainstream: Social exclusion in mobile families from home-school partnerships. *Scottish School Board Association, Dumfries: Millennium Books.*

Jordan, E. (2000c) The exclusionary comprehensive school system; the experience of showground families in Scotland. In: Danaher, P. A. (ed.) Mapping international diversity in researching Traveller and nomadic education, *International Journal of Educational Research,* 33 (3), pp. 253–263.

Jordan, E. (2000d) The inclusive school; effective education for secondary age Travellers. In: Hornberg, S. (ed.) *Die Schulsituation von Sinti und Roma in Europa.* Frankfurt am Main: Iko Verlag.

Jordan, E. (2001a) Interrupted learning: The Traveller paradigm. *Support for learning*, 16 (3), pp. 128–134.

Jordan, E. (2001b) Exclusion of Travellers in state schools. *Educational Research*, 43 (2), pp. 117–132.

Jordan, E. (2001c) From interdependence, to dependence and independence home and school learning for traveller children. *Childhood*, 8 (1), pp. 57–74.

Jordan, E., and Holmes, P. (1997) The interrupted learner; whose responsibility? In: Bastiani, J. (ed.) *Home-School work in multicultural settings*. London: David Fulton, pp. 89–94.

Jordon, E., and Padfield, P. (2002) *Interrupted learning: Laptops and their communicative possibilities*. Edinburgh: Scottish Traveller Education Programme.

Jordan, E., and Padfield, P. (2003a) *"Are these really for us?" Laptops for teachers of pupils educated in outwith school settings*. Edinburgh: School of Education, University of Edinburgh.

Jordan, E., and Padfield, P. (2003b) Education at the margins; outsiders and the mainstream. In: Bryce, T. G. K., and Humes, W. M. (eds.) *Scottish education: Second edition post devolution*. Edinburgh: Edinburgh University Press, pp. 836–841.

Jordan, E., and Padfield, P. (2004) *Issues in school enrolment, attendance, attainment and support for learning for Gypsy/Travellers and school-aged children and young people based in Scottish local authority sites*. Edinburgh: Moray House School of Education, The University of Edinburgh.

Knowles, G., and Lander, V. (2011) *Diversity, equality and achievement in education*. London: Sage.

Ladson-Billings, G. (1992) Reading between the lines and beyond the pages: A culturally relevant approach to literacy teaching. *Theory into Practice*, 31(4), pp. 312–320.

Lloyd, G. (2005) *'Problem girls': Understanding and supporting troubled and troublesome girls and young women*. London: Psychology Press.

Lloyd, G., and McCluskey, G. (2008) Education and Gypsy/Travellers: 'contradictions and significant silences'. *International Journal of Inclusive Education*, 12 (4), pp. 331–345.

Lloyd, G., and Norris, C. (1998) From difference to deviance: The exclusion of Gypsy-Traveller children from school in Scotland. *International Journal of Inclusive Education*, 2(4), pp. 359–369.

Lloyd, G., and Stead, J. (2001) 'The boys and girls not calling me names and the teachers to believe me'. Name calling and the experiences of travellers in school. *Children and Society*, 15(5), pp. 361–374.

Lloyd, G., and Stead, J. (2002) Including Gypsy Travellers in education. *Race Equality Teaching*, 21(1), pp. 21–24.

Lloyd G., Stead, J., Jordan, E., and Norris, C. (1999) Teachers and Gypsy Travellers. *Scottish Educational Review*, 31(1), pp. 48–65.

Lloyd, G., Stead, J., Jordan, E., and Norris, C. (2010) Teachers and Gypsy Travellers. In: Rix, J., Nind, M., Sheehy, K., Simmons, K., Parry, J., and Kumrai, R. (eds.) *Equality, participation and inclusion 2: Diverse contexts*. London: Routledge, pp. 162–181.

McCluskey, G., and Watson, T. (2012) Gypsies, Roma, travellers: Teachers making a difference. In: Arshad, R., Pratt, L., and Wrigley, T. (eds.) *Social justice re-examined: Dilemmas and solutions for the classroom teacher*. Stoke-on-Trent: Trentham Books, pp. 179–192.

McCluskey, G., Kane, J., Lloyd, G., Stead, J., Riddell, S., and Weedon, E. (2011) Teachers are afraid we are stealing their strength: A risk society and restorative approaches in school. *British Journal of Educational Studies*, 59(2), pp. 105–119.

McKinney, R. (2001) *Different lessons: Scottish Gypsy/Travellers and the future of education*. Scottish Travellers Consortium.

McKinney, R. (2003) Views from the margins: Gypsy/Travellers and the ethnicity debate in the new Scotland. *Scottish Affairs*, 42(Winter), pp. 13–31.

Myers, M. (2018) Gypsy students in the UK: The impact of 'mobility' on education. *Race Ethnicity and Education*, 21(3), pp. 353–369.

Myers, M., and Bhopal, K. (2009) Gypsy, Roma and Traveller children in schools: Understandings of community and safety. *British Journal of Educational Studies*, 57(4), pp. 417–434.

Myers, M., and Bhopal, K. (2018) *Home schooling and home education: Race, class and inequality*. London: Routledge.

Myers, M., McGhee, D., and Bhopal, K. (2010) At the crossroads: Gypsy and Traveller parents' perceptions of education, protection and social change. *Race Ethnicity and Education*, 13(4), pp. 533–548.

Nisbet, I. (2014a, 21 May) Personal communication. Head of Education Law, Govan Law Centre, Lecture, TENET Seminar.

Nisbet, I. (2014b, 2 September) Personal communication. Head of Education Law, Govan Law Centre, Recorded Interview.

O'Hanlon, C., and Holmes, P. (2004) *The education of Gypsy and Traveller children: Towards inclusion and educational achievement.* Stoke on Trent: Trentham Books.

Oswald, C. (2014, 9 November) Personal communication. Head of policy (Scotland) Equality and Human Rights Commission, Email interview.

Ozga, J. (2000) *Policy research in educational settings.* Buckingham: Open University Press.

Padfield, P. (2005) Inclusive educational approaches for Gypsy/Traveller pupils and their families: An urgent need for progress? *Scottish Educational Review,* 37(2), pp. 127–144.

Padfield, P. (2006a) *Learning at a distance supported by ICT for Gypsies and Travellers: Young peoples' views.* Edinburgh: University of Edinburgh.

Padfield, P. (2006b) *Impact of the national guidance: Inclusive educational approaches for Gypsies and Travellers, within the context of interrupted learning, schools and practice.* Project 7 Final Report. Edinburgh Moray House School of Education. Edinburgh: The University of Edinburgh.

Padfield, P. (2008) Education at the margins: Learners outside mainstream schooling. In: Bryce, T. G. K., and Humes, W. M. (eds.) *Scottish education: Beyond devolution,* 3rd ed. Edinburgh: Edinburgh University Press, pp. 777–782.

Padfield, P., and Cameron, G. (2009) Inclusive education for children and young people with interrupted learning in Scotland. In: Danaher, P. A., and Kenny, M. (eds.) *Traveller, nomadic and migrant education.* London: Routledge, pp. 24–29.

Pring, R. (2004) *Philosophy of educational research.* 2nd ed. London: Continuum.

Rayner-Canham, M. F., and Rayner-Canham, G. (2008) *Chemistry was their life: Pioneering British Women chemists, 1880–1949.* London: Imperial College Press.

Richardson, J. (2006) *The Gypsy debate: Can discourse control?* Exeter: Imprint Academic.

Save the Children Scotland. (2005) *Having our say.* Available at: http://www.gypsy-Traveller.org/your-family/young-people/educational-reports-and-resources. Accessed November 2012.

Scottish Executive. (2007) Advisory Committee on Scotland's Travelling People's. Appendix C Advisory Committee Recommendations 1971–1999. Publication date November 21, 2000. Available at: https://www2.gov.scot/Publications/2007/05/22093426/16. Accessed 24 February 2013.

Scottish Office. (1982) *The third term report 1979–1981.* Edinburgh: The Scottish Office/HMSO.

Scottish Office. (1992) *The sixth term report 1989–1991*. Edinburgh: The Scottish Office/HMSO.

Scottish Office. (1995) *The seventh term report 1992–1994*. Edinburgh: The Scottish Office/HMSO.

Scottish Office. (1998) *The eighth term report 1995–1997*. Edinburgh: The Scottish Office/HMSO.

Scottish Office. (1998) *Travelling people in Scotland: Report on seasonal count, July 1998*. Edinburgh: The Scottish Office/HMSO.

Scottish Office. (2000) *The ninth term report 1995–1997*. Edinburgh: The Scottish Office/HMSO.

STEP. (2013) Scottish Traveller Education Programme, The University of Edinburgh. Available at: http://www.step.education.ed.ac.uk/travelling-communities-in-scotland/. Accessed September 2012 to November 2014.

STEP. (2015) Scottish Traveller Education Programme, The University of Edinburgh. Available at: http://www.step.education.ed.ac.uk/travelling-communities-in-scotland/. Accessed September 2012 to November 2016.

The Scottish Executive. (2001) *Race equality advisory forum final report, making it real, a race equality strategy for Scotland*, October 2001. Available at: www.gov.scot/Publications/2004/06/19566/39689. Accessed 24 February 2013.

The Scottish Executive. (2004) *A curriculum for excellence*. Edinburgh: The Scottish Executive/HMSO.

The Scottish Executive. (2005) *Delivering for Scotland's Gypsy/Travellers: An updated response to the equal opportunities committee inquiry into Gypsy Travellers and public services 2001*. Available at: www.gov.scot/Publications/2004/06/19513/39159. Accessed 25 February 2013.

The Scottish Executive. (2006) *Report of the Gypsies and Travellers strategic group*. Available at: http://www.gov.scot/Topics/People/Equality/gypsiestravellers/strategy. Accessed 24 February 2013.

Tomlinson, S. (2008) *Race and education: Policy and politics in Britain*. Berkshire: Open University Press.

Tyler, C. (2005) *Traveller education: Accounts of good practice*. Stoke-on-Trent: Trentham Books.

Wilkinson, R., and Pickett, K. (2010) *The spirit level. Why equality is better for everyone*. London: Penguin.

Winch, C., and Gingell, J. (2008) *Philosophy of education: The key concepts*. London: Routledge.

4

Gypsies, Travellers and Intersectionality

As demonstrated in the last chapter, researchers have yet to fully explore the educational experiences of Gypsy and Traveller girls in Scotland and to ask why many girls do not formally attend school after the age of 12. Conversations with teachers, charity workers, liaison officers and other stakeholders who work in the field, offer a range of explanations and reasons that aid understanding of the data. However, the voices and experiences of the girls are missing, silent and unheard in these dominant explanations, and it is an intention of this study to redress this imbalance in order that we may respect and understand more clearly the issues that affect their education.

This chapter reflects the researcher's experiences in grappling with an intricate melange of power, myths and history, identity, assumptions, prejudices, and policies in exploring truths and gaining insights into societies that at one level wish to remain unseen. The research process had a nested narrative of its own that reveals the complexities and sensitivities involved in working with communities that have been marginalised for centuries and to whom the researcher does not herself belong. The chapter draws attention to some aspects of the research design and methodology and the complications faced, some of which

G. Marcus, *Gypsy and Traveller Girls*, Studies in Childhood and Youth,
https://doi.org/10.1007/978-3-030-03703-1_4

are of course not unique to certain types of social research. I highlight challenges around gaining access to research participants and the ethical considerations surrounding research with children from minority ethnic backgrounds.

I begin with an explanation of and justification for the use of a black feminist intersectional framework in which to situate and analyse the narratives of the Gypsy and Traveller girls I met. At a presentation I gave on black feminist thought to an audience composed largely of black feminists, I was asked how intersectionality is connected to 'these white girls' and why I chose to use this framework that some rightly felt belonged to them.

The term 'intersectionality', which will be defined below, and its use has now been co-opted into the everyday language of policy and research in such a way that erases its origins in African American women's struggles for emancipation, and worse still, excludes racial oppression as a key element. In this chapter, I argue for its proper application and its power as an alternative multidimensional approach to uncover social truths, using the voices and experiences of black feminists. In keeping with this feminist stance, I consciously steer clear of the great white male sociologists and philosophers like Durkheim, Weber, Bourdieu.

What Is Intersectionality?

The term intersectionality is now banded about freely and loosely, watered down and stripped of its history. Intersectionality centres the experiences of women of colour, and Black women in particular, in feminist theory and emancipatory practice. Intersectionality challenges mainstream feminism by displacing essentialised notions of women and the universalisation of white middle-class women's experiences. At times viewed today as 'the brainchild of feminism and gender studies', intersectionality is also a political challenge to white supremacy in feminist politics and feminist social science (Mirza 2013: 405; Bilge 2014).

The concept is not a new one as it first took root as a response to the experiences of Black women in the United States, their pernicious subjugation and subsequent struggles for freedom and recognition (Crenshaw 1991; Collins 2000; Yuval-Davis 2011; Bassel and Emejulu 2014; Bilge 2014). In 1851, Sojourner Truth, an African American abolitionist, women's rights campaigner and suffragette, disrupted the tenacious idea that only white women are 'women' in her famous speech *Ain't I a Woman?* (Truth 1851). At the Ohio Women's Rights Convention, she asserted that a Black woman, when viewed as a slave or as property, is devalued, dehumanised and oppressed by racism, but also sexism. Truth argued that there are different ways of being a woman, but male and female white supremacy erases different manifestations of what it is to be a woman:

> That man over there says that women need to be helped into carriages, and lifted over ditches, and to have the best place everywhere. Nobody ever helps me into carriages, or over mud-puddles, or gives me any best place! And ain't I a woman? Look at me! Look at my arm! I have ploughed and planted, and gathered into barns, and no man could head me! And ain't I a woman? I could work as much and eat as much as a man – when I could get it – and bear the lash as well! And ain't I a woman? I have borne thirteen children, and seen most all sold off to slavery, and when I cried out with my mother's grief, none but Jesus heard me! And ain't I a woman?… If the first woman God ever made was strong enough to turn the world upside down all alone, these women together ought to be able to turn it back, and get it right side up again! And now they is asking to do it. The men better let them. (Truth 1851)

Racism and sexism marginalise and exclude Black women, but so do white feminist struggles. Truth's speech reflected the view that 'women' are the same in some ways, yet different. In 1989, Crenshaw (1989, 1991), an African American critical legal studies theorist, brought this argument to the fore. In her article *Mapping the Margins: Intersectionality, Identity Politics, and Violence Against Women of Color*, Crenshaw formally introduced the term 'intersectionality' to address the fact that the experiences and ongoing struggles of African American women were not being critically considered in feminist and anti-racist discourse. She contended that both race and gender be interrogated to observe how these two categories interact to shape the lives of women who are not white:

> Feminist efforts to politicize experiences of women and antiracist efforts to politicize experiences of people of color have frequently proceeded as though the issues and experiences they each detail occur on mutually exclusive terrains. Although racism and sexism readily intersect in the lives of real people, they seldom do in feminist and antiracist practices. (Crenshaw 1991: 1242)

Using an Intersectional Framework

There has long been interest, both politically and theoretically, in exploring the complex relations between identity, hierarchical power and subordination (Freire 1970, 1985; hooks 1981; Spivak 1988; Butler 1990, 2004; Foucault 1997). Intersectional approaches to social locations have stressed the interdependence between different kinds of divisions, as well as the tensions and contradictions within and across these social categories. The traditional unidimensional approaches to investigating experiences of discrimination, particularly within marginalised communities, are at times inadequate. Discrimination is 'not additional or multiplicative, but expresses a specific interplay between different 'axes' that cannot be reduced to the sum of its parts' (Farris and de Jong 2014: 1507). Race, class, gender, age, nation, sexuality, ethnicity form different axes.

In this book, discrimination is defined as acts of exclusion, subordination and oppression. These terms are not synonymous. Exclusion involves barring or restricting someone from belonging or taking part. Subordination implies that a person is placed or viewed as being in a lower rank, made subservient and suggests a loss of equal status. Oppression, on the other hand, suggests that there is not only an element of injustice but harsh or cruel domination. Within the context of African American women in the United States, Collins (2000: 4) contends that oppression 'describes any unjust situation where, systematically and over a long period of time, one group denies another group access to resources of society'. African American women have been and continue to be systematically oppressed economically, politically and ideologically (Collins 2000: 4). hooks (2015: 5) explains that 'being oppressed means the absence of choices'.

Exploring the intricacies of such issues through a single lens—such as race, gender or class—is likely to produce simplistic and skewed findings. Intersectionality is not just good research practice or a necessary heuristic device for understanding issues of power and inequality, but is increasingly viewed as a research paradigm in its own right. Drawing on the work of key proponents of this methodological approach (Crenshaw 1991; Collins 2000; Brah and Phoenix 2004; Yuval-Davis 2006; Davis 2008; Mirza et al. 2010; Bilge and Scheibelhofer 2012; Anthias 2013), I propose that an intersectional framework is ideally suited to critically exploring the educational experiences of Scottish Gypsy and Traveller girls.

Differences in Interpretation

Intersectionality is a contested concept and is defined and interpreted in different ways. Collins (1993, 1994, 1998, 2000, 2001) who writes extensively on the idea refers to intersectionality as a 'matrix of domination' (2000: 276) reflecting various spheres of power—structural, disciplinary, hegemonic, and interpersonal. These four spheres are systems of power that produce 'sites of oppression' within gender, race, class, and other inequalities, but crucially they 'mutually construct one another' (Collins 2000: 203). Writing in relation to the lives of Black women, Collins explains that the four dimensions of power cannot be interrogated in isolation, but interweave to affect the social, political and economic lives of Black women. The combined interactive power of the four spheres—in social institutions like schools (structural), by the State and its bureaucratic institutions like prisons (disciplinary), within ideology and culture in families and communities (hegemony), and at the 'level of everyday social interaction'—diminishes the potential of Black women to succeed and flourish in their own right (Collins 2000: 277).

The recognition and interrogation of these intersections are at the heart of intersectional research according to Collins.

Naples (2009: 570) asserts that these spheres of domination are not necessarily static and rigid systems of oppression. Prins (2006: 6), like Collins (2000: 131), argues that individuals have agency; their identities, experiences and worldview also play a role. The four spheres of domination interact with individual and group agency to construct systems of power and oppression. Naples (2009: 570) refers to this approach as interactional. For example, a Gypsy or Traveller woman's oppression may be related to and dependent upon the subordination of a Gypsy or Traveller man. Their subordination may in turn be related to and dependent upon domination by the family, cultural expectations within the group and by other forms of structural oppression. A Gypsy and Traveller girl's social location as a woman may not be the prime factor affecting her educational experience, but it is an important one to consider. A relational or interactional approach is a more nuanced one to intersectionality and is one that is considered in this study. In this sense, I agree with Cho's et al. (2013: 795) definition of intersectionality as an 'analytic sensibility'—sensitizing us to the multiplicity and complexity of inequality.

Carbado et al. (2013) maintain that intersectionality is today viewed as 'a method and a disposition, a heuristic and analytic tool'. It has represented Black women's struggles, and continues to do so, but has 'moved' beyond to involve other local, national and international efforts for change. 'Actors of different genders, ethnicities, and sexual orientation have moved intersectionality to engage an ever-widening range of experiences and structures of power' (Carbado et al. 2013: 305). However, Bilge (2010, 2013, 2014), Bilge and Scheibelhofer (2012), Mirza (2008, 2009, 2013), and Mirza and Gunaratnam (2014) contend that intersectionality, especially within academic disciplines, has become entwined with neoliberal, postracial politics. They warn against the dangers of not acknowledging the origins of intersectionality in the North American Black women's struggles for emancipation, and the erasure of race from our understandings of injustice 'through denial, reductionism and disassociation' (Bilge 2014: 2). Intersectionality has been 'undone' and Bilge (2013) argues, needs to be 'saved' and 're-politicised'. Mirza (2015: 3) points to the 'normative absence and the pathological presence of [groups] of racialised women collectively assigned as "other"'. As was similarly argued previously by Collins (2000), Mirza advances the idea that intersectionality's function is to continue to critically disrupt and problematise

> the dispersed flows of domination and subordination in which cultural patterns of oppression and privilege are not only interrelated, but bound together and influenced by the cross-cutting systems and structures in society. (Mirza 2015: 3)

Crenshaw (1989) refers to her understanding of intersectionality as 'one way' of approaching it and only 'provisional', envisaging its 'indefinability' as a theoretical fixture and the challenges of containing its use within a single discipline of academia or for a single purpose. Carbado et al. (2013: 304) explain the different ways in which intersectionality has been defined and put to use—across disciplines, national borders, to engage women of colour, women in the Global South, even examining Black men's experiences and advocating the need of gender equity between Black women and Black men. They conclude that 'the theory is never done' and that 'there is potentially always another set of concerns to which the theory can be directed, other places to which the theory might be moved, and other structures of power it can be deployed to examine' (Carbado et al. 2013: 304). They suggest that it does not make sense to try to 'frame' it, and 'anthropomorphize the concept as its own agent replete with specific interests and tasks that reflect its capacity and fundamental orientation' (2013: 304). Carbado et al. (2013: 304) propose that an alternative approach to defining intersectionality is to assess what it does, and 'what else the framework might be mobilized to do'. This I believe is what makes this framework so powerful and relevant.

Intersectionality allows us to see women in their particular context, without minimizing the effects of differences between different forms of subjugations or concealing one form in another. Rather, each form of oppression informs the other. Mirza (2015: 4) also concedes that 'it is only by attention to situated localised accounts of "marginalised lives" that we can reveal the ways of "being and becoming" a gendered, sexed, raced and classed subject of materialist discourse…[it] valorises situated experience which is at the heart of black feminist epistemology'.

Intersectionality and Gypsy and Traveller Girls

Convinced by the works of Carbado et al., Crenshaw and Mirza, my study asserts and demonstrates that it is possible for intersectionality as a theoretical framework to acknowledge the origins of the concept in Black women's emancipatory struggles, and still 'mobilize' to critically examine the experiences of different kinds of marginalised women. In my case, I was seeking to apply an intersectional framework to a group of racialised and marginalised 'white' women— Gypsy and Traveller girls in Scotland. Intersectionality's construction as both a theoretical framework and a strategy for emancipatory struggles is what I find appealing as a researcher.

Given my earlier discussion on definitions of intersectionality and what it does, Davis' (2008) definition embraces the interactions between political structures, communities and individual agency, in affecting inequality and injustice through the connections between one or more axes of injustice. I have chosen to define intersectionality as the 'interaction between gender, race, and other categories of difference in individual lives, social practices, institutional arrangements, and cultural ideologies and the outcomes of these interactions in terms of power' (Davis 2008: 68). Intersectionality is about recognizing the different social, economic and political consequences for specific groups of people who are oppressed in multiple ways because of their race, ethnicity, gender, class, sexuality, disability, and age. However, race is a crucial aspect, and cannot be denied or ignored.

This book highlights how the fusion of ethnicity, race, gender, and class has served to undermine Gypsy and Traveller communities over the centuries. The curious racialization of Gypsy and Traveller communities, subject to what Crenshaw (1991: 1261) calls 'patterns of othering' in the media and in popular consciousness as a minority white population in Scotland, was also explored. The research problematizes what it means to be 'white', and to be a 'white woman' living within 'simultaneously interlocking oppressions', that collectively serve to marginalise and silence lives (Combahee River Collective 1977; hooks 1981; Brah and Phoenix 2004).

Crucially, one of the strengths of intersectionality is that it recognises 'within-group diversity ... and the limitations of groups within categories to self-identify in a personally relevant or empowering way' (Hancock 2007: 75). Just as there are tensions between dominant and subordinated groups, there are also tensions within these groups that need to be explored. Gypsy and Traveller girls may be considered 'white' and Scottish, because their physical characteristics do not mark them as being visibly different; but within the population of Gypsy and Traveller girls there are multiple differences, the most potent being whether a Gypsy and Traveller girl leads a completely nomadic or semi-nomadic lifestyle, whether she lives in a trailer on a council run Traveller site, a privately owned site, in a house or flat.

Furthermore, it is not just women of colour who experience oppression by powerful systems that promote inequalities. Being 'white' should be problematised. There are hierarchies of whiteness, and some 'white people' are excluded and oppressed by the very system and dominant practices of whiteness in Scotland that protect the interests of privileged white groups. Being part of or being excluded from being 'white' is a complex historical social construct.

The category 'white' is a relatively new concept and a category constructed within the history of Europe, America's colonies, and the United States. According to Dyer (1997), whiteness is not a race, but a socially constructed invisible physical, mental and emotional image of what being human looks like. All other peoples are measured against this norm. Whiteness consists of a body of knowledge, ideologies, norms, and particular practices, which affect how white people, think about race and racial identities, how they operate and relate to others in the world, and what they believe to be their place in it. Whiteness is shaped and maintained by the power of long established social institutions that encompass a 'matrix of domination' (Collins 2000: 276). Individuals and groups who are white, also play their part, consciously or dysconsciously, to preserve, cultivate and habituate these institutions. However, white people are not a homogeneous group.

Whiteness is a dynamic process of social and cultural influences, and the mélange of people who are accepted as white, or who occupy the upper echelons of the hierarchies of whiteness, are not fixed in time and place. In reality, a small minority of the white elite control most of the group's power and resources. Representations of whiteness are constructed, insidious and problematic for some white people and people of colour. Johal (2005: 273) argues that white people 'hold a pigmentary passport of privilege that allows sanctity within the racial polity of whiteness'. Whilst 'people of colour across all differences' do not hold this passport, the picture is more nuanced. Not all white people are entirely privileged.

The persecution of Gypsies and Travellers in Scotland and in the UK is well documented. For centuries they have been socially constructed as degenerates. They are deeply embedded in the lowest ranks within the hierarchy of whiteness. However, Clark (2006: 7–8) points out that there is an 'ethnicity conundrum' because 'the majority (settled) society tends to regard Scottish Gypsies and Travellers as not constituting an ethnic group (but they are white?)' whilst others (academics and policymakers) do. Perceived as being part of 'the dangerous classes' (Morris 1994: 16) by the white majority, whilst also being ascribed the socio-legal status of separate ethnicity in 2008, Gypsies and Travellers are entangled in a convoluted web of race, ethnicity and class made more complicated by their own processes of community and individual self-identification. Gypsies and Travellers are white but also racialised as problematic Other.

The use of an intersectional framework exposed and challenged discriminations within the educational experiences of Gypsy and Traveller girls—racisms, sexisms, class oppression and ageism. Not unlike critical race theory, it has the potential to challenge and displace the dominant ideologies and principles within our education system in Scotland such as, 'objectivity, neutrality, meritocracy, gender and colour blindness, race and gender neutrality and equal opportunity' (Solorzano 1998: 122). Intersectionality demonstrates that the particular context of the educational and lived experiences of Gypsy and Traveller girls (and boys) is authentic, varied, variable, and worthy of genuine understanding.

It was ideally suited to critically explore the heterogeneous educational experiences of the Gypsy and Traveller girls I interviewed. Prima facie, various surveys and reports show that racism and racist bullying is a major problem experienced by Gypsy and Traveller pupils (Save The Children Scotland 2005; Amnesty International 2012a, b). However, it would have been too simplistic to assume that racism is all that they encounter, and that racism is the main cause for non-attendance and low attainment, especially at secondary level. It was important to explore whether there are other systems of exclusion, subordination and oppression that interact together to affect their lives and experiences.

Within an intersectional paradigm, there are fewer possibilities for both participant and intersectional 'invisibility', revealing the heterogeneity of identities, representations and experiences; and exposing the entangled relations between privilege and marginalisation across multiple levels. Matsuda (1991, cited in Crenshaw 1991: 1245) calls this inquiry 'asking the other question'. Where gender biases exist the researcher asks, 'Where is the race bias in this?' and where there is a race bias, one asks 'Where is the gender bias or patriarchy in this?' The researcher is always looking for other forms of discrimination that accompany the one obvious bias. This study aimed to explore if in some ways the experiences of Gypsy and Traveller girls may be similar to more privileged white girls and women, or British Muslim girls, and if in other ways, they may experience discrimination like Gypsy and Traveller boys and other men of colour do. The point is that no one group's experiences of privilege and oppression are entirely separate, exclusive and confined within that group (Crenshaw 1991: 1242), but it is nevertheless important not to fuse one group's experiences with another, and seeing them as one and the same. Homogenising experiences of subordination betrays the plight within individual and group shared narratives. Collins (2000: 287) warns that 'oppression is filled with contradictions because a matrix of domination contains few pure victims or oppressors'. She asserts that 'every individual derives varying amounts of penalty and privilege from the multiple systems of oppression which frame everyone's lives' (Collins 2000: 287). No one group has a monopoly over a type of oppression that is exclusive only to them.

Challenges of Intersectionality

There are several challenges associated with intersectionality, both as a research paradigm and tool for analysis (Davis 2008: 1). In their research comparing the effectiveness of uni-dimensional and intersectional approaches in studying marketing and media imagery, Gopaldas and DeRoy (2015) suggest that an intersectional approach to analysis is more complex, time-consuming, and the findings are challenging to summarise. They also suggest that larger datasets may be needed to account for all intersections' (Gopaldas and DeRoy 2015: 356). However, it is precisely this complexity in the educational experiences of Gypsy and Traveller girls and the heterogeneity of their narratives that, as a researcher operationalising intersectionality, I am interested in exposing and understanding.

Naples (2009: 567) warns that it is 'not enough to assert that one's study is intersectional … a researcher must specify and reflect on which aspects of intersectionality are brought into the frame and which ones are left out or treated less centrally in the analysis'. There could potentially be a long list of social divisions, but it is equally vital not to be reductive or to generalise too loosely (Butler 1990; Knapp 1999), as deconstruction and the individualization of difference could make it difficult for political mobilization to take place (Anthias 2013: 4).

Whilst I hope that my research will be transformative by making a significant contribution to the debate on the experiences of Gypsies and Travellers, I cannot claim that the research participants, the Gypsy and Traveller girls, had this aim in mind. This work was not a piece of participatory action research with young Gypsy and Traveller women. I was not aware and have not been made aware of community activism, or a concerted force of opposition, run solely by Gypsy and Traveller women in Scotland. This research aims to be transformative, but only in a limited sense, in that it is 'not [as yet] part of a social movement' (Carbado et al. 2013: 305).

Anthias (2013) presents a useful summary of the limitations of an intersectional framework. Particularly significant, in my view, is 'the impossibility of attending analytically to the plurality of categories [and] individual differences' (Anthias 2013: 4). Deciding what to leave in and what to leave out requires careful consideration. Another important point she raises is that the idea of intersectionality 'suggests that what takes place is similar to what happens at an intersection (where things collide or crash together) […but it] might not be a product of the intersection at all but may [only] be manifested in that space' (Anthias 2013: 11). The researcher needs to be careful not to be misled. Not all points of intersection produce problems of subordination and oppression. Anthias (2013: 13) also advances a valid question about the challenges in dealing with the inequality of women within their own communities and within their own families, i.e., outside what is usually thought of as the public domain. Entering into the private world of family and close-knit community relations raises issues about just how much public bodies can do to predict and prevent combinations of intersecting inequalities.

An intersectional paradigm allowed for a critical appreciation of the connections between the Gypsy and Traveller girls' lived educational experiences, current policy, legislation and practice. The research relied on an interactional and relational approach to intersectionality. It aimed to be transformational, but in a limited sense. Gender, class and age are considered principal categories or axes of inequality and injustice, although class did not feature overtly in the girls' narratives. Race and ethnicity, and the processes of racialisation that Gypsy and Traveller communities have been subjected to, are not denied but are critically explored in problematising the social, cultural and historical construction of 'whiteness'.

However, as I was to discover, issues of trust, broken over centuries of persecution, were a central underlying theme, which made it a challenge to meet and talk with Gypsies and Travellers.

Gaining Access

I could not have gained access without the trust and support of the few gatekeepers who paved the way. It took over a year to locate a Gypsy and Traveller girl willing to be interviewed, and then considerable networking to have finally conducted interviews with 13 Gypsy and Traveller girls. It would have been useful to meet the participants more frequently for greater collaboration, to have met all their families, but circumstances were prohibitive. Only one Local Authority granted permission to interview pupils. It took nearly three years of networking and negotiation to gain the trust of the girls from Article 12 and arrange a date for the focus group to take place. They eventually agreed to a focus group discussion. It took six months and Freedom of Information requests to get relevant documents from all 32 Local Authorities.

The gatekeepers who were willing to support the research facilitated each meeting and made introductions. They were present in the meeting 'space' when the research and consent form were explained, but were not present at any of the interviews. They provided a safe conduit for both the girls and me. They also helped to check the girls understood what was said and that they were comfortable to carry on. This verbal introduction and explanation was recorded as part of the ethics process, which I will discuss further below. The audio-recorder was then turned off before the interview, and I asked them again if they were ready and happy for me to record their voices as we 'chatted'.

Gaining access to participants, however, posed a significant challenge to the research in several ways. Within a few months of starting my research, I encountered barriers of silence. Firstly, stakeholders displayed a certain apprehension or unease about speaking with me about their work with Gypsies and Travellers. Within my own institution, politics and old disagreements amongst staff about funding and research led to subtle walls of silence and non-cooperation from certain departments. Even though one organisation in particular had collated documents, researched information and had daily access to relevant networks and Gypsy and Traveller communities, proactive dialogue and support for my research only trickled in my direction, and was almost absent.

Secondly, stakeholders and potential gatekeepers from a range of government organisations and charities whom I approached were predominantly reluctant to give interviews or provide access to Travelling Communities. Stakeholders who agreed to meet were not only reluctant, but also afraid to be identified. Some officials talked about being contractually bound not to 'say anything bad about the council' or were afraid of inadvertently being accused of being a 'whistle-blower', or 'losing funding' (Anon. Teacher 2 2014, Personal communication). One high-ranking official explained she had been warned not to upset the status quo; because of the work her team were doing to counter racist attitudes and practices in the workplace towards Gypsies and Travellers. Her colleague nodded in agreement (Anon. Head of charity 2 2014, Personal communication; Anon. Charity Liaison Officer 2014, Personal communication). Another mentioned that she had to sign an agreement not to 'share' a report she wrote that was perceived as being critical of a major educational project (Anon. Teacher 3 2014, Personal communication). Certain reports could not be made available for public scrutiny. I noted the complex culture of silence—the absence of speech and lack of communication, possibly implying concealment and secrecy. I was perplexed as to why this was the case.

When I shared my research focus with some stakeholders I also faced well-intentioned discouragement. Some responded with the following generalised views. One explanation cited was that the girls will already have left school and be married with children. Another explanation for not granting access was that their families would never allow the girls to speak to a researcher. Also in conversation with one stakeholder, it was suggested my ethnicity would be a problem as I look like a Roma 'and they [Travellers] don't like Romas'. I was warned never to be on my own with a Traveller on a Traveller site (Anon. Academic 2 2013, Personal communication). Another gatekeeper confirmed this view that the colour of my skin might be a problem (Anon. Teacher 1 2014, Personal communication).

One potential gatekeeper was sympathetic to my predicament, but advised I could not possibly succeed in finding answers to the research question because 'the girls are only interested in marriage and having babies, so there is no point as the girls have no ambitions or aspirations… you won't get any data, you are wasting your time' (Anon. Academic 1 2013, Personal communication). This gatekeeper was part of an established network that works directly with Gypsy and Traveller families, and so not only had knowledge and experience, but access.

Many gatekeepers were reluctant to initiate contact or to get involved with the research in any way. However, to compound matters, there were also walls of silence and fear from some of the Gypsies and Travellers I did meet. Gypsies and Travellers who refused to take part in interviews were suspicious and afraid they might get into trouble with the authorities because their children were not in school (Anon. Traveller mother 1 2014, Personal communication). They also admitted they did not see the point of talking, as nothing was going to change for their families and communities (Anon. Traveller mother 1 2014, Personal communication; Anon. Traveller man 2014, Personal communication).

The idea that communication and dialogue would be helpful seemed to be discounted. Gypsies and Travellers in Scotland are unwilling to self-identify out of fear (EHRC 2015), but also as a strategy to retain a measure of control from interference from the State. The inability of twice-yearly counts and various other statistical data, including the most recent national Census, to gather accurate data reflects their passive retaliation, which is problematic for government. The fact remains that even the exact population figure of Scottish Gypsies and Travellers are unknown. Unlike other minorities, Gypsies and Travellers in Scotland are not always easy to identify, because their ethnic difference is often not physically visible to others. Their invisibility is another form of silence. Whilst it is a major obstacle to a researcher keen to understand the experiences of these marginalised peoples, to Gypsies and Travellers it is arguably a tool of resistance and 'community formation' (2003: 49). As one experienced planning official stated, 'they are not called "the people of the mist", for nothing!' (Anon. Planning Advisor 1 2014, Personal communication).

It was especially heart breaking to hear the story of a 70-year-old woman who used silence to remain quiet about her identity for over 50 years. She was ostracised and also excluded herself from her Traveller family, choosing instead to 'pass' as a non-Traveller. She disclosed how she remained hidden and silent out of fear, but also in order to 'learn to read and write', pursue her love of learning, and 'be independent', free from persecution (Anon. Traveller woman 2015, Personal communication). Traveller writer, Jess Smith (67), also talked about being ostracised by her family, because she chose to write about her community, to break the silence. She believes her novels, stories and ballads cost her dearly, but she maintains it is a sacrifice she is willing to make to promote greater understanding (Smith 2014, Personal communication). Silence, fear, conflict, and tension are intertwined in their narratives.

Undeterred and determined to gain a wider perspective, I visited several Traveller sites across Scotland and spoke to various professionals from education, social work and health on the work that they do with Gypsy and Traveller communities. I attended the Gypsy Lore Conference in Glasgow in October 2013 and, through the Scottish Government's recent Roma Mapping exercise (12th August and 4th October 2013), I met and networked with social workers, youth workers, health professionals, and other practitioners in the field. Planning Aid Scotland (PAS) provided useful insight into the accommodation issues affecting Gypsies and Travellers (Planning Aid Scotland 2014, Personal communication). In speaking with various professionals and stakeholders, there was a strong sense of the ethical dilemmas they experience and the complexities they face in understanding culturally remote groups. As previously mentioned, I gathered policies, recommendations or guidelines used by Scotland's 32 local authorities in trying to address the specific needs of pupils from Travelling Communities. Educational attainment data was obtained and gleaned for relevant evidence to support the government's understandings of the current experience of Gypsy and Traveller pupils.

Trepagnier (2006: 72) argues the silence and passivity … of 'well-meaning White people' who consider themselves non-racist and who work with minority ethnic groups, can help to perpetuate racial divisions in society. Many acknowledged the racism towards Gypsies and Travellers, within the rank and file, even amongst their colleagues. It was particularly interesting to listen to the discourse and rhetoric used by these professionals when I spoke with them. Consciously or dysconsciously, in the name of 'diversity', nearly all were keen on assimilation rather than integration—a dualistic them/us, majority/minority rhetoric, rather than a pluralistic approach to living a shared 'good life' in a democracy. The Other was in conflict with the dominant majority culture and posed problems for various institutions and frontline services.

Dialogic approaches to conflict resolution were rarely mentioned in the conversations I had with the stakeholders and professionals I met.

Silence can be a powerful tool of control—used to avoid, muffle, suppress, degrade, and marginalise. Equally, it can be a tool for defence and protection, 'to sever ties with fellow citizens' (Ferguson 2003: 51). Its impact and consequence depends on the motives of the individual, community or organisation putting it to use.

In my view, the opinions and passivity of some of the gatekeepers I met, add to the stereotyped images and paternalistic assumptions that maintain these unequal partitions in society. There is no room for dialogic forms of cooperation and communication as their care is part of the control (Clark 2008: 65). In the long term, these institutional silences and barriers are detrimental to the lives of Gypsy and Traveller girls, as they help to conserve the status quo. The issues surrounding the role of gatekeepers, the power they wield and the knowledge they inadvertently conceal within their ranks could be examined more closely in a future study.

With the help of gatekeepers, who were sometimes present during the start of the interviews, research participants selected the setting and environment for both individual interviews and the focus group discussions. Informal places outwith schools and their local area, easily accessible by public transport, were suggested as comfortable, 'safe' venues in order to ensure anonymity, confidentiality and safety of the participants. I met the girls in cafes, country hotels, their homes, and youth and sports centres. The summer period provided a challenge as some of my contacts were away 'shifting' (travelling). Each interview lasted from 60 to 90 min, but I was frequently invited to chat informally with the participants, their parent or with the gatekeeper present. Each meeting tended to last several hours and afforded much data in the form of field notes.

Interviews and discussions were audio recorded, fully transcribed by a skilled audio typist familiar with Scottish accents and dialects, and then checked for accuracy by me. Each transcript was therefore a verbatim record of the interview and a source of evidence for data audit (Drever 2003: 60).

Ethical Considerations

The study I conducted adhered to rules as set out by the institution at which I did my doctoral research—Moray House School of Education Ethics Committee and British Educational Research Association guidelines (BERA 2011). The core principles of anonymity, confidentiality, safety of participants, informed signed consent, and the freedom to withdraw acted as a crucial guide throughout the 13 interviews I conducted and the focus group discussion with four Gypsy and Traveller girls held subsequently. There was no financial or material gain to be had by this research. Neither was there any conflict of interest as outlined by the University's policies.

Whatever a researcher's view might be about the existence and extent of truth, it is vital that researchers 'take care and they do not lie' (Williams 2002: 11). This is first and foremost the fundamental standard to which my work adhered. Angen (2000: 39) argues it is important that the research is ethically valid from the outset, and the researcher has 'moral integrity'. Validation is much a moral issue as it is one of trustworthiness.

Working with members of the Gypsy and Traveller communities as an outsider has its unique challenges. Weckman (1998), a Finnish Gypsy activist, warns the outsider against the limitations of attempting to represent the experiences of a group or groups. Donna Haraway (1988: 586), a feminist philosopher of science, in her article on situated knowledge also warns against 'essentialising' or 'fetishizing' the experiences of women on the margins ('Third World Women'). She states that 'critically positioning' one's own 'partial connection' or 'partial perspective' as an outsider is 'the key practice in grounding [claims to] knowledge' about others (Haraway 1988: 586–587). I am not a Gypsy or Traveller girl, neither am I professing to perfectly understand and represent her experience.

Gypsies and Travellers in Scotland are varied, inter-related and dynamic groups. They have different languages, customs, traditions, and histories. Prior research into these subtle differences helped me to be sensitive to customs and rituals, especially when visiting their homes.

For example, I brought a gift as appreciation for being invited into their trailer, I offered to remove my footwear, and I dressed conservatively. I greeted male members of the family formally but did not converse with them unless they chose to speak with me. None of them did.

Particular attention was paid to the ethics surrounding working with young people, who could also be potentially vulnerable because of their ethnicity or gender. The Gypsy and Traveller girls I interviewed were aged twelve years and above, and might be deemed 'vulnerable' because of their community's minority status, the rules of behaviour and social engagement within their communities, and the sensitivity of the topics that were exposed for discussion. The Moray House School of Education Ethics Form (2012: 4) implied that research participants with an ethnic 'minority status or their otherwise disempowered position in society constitute a vulnerable group'. Whilst it is essential to take special care when working with young people, as a minority ethnic woman, I question and refute the assumption that participants from ethnic minority communities are necessarily 'vulnerable' and that they should be treated as such from the outset. I also question and refute that being an ethnic minority woman automatically compounds one's vulnerability. This form has since been updated and revised.

Samantha Punch (2002) who has worked extensively with children across majority and minority world contexts suggests working with young people can be unpredictable and is not the same as working with adults. There were several factors that helped me to elicit their accounts in an ethical way. First and foremost, years of practice working with children in schools, together with experience as a headteacher, chairing meetings, enabled me to ensure the girls had fair and equal opportunities to talk. Moreover, I like the company of children and enjoy being with them. Second, I listened sensitively to what they had to tell me. In my experience, children sense when a person is not engaging with them genuinely. I valued their knowledge and the power of their testimonies. I was not there to judge or cast aspersions about why they were not in school, or to criticise their choices, lifestyle, or community. Patronising language was not used. My professional experience was also helpful in managing the focus group, playing the role as guide and moderator. Finally, being aware of and sensitive to their culture and their parents' expectations supported both the type of questions I asked and the way in which I asked them. I decided not to include, for example, topics about puberty, sex or their sexuality.

At a talk I gave recently about this research, I was questioned about why I 'chose to exclude topics on sex and sexuality' by a man in the audience who self-identified as 'gay Roma'. Had the girls brought up issues about their sexuality I would have addressed and included these findings in my work. None of them did. Instead in asking them about their experiences, their powerful accounts of racism, gender and age discrimination were running intersecting themes that they placed on the agenda for me to explore critically. Issues of class were not highlighted by them. In their view, they faced discrimination because of their race and gender, and their age put them at a disadvantage in challenging such experiences, regardless of their class.

The questions I asked were not 'leading', kept sufficiently neutral to give space to the girls to voice their narratives. My role as researcher was to explore, understand and to critically analyse, but not to present an alternative or better view from my supposed privileged perspective. Having been invited into their homes, based on trust, and being aware of their youth and my power to disrupt, I was careful not to de-stabilise their world, upon my leaving. This was my ethical choice for this research. Another study conducted by another researcher with different aims might necessarily have been handled differently.

In other words, 'the key ethical issue is what limits ought to operate on the building of relationships with participants' (Hammersley and Traianou 2012: 116). I worked hard to minimise my role and power as researcher, to gain trust and to ensure they felt at ease, but I also ensured I maintained a respectful distance. I wanted the girls to feel comfortable and relaxed talking with me, and in doing so, the fact that I was a researcher might have become 'submerged in their perceptions' (Hammersley and Traianou 2012: 116). Within the interview 'space', I was not their personal friend, but a momentary one-woman audience listening, with care and compassion, to their account of their educational experiences.

Separate consent forms were devised and approved by the School of Education Ethics Committee—one for young people aged 16 and over and one for parents of young people under 16. I verbally explained the information guide to all participants and their parents. In case a participant could not read, did not wish to sign or give written consent, permission was sought, in advance, from the Ethics Committee to allow audio-recorded verbal consent. I argued that in situations where research participants traditionally mistrust and have a fear of 'authority', accepting an audio-recorded verbal consent could be an acceptable alternative. I have met several Gypsy and Traveller women, some of whom lead successful lives, who cannot read or write. Allowing a person's level of literacy to dictate method of consent, was unfair and unnecessary, when flexible alternatives might be negotiated. Consent was provided in three ways—signed by the participant or parent, signed by the gatekeeper on behalf of the parent or verbal consent was given and digitally recorded.

All participants, regardless of age, were given the choice to be interviewed with their mother present, out of a respectful acknowledgement of the social rules Gypsy and Traveller girls abide by, rules set by their families and communities. All participants were interviewed in safe, neutral environments of their choice. In addition, in accordance with legal guidelines, I applied to be a member of the Protecting Vulnerable Groups Scheme and this was approved before I began fieldwork. Furthermore, it has been argued that it is critical to encourage participants 'to draw their own boundaries of privacy and emphasise participants' prerogative to withdraw materials from the study at any time' (Daly 1992: 10), and this was articulated throughout the interviews.

This research explored issues of discrimination, racism, bullying, and other negative factors that could impact on these young participants. They might be reluctant to voice their concerns if there was a risk of being identified by their families, community and the readers of this book. There was a possibility a participant would face criticism or potential alienation from their community because they have participated in the research. Through the consent form and detailed explanation, all participants were made aware that they have a right to anonymity and confidentiality. Issues of anonymity and confidentiality can conflict with the need to present salient findings, and I was vigilant to balance the thirst for revealing data with the ethics of preserving my integrity and commitment to the girls I interviewed. Various steps were taken to minimise the risk of exposure and these procedures were negotiated carefully with the participants themselves and/or their parents. For example, meeting in a setting that is within easy reach by transport but outwith the local area of residence, gave added protection to each young person. All participants expressed their wish not to be named, but agreed to the use of a pseudonym of my choice. The participants were not told their pseudonym. Stringent steps were taken to ensure their identities would be 'difficult to recognise'; in other words, they will not be 'identifiable' in transcripts and publications related to the research (Hammersley and Traianou 2012: 127). They would not be identified even at the expense of losing valuable data. Assurances of anonymity and confidentiality are necessary, but in reality, not an absolute guarantee against exposure.

Two participants ('Skye' and 'Rona') critically explored the impact and need for anonymity. We talked about the advantages and disadvantages of disclosing their identity. They felt they should be open and honest about who they were because they had nothing to hide. They reported they had both consented in the past to have their identities revealed in other publications. One girl who was over 16 years old consulted the gatekeeper. I spoke with the mother of the girl who was under 16 years. We decided jointly that they should remain anonymous, like the other participants, for their safety. Hammersley and Traianou (2012: 130) reason, 'those who ask to be named will not always recognise the dangers involved. And naming some people may increase the likelihood that others can be identified … exposing them to the danger of various harms'. Had these young participants insisted on being named, which they had every right to assert, this would have raised questions about their safety and who has control over the research data (Grinyer 2009; Hammersley and Traianou 2012). I also explained to the girls that not being named could present greater freedom to speak more openly about issues affecting their lives, without fear of offending their family or community. It would be a less complicated, uniformed approach. They were also advised of their right to withdraw at any time during the course of the study, without penalty or a need to explain their reasons for withdrawal. The issue over who has access to the information they provide was made clear from the outset and regularly highlighted as part of the discussions during interviews.

Participants were also given a choice as to whether they agreed to be photographed or to take part in video-recorded interviews. It was made clear that these images might be used later in an exhibition organised by me. They all declined to be photographed or video recorded. I adhered to their wishes.

I am aware of some of the risks involved in conducting research with young people and/or marginalised minority groups, but it was only through preliminary and ongoing discussion and negotiation with the Gypsy and Traveller girls, their parents and gatekeepers that I gained a clearer understanding of any physical, emotional or social harm that they might encounter. All participants and their parents were informed that I would be unable to keep 'secrets' in circumstances where someone could be in danger. I explained that the consent form clearly states the situations under which confidence cannot be kept, and the procedures I would have to follow to ensure the safety of participants or someone whom they knew. No child protection concern, or abusive situation was raised during fieldwork. Through constant awareness and monitoring of the potential for harm and 'unfair exploitation', I was able to safeguard the wellbeing of the participants throughout the research process. Their safety and wellbeing was paramount, as was mine. Ethical research is about *behaving* ethically and fairly, out of respect for the participants involved 'in the face of uncertainty, risk and moral complexity' (Back 2007: 97).

Griffiths (1998: 97) maintains that, as 'there is no hope of doing perfect research', it is not possible to be perfectly reflexive or ethical. So, by critiquing my own values and the integrity of my position, I have tried to ensure the authenticity of my work and be 'vigilant about [my] practices' (Spivak 1984–1985: 184). The use of my own field diary and interview notes, not only left a research trail to analyse findings subsequently, but also allowed for personal, candid reflections, which were used to inform the mechanics of the research and its outcomes (Punch 2012).

Finally, in a study of communities where discrimination is widely reported and acknowledged, a researcher needs to do more than describe or explore experiences. It is crucial to offer a critique of the hegemonic power of imbalances between dominant and subordinated groups. Luker (2010: 34) argues that as social beings we construct meaning out of our experiences. However, we are 'constrained by (and in some cases facilitated by) the social, and all too often the social is invisible to [us]'. It is the role of the responsible researcher to try 'to see those things that people in everyday life cannot [see]' (Luker 2010: 34).

Whilst I shared certain experiences with them, having different social locations and perspectives also allowed me to see the girls' experiences in a different light when analysing the data. In my role and identity as practitioner researcher, it is important that educators at all levels, from nursery to tertiary, ought to question educational policy and practice, to challenge the uncomfortably controversial, to take sides and 'get off the fence' (Griffiths 1998).

As mentioned earlier, 'the politics and epistemology of partial perspectives' undergirds this study (Haraway 1988: 584). My personal experiences, assumptions and views on racism and gender bias, on education and travel, have impacted on the research process and in my interpretation of the complexities of the multiple realities involved. I was also conscious of my status, power and 'co-optedness' within the education systems that I have been, and continue to be part of. I am partially a product of the system, which some in Gypsy and Traveller communities reject. Mindful of Inken's (2014: 266) advice when critically observing alternative forms of doing and thinking, I acknowledged and used my perspectives and experiences to problematise existing 'understandings of power, inequality and difference … firmly supported by the [decolonising] epistemological foundations of intersectionality'.

References

Amnesty International (2012a) *On the margins*. Available at: http://www.amnesty.org.uk/sites/default/files/amnesty_international_on_the_margins_2012.pdf. Accessed 8 May 2013.

Amnesty International (2012b) *Caught in the headlines*. Available at: http://www.amnesty.org.uk/sites/default/files/amnesty_international_caught_in_the_headlines_2012.pdf. Accessed 8 May 2013.

Angen, M. J. (2000) Evaluating interpretive inquiry: Reviewing the validity debate and opening the dialogue. *Qualitative Health Research*, 10(3), pp. 378–395.

Anon. Academic 1 (2013, April 18) Personal communication. Conversation and notes.

Anon. Academic 2 (2013, April 15, August 12) Personal communication. Discussion, interview and notes.

Anon. Charity Liaison Officer (2014, September 10) Personal communication. Recorded interview.

Anon. Head of charity 2 (2014, September 10) Personal communication. Recorded interview.

Anon. Planning Advisor 1 (2014, October 8) Personal communication. Recorded interview.

Anon. Teacher 1 (2014, April 30) Personal communication. Interview and notes.

Anon. Teacher 2 (2014, May 21) Personal communication. Conversation at TENET seminar, Edinburgh.

Anon. Teacher 3 (2014, June 18 and September 17) Personal communication. Discussion, interview and notes.

Anon. Traveller man (2014, June 10) Personal communication. Conversation and notes.

Anon. Traveller mother 1 (2014, June 10) Personal communication. Conversation and notes.

Anon. Traveller woman (2015, August 15 and October 6) Personal communication. Telephone interview and notes.

Anthias, F. (2013) Intersectional what? Social divisions, intersectionality and levels of analysis. *Ethnicities*, 13(1), pp. 3–19.

Back, L. (2007) *The art of listening*. New York: Berg.

Bassel, L., and Emejulu, A. (2014) Solidarity under austerity: Intersectionality in France and the United Kingdom. *Politics and Gender*, 10(1), pp. 130–136.

BERA. (2011) Revised ethical guidelines for educational research [Online]. Available at: https://www.bera.ac.uk/wp-content/uploads/2014/02. Accessed 5 January 2014.

Bilge, S. (2010) Recent feminist outlooks on intersectionality. *Diogenes*, 57(1), pp. 58–72.

Bilge, S. (2013) Intersectionality undone. *Du Bois Review: Social Science Research on Race*, 10(2), pp. 405–424.

Bilge, S. (2014) Whitening intersectionality. *Racism and Sociology*, 5, p. 175.

Bilge, S., and Scheibelhofer, P. (2012) Unravelling the new politics of racialised sexualities: Introduction. *Journal of Intercultural Studies*, 33(3), pp. 255–259.

Brah, A., and Phoenix, A. (2004) Ain't I a woman? Revisiting intersectionality. *Journal of International Women's Studies*, 5(3), pp. 75–86.

Butler, J. (1990) *Gender trouble and the subversion of identity.* New York: Routledge.

Butler, J. (2004) *Undoing gender.* New York: Routledge.

Carbado, D. W., Crenshaw, K. W., Mays, V. M., and Tomlinson, B. (2013) Intersectionality. *Du Bois Review: Social Science Research on Race*, 10(2), pp. 303–312.

Cho, S., Williams, K., and McCall, L. (2013) Towards a field of intersectionality studies: Theory, applications and praxis. *Signs*, 38(4), pp. 785–810.

Clark, C. (2006) Defining ethnicity in a cultural and socio-legal context: The case of Scottish Gypsy-Travellers. *Scottish Affairs*, 54, pp. 39–67.

Clark, C. (2008) Introduction themed section care or control? Gypsies, travellers and the state. *Social Policy and Society*, 7(1), pp. 65–71.

Collins, P. H. (1993) Toward a new vision: Race, class, and gender as categories of analysis and connection. *Race, Sex and Class*, pp. 25–45.

Collins, P. H. (1994) Shifting the centre: Race, class, and feminist theorizing about motherhood. *Mothering: Ideology, experience, and agency*, pp. 45–65.

Collins, P. H. (1998) *Fighting words: Black women and the search for justice* (Vol. 7). Minneapolis: University of Minnesota Press.

Collins. P. H. (2000) *Black feminist thought. Knowledge, consciousness and the politics of empowerment.* London: Routledge.

Collins, P. H. (2001) The social construction of black feminist thought. *Feminism and race*, pp. 184–202.

Combahee River Collective (1977) The Combahee River Collective Statement. *Capitalist patriarchy and the case for socialist feminism*, pp. 362–372.

Crenshaw, K. (1989) Demarginalizing the intersection of race and sex: A black feminist critique of antidiscrimination doctrine, feminist theory and antiracist politics. University of Chicago. *Legal Forum*, 140, pp. 139–167.

Crenshaw, K. (1991) Mapping the margins: Identity politics, intersectionality, and violence against women. *Stanford Law Review*, 43(6), pp. 1241–1299.

Daly, K. (1992) The fit between qualitative research and the characteristics of families. In Gilgun, J. F., Daly, K., and Handel, G. (eds.) *Qualitative methods in family research.* Thousand Oaks, CA: Sage, pp. 3–11.

Davis, K. (2008) Intersectionality as buzzword: A sociology of science perspective on what makes a feminist theory successful. *Feminist Theory*, 9(1), pp. 67–85.

Drever, E. (2003) *Using semi-structured interviews in small-scale research: A teacher's guide.* Glasgow: The SCRE Centre.

Dyer, R. (1997) *White.* London: Routledge.

EHRC. (2015) Developing successful site provision for Scotland's Gypsy/Traveller Communities. Available at: https://www.equalityhumanrights.com/sites/default/files/successful_site_provision_scotland.pdf. Accessed 21 April 2015.

Farris, S. R., and de Jong, S. (2014) Discontinuous intersections: Second-generation immigrant girls in transition from school to work. *Ethnic and Racial Studies*, 37(9), pp. 1505–1525.

Ferguson, K. (2003) Silence: A politics. *Contemporary Political Theory*, 2(1), pp. 49–65.

Foucault, M. (1997) What is critique? *The Politics of Truth*, pp. 23–82.

Freire, P. (1970) *Pedagogy of the oppressed.* New York: Continuum.

Freire, P. (1985) *The politics of education: Culture, power, and liberation.* Westport: Greenwood Publishing Group.

Gopaldas, A., and DeRoy, G. (2015) An intersectional approach to diversity research. *Consumption Markets and Culture*, 18(4), pp. 333–364.

Griffiths, M. (1998) *Educational research for social justice: Getting off the fence.* Buckingham: Open University Press.

Grinyer, A. (2009) The anonymity of research participants: Assumptions, ethics, and practicalities. *Pan*, 12(1), pp. 49–58.

Hammersley, M., and Traianou, A. (2012) *Ethics in qualitative research: Controversies and contexts.* London: Sage.

Hancock, A. M. (2007) When multiplication doesn't equal quick addition: Examining intersectionality as a research paradigm. *Perspectives on Politics*, 5(1), pp. 63–79.

Haraway, D. (1988) Situated knowledges: The science question in feminism and the privilege of partial perspective. *Feminist studies*, 14(3), pp. 575–599.

hooks, b. (1981) *Ain't I a woman: Black women and feminism.* Boston: South End Press.

hooks, b. (2015) *Feminist theory: From margin to center.* London: Routledge.

Inken C. E. (2014) Connecting intersectionality and reflexivity: Methodological approaches to social positionalities. *Erkunde*, 68(4), pp. 265–276.

Johal, G. S. (2005) Chapter thirteen: Order in KOS on race, rage, and method. *Counterpoints*, 252, pp. 269–290.

Knapp, A. (1999) Fragile foundations, strong traditions, situated questioning: Critical theory in German-speaking feminism. In M. O'Neill (ed.) *Adorno, Culture and Feminism*. London: Sage, pp. 119–140.

Luker, K. (2010) *Salsa dancing into the social sciences: Research in an age of infoglut*. Cambridge, MA: Harvard University Press.

Mirza, H. S. (2008) *Race, gender and educational desire*. London: Institute of Education: University of London.

Mirza, H. S. (2009) Plotting a history: Black and postcolonial feminisms in 'new times'. *Race Ethnicity and Education*, 12(1), pp. 1–10.

Mirza, H. S. (2013) 'A second skin': Embodied intersectionality, transnationalism and narratives of identity and belonging among Muslim women in Britain. *Women's Studies International Forum*, 36(February), pp. 5–15.

Mirza, H. S. (2015) Harvesting our collective intelligence: Black British feminism in post-race times. *Women's Studies International Forum*, 51, pp. 1–9.

Mirza, H. S., and Gunaratnam, Y. (2014) 'The branch on which I sit': Reflections on black British feminism. *Feminist Review*, 108(1), pp. 125–133.

Mirza, H., Ali, S., Phoenix, A., and Ringrose, J. (2010) Intersectionality, Black British feminism and resistance in education: A roundtable discussion. *Gender and Education*, 22(6), pp. 647–661.

Moray House School of Education. (2012) Moray House School of Education Student Application Form. Available at: http://atate.org/mscel/assignments/Dissertation-Ethics-Form-Tate.pdf. Accessed 5 January 2013.

Morris, L. (1994) *Dangerous classes. The underclass and social citizenship*. London: Routledge.

Naples, N. A. (2009) Teaching intersectionality intersectionally. *International Feminist Journal of Politics*, 11(4), pp. 566–577.

Planning Aid Scotland (PAS). (2014, September 14) Personal communication. Conversations, discussions conference notes and materials, Edinburgh.

Prins, B. (2006) Narrative accounts of origins A blind spot in the intersectional approach? *European Journal of Women's Studies*, 13(3), pp. 277–290.

Punch, S. (2002) Research with children: The same or different from research with adults? *Childhood*, 9(3) (August), pp. 321–341.

Punch, S. (2012) Hidden struggles of fieldwork: exploring the role and use of field diaries. *Emotion, Space and Society*, 5(2) (May), pp. 86–93.

Save the Children Scotland. (2005) *Having our Say.* Available at: http://www. gypsy-Traveller.org/your-family/young-people/educational-reports-and-re-sources. Accessed November 2012.

Smith, J. (2014, May 14) Personal communication, Traveller writer and story-teller, Recorded interview.

Solorzano, D. G. (1998) Critical race theory, race and gender microaggres-sions, and the experience of Chicana and Chicano scholars. *International Journal of Qualitative Studies in Education,* 11(1), pp. 121–136.

Spivak, G. (1984–1985) Feminism, criticism and the institution. *Thesis Eleven. A Socialist Journal,* 10(11), pp. 175–187.

Spivak, G. (1988) Can the subaltern speak? In: Nelson, C. and Grossberg, L. (eds.) *Marxism and the interpretation of culture.* Urbana and Chicago: University of Illinois Press, pp. 271–316.

Trepagnier, B. (2006) *Silent racism: How well meaning white people perpetuate the racial divide.* Boulder: Paradigm Publishing.

Truth, S. (1851, May 29) Ar'nt I a woman? Women's Rights Convention, Akron, Ohio.

Weckman, S. (1998) Researching Finnish Gypsies: Advice from a Gypsy. In: Tong, D. (ed.) *Gypsies: An interdisciplinary reader.* London: Taylor and Francis, pp. 3–10.

Williams, B. A. O. (2002) *Truth and truthfulness: An essay in genealogy.* Princeton: Princeton University Press.

Yuval-Davis, N. (2006) Belonging and the politics of belonging. *Patterns of prejudice,* 40(3), pp. 197–214.

Yuval-Davis, N. (2011) *The politics of belonging: Intersectional contestations.* London: Sage.

5

'I Am Not Big, Fat or *Just* Gypsy': The Racialised and Gendered Experiences of Gypsy and Traveller Girls in School

This chapter is divided into six parts and here I address the main research question: *How do Gypsy and Traveller girls frame their educational experiences?* I begin with a brief explanation of the types of educational establishments to which the Gypsy and Traveller girls had access. I then foreground the girls' own definitions and understandings of education and learning respectively, as it forms a useful backdrop upon which the tapestry of their experiences is woven. The next sections highlight their positive experiences, and the challenges and obstacles they face. The challenges and barriers are split further into two categories—their friendships with peers and relations with school staff. Both have an impact on their attendance, exclusion, achievement and attainment.

Their educational experiences vary and are not homogenous. They share some common experiences, but there is no single narrative. The term 'most' signifies eight or more out of the thirteen participants. Most of the girls cite negative experiences at school and are deterred from attending mainstream educational settings because of:

© The Author(s) 2019

G. Marcus, *Gypsy and Traveller Girls*, Studies in Childhood and Youth,
https://doi.org/10.1007/978-3-030-03703-1_5

- Racism and bullying by peers and school staff
- Lack of respect, support and understanding from school staff
- Gender discrimination from school staff who are primarily women
- Fear and lack of trust of school staff

Self-exclusion from mainstream educational settings enables the girls and their families to assume control and reflects a form of 'weak power' (Hall 1991). Their accounts disrupt the anecdotal myth perceived by the public and even within education, that *all* Gypsy and Traveller girls do not attend school beyond age 12. Success in attainment and achievement increases where the girls have positive experiences with non-Traveller peers, school staff who demonstrate support and fair expectations, without bias and consistent attendance in school with little or no interruption.

Throughout, I reflect on and synthesise the girls' views with the existing literature in the field and my own views, using the intersectional approach discussed in Chapter 4. I have included comments from the focus group discussion with Article 12, as these form part of the data I collected. However, as stated in the methodology chapter, the discussion helped to strengthen findings from the 13 interviews. Where appropriate, comments from stakeholders are included to compare and contrast different points of view, but not to undermine or question the veracity of their perspectives. The final part highlights silences, tensions and contradictions in their accounts, and summarises the main points in the chapter.

Throughout the research process, I was aware of Spivak's (1988) thoughts about representation and *re-presentation*. I reiterate that I am not representing the girls, but I acknowledge that *re-presenting* the voices of historically muted minority ethnic women is challenging. I cannot reflect a perfectly accurate picture of the girls' experiences, as they would tell it, despite the use of ad verbatim quotes. My perspectives, experiences and subjectivities influence, to a certain extent, what I elect to present in these findings. In doing so, I heed Spivak's advice that researchers must 'learn that their privilege is their loss' (1988: 82). The purpose of this chapter is to re-present their narratives with care and to critically contextualise their perspectives within wider themes at play—the institutions and structures that help to influence their lives.

In her book *On Being Included: Racism and Diversity in Institutional Life*, Sara Ahmed offers a helpful definition of what an institution is. She argues institutions are not fixed entities or 'containers', but that they are 'processes or even effects of processes' (Ahmed 2012: 20–21). Just as institutions emerge and take form, they also constitute 'routines, procedures, conventions, roles, strategies, organisational forms, and technologies' (March and Olsen 1989, cited in Ahmed 2012: 21). An institution, in other words, is an object (a noun) and an act (a verb). I offer the argument that a school and the education system, from which it gains its energy, are both live institutions. I offer one definition of 'education' as being the formal 'systems, structures and processes' of learning (Bartlett and Burton 2007: 59). These systems, structures and processes exist, develop and become routines of habit, to both create and mould institutions. Some of these habits and routines are overt, but others are hidden, subtle. For example, the aims, principles and content of the school curriculum are written and published, but there is also the hidden curriculum of unintended learning experiences. Education systems and schools, as institutions, are not homogenous. This book is concerned with the Scottish education system as an institution and the different schools that constitute it.

Types of Schools

As a quick guide, Table 5.1, shown below, captures the variety of educational settings accessed by the girls from the age of five. This table displays the value the girls place on education and learning and links to the accounts they provided about attendance or non- attendance in schools. The table shows that all went to primary school, but most experienced varying periods of interrupted learning. Most had negative experiences.

There are several types of educational facilities available to Gypsy and Traveller pupils in Scotland—state primary and state secondary schools; local authority mobile units or portacabins located on Traveller sites; part-time local authority provision held outwith school premises; further education colleges; home education and private tutoring. None of the girls I met attended private schools. However, based on my

Table 5.1 Educational settings and quality of experience

Name	Age	Primary	Experience at primary	No. of primary schools attended	Secondary attendance	Experience at secondary	Local authority (LA) mobile unit	Experience at mobile unit	Other LA post primary	Experience at other LA	FE college	Experience at FE college	Home or private tutor
May	12	✓	–	12					✓	+			
Cara	12	✓	–	5					✓	+			
Ailsa	13	✓	Mixed	3					✓	+			
Islay	13	✓	–	8					✓	+			
Dana	13	✓	–	5					✓	+			
Fara	13	✓	–	13									✓
Skye	15	✓	+	1	✓	+							
Vaila	15	✓	+	3							✓	+	
Shona	16	✓	–	2			✓	Mixed					
Iona	16	✓	–	13									✓
Kilda	18	✓	–	2*			✓	Mixed					
Rona	19	✓	+	1	✓	+					✓	+	
Sandray	22	✓	+	1	✓	+					✓	+	
Total: 13		13			3		2		5		3		2

+ Means positive experience; – Means negative experience; Mixed experience; LA—Local authority; FE—Further education experience working in a private school, and from conversations with health visitors and several local authority teachers, I am aware that there are Gypsy and Traveller girls (and boys) who do attend private schools. I was unable to secure interviews with these young people.

There are no separate schools for Gypsy and Traveller pupils in Scotland. However, of the thirteen girls I interviewed, five aged between twelve and thirteen years, attended a local authority managed out of school provision based in a building used by a youth social club. This out of school provision is supposed to cater for the needs of Gypsy/Roma/Traveller pupils aged twelve to sixteen years in that Local Authority, although there were no Roma pupils in attendance. I was given to understand that it is jointly funded by a charity and because of a limited budget is only accessible two days a week. The opportunity to increase their attendance at the 'school' or centre is not available to the Gypsy and Traveller pupils at present (Anon. Quality Improvement Officer Inclusion 2014, Personal communication).

For confidentiality reasons, I am unable to name the Local Authority or the location of this centre, as this could lead to the identification of the pupils I interviewed. For convenience I refer to this particular provision as a 'youth centre' throughout the book. The learning activities managed by local authority appointed teachers during the day for Gypsy and Traveller pupils at the centre are separate from the evening leisure activities provided by the youth centre staff for all young people living in the area.

In the next chapter, the girls' additional reasons for not being able to attend school more than the two days are explored. Skye (15) is currently attending a local state secondary school. She has been continually enrolled in school since nursery.

Another young woman, Rona (19), attended her local state run secondary school and attended one primary school. She has been to a further education college and is currently an apprentice at a beauty and hairdressing salon. Like Skye and Rona, Sandray (22) only attended one primary and one secondary school. She studies music at a further education college and hopes to go to university. Vaila (15) also attends courses at a further education college, despite initially being encouraged by her parents to stop school when she was twelve years old.

Vaila attended three primary schools, but skipped secondary education. Kilda's (18) education was the most markedly interrupted because of a serious illness when she was five. She never formally returned to school, preferring instead to access some learning intermittently from the local authority Traveller Education Network (TENET) teacher that visits the site on which Kilda lives. Her sister, Shona (16), occasionally attends in the same setting. Fara (13) and her sister, Iona (16) continue to be 'home educated' after leaving primary school. More detailed profiles of the girls can be found in Appendix A.

Definitions and Understandings of Education and Learning

At the start of each interview, I engaged each participant in an informal chat to help create a comfortable environment and tone in which to converse. A range of questions was broached to get to know each Gypsy and Traveller girl, and gather some background information about her family and school. I shared brief information about myself as most of the girls asked me questions too. These initial discussions led to conversations about previous school experience, what the girls understood by the term 'education' and how important it was to them.

None of the girls could immediately offer a clear-cut definition of the term 'education', except that in their opinion this was what took place within a formal setting of a school, with teachers. Iona remarked being in education is being 'a wee bit under pressure like if you dinnae do what you are told to do… they check you for that'. The discussions that followed gave rise to a range of subsidiary questions that helped to further explore their ideas and perceptions. Most explained they had a 'bad education' and negative educational experiences, but they all declared they valued a 'good education' in school. Ailsa, for example, stated that she had a 'good education' at times, but could not explain what that entailed. 'I am not sure…I'd learn math!' (Ailsa). Like Ailsa, most of the girls found it difficult to explain exactly what they meant by a good education. In trying to explain, their answers initially tended to include examples of what was useful to know like Maths or Reading. Outdoor education was cited several times as an example of good education because, as May (12) noted, it was 'suffocating' to be indoors in a classroom all day.

Their difficulty in defining education may be reflected in Winch and Gingell's (2008: 78) argument that the term 'education' is problematic. If educationalists find it challenging to define, it is unsurprising that pupils do too. Education is subjective, complex and difficult to measure. It is arguably even more of a struggle when pupils experience negative, exclusionary and confusing practices at school. Interestingly, in attempting to explain what education is to them, the girls chose to attach a binary moral value to it instead—good or bad. Their judgement supports Pring's (2004: 12) contention that education is a moral activity based on culture and values. Pupils in school are not exempt from reproducing this binary.

An education in school was viewed as a privilege. Most of the girls alluded to their right to an education. The focus group from Article 12 went further and argued emphatically that they believed they had a right to a good education, but that this was systematically denied them. Many of the girls said they could learn better if their experiences were positive. Dana explained why she chooses to attend the youth centre:

> The teacher does want us to be clever, but she wants us to come here and make…maybe do something, like…we want to take a beauty course and she wants us maybe to learn something out of it. Because like for Mrs 'X' and Mrs 'Y' they're listening to us, helping us, we've got like the highest respect for them, but in school it's bad. Yeah because they take time for us but in the normal school I didn't feel like they had time…yeah of course they had time but I felt rushed, but in here it's like different. I've got time for them and I've got the highest respect for them. I can talk to them about any problems I have as well. Yeah anything!

Instead, as is highlighted in detail later in this chapter, prejudice, discrimination, bullying, and lack of support were all cited as reasons for an infringement of their right. The moral nature of education—good or bad as articulated by the girls—is also, for them, a matter of social justice. Their perceptions further reinforce the idea that education is not a neutral process. Gewirtz (2006) stresses the 'multi-dimensional nature of justice', the diverse value systems of the different agencies involved in educational activity—individual, family, local and national. Teachers, schools, local authorities and national government may all claim that they provide good, if not excellent, standards and experiences of education, but some children and their families may not agree based on their own moral and cultural values. The girls' definition of their education as good or bad is largely adjudicated by the moral and cultural norms of their families and communities, which in comparison could conflict with institutional interpretations of what is good, just and fair.

In our discussions, the girls tried to explain education in terms of its aims or usefulness. All girls registered that there were benefits to getting an education and that it is a means to an end. For example, Sandray explained—'I want to do music, I wanted to learn music, and that's why I went to college and that's why I've done my degree. And that makes me happy'. Vaila made clear that 'as soon as I turn 16 I'm hoping to start trying to work in a salon even just like sweeping floors and things and then work my way up because a lot of Travellers nowadays is actually getting jobs and getting better education. It's easier to get jobs if you have an education'.

When asked what these benefits were, nearly all the girls mentioned the need to acquire basic skills to read, write and do math, as they understood these were necessary skills for life. However, with the exception of Ailsa, the four girls I interviewed who attended the youth centre part-time, did not see the need for learning beyond the basics mentioned above, because they planned to marry and bear children within a few years. They were clear that the aim of getting an education was not to prepare them for work, but to enable them to socialise with other Travellers—'I guess we're getting an education other than going to high school but at the same time we get to see our friends here' (Islay). She said her parents would not want her to 'know too much' like Traveller children do. May appreciated being only 'with my own kind' at school. Dana explained further, 'we are really happy here because like when I'm at home I don't get nowhere and I have to sit on the site, like we're in the trailer all day but then you come here you're actually somebody, like you're talking to somebody'. For these girls there were, as Winch (2002) would argue, certain individual and social advantages to gaining an education.

Shona and Kilda, who attend lessons intermittently in a portacabin based at their Traveller site, remarked that they needed to learn to read in order to use their smartphones. Incidentally, Dana revealed her ability to read and write improved when she got a smartphone:

> But then when I came to Primary 7 I got a Blackberry and then that's when I started getting good at writing because I was always texting people and whatever, that's when I started to come around and then when I came here [the youth centre] I improved a lot. Like texting and all that. And better speller yeah.

Shona and Kilda admitted using their smartphones to learn to read and write ultimately led to learning how to drive. When I met them, they had just received help from the local health visitor to fill in their applications for a provisional driving licence. They both admitted that being able to drive gave them some freedom from the confines of their Traveller site. As Kilda notes, 'a lot of girls pass their test and get their cars, a car! And they go and see stuff like what all the Travellers do, like all the Travellers on a Sunday…all the Travellers go and meet up'. For Kilda and her sister being able to drive was key. They thought driving was a skill that was accepted and valued by their family. It would bring them direct benefits that would fit in with community expectations and boundaries. A report by Cemlyn et al. (2009: 44) highlights the importance of driving theory lessons in breaking down barriers, encouraging learning in 'literacy and computing' for 'employment and economic inclusion'. The girls view the aims of education as extrinsic and utilitarian, and here education serves a rudimentary purpose (Winch 2002). Most think mainstream education is not 'an intrinsically valuable activity', neither is it seen by some of the girls as having substantial extrinsic value, leading to a 'worthwhile occupation or to earn a living' (Winch 2002: 102). The focus group believed 'there's a misunderstanding from the education system that Gypsy/Travellers don't want to learn, they don't want an education and that's not the case… every young person that we've met has expressed an interest in education in one way or another'.

Four of the girls, however, stressed the importance of 'getting an education', getting 'qualifications', and mentioned going to college because this led to a career and greater independence (see shade in Table 5.1). They talked about the need for Traveller women to become more independent from Traveller men by earning their own income. Vaila reasoned that 'getting qualifications is going to help you get a job a lot better'. Iona, despite choosing to leave school at 13 years, reflected, 'you want to be independent from everybody else' and advised that being able to read and write helps a person to 'always check the small print!' On the contrary, she did not believe that being at school was the only path that led to independence. The girls from Article 12 agreed. Gypsy and Traveller girls seem to have a different and competing definition of education than the dominant way it is represented in Scotland. Is there a space in school to reflect these differing needs? However, it is important to recognise that their views are similar to other groups. It is not uncommon to think that education is instrumental, designed to help you get a job and navigate the world.

Similarly, Sandray took pains to point out that even though her father had never attended school, and could not read or write, he was a 'very intelligent man'. He is knowledgeable 'about certain subjects and about his way of living'. She explained that being educated in school was not the only form of education and that there are different types of 'educated people':

> You know… because Travellers are 'nae educated right in the way of reading and writing numbers, but they can get money, they can survive, they can build a home from scratch for themselves, they can get cars, they can get anything because they are very wise to that point but they didn't have to go to school to know that, you know? So that's what I think educated is like having the experience of being able to work out how to get money or how to solve a problem, or…not necessarily reading or writing but actually being able to take in… learn quickly… that's what I believe knowledge is.

This is a vital piece of evidence which confirms Gypsies and Travellers' internal pride in their own alternative or additional skills. Gypsies and Travellers emphasise many alternative economic skills, in 'knowing the local economy and local people; manual dexterity, mechanical ingenuity; highly developed memory; salesmanship and bargaining skills' (Okely 1979: 23).

The question and discussions about the meaning and importance of education led to what the girls understood by the term 'learning' because all the girls, including those from Article 12, used the term more naturally in conversation. They not only offered a clear explanation of what they meant by learning, but specified what type of learning they appreciated and, crucially, made a distinction between learning in school and learning at home. Shona argued that, 'learning is about rights and wrongs and showing us about being safe'. Islay expressed pity for non-Traveller children because all their learning takes place indoors, in contrast to the expanse and variety of learning she experiences, a privilege that comes with being able to travel—learning languages, seeing new places, meeting different people as we can see in this exchange:

> *GM (Researcher)*: So what do you think learning is then, how would you define it, what is learning to you?
> *Fara*: The way of going up in life if you want...the more you learn the more you can do, your possibilities are endless if you're constantly learning.
> *GM*: And do you think the only place to learn Fara is in school?
> *Fara*: No!
> *GM*: Okay so you can learn outside of school as well?
> *Fara*: Aye! If you're careful with the way you think and the way you like...the way you...what's the word um...Reason? You learn from what's around you.

School was not the only place to learn, one can learn from home and family. All the girls made sharp distinction between the education they receive within a school setting and the continuous learning they receive from a young age from their parents, families and communities. The latter seems to play a powerful role in their lives, and the girls are conscious of its value. All talked about how much they learn when they 'shift' or travel; they enjoy learning outdoors but feel constricted being in a classroom. Lee and Warren (1991: 322) assert that education within schools is not sufficient—'Rather than look to the provision of more and more mainstream opportunities for Romani children - that is, to ask what can we do for them'—there is some value in looking beyond stereotypes and asking: 'What can we learn from the Romanis?'. The girls' accounts reveal that school does not necessarily fit all their needs and their society's, but that their education at home provides them 'with a degree of independence, work satisfaction through non-alien-ated labour, family solidarity and cohesion and group survival' (Lee and Warren 1991: 322).

The girls at the youth centre stressed that it was more important that they learned to be good homemakers with the necessary cleaning, cook-ing and child-rearing skills. They are trained to do these tasks by their families. All the girls have responsibility for looking after their younger siblings, except Vaila and Sandray who are the youngest in their family. All recognised the importance of these core, nurturing skills and unre-servedly acknowledged that they learned a lot from their parents and families. Iona summarised, 'at home you've got life lessons, at school you've got learning lessons, some skills at school, here [at home] its life lessons… lessons for life'.

Most observed that a valuable education, would be a flexible one that involves being at school for some of the time, in some cases just to get the basic skills, in combination with lifelong learning experiences at home and when they travel most of the year. In their eyes, school is temporary but the learning that is passed on to them by their commu-nities is permanent and is very much part of who they are and where they have come from, their ancient traditions and lifestyles.

However, slightly more than half of those interviewed stated they set equal value to the learning they received from family, community and school:

> *Sandray*: I would just say it's both equally great because I've been taught so much about my heritage, and the way of life, and I'm proud of that and you know how to get money and how to hawk, and how to do things like that. I could do that.

GM: So one is not better than the other?

Sandray: No I would'nae say so. I would say they're both equally important.

GM: Yes and so if you didn't have one of them you would then feel less of a person maybe, would you, or would you feel -

Sandray: If I didn't have education then *I would'nae know any better would I*? I mean education as in grades and stuff like that, I would'nae know any better anyway would I? So...*but I'd still survive -*

GM: Because you're a Traveller!

Sandray: Because I'm a Traveller you know! [Laughter] I'm not meaning to be like ...funny...

GM: No I absolutely get where you're coming from!

Sandray: It's the best of both worlds for me.

Rona, Skye, Vaila, and Sandray, seemed to have an instinctive understanding of the potentially life changing value of a formal education in school:

Because the more education I learnt and the more people I met in college and school I questioned who I was and what I wanted to do...I was getting an education it just opened my mind up a bit more...I'm glad that I've had the education I've had because I would never ever restrict my kids or anybody, I'd encourage education as much as possible. (Sandray)

In the focus group discussion one girl mentioned that she wished she had the opportunity to re-visit school, as she believed her opportunities were now limited—'I wish I had'nae walked away. I would like to go to school again...I think I have lost out a bit you know'. However, through her work with Article 12, she has been presented with a chance to empower herself and her community. The others in the group agreed.

Sandray's response below, demonstrates the complexity of the situation for Gypsy and Traveller girls. She, like some of the other girls, values the education in school, but it also impacts on her identity, family:

But I felt like...I don't know if you want to ask me this later but I felt like I was two people when I was growing up... So I felt like I was torn between 2 lives.

I'd encourage education as much as possible however, it will'nae keep the traditions on if people are exposed to a lot of education. That's the only downfall to it. There won't be a community anymore, like say if everybody knows everything about Gypsies, and they know everything about everything else it would'nae be a community otherwise would it? It would'nae be like a private community. It would be too mixed up so I don't know what to do.

This last observation that Sandray offered indicates that learning at school and at home with her community, impacted on her sense of identity and her friendships. Some of the girls, and Sandray in particular, acknowledged that both settings present challenges, tensions and contradictions in different ways and for different reasons. The focus group discussion confirmed that their work in Article 12 meant that, as young women, they had to balance finely their obligations to the organisation and still meet their families' expectations to behave appropriately according to traditional standards.

On the other hand, the girls at the youth centre and the two sisters that intermittently attended lessons at the portacabin on their site (see Table 5.2), stressed that it was more important that they learned to be

Table 5.2 Views on the importance of learning at home and at school

Name	Home/family education more important	School more important	Both important
May	✓		
Cara	✓		
Ailsa			✓
Islay	✓		
Dana	✓		
Fara			✓
Skye			✓
Vaila			✓
Shona	✓		
Iona			✓
Kilda	✓		
Rona			✓
Sandray			✓
	6	0	7

good homemakers with the necessary cleaning, cooking and child-rearing skills. They are trained to do these tasks by their families. I wondered if these girls, who had not perhaps experienced continuous formal education in school, felt they were missing out and if they 'knew any better', as suggested by Sandray. It was difficult for me to ascertain just how much choice most of the girls had and even if they thought they had the freedom to choose, how would they judge if they were being unduly influenced. Like children and young people from all ethnic backgrounds, they will be guided by their families' values, expectations and aspirations.

Iona and Fara said they valued both learning at home and at school but they elected not to go to secondary school. They told me that they exercised their individual freedom to refuse opportunities offered in secondary schools and embraced other educational activities from home. Fara and Iona are the only girls who asserted their right to reject what they perceived as an education system that was inflexible, bigoted and unkind.

> *GM*: So you've been to around 13 schools you said? So why girls are you both not in school today? Why are you not there?
> *Iona*: We've had enough!
> *GM*: Yeah okay! Yeah I can understand that.
> *Iona*: That's basically it, we've had enough and maybe out of them 13 we've had 2 where we felt like we fitted in for a while. Why should we put up with it?

Whilst they have been discriminated against, this is also a result of having strong cultural values and boundaries, set as different from the dominant culture.

Pring (2007: 509) discusses the role of 'the common school' in unifying children from different cultural and socio-economic backgrounds:

> Given the changed economic and social conditions in which we live, there is a need to expose children from a limited and limiting cultural framework to one that broadens their horizons.

However, he warns against picking out certain ways of knowing as being better than others, and forcing pupils to conform. A common education system or school may be a convenient means of assimilation and social cohesion, but it presupposes a hierarchy of knowledge and cultures. Education in schools is structured, attendance is mandatory, dedicated to certain subjects, homework and exams. The aim is to succeed academically to progress to higher education, get a good job and contribute to the economy. It does not easily allow for deviations or alternatives, and does not account for learning that takes place at home and in the community (Bhopal 2018). Travelling cultures might argue that an education in a mainstream common school is not important and might be dangerous to their traditions. Who decides what is best? Does this not perhaps then affect the community's and individual's right to choose, freedom to live their lives as they see fit? Ought everyone be forced into a specific model of what his or her cultural framework should be? Is it the role of education to control, direct and prevent choice?

> The common school, therefore, would seek to first understand and respect the different cultural traditions that the young people bring with them into the school; second, to reconcile those cultural differences, which, if ignored, fragment the wider community so that it is no community at all. (Pring 2007: 510)

A report on inequalities faced by Gypsies and Travellers by Cemlyn et al., confirms this view that 'while social inclusion is a valid aim, it needs to be on the basis of cultural validation and respect, and to support rather than detract from educational aims' (2009: 101). Some girls had positive experiences in school and, from their accounts below, where there was, as suggested by Pring (2007), respect for difference, acceptance of diversity and reconciliation of ideas, the school community helped these girls to thrive.

School Experience—Positives

As Table 5.1 reveals, only four out of the thirteen participants described having positive experiences in school. Skye, Rona and Sandray went to one primary school and one secondary school. Vaila attended three primary schools because her family moved to a new house each time, which is not atypical. However, out of the four who had positive experiences, Vaila did not attend secondary school, and these reasons are considered further in the next chapter. The girls stressed that they enjoyed being at each stage of school—primary, secondary and further education college.

The four girls explained that a reason they enjoyed being in education was due to the good relations with their peers. They made friends with Traveller and non-Traveller pupils alike. There is something intrinsically life forming and sustaining about school friendships (Ladd et al. 1996; Hartup and Stevens 1997). Rona and Skye were adamant that bullying and name-calling were not problems they encountered. They asserted:

> *Rona*: Never! I've never experienced any of that!
> *Skye*: Never! Everyone like knows we are Travellers and that we live on a site… nobody cares; there's been no hassle like.

They were happy to attend school, 'to mix with non-Traveller friends' (Rona). They both reasoned that this was because of their 'attitude' and their family's support and encouragement to be 'open and friendly to other [non-Travellers]' (Skye). The girls emphasised the importance and benefits of socialising with peers from both the Traveller and non-Traveller communities.

Rona and Skye explained they chose not to attend the mobile school just for Travellers made available on their site, but attended the local state school. 'Why would you wanna be with Travellers all the time… it's so boring!' (Skye). Her parents asked her whether she wanted to attend secondary school, giving her the freedom to decide:

> I was asked whether I wanted to go to secondary school and I said yes because like it's the normal thing to do…like my sister didn't ask any of her kids if they wanted to go to school… they just went. (Skye)

Skye's comment perhaps suggests that attitudes and aspirations are changing and that younger Gypsies and Travellers might be beginning to view education and school differently.

Vaila remarked that 'it was quite nice to actually socialise with other people other than Travellers to learn about their lifestyle as well', even though there was the occasional name-calling, 'if you did anything wrong they'd [Traveller pupils] end up going 'Oh this is a tink thing!'' (Vaila), but she pointed out that in contrast non-Traveller peers would not racialise each other in disputes—'They would probably just laugh at them' (Vaila). The four girls stressed that they socialised with friends, Traveller and non-Traveller, both in school and outside school. They visited each other's homes and families. In each interview, unprompted, the girls compared their social experience to that of 'cousins' and other members of their family, who 'refuse to mix with non-Travellers' (Vaila). Skye and Rona echoed, 'we are unique!' Their explanations for this difference in attitude and experience are discussed in the next chapter.

Another reason cited for positive school experiences by all four girls was that their teachers were supportive—'They just treated me like everyone else really' (Vaila). All four explained that they were motivated to learn, did well at school and attained good results throughout. Rona, Vaila, and Sandray, who subsequently attended courses at college, each said they particularly appreciated the freedom of being at college, being able to choose courses to pursue, and their greater control over their learning. They pointed out that the relationship between staff and pupils at the college seemed more relaxed and less autocratic.

As highlighted in previous chapters, difficulties getting accurate population figures in the recent 2011 Census and anecdotal evidence suggest that some, if not most, Gypsies and Travellers do not reveal their real ethnic identity. A few interviews with adults supported this trend, and this silence is examined further below. It is encouraging to observe that all four girls willingly disclosed their Traveller identity at school, and stated that whilst some peers were surprised to discover their ethnicity, it did not affect relationships adversely.

A few of them were kind of shocked at first, I've never really met a Traveller they kept saying so they were kind of interested to know like how we were different to them, like our rules to their rules. (Vaila)

Vaila and Sandray sensed that their non-Traveller friends were at most curious about Travelling culture, and the staff at the colleges were seen to be supportive, despite their ethnicity.

May (12), Cara (12), Islay (13), Ailsa (13) and Dana (13) who attend school two days a week at the youth centre, all mentioned how much they appreciated the positive learning environment there. Being able to socialise in a school setting with only Traveller pupils was perceived as an advantage and as Dana clarified, 'we're separate from everybody else anyways!' She thought having a school for Travellers is a good idea. The girls drew attention to their teachers' kindness and support in helping them to learn. They appreciated their teachers' respect for their family and ethnicity.

> The teachers just like doing this for us… they're listening to us, and help-ing us, we've got like the highest respect for them Yeah from my family too… because Mrs 'X' she teached all my aunties and all my cousins and everyone so she knows my family. She knows me since I was born. (Dana)

May made clear that she 'likes it more because they [the teachers] understand where you're coming from'. Islay believed the youth centre is a 'really good school' because:

> All the class children get one-on-one time and its really good…I guess we're getting an education other than going to high school but at the same time we get to see our friends here. But this is better than high school because…see here… like all the staff are kind

Below is the flow of conversation between Cara, Islay and me about the benefits of learning at the youth centre:

> *Cara*: Uh huh we're comfortable here.
> *Islay*: You can be yourself.
> *Cara*: You can be yourself yeah.
> *GM*: And you're not judged?
> *Cara*: No!

GM: Do you feel safe here?

Cara: Yeah. We feel very safe here. They're [the teachers] nice, they are really nice.

Islay: They're close to us, you know.

Cara: Uh huh, they are, and then like if you need help they will come and help you. And they'll take their time. They'll help you and they'll learn it with you, but like when you're in primary school and high school they won't take their time and help you because they've got that many people and they've got to get around all of them. And they won't take time and learn you, but here they will.

Whilst most of the girls described their experiences in mainstream primary school as negative, five of them from the youth centre echoed some of the positive experiences recounted by Rona, Skye, Vaila, and Sandray. Ailsa was the only one who maintained that her experiences were mixed. When she had a good experience in a mainstream primary school, her reasons largely reflected the ones listed by Rona, Skye, Vaila, and Sandray, although she was rarely allowed to mix with her non-Traveller peers after school hours. Her work improved and she did well in these school settings. Her experiences at the youth centre were also positive. However, in mainstream schools where she had negative experiences, she acknowledged that there were both challenges and barriers that were distressing and difficult to overcome.

Uh…I'm glad I go [to the youth centre]. It's good that I get an education. But I did want to go to secondary school and I didn't because I wanted a really good education, I wanted to get through to college and uh…but I didn't want anything bad to happen so I think this is a good situation. (Ailsa)

Learning at the youth centre is a safe compromise for the Gypsy and Traveller girls. The further education colleges attended by Vaila, Sandray and Rona provided flexibility and choice. The girls seem to have had encouraging and successful experiences because of three key issues:

1. They had positive experiences with non-Traveller peers.
2. School staff demonstrated respect, support and fair expectations, without bias.
3. They had consistent attendance in school with little or no interruption.

Furthermore, 'no one school or college can deliver to all young people the education and training they are entitled to' (Pring 2007: 520). What is needed, what these girls have accessed and what seems to have worked better in some cases are a variety of learning centres (not just mainstream schools), working to provide a range of experiences that enable these young people to feel safe and fulfilled. The flexibility in educational provision that most of the girls said they would like to have might be a way forward to build consensus and trust. The Report of the Gypsy/Traveller Strategic Group (The Scottish Executive 2006: 9) recommends that educational provision should be flexible—a 'mechanism for accrediting informal learning should be developed [and the] Scottish Executive should develop a strategy on Gypsy and Traveller learning covering school, out-of-school, further and higher education'. Whether these experiences reflect an academic standard of quality is another issue, and will be discussed further in the section where relations with staff are explored.

I will now turn to explore the girls' explanations of the challenges and barriers they faced in formal educational settings.

Challenges and Barriers

There are no research findings in Scotland that examine what Gypsy and Traveller girls in particular experience as challenges and barriers in school. The girls I interviewed were asked to voice their concerns and perceptions. Each girl was asked if there were any problems they faced in school that made their experience difficult. The challenges that the girls identified can be categorised into two main themes—their interactions with their peers and their relations with teachers, headteachers and occasionally playground assistants. I asked them to explain the nature of their experience, to describe what happened, how they felt about it, and how they coped.

Friendships

Table 5.1 shows that eight out of the thirteen girls experienced negative problems particularly with friendships and their relationships with peers at school. None of the four girls in the focus group had positive experiences in school. The girls cite three reasons for the negative impact on their social life in school—name-calling, bullying and racist attitudes. All eight girls reported they were called names and when asked why they thought this was happening, they all believed it was because they were Travellers. The girls described being called 'Gypo', 'pikey', 'tink' 'stinking Gypos'. As Fara recounted, 'well one of the things was… "Go back to where you came fae, you dirty black pikey"'. Iona described the kinds of words used to being likened to 'the scum of the earth, rats, you know like the lowest of the low'. Fara and her sister Iona both believe that these insults 'must be coming from their parents I would think or older children they're with… yeah because you're not born with these words in your mouth are you?' In the interview, I recalled Mandela's (2004: 784) words about not being born to hate, but taught to hate. Iona laughed and interjected, 'I know they're only children but some of them look quite dodgy to be around and you do get cruel ones'.

Unlike the rest of the girls, Kilda and Ailsa both used the words racist or racism to describe what was happening to them. In labelling the discrimination as 'racist' their analysis seems quite sophisticated in my view, as it serves to transfer the problem away from them as individuals and to the perpetrators. It is not that Kilda and Ailsa see anything wrong with who they are, but that the name callers are the ones with the problem of being unable to accept that people are not only different, but have a right to be so.

Kilda: I've been called pikey, a gypo, pikey smelly bastards... even Gypsy! There's like all these children against us because we're Gypsies. And they call us it all the time as we walk passed, we'd be Gypsies!
GM: But you don't call yourselves a Gypsy you call yourselves Travellers?
Kilda: Travellers!
GM: Is the word Gypsy a bad word?
Kilda: Racist! It's just racist!

Ailsa was clear to point out that this did not happen in every school she went to:

Ailsa: Well I was in two schools before and they were fine, but I moved to another one and some people in the school were racist.
GM: In what way? What were they doing?
Ailsa: Like...they were calling me names.
GM: Why?
Ailsa: Because I am a Traveller!
GM: So did they know you were a Traveller? How did they know you were a Traveller?
Ailsa: Because the other Travellers who was in the class I was related to them.
GM: Oh I'm very sorry to hear this because it must make you feel really upset like you said. And of course you never forget these experiences do you?
Ailsa: *It doesn't always happen.* Um...well my parents were afraid of racism because it's worse in secondary school.

Ailsa's last comment about her parents' fears about racism in secondary school being *worse* is a telling indictment of the situation experienced by some pupils and their families. Perhaps drawing on their own experiences or the experiences of their family and kinship networks, there appears to be a perception that racism happens in primary school, but that it will intensify when the children go to secondary school. Such fears are discussed further in the next chapter alongside the other concerns that Gypsy and Traveller families have about sending their girls to school. The focus group all reported they had experienced racist bullying. One in particular seemed to have a rough time:

I was bullied as soon as I went into school, in Primary 2 — Well they would notice you were different, the site was like about half a mile away from the...the school and when I got there in Primary 2 they just started... coming around you, bullying you and see if somebody came to play with you, I can remember people bullying them too. That happened right up till I left. I made it to Primary 5! [Laughter] (Member of Focus Group)

However, the focus group believed being away from school for periods of time did not help either. It made Gypsy and Traveller pupils vulnerable to being considered stupid because they could not do the work they had missed:

Like say if you shift away for a while and you've missed out a big chunk, or even if it's only a couple of weeks or whatever you've missed out this chunk of school, when you go back you feel so behind everybody else, and then you get made a fool of for that. (Member of Focus Group)

They agreed that because most Gypsy and Traveller children do not attend nursery school, it is more difficult for them to assimilate into primary. 'But when it comes to primary school they've never been to nursery, never mixed with a settled community, they've been among their own. So it's like taking you out of your comfort zone and thrown in at the deep end' (Member of Focus Group). Of the eight girls who were unhappy at school, none of them cited interrupted learning as a problem for them, but on the contrary it was the bullying that caused them not to attend in the first place.

For the majority of the girls I interviewed, school was seen to be unsafe and risky. I asked each of the girls to describe how it felt to encounter such powerful, derisory language. Ailsa disclosed that it made her feel angry and that no one liked her, 'I felt that no one cared and everyone hated me'. When asked why she assumed 'everyone' hated her, she explained the humiliation she felt in response to racist bullying and revealed how her peers toyed with her mind:

GM: Everyone? Even the people who liked you?
Ailsa: I wasn't sure because they were nice but sometimes they just ignored me.

> *GM*: So it was almost like games, you weren't sure how they were going to react.
> *Ailsa*: Yeah I lost some friends because of it. Like I was great friends with them and then I told them [I was a Traveller] and then now they don't want to be friends.
> *GM*: If someone didn't like you because you were a Traveller what would you say to them?
> *Ailsa*: Not sure... *I get it all the time* – I would say I'd rather be a Traveller.

Note the subtle contrast or contradiction between the italicised statement in the previous exchange and the one last statement above, which perhaps reveals the state of confusion and distress that comes from being subject to racist bullying. Ailsa's descriptions of her experiences with her peers at school are all the more poignant because she is the one child that assesses her experiences as 'mixed'. Despite what seems deeply wounding, she does not reject her experiences at school as being entirely negative. The depth of distress experienced by these eight girls was summarised powerfully by Kilda:

> It wasn't really fair. It makes us feel like we must not be human because everybody's human... We're the same as everybody else in this world do you know what I mean? Just because we live a different...style from everybody else.

She goes on and uses the colour of my skin as an example:

> The same as what I like see how you's are colourful, the way I look at it is when you get cut you bleed the same as us so it's no different, do you know what I mean? Nobody's different — nobody! We're all the same so I don't treat anybody differently; do you know what I mean? (Kilda)

The girls' accounts of these experiences at school suggest that 'whiteness' and 'Scottishness' are unstable markers. In fact, concepts like 'Scottishness', 'Englishness' or 'Britishness' are in fact difficult to define and in my view aligned more with the rhetoric of race and xenophobia as these terms set up barriers between 'us' and 'them'. The girls do not look or sound visibly different to other White Scottish people, and yet derisory comments from non-Traveller pupils racialise them as an Other to be despised.

Their experiences echo the statements in reports highlighted in Chapter 3 that racism and racial discrimination continues to be a problem in Scottish schools. The 2005 survey by Save The Children highlighted 92% of young Gypsies and Travellers in Scotland have been bullied or called names because of their ethnic identity. The Scottish Social Attitudes Survey (Scottish Centre for Social Research 2010) confirmed that there are negative and racist views towards Gypsies and Travellers. A recent report on prejudiced-based bullying in Scottish schools (EHRC 2015b) also highlighted the seriousness of the problem.

Significantly, the existing academic literature on the education of Gypsies and Travellers in Scotland, highlights the problem, but does not directly investigate bullying and racism in schools; preferring to explore pedagogical strategies for coping with interrupted attendance, special needs, and behavioural challenges, reflecting ethnocentrism. This lacuna may suggest that the problem of racial discrimination in Scottish schools is perceived as taboo and requires an in-depth exploration of institutionalised and everyday racism against Gypsy and Traveller young people—especially young women. This lack of attention to Gypsy and Traveller young people's experiences of racism can be seen as a form of silence that perpetuates the existing inequalities faced by some Gypsy and Traveller pupils, and particularly those who identify their ethnicity.

Coping Strategies

In my conversations with the girls, I asked each of them how they dealt with such painful encounters with their racist peers. In this extended response, Fara recounted how she perceived the bullying that took place. Note how she identifies the various stages of harassment, her strategies for coping and the underlying stress that ensues:

> Whatever they say and it's alright the first time but they repeat it and repeat it and repeat it until it rings in your head and then you get really annoyed and you think about saying something back and you think

should I do this or are they just going to come and hit me with more? But me and Iona are not really the aggressive type, she's a wee bit more feisty than me but…I'm not…I try and avoid everything and try and hide in the shadows… Because if you don't you're just sitting there waiting for them to beat you. It's a time bomb. You're a sitting duck! And if not, you've got to try and stand up for yourself and I'm not very good at that! (Fara)

The experiences are at first 'alright' then 'they repeat it and repeat it and repeat it'. The repetition suggests it is unbearable. Note the self-introspection—Fara and her sister are not 'the aggressive type', and they are reluctant to retaliate or lash out, although one is 'a wee bit more feisty'. Her account reveals her fear and some conflict between not allowing themselves to be 'sitting ducks' and ignoring the behaviour hoping it will pass.

The girls' strategies for coping with bullying, racist or otherwise, ranged along a crescendo of seriousness from initially ignoring the insults, hiding away, walking away, 'standing up', telling staff in school in order to get help when it seemed to get unbearable, and finally not telling staff in school even when physically beaten by other children. These various coping strategies were also listed in the focus group discussion. Dana revealed she would never tell her teacher if there were problems in the playground because 'we don't grass'.

All the eight girls, however, discussed these incidents with their parents, but only a few parents intervened by speaking to a teacher or headteacher. Some parents decided to speak to the parents of the bullying child. The girls noticed that when their parents did ask for help, they too were ignored or promises by staff to deal with the issues were not honoured. As Fara admitted, 'in most of the cases it [having their parents intervene] doesn't help'.

Like their children, parents stopped reporting the incidents and moved on to another school or withdrew their child from education to avoid conflict or as one parent put it 'We did'nae want trouble'. Iona echoed this idea, 'if the girl couldn't ignore it, to try and find help about it, and if that did'nae work for her to leave and get home tutored, or a different school and try again'. Note the choice of phrase 'try again', which may allude to a sign of hope, resilience and perhaps the need to keep moving on in search of better experiences.

This is one reason why attendance amongst Gypsy and Traveller girls is poor, or non-attendance might be a more palatable option for Gypsy and Traveller girls and their families. Self-exclusion is a coping strategy and minority cultures, keen to preserve their dignity and power, do self-exclude for safety and the comfort of those who accept them. There has been relatively little research into the use of self-exclusion as a positive tool. Exclusion tends to carry negative connotations. As a woman of colour, when I worked in the education system and experienced subtle everyday racism, I self-excluded, just like the girls in this study, in order to cope. If one is not included, self-exclusion might be a more viable alternative. Most of the girls I interviewed who spoke of racist bullying in the primary schools they attended excluded themselves from mainstream secondary education as a form of protection. As I demonstrated above, very few of the girls said they reported the bullying to their teachers because if they did, staff would not listen or care. They feared being punished for speaking up. They said they often preferred to stay silent. Ahmed (2012) highlights such experiences of exclusion, a sense of not belonging, silence, humiliation and fear in her study of minority ethnic experiences in institutional spaces. There is no space in which to feel included in the schools that the Gypsy and Traveller girls attended. Institutional whiteness in schools is part of the hidden curriculum and can be debilitating for minority ethnic pupils.

Arguably by remaining silent and by self-excluding, the girls and their families, like other minoritised groups, have managed centuries of persecution and survived. Gypsies and Travellers use silence and self-exclusion to their advantage, and in this way silence is not 'merely an impediment to community' (Ferguson 2003: 50). The idea that power and control only exists in the hands of governing institutions is refuted. Ladson-Billings (1996: 85) contends that 'silence can be used as a weapon…silence can be used as a means of resistance that shuts down dialogic processes'. The power of individual human agency ought not to be underestimated. Here Stuart Hall's (1991) idea about 'weak power', and Belton's (2013: 287) argument that the 'socially excluded might exclude the included' are being played out in their narratives about how they cope with discrimination faced in schools. Only four out of the thirteen girls remained in further education after primary, the others, given their negative experiences, felt compelled to reject mainstream education.

Another coping strategy suggested was to be at the youth centre with other Traveller children so that they do not have to 'blend in or change'. 'No I think most people think to blend in is good but…I prefer to be different' (Cara). Some girls favoured the idea of having a school just for Travellers because they believed they are, and want to be, 'separate from everybody else'. Even though all the girls I spoke with agreed that school presented them with a chance to socialise, five stated it was a chance to socialise with their peers from the Travelling community. They did not see the need to socialise with non-Travellers and the Gypsy girl, May, was particularly adamant that her community should live separately to other communities:

> I'd rather stay with my own kind… because like I'm with my own kind and I'm not like mixing because they don't understand me and I don't understand them, like not being disrespectful or anything. (May)

Of the thirteen girls I interviewed, eight strongly asserted their right and need to live apart from the rest of society because 'we are different…it's like all my kind here and if we are not mixing then there's no trouble' (May). Being different can lead to conflict, but being apart can accentuate opposition as is suggested in the poem entitled *Scotia Bairn* by Traveller, Jess Smith (2002):

> We are different, you and I: I am the wind in your hair; you are the voice of mistrust.
>
> I am the blue Atlantic as she thrusts her watery fingers into Scotland's west coast.
>
> You are the gate that stops me from entering the forest.
>
> I am the grouse in the purpled heather; you are the hunter who denies me my flight.
>
> I am the salmon as she leaps to her favourite spawning stream; you are the rod who would end my epic journey.

The girls preferred to self-exclude because they lacked the trust, ability or support to participate across cultures or were afraid to do so. I make several observations about why the girls express a preference for self-exclusion rather than participation. They have learnt from staff and non-Traveller pupils that they do not belong and this is part of their education within a hidden curriculum. Centuries of segregation, either enforced or through choice make it challenging for Gypsy and Traveller communities, families and their children to build bridges with the outside world. This seems entirely understandable. Even Traveller sites, often situated on the outskirts of towns and villages, ghettoise them. They are not allowed to use land which is profitable for housing, but note that sites are still near towns because their economy is interlinked with and provides services to non-Travellers. On the other hand, the majority Scottish population and their children may find it challenging to connect with Gypsies and Travellers. Fear and racism are potent partitions.

A minority of the girls in my study expressed the opinion that Travellers and non-Travellers can never live together harmoniously, which stems from a loss of hope in the school as an institution. Sandray pointed out that Travellers not only see themselves as being different but better than non-Travellers. 'You feel like you're superior to everybody around you because you've got your own language, you've got your own ways, you dress your own way, its just... It's just a good feeling'. However, she revealed her dilemma and added, 'I'm not going to lie... to me it's not [real] because there's a real world out there, you cannae just stay in your bubble'. Self-exclusion, in this context, is preferable to participation.

I asked the girls if there was ever a time they hit someone who had insulted them. Fara remarked that if someone hit her she would hit back in defence, especially if the child insulted her family—'Give them a shove off and then try and run'. Islay admitted she did once 'beat someone up' because the child insulted her family, and that was one step too far for her, but she said she was excluded as a result. According to her, the instigator went unpunished. The others commented that if they did hit a non-Traveller child they think they would be the ones in trouble with teachers. Ailsa talked about her cousin who was being hit by other children, 'so he started fighting back and he got into a lot of fights and got excluded'. Cara recounted 'they never take our side'.

> I'd tell the teacher about it, and the teacher would do nothing about it... they didn't believe us. They thought we were telling lies because there's a lot of children...we're the only Gypsies there. (Kilda)

According to the Scottish Government (as at February 2016) in 2012/2013, the rate of exclusion per 1000 pupils was 34 for White Scottish pupils, but 58 for White Gypsy/Traveller pupils. In 2014/2015, the rate of exclusion per 1000 pupils was 29 for White Scottish pupils, but an increase to 75 for White Gypsy/Traveller pupils. Given their relatively low share of the general student population, the figures suggest that White Gypsy/Traveller pupils are not only the most excluded group, but that the number of exclusions has increased. Interestingly, the number of exclusions for white pupils has fallen considerably since 2006, but the reverse is true for White Gypsy/Traveller pupils.

Although only one of the girls I interviewed reported being excluded, these figures reveal a worrying trend that merits further investigation. Gypsy and Traveller pupils may be excluded because they are more badly behaved than other pupils—'violent and disruptive' as some research suggests (Cullen et al. 1996; Lloyd and Norris 1998)—or they may be discriminated against. Lloyd and McCluskey (2008: 335) allude to the problem of 'disproportionate disciplinary exclusion [alongside] racist harassment and bullying'.

In 2013, self-identifying White Gypsy/Traveller pupils, to use the government's statistical category, formed only 0.2% of all pupils in primary and 0.07% of all pupils in secondary. These figures have minimally changed, if at all. A report on the inequalities faced by Gypsies and Travellers confirms both the girls' experiences and the statistics cited above—'participation in secondary education is extremely low, discrimination and abusive behaviour on the part of school staff and other students are frequently cited as reasons for children and young people leaving education' (Cemlyn et al. 2009: v).

The term 'White Gypsy/Traveller' is the Scottish Government's category on Census forms and statistical data from 2011 onwards.

Other government reports still refer to these communities as Gypsies and Travellers with no hue attached. Again, I note the ethnicity conundrum that Clark (2006) refers to. Gypsies and Travellers are under the category 'White' on the Census Household Questionnaire (see Appendix C), yet they are legally considered a separate ethnic group, a minority, and in addition they can be racialised by the majority White Scottish population as being Other. I am curious if the colour white implies a binary opposition to the colour black, and wondering which box a self-identifying Black Gypsy/Traveller in Scotland would tick on the Census form. As one is only allowed to 'tick one box', anyone who identifies as Scottish and Gypsy/Traveller, which is entirely conceivable, faces a personal conundrum.

There is a caveat that concerns the validity of these statistics. All of these figures have to be interpreted based on Gypsies and Travellers who choose to reveal their ethnic identity, and can only be relevant within this context. There could be many more Gypsy and Traveller pupils than the figures suggest (Lloyd and McCluskey 2008; EHRC 2015a).

The eight girls' accounts of the challenges they face in trying to socialise with non-Traveller pupils in the schools they attended, are arguably more difficult to overcome because of the perceived lack of support from agents within the school system. Research has shown that racist oppression can have a detrimental effect on the lives of children as they are constantly made to feel inferior to the rest of the population and treated like second-class citizens (Collins 1994; Lorde 2007; Sue et al. 2007; Cemlyn et al. 2009). Through systematic and everyday racial insult, assault or invalidation, unhappiness in school and being exposed to physical and psychological exclusion can be damaging to an individual's self-esteem and their academic competencies (Coll et al. 1996; Sue et al. 2007; Cemlyn et al. 2009; Heaslip 2015). It acts as a barrier to learning with joy in a safe environment. For example, a report by Cemlyn et al. (2009: vi) points out that 'there is an increasing problem of substance abuse among unemployed and disaffected young [Gypsy/Traveller] people'. A 2012 report by MECOPP, as highlighted in Chapter 2, shows concern for the physical, emotional and mental wellbeing of Gypsies and Travellers. With tears in her eyes, May, who at twelve years of age is the youngest research participant, declared she would never forget the humiliation, the name-calling and bullying.

Relations with Staff

The girls' problems with friendships, peer-group tensions, difficulties related to name-calling, bullying and racism add to the tensions with school staff, and vice versa. The same eight girls (see Table 5.1) who reported negative or mixed experiences in school gave reasons why, in their view, their relations with teachers and head teachers were poor. They describe feeling unsafe, threatened and having lack of trust. The eight girls recalled accounts of not receiving support from the school in dealing with problems in the playground, and problems with school-work. The most striking element of teacher behaviour they stressed was a lack of respect for Traveller culture, their family and the girls as individuals because of their ethnicity.

Young Gypsy and Traveller people in fact identified these problems in a report when they were asked to make a wish list that would help improve their lives in schools (Cemlyn et al. 2009). The Report of the Gypsy/Traveller Strategic Group recommended 'authorities accept Gypsies/Travellers and not to treat them differently to the rest of the community' (2006: 13). They asked that their difference be recognised, valued, respected. Aspirations towards diversity and equality, and the subsequent use of these terms in institutional documents and reports, help to tick the box of political correctness. These principles become performance indicators towards achieving excellence. Ahmed states that the term diversity in particular has replaced earlier terms such as equal opportunities and antiracism (Ahmed 2012: 52). The young Gypsy and Traveller people have asked these institutional stakeholders to learn to respect Gypsies and Travellers as different, but not to penalise them for it or force them to assimilate in ways that run contrary to their lifestyle and identity—valuing their humanity and their otherness. 'Diversity aims to recognise, respect and value people's differences to contribute and realise their full potential by promoting an inclusive culture for all' (University of Edinburgh 2016).

The challenge for teachers, schools and other institutions like the Scottish Government, and local authorities that provide key public services is to promote and practice diversity and indeed excellence, without emptying it of content and meaning (Ahmed 2004: 108).

Some of the girls were asked if their negative experiences stemmed from the teachers or pupils. Their nuanced response follows:

> *GM*: So are these experiences that you've had where they have been negative experiences are they mostly from the teachers or the kids?
> *Iona*: The kids!
> *GM*: The kids! And so the kids are worse than the teachers? Not the teachers worse than the kids?
> *Fara*: No! No! But the teachers could be a wee bit more helpful when it comes towards the kids.

I asked the focus group what they thought. Some members of the focus group believed teachers were just as bad as the pupils and some thought they were worse because 'as adults they could have done more and they should have' (Focus Group).

> Like when the weans were saying something wrong to you the teacher did'nae discipline them, it was just that's bad! They did'nae get disciplined and we felt like the bad ones so at that point I would say the teachers were worse because if the weans were checked and told it was wrong maybe they would'nae have kept doing it. (Member of Focus Group)

Another member of the group highlighted the problem of inertia and recalled that she 'had one teacher in high school who was really nice but he could have done more. I was telling them the problems and they were like not fixing it. They'd say okay we'll get on it but two years later and I'm still getting bullied so'. Yet another, however, related:

> I had one teacher who literally she had my older sister, my brother, then me and she hated us! She literally…she did'nae hide that she had a problem with Travellers and she used to say things, she used to put me to the head teacher and go she's thick, she cannae learn. (Member of Focus Group)

They do not tell stories of teachers being 'a wee bit more helpful', caring about them, rejoicing in their success, and putting in extra effort. Their teachers seemed unable or unwilling to protect the girls when bullied, or to embark on the crucial opportunity to directly address racism in the school. Rather they seemed to have stuck to their comfort zone of doing nothing or very little, than experience the discomfort of using the curriculum to challenge hegemonic practices and attitudes (Boler 1999: 176). An EHRC report into prejudiced-based bullying in Scottish schools reflects this reluctance (2015b: 40). The teachers here seemed to lack genuine investment, not only in the girls' progress, but also in addressing the ignorance of non-Traveller pupils. There is a disconnect which, as a teacher myself, I believe to be a tragic waste of both their potentials and the teachers' sense of fulfilment in inspiring the lives of all pupils. On a structural level, teachers seem to have lost the chance to disrupt 'the inertia which has characterised the system', contributing instead to the existing conditions, rather than taking action for positive change (Allan 2003: 300; hooks 1994).

Ailsa recounted how one of her teachers accused her of stealing resources, 'and she always believed that I was taking the stuff out of the class…so the kids used to go up to the teacher and tell them I was stealing too'. She revealed that they threatened to call the police and she was 'really frightened'. Police routinely presume Gypsy and Traveller communities are likely to be engaging in criminal activity, than be victims. Gypsy/Traveller Liaison Officers (GTLOs) have been known and are used by the police to act as informants.

As a result of a serious illness Kilda lost her hair. She was bullied in school aged five, because she was an ill Traveller with no hair:

> A lot of children used to say Ha-ha you've got cancer! And I used to get a lot of that so I didn't really go back because I would get made a fool of because I didn't have no hair. So I never really went to school that much. And I'd go and tell the teacher about it but nothing would ever get done about it. (Kilda)

All eight girls disclosed that they were afraid of 'detention'. If non-Traveller pupils told on them, they would get detention. Ailsa explained in detail her fear of being punished and of not being believed by her teachers, not trusting her word over that of non-Traveller pupils. This exchange suggests that non-Traveller pupils' words had more weight with teachers:

Ailsa: Yeah well they used to go up to the teacher and tell them I was stealing, like they used to say that I was taking their pencils and stuff but everyone in the class has a pencil but they'd think that my pencil was theirs because they have the exact same kind. But...

GM: Because you were a Traveller they thought you would be stealing as well?

Ailsa: Yeah and people used to come up to me and tell me if they caught me stealing they'd phone the police! But I told them I didn't do that.

GM: But you must have been really frightened? When someone says that to you?

Ailsa: Yeah I was!

GM: And did the teacher believe them?

Ailsa: I told them... well...I had two teachers in Primary 7 and the first teacher she didn't believe them that I would do it but the second teacher she did and she always believed that I was taking the stuff out of the class and...

GM: And what other...can you give me more examples, so they accused you of stealing, they didn't like you because you were a Traveller, what else...what sort of other things did they do?

Ailsa: Um...they used to take my stuff and they used to ruin them, and like they used to take my jacket and put it outside and hide the stuff in places and I couldn't find them. That's what they used to do. But they used to say I did things to them.

GM: And did this happen to the other Traveller children in the school as well?

Ailsa: Uh...yeah my cousin was in the same class as me and um... he would get into fights because of it, because they used to be racist towards him and they used to start hitting him so he started fighting back and he got into a lot of fights.

GM: Was he blamed for it because he was getting into fights?

Ailsa: Yeah he was blamed for it. For standing up for his self.

One member of the focus group revealed she did not let anyone know her ethnicity because she was 'terrified' she would be bullied.

I can remember I would'nae say I was a Traveller because I was terrified
and my mum used to always put it in my head that...don't speak about it
because you're making it worse for yourself just act normal.

However, the other members said that the non-Traveller pupils and
teaching staff always found out somehow, and that it was difficult to
hide their ethnicity especially if one lived on the local Traveller site.

May felt the teachers in the youth centre she currently attends are
better than the teachers in the many primary schools she attended in
the past, because the former 'don't treat you like you're different, they
treat you like you're normal, like a normal human being and they
don't like annoy you and *don't like choose sides*'. Like Ailsa, she believes
that teachers in her primary schools took sides and preferred the
non-Traveller pupils. Islay recalled the confusion over when and why a
pupil was in detention:

You did nothing you just sat in the room, when I wasn't doing like science or RME they brought me into the room where the high school office
was and there was like a detention room. Like [Stewart], my brother
[Stewart], when he was in detention that's where he went but you sit
there and you don't do nothing.

May said that when, in the past, she did get into trouble in schools she
was not excluded because as one headteacher believed 'it would be too
much of a holiday':

GM: Who said that?
May: My head teacher... in my other school. She said it would be too
    much of a holiday!
GM: In any of the arguments that you've been in has the other person
    you were arguing with been excluded?
May: No!
GM: Right so no one was excluded and you were told it would be too
    much of a holiday for you to have been excluded?
May: Yeah. A holiday.

According to Lloyd et al. (1999: 5), the teachers they interviewed
believe 'one of the major issues is truancy'. Yet most of the girls believe

that there is a lack of understanding if they are late or absent for a few days. According to the girls, the schools 'never bother to check' why the girls are absent—'nobody cares!' (Cara). If truancy is indeed a major problem, as suggested by staff, then why do the girls I interviewed highlight some schools not following up on absence?

Given a combination of several reasons—the stereotyped perception that Gypsy and Traveller pupils attend intermittently, or play truant; that some Gypsy and Traveller parents may not be contactable by phone; that some schools may be overworked and understaffed—it may be understandable that staff are prepared to turn a blind eye or alternatively as Cara believed 'nobody cares'. As a former head teacher, I am aware that there are strict safety guidelines in place in some local authorities. If a child is absent, and a parent has not informed the school by a reasonable time in the morning, it is the duty of the school to check that the child is safe with his/her parent or family, and to log that call. Schools should act dispassionately as an extra safeguard in the interest of the pupil, whatever their views on a pupil's previous attendance record. A pupil's safety should be priority.

There seems to be a problem with the way some teachers speak to the girls. Cara exclaimed, 'I am sick of [teachers] shouting at you every day for nothing so… I don't know because if you didn't do the work then they would all shout at you and like send you to the headmaster's office but it's their fault because they wouldn't help us'. Islay believed it is 'because…we're Travellers and they don't like us and they think we're dumb!' Cara emphasised, 'I just didn't like school! I don't like *any* school!' I sensed Cara's loss of hope in her teachers and the system. Iona and her sister Fara both chose not to attend secondary school. They have many interests that they pursue at home with a lot of enthusiasm and effort, and this is discussed in Chapter 7. Both sisters had been to 13 different primary schools and encountered many challenges and barriers to their learning.

> *GM*: So you've been to around 13 schools you said? So why girls are you both not in school today? Why are you not there?
> *Iona*: We've had enough!

Their accounts of their relationships with staff indicate that teacher attitudes, the lack of support and care, deep-seated fear and mistrust, is not only a challenge but a barrier to their continuing education. Iona's comment above resonates with Ahmed's (2012: 36) reminder about the 'weight of tiredness' that comes from being exposed to institutional spaces of whiteness. It is tiring to have to try to fit in, to have to be the one who has to bear the burden of being different, of accepting the hostility, whilst being expected to change in order to integrate better. The name-calling, bullying and racism from non-Traveller peers may, at the very least, be defined as a challenge that could be overcome, but the lack of support from teachers in helping to battle these injustices serves as a powerful barrier to learning and happiness in school. It is one of the main reasons for poor attendance and non-attendance. The level of support given seems to have a direct co-relation to a lack of achievement and attainment.

> I tried to learn but the teachers would just tell you to go and sit back down but every time you got stuck in…that's how you couldn't really… like…when you got…when you done it all she'd mark it wrong but then…it was right, well some was right and some was wrong but she'd make out…then I'd have to do it all again the same page! But like 3 times! They don't help! (May)

Lloyd et al. (1999: 1) interviewed teachers, Gypsy and Traveller parents and pupils in order to ascertain 'how schools in Scotland perceive and respond to the culture and behaviour of Traveller children, in respect of behaviour, exclusion and difference'. Their findings mostly highlighted teachers' views of the difficulties and problems posed by Gypsy and Traveller pupils. Where the teachers identified 'lack of cooperation in class, e.g. not following instructions and learning difficulties', the girls I interviewed talked about lack of support. Where the teachers mention difficulties in 'style of addressing adults and sense of justice' or 'local poverty and delinquent subcultures', the girls reported a lack of care and respect (Lloyd et al. 1999: 5).

Out of a list of issues, the teachers in this study share only two concerns in common with what the girls have reported—'problems with friendships / peer group relationships [and] name-calling / bullying of Traveller pupils and fighting' (Lloyd et al. 1999: 5). The teachers were concerned by Gypsy and Traveller pupils' 'lack of cooperation in class, late coming and absence' (Lloyd et al. 1999: 5). They described problems to do with interrupted learning in addition to specific learning difficulties. Lloyd et al. (1999:5) found that teachers reported several other 'difficulties' with Gypsy and Traveller pupils—difference in style when addressing adults, 'difficulties associated with transition to secondary school, difficulties deriving from travelling life and being on a site, local poverty and delinquent subcultures'.

The problems and difficulties cited above reveal how much Gypsies and Travellers are perceived as a problem by staff, how challenging they feel these pupils are to manage, and the conflict between teachers and pupils' perceptions. Lloyd et al. (1999: 14) contend that the teacher's responses throw into question the ability of schools to respond to these challenges appropriately:

By seeing these issues in individual terms, by not recognising difference, schools may continue merely to focus on behaviour, rather than explore the institutional response of the education system to a marginalised community.

In a study of British Muslim girls and the dynamism of their family values, Basit (1997: 436) also found that:

Teachers are constantly struggling to make sense of the social world of their ethnic minority pupils and are effective when they understand the dynamics of the ethnic minorities' religions and cultures and teach within that framework without exerting pressure...to conform to the majority norm.

Ahmed's (2012: 35) work on diversity in institutions echoes this point—'certain communities' are not reached by institutions and, in this case, the institution of school and the education system. Their statements reveal that the schools they attended do not or are unable to include Gypsy and Traveller communities, and the institutions are perceived as excluding them. The problem manifests itself in several ways. First, many existing studies as discussed in Chapters 2 and 3 show that, teachers and schools view Gypsy and Traveller families and their children as a problem, because the families resist being included within existing structures of the school and education system. Second, the teachers and schools do not view the institution as having a problem or being a problem. Third, the families and their children view the system as a problem because teachers and schools are unable and / or unwilling to include them. Gypsies and Travellers and their children experience the institution as it is. The teachers in these schools are part of the institution, and arguably institutionalised.

Ahmed (2012) explains this disconnect and the inability of institutions like schools and the people who work within it to 'see' and 'listen' to what is actually happening. Citing Sullivan (2006: 1), Ahmed (2012: 35) argues that as an institution of whiteness, school culture is 'a habit insofar as it tends to go unnoticed', the culture of whiteness is 'invisible' to those who are within it. 'When things become institutional they recede… to become routine or ordinary…becomes part of the background for those who are part of the institution' (Ahmed 2012: 21). Teachers who are part of this world become involved with routines and habits in such a way that 'they recede from consciousness' (Ahmed 2012: 21). As Back (2007: 5) asserts in his monograph *The Art of Listening*, 'the capacity to hear [and to see] becomes damaged and is in need of repair'.

It is only those who are excluded or who cannot fit in or are perceived as being part of that problematic 'certain community' that can see what is going on. Hence the importance of teacher training that reveals these habits, deals openly with issues of diversity not just as a paper exercise, but as a genuine attempt to change and embrace new perceptions; learning different ways of seeing and doing. The focus group emphasised the need for better teacher training and for teachers to be 'more culturally sensitive'. One member suggested 'that it becomes mandatory in all primary and high schools that there's awareness raising about Gypsy/Traveller culture and its part of your social awareness…it becomes a module within the curriculum'.

Rona and Skye alleged the curriculum offered at local authority mobile or portacabin schools was deliberately made simple for Traveller children 'as if they were too thick to understand', and they considered behaviour in these schools poor. 'We've got like a portacabin and a teacher used to come down and go in twice a week for the kids from the site' (Rona). 'And there was like limits…there was like limits! Because like the…in normal school it's like um…you can…they'll help you do whatever you want, whatever you want to achieve (Skye)'. In one such portacabin school I was at, teachers used magazines like *Heat* and *Take A Break* to teach Literacy because the girls were interested in the material. Other teachers I had spoken to highlighted this strategy.

As an experienced teacher aware of the breadth of the Scottish curriculum and quality of resources offered in many Scottish mainstream schools, I was disappointed with the quality of the material on offer to these Traveller girls. Whilst I understood the challenges faced by the teachers in their attempt to encourage pupil interest and attendance, I wondered if the use of high quality material for Literacy, particularly targeted at reluctant readers, for example, might have been more appropriate from an educational perspective. There are websites about Gypsy/Roma/Traveller history and culture, which could be used as materials for discussion and writing. For the teachers, maintaining attendance was a key priority, quality of provision perhaps deemed secondary under the circumstances. However, the lack of appropriate resources and their teacher's priorities seems to reinforce again their lack of access to a menu of opportunities that other pupils in mainstream education would have access to.

One member of the focus group complained that when she decided to go to secondary school she was placed in a classroom on her own:

> All they were doing was giving me a chess thing and saying on you go and learn how to play chess, here's some paper why don't you colour paper in. In the first year I was in the Standard Grades for a good few of my classes, so in second year I still knew stuff so I could have went back in the classes, but they just left me with a chess table sitting playing chess.

One mobile teaching unit (portacabin) on a Traveller's site I visited, reflected the problem underscored by Rona and Skye about the levelling down of standards and expectations for Gypsy/Traveller pupils. The health visitor in charge reported there were two main activities on offer—art and cooking. There was not always a teacher on the site. Apart from a few computers, the 'school' was poorly resourced compared to my experience of mainstream classrooms. The quality of literacy materials was poor, comprising mainly magazines and an odd collection of second-hand books (see Figures 5.1, 5.2, and 5.3).

Kilda described how she felt about the work she did in the brief time she was in primary school:

Fig. 5.1 Shelf of resources at mobile learning centre Traveller site

Fig. 5.2 Ovens, stoves and a fridge for cookery classes at mobile learning centre Traveller site and some artwork on display

Fig. 5.3 Example of artwork done by a Gypsy/Traveller pupil at mobile learning centre Traveller site

I'd always be like…the last one [worst in the class], because they would give me easier homework, like easier stuff to do than the rest of the children. But me myself I found it unfair but I couldn't do it, I found it unfair because they were giving me easy stuff and the rest of the children was getting all theirs and they were just moving up.

Kilda perceived what her teachers might have considered necessary support by giving 'easy stuff', as 'unfair'. Her comment is complex and seemingly contradictory. She recognised that she was worst in the class ('the last one'), thought other pupils were getting work that was appropriate to their age and stage, but that she was getting 'easy stuff'. Yet, she admitted she could not have done the work given to other pupils, but still perceived it as not fair because they were progressing further and faster. As a teacher and headteacher, I have witnessed many instances of staff coping with pupils' needs with 'easy stuff'. Overworked and under pressure, with little extra support in class due to limited budgets in the education system, teachers might be forgiven for employing such strategies, but the long term impact on a child's self-esteem and motivation cannot be ignored. What could be lacking is supportive communication with pupils—words of encouragement, nurturing of their self-esteem. I think that what Kilda perceived as 'unfair' might be more to do with a sense of feeling less worthy, less clever, less included. This contrasts with hooks (1994) description of how some of her teachers were 'on a mission' to uplift her sense of being, and I suggest that this is what is missing in Kilda's educational experience. The perceived lack of support is not uplifting but lowers her spirit. In the following extended exchange Kilda explains why she might be deemed 'not good enough':

Kilda: Because I couldn't read and write.

GM: Okay and you hadn't learnt up to that point when you were ill, can you read and write now?

Kilda: Yeah I can a little bit, it's not as good but…

GM: You're getting there.

Kilda: I can spell some words, I can't spell them but if you put them in front of my face I could read them. It would take me a bit of time to do it but I still do it.

GM: But fair enough you do it yeah and the maths as well so if you went to a shop are you able to do shopping, and spend money, and buy things with money and not get cheated?

Kilda: Yeah I can do all that yeah.

GM: You can do all of that so actually you're quite good!

Kilda: I've got some experience. It's like they say if you don't learn yourself…if you can't get help learn yourself.

GM: Yeah exactly! So you're learning it yourself, so you think...do you think the teachers in school could have helped you more, Kilda?
Kilda: Yeah they could have, yeah.
GM: Why do you think they didn't help you as much as they could?
Kilda: Well because I'm a Traveller, to be honest. The teacher would do nothing to help!

I found it difficult to listen to her account and sensed her lack of self-esteem, her struggle to define why she was not good enough and why she was. 'To be honest I feel proud of myself... We don't put ourselves down for anybody' (Kilda). In Chapter 7, I discuss this theme in connection with her understanding of what it means to be successful.

As noted above, most of the girls believe that teachers in mainstream primary or secondary schools do not support them or treat them differently because they are Gypsies and Travellers. The girls think that their ethnicity sets them apart from other students, but they do not use the term racist or racial discrimination to describe their teachers' attitudes and behaviour towards them. The focus group confirmed that teachers could be prejudiced towards Gypsy and Traveller pupils, as is demonstrated in this example they cited about 'a teacher in a proper school'. Jill is their peer leader and is not a Gypsy and Traveller:

> *F1*: We were there as Article 12, to do a workshop for all these students or children in the school and this woman was taking us to the class, so we were all walking alongside Jill and she was speaking away to Jill and she went um...what was it she said?
> *F3*: "Are they here to learn or something?" Are they here to learn!
> *F2*: Something along the lines —
> *F3*: "Can they even read?" [The teacher asked Jill]
> *Jill*: Can they read? Are they here to do their...to learn and...you know the thing that was really insulting about it is that all the girls were in earshot of this question! It was extremely patronising and she could have quite easily have asked why are you here, what are you doing? And was kind of completely shocked when I said to her no they're doing...they're delivering this workshop.

F4: That was in the actual school and I think we learnt from those workshops the teachers perhaps needed a bit more awareness raising than the pupils!

Based on the evidence, it is fair to conclude that most of the girls I interviewed experienced racist bullying from their non-Traveller peers, alongside forms of 'silent racism' within the formal school structure and from staff in particular. The teachers may be 'well-meaning White people' who consider themselves non-racist (Trepagnier 2006). However, there is much evidence that White teachers are not as racially literate as they should be (Sleeter 2001; Solorzano and Yosso 2001; Ladson-Billings 2009). Their silence and passivity in the face of racist bullying experienced by Gypsy and Traveller girls, has deterred the girls from attending school, affected their achievement and helped to perpetuate harmful divisions. Deflection, denial and ignorance preserve everyday and institutional racism, which remains invisible especially to those who benefit from it (Essed 1991; Trepagnier 2006; Picower 2009).

Recalling Matsuda's advice to look for other forms of discrimination that accompany the one obvious bias by 'asking the other question', I was inclined to ask whether alongside the racism, there was indeed some elements of gender bias (1991, cited in Crenshaw 1991: 1245). I reiterate that not all the girls had negative experiences in school, and it is useful to consider the ingredients that help to create positive experiences as explained above. However, what was not as obvious or expected at first was the small possibility that the girls experience what Farris and de Jong refer to as 'gendered disadvantages' (2014: 1505).

It could be argued that differences in treatment based on gender bias is perhaps not an issue because the girls do not use terms like sexist or gender discrimination to describe the lack of support in school. Furthermore, teachers could treat Gypsy and Traveller boys in exactly the same way as Gypsy and Traveller girls. Ailsa claimed that her other Traveller friends and her own brother were treated poorly by staff and non-Traveller pupils. Therefore, I could infer that Gypsy and Traveller boys might have similar experiences as described by the girls.

Incidentally, Rona and Skye do use the terms racist and sexist to describe the different attitudes and expectations within their culture, and this is discussed in the next chapter. Skye said, 'I am not big, fat or *just* Gypsy'. Their comments reflect my argument that most of the girls I interviewed may not be as readily aware of gender inequalities as they are of racial discrimination. Based on their community's experiences with the majority Scottish population, the girls are perhaps more adept at identifying race bias.

However, like racism, sexism can be overt or 'subtle' (Benokraitis 1997). Nieto-Gomez (1997: 97) provides a useful definition:

> As being part of the capitalist ideology which advocates male suprema-cist values. These values define the nature of women and men in respect to being superior or inferior. Men are defined as "naturally" stronger, more logical, and able to economically provide for others. Women are defined as "naturally" dependant, childlike, and therefore always in need of authority. Her primary functions are to secure others as a wife and a mother since her primary abilities are to conceive, procreate and nurture.

Sexism involves institutionalised male privilege and domination over women. This patriarchy, however, can equally be practised and perpet-uated by women. Within the field of feminism, itself a contested con-cept, the relationship between men and women, and amongst women, is understood and defined in different ways; made more complex when issues of race, class, age and other inequalities intersect. However, hooks (2015: 5) maintains that 'sexism has not meant an absolute lack of choices' and that 'many women in society do have choices (as inade-quate as they are)'. She contends that not all women view gender dis-crimination as a form of oppression (hooks 2015: 5).

As the next chapter reveals, deeply embedded traditional expectations within their own families on performing gender specific roles, implies that they may be culturally conditioned not to wholly recognise gen-der inequalities. 'Through the socialisation process children are taught to act within the institutions of their parents' (Trepagnier 2006: 65). However, this does not mean that gendered discrimination is not a problem. What is more, most of the girls are adolescents, still in their formative years; arguably too young to specifically brand infringes on their freedom and potential as women and human beings. Just as they seem afraid to question or oppose their teachers in school, they might be equally unsure about criticising their cultural traditions at home. Like other young people, their youth puts them at a disadvantage and in a position of less power compared to the powers within the structural institution of school and hegemonic institution of family and culture (Collins 2000).

Returning to Matsuda's advice, there are indeed several reasons why the girls might be gender disadvantaged and experience 'subtle sexism'. First, there is limited but growing evidence that teachers can and do make decisions based on their own individual gendered assumptions, especially towards girls who are visibly from minority ethnic backgrounds or racialised as Other. Farris and de Jong (2014: 1511), for example, highlight problems for second-generation immigrant girls in the UK and Europe, who experience 'inadequate educational environments…[that serve to] reinforce initial gaps and creating what some authors have called segregation'. The mobile learning units or portacabins, situated on council run Traveller sites on the periphery of towns and cities, arguably offer inferior education and reinforce the poverty that often exists in these 'educational ghettos' (Maurin 2004 cited in Farris and de Jong 2014: 7). Basit (1997: 426) highlights other studies that attest to this gendering. 'Girls of Asian and Afro-Caribbean origin feel that less is expected of them because of their race… [and] research indicates that some teachers feel frustrated at having to teach…children who have alien ways' (Wright 1986; Basit 1997: 426).

Farris and de Jong (2014: 1511) refer to this phenomenon as 'teachers "reinforcing" paths'. It is interesting that none of the girls I interviewed aspired to professional employment. Only two girls mentioned going to university. Bancroft et al. (1996) found that university or college attendance was very uncommon. Most either recognised that they had to be married and have children, or possibly combine that with a vocational career in hairdressing, beauty therapy or in two specific cases, a career in music and art, all of which may be considered soft choices (Farris and de Jong 2014). This theme is discussed further in Chapter 7 on their future aspirations.

Secondly, earlier in this study I quoted stakeholders who believed all Gypsy and Travellers girls are destined to be married and have children from a young age. According to those stakeholders, the girls are not interested in school and certainly not interested in making the transition from school to work; the girls apparently have no ambitions or aspirations beyond caring for their husbands and children. One teacher I interviewed admitted she deliberately did not spend too much time producing resources for the girls, because they were not likely to attend if required to stay at home that day to look after siblings or cook (Anon. Teacher 1 2014, Personal communication). As mentioned earlier, in one portacabin I visited a teacher who used popular women's magazines to teach the girls to read because it is what she believed captured their interest. There is some evidence from research reviewed in this study that suggests teachers may hold stereotyped ideas on gender and do not hold high expectations for the Gypsy and Traveller girls in their classrooms.

As highlighted in the educational literature in Chapter 3, Lloyd (2005) discusses the experiences of Gypsy and Traveller girls within the context of emotional and behavioural disorder (EBD), stating that Scottish Gypsy Traveller girls in particular who got into trouble in school, negotiated and resisted labels of ethnicity and gender (2005: 129). She argues there are 'pressures on Gypsy and Traveller girls to defeat the prejudiced and stereotyped expectations of some teachers' (2005: 133). Teachers she interviewed in the study said they valued those [girls] who attempted to minimise difference (2005: 129). Note the gendered nuances and clichéd implication that Gypsies are dirty, in the statement uttered by one teacher who said she appreciated it when:

> They [Gypsy and Traveller girls] were very acceptable, they were nicely dressed, they turned up nice, they didn't make themselves different in any way… they were actually very clean and tidy… they didn't make themselves out to be Tinker girls… their hair was nice and what not. (Lloyd et al. 1999: 5)

One member of the focus group stated that 'I think it's a lot easier for lassies at school than what it is for boys, because they are more likely to behave, follow rules and refrain from "talking back" or challenge authority' (Member of Focus Group). The other girls agreed.

Yet when Gypsy and Traveller girls 'acted up' they were defined as deviant and were subject to disciplinary exclusion. Lloyd (2005: 126), problematising the label 'EBD girls', proposes that the voices of so-called 'problem' girls need to be heard, and that teachers need to 'recognise the individual complexity of their lives'. Most of the girls I interviewed feared retaliating against the bullying in the playground. One was excluded for hitting a child who insulted her family. The girls reported being sent to detention for daring to talk back to their teachers. The fear and silencing further reinforces socialised norms of acceptable ways to behave as women; that as girls they ought to remain hidden, bear whatever problems come their way or self-exclude, as many have done. To speak up or fight back could be perceived as bad behaviour and insubordination. The next chapter discusses how even within their own cultures, some of the girls play silent roles and there are limits to their ability to voice their concerns and aspirations.

Moreover, as Farris and de Jong (2014: 1512) point out, 'when the terms of comparison become the female school population in general, the situation immediately appears less positive'. Scottish Government statistics (as at February 2016), although limited, do paint a picture of gender disadvantage. Due to the small number of leavers who are White Gypsy/Traveller girls, statisticians have created an average of attainment for 2011/2012, 2012/2013 and 2013/2014 leavers. According to the attainment data based on gender and ethnicity, White Gypsy/Traveller girls do not fare as well as White Scottish girls. There were on average 24,938 female leavers, but only 14 of those were White Gypsy/Traveller girls. Only 44% achieved one or more awards at Standard Grade Credit, Intermediate 2, or National 5, compared with 85% White Scottish girls. The statistics reveal a trend of non-attendance and/or low performance within the gender. The girls seem under-represented in secondary school and potentially in paths leading to higher education, and they have higher dropout rates compared to White Scottish girls. This could be entirely due to family and cultural factors, or there may be other factors at play.

Within the school structure, the evidence from the girls' perceptions that learning is levelled down, that teachers are 'unfair', that the girls are 'shouted at' or put in detention for no justified reason, that their word does not hold as much weight as that of their non-Traveller peers, together with some of the gendered language used by teachers to describe Gypsy/Traveller girls in Lloyd's et al. (1999) and Lloyd's (2005) studies, all suggest that the girls from these communities suffer some gender discrimination.

In Chapter 4, I argued that one of the merits of using an intersectional framework is that it can uncover 'within group diversity'. It would be interesting to establish with greater certainty, as in Farris and de Jong's (2014) study with second-generation immigrant girls in Europe, and as the statistics above suggest, if Gypsy and Traveller girls are disadvantaged or discriminated against in school because of their gender, and not only because of their race. According to the Census in 2011 (The Scottish Government 2015), Gypsies and Travellers in Scotland were on average younger compared to the population as a whole. Yet 50% aged 16 and over had no qualifications. The statistics do not reveal how many are Gypsy/Traveller women. Other pertinent questions that in my view should be explored in greater depth include—are they also 'disproportionally unemployed; [do they] work in precarious jobs; experience longer waiting times before obtaining their first job; are overqualified for their jobs; or are forced to become self-employed due to lack of access to the mainstream labour market?' (Farris and de Jong 2014: 1515).

Towards the end of each interview I asked each girl what kind of school they would wish for if they had a magic wand. Some girls struggled to answer the question. Ailsa said she wanted to be treated like everyone else so that she could have a good education. Fara's response in particular was surprising, as this extended exchange reveals:

> *GM*: If you had a magic wand and you could create a school that was not like all these other places that you've been to would you use your magic wand to create that school and would you go to it?
> *Fara*: No.

GM: Why not Fara?

Fara: Because it would'nae be normal because like see from the schools you get bullied you learn from it because...

GM: Tough lessons to learn though...

Fara: Aye they are. But still you learn because if you go to one school and everybody's nice to you you're like...if you go to another school you think everybody's going to be nice to you so you try and make pals with as many folk as you can and if they all dinnae want to be pals with you... you know who the bullies is.

GM: So actually what you're wanting is to go to a normal school where if there is a problem you get support? So that's better than a perfect school where there are no problems?

Fara: Aye! Aye! That's what I would prefer like.

Like many of the girls I interviewed, Fara's response above is an example of their mature outlook, their ability to reason and articulate their thoughts, their consideration for others demonstrated throughout the interviews. Her response is particularly powerful in that her experiences and understandings make her unable to countenance even dreaming of such a 'harmonious' future. Her prior experiences at school force her to be pragmatic. Fara is willing to accept that there will be challenges but she just wants her teachers to do their job—respect and support her, educate her to her full potential, appreciate her Traveller identity.

Overall, I was struck by their knowledge and attitudes about education and learning, and how that contrasted with the dominant discourses about education in Scotland. In my discussion with the girls from Article 12 similar observations about staff in schools were made. None of them reported that in the schools they attended staff were supportive:

F1: I think the teachers could have done more, I really do think – as adults they could have done more. I think they should.

F3: I think there should be one of the meetings with the parents, like I think maybe the teachers taking them into discuss like their learning because when I was at school they never like...I think there should be like leaflets, or even like wee packages to take away like when... if you're going out in the trailer, or like a teacher there to help you because I would'nae mind going to class to be with somebody that would be there for me, to help me and understand the way.

F2: I would say the teachers were worse [than non-Traveller pupils] because if the weans were checked and told it was wrong maybe they would'nae have kept doing it. I was telling them the problems and they were like not fixing it. They'd say okay we'll get on it but 2 years later and I'm still getting bullied.

I was reminded of the paper by Lloyd et al. (1999) in which teachers cited a list of nine major issues they faced when teaching Gypsy/Traveller pupils and, most poignantly, the last in the list refers to the pupils as being part of 'delinquent subcultures'. Such harmful language and attitudes reinforce arguments that dominant systems of knowledge ought to be deconstructed and decolonised; and that alternative and indigenous systems of knowledge should be better recognised as equally valid (Spivak 1995; Freire 1998; Pring 2004; Mirza 2008, 2009, 2013, 2015; Mirza et al. 2010; Bilge 2014). The girls' understanding of education and learning is linked to their understanding of the kind of culture and society in which they live. In the next chapter on family expectations, the girls reveal that their love and respect for family is fundamental to their learning. The strong connection to their community echoes hooks (1994) idea that education ought to shift from a 'thing oriented society' to a 'people oriented society', arguing that the values of love, generosity, and care are so fundamental to learning and teaching.

The main aim of this research was to highlight how Gypsy and Traveller girls frame their educational experiences in Scottish schools. Their perceptions of their peers and teachers are reflected in the scholarly works and government reports highlighted in the literature review. The racial discrimination experienced by most of the girls in school was not surprising. However, the depth of the emotional and mental injury felt by the girls who reported such abuse was shocking to listen to and absorb, particularly because as many of these girls are still in their formative years—children under the age of 16. The girls' narratives reflect nearly all the feelings of vulnerability that Heaslip (2015: 3–4) highlights in her study—that of being an outsider, how they are perceived, feeling discriminated against and threatened by their peers and staff. One would expect the girls to feel powerless, and perhaps at times they do. Yet they resist the pressure to conform to live a particular way of life. I did not sense that the girls felt overcome; or any 'ambiguities' over their identity as is suggested in Heaslip's work on the experiences of vulnerability from a Gypsy and Traveller perspective. Instead, the girls (and their parents) were willing to quietly oppose the system by refusing to attend school, through self-exclusion. In the next chapter, vulnerabilities within the family and community, as disclosed by Heaslip's participants (2015: 3–4), are discussed and reflect a different perspective.

One could argue that we all face injustices in school, that the girls exhibit too much sensitivity, lack perseverance and should have tried harder to overcome the discriminations they faced. Many others have and continue to do so. In an interview with one teacher she remarked, 'yes they have difficulties, but they do not have commitment to their education' (Anon. Teacher 6 2014, Personal communication). However, such arguments distract from what is fundamentally reasonable and human. No child should experience racial discrimination in school. The situation the girls describe is unacceptable and must not to be tolerated in Scottish society. 'In the climate of a history of rejection it is not surprising that many children from Gypsy, Roma and Traveller families do not achieve in school' (Knowles and Lander 2011: 106). Lloyd and McCluskey (2008: 336) recommend a 'need for a more multi-layered understanding that locates this educational failure within social and economic context of Gypsy and Traveller lives and in institutional racism of schooling'. Added to that is a possibility that the girls also experience gender disadvantage within the system, even though they do not directly label their experiences in school as sexist.

The resulting tensions and contradictions within the data, the girls' voices and the current literature are discussed below. hooks (1994: 244) argues that she is 'turned on by subjectivity that is formed in the embrace of all the quirky conflicting dimensions of our reality'. The findings in this study are just that—subjective, quirky, conflicting—and nevertheless deeply relevant.

Silences, Tensions and Contradictions

There were several matters that were not brought up in discussion and left unsaid. There were no references to sexuality or sexual harassment. There were no discussions about sexual identity. Most of the girls did not talk about their socio-economic circumstances, except Sandray, Vaila, Fara and her sister Iona. Table 5.3 shows the type of home each participant lived in and their family circumstance.

Sandray, Vaila, Fara, and Iona either lived in a house or in trailers on privately owned land (see dark shaded cells in Table 5.3). Their families seemed visibly well off. May said she lived in a 'bungalow in the middle of no where'. The two sisters, Kilda and Shona, whom I visited in their sparsely refurbished trailers shared with five other siblings and their parents, and Ailsa whom I was told lived in emergency housing with her mother and three siblings (see light shaded cell in Table 5.3) clearly faced challenging living conditions. Apart from these girls, it was diffi-cult to ascertain if the other five girls were living in relative comfort or

Table 5.3 Family circumstances and type of housing

Name	Age	Family life	Type of home
May	12	M/F/Ext	'Bungalow'
Cara	12	M/Ext	LA Traveller site
Ailsa	13	M	Council flat (emergency housing)
Islay	13	M/F	LA Traveller site
Dana	13	M/Ext	LA Traveller site
Fara	13	M/F	Private site/rent house (Winter)
Skye	15	M/F/Ext	LA Traveller site
Vaila	15	M/F/Ext	Private site
Shona	16	M/F	LA Traveller site
Iona	16	M/F	Private site/rent house (Winter)
Kilda	18	M/F	LA Traveller site
Rona	19	M/F/Ext	LA Traveller site
Sandray	22	M/F[a]	House

[a]Mixed ethnicity—Gypsy and non-Traveller parents
M—Mother; F—Father; Ext—Extended family; LA—Local authority

poverty. As Table 5.3 demonstrates, there is no consistent direct correlation between a participant's family composition, the type of home they live in and their socio-economic circumstance. Neither could I assume that those living on a Local Authority Traveller site were all poor.

Most of the girls were silent on this issue. To break this silence and ask would have been an intrusion and potentially embarrassing for the girls. Therefore, the potential intersecting inequalities that arose as a result of poverty and class, and the impact of such difficulties on their education are not explored in this study.

The girls I interviewed did not use the term 'interrupted learning' and never mention that their travelling lifestyle impacts on their schoolwork and experiences. However, the focus group did highlight it as being an issue. Yet much has been written about this phenomenon, and the educational experiences of Gypsy and Traveller pupils tend to be associated with the consequences of interrupted learning (Jordan 2000b; Jordan and Padfield 2003a, b; Padfield 2008). Some research highlights that teachers in schools view Gypsy and Traveller pupils as problematic because their travelling lifestyle interrupts their studies and results in other associated difficulties in school (Lloyd 2005).

The girls do not report having to use computers or information technology to help with learning outside school. From my observation and based on their conversations with me, many of the girls come from families that are not well off. In the homes that I visited, few had computers. In fact, only two out of the thirteen girls said they owned a computer but even then, they explained parents strictly monitored access. The focus group noted this was not unusual or restricted to Gypsy and Traveller communities. 'It's the same as everybody though, not every single person has got a computer, a laptop—It's just normal society, and not everybody has got it' (Focus Group).

Lloyd and McCluskey (2008: 339) claim that 'there has been widespread staff development to promote understanding and stronger policies of discrimination and diversity in schools'. They do acknowledge that 'many local authority staff may not still realise that this applies to Gypsy/Travellers' (2008: 339). However, it would have been useful had they listed some evidence for these claims. On the contrary, according to an evidence-based report *Minority Ethnic Pupils' Experiences of*

School in Scotland (MEPESS) (Arshad et al. 2005) teachers still receive little to no training on how to handle diversity and discrimination. They are still ineffective in general with tacking anti-racism and recognising difference (Arshad et al. 2005). The issue is compounded in the case of Gypsy/Traveller pupils. Cemlyn et al. (2009) reveal that teachers lack confidence to identify and handle racist bullying in schools, as supported in a report by the EHRC (2015b: 4–5). The report found that teachers 'may not view such duties as relevant to their role' (2015b: 40). This attitude reveals a lack of recognition by these teachers of the 'agency', 'mobility' and 'privilege' that has been afforded them by deeply embedded structural systems that favour their 'whiteness' and indeed students who are considered white (Ahmed 2004: 11). The attitude and behaviour of teachers and schools maintain and reinforce the existing power of whiteness and hegemony in society; it is naturalised.

Clark (2006) reminds us of the 'ethnicity conundrum', in which the majority of Scottish population do not view Gypsies and Travellers as a separate ethnic group, yet there is much evidence that they have been racialised as deviant Other. Clark was instrumental in winning the court case which recognised Gypsies and Travellers as an ethnic group. Class, ethnicity and race are curiously intertwined in perceptions of Gypsies and Travellers. Lloyd and McCluskey (2008: 339–340) recognise the 'denial of difference; denial of the complexity of identity or that 'difference is construed as deviance'. These contradictions might help to explain why staff were unable and unwilling to recognise racist name-calling and bullying when reported by the girls. Nevertheless, such denial and ignorance are harmful to Gypsy/Traveller pupils, and constitute negative learning experiences for non-Traveller pupils who will continue to perpetuate such hate (Mandela 2004). All pupils are in fact being let down, but in different ways. By denying and not defending the validity of Gypsy/Traveller cultures, staff 'silence the issue for schools' (Lloyd and McCluskey 2008: 341). As their research suggests, by perpetuating a deficit model of practice rather than employing a social model to understand problems faced by Gypsy/Traveller pupils, the teachers become part of the problem, and not the solution. Equally, out of fear, most of the girls I interviewed met the problems they faced with silence, and so the difficulties are preserved and endured. Gypsy and Traveller pupils continue to be part of the 'educationally under-served population' (Hancock 2007: 75) and there still remains a social moat between them and their non-Traveller peers.

It would appear from my data, racism and bullying by peers, lack of respect, support, and understanding from school staff, alongside fear and lack of trust, account for reasons why most cite negative experiences at school and are deterred from attending mainstream educational set-tings. These experiences have had an enduring impact on most of the girls; education spaces are viewed as unsafe and risky. What was some-what unexpected were the translucent instances of gender discrimina-tion from school staff who are primarily women, reinforcing the idea that patriarchal systems can be perpetuated by men, but also women who consciously or dysconsciously accept and propagate the status quo. All classrooms have children with different needs and who come from a variety of backgrounds, where external socio-economic influences impact on their achievement in school. Knowles and Lander (2011: xii, 12) reason that the onus lies on teachers to recognise this and act fairly and respectfully with all children and their families.

It was especially compelling to discover the ways in which most of the girls coped with these negatives experiences. By staying hidden, invisible and silent, or through self-exclusion from mainstream educa-tion, the girls and their families assumed a measure of control; reflect-ing Hall's (1991) argument that this sort of behavior reflects a form of 'weak power'. Self-exclusion through non-attendance or intermittent attendance is disapproved of within mainstream education, but is in many cases a chosen course of action by the Gypsy/Traveller girls I met.

Following centuries of subordination and exclusion, even the mod-ern-day education system on its 'journey to excellence' can still per-petuate socially unjust community norms that embed and invisibilise racist and sexist beliefs and practices. Collins (2000: 277) maintains that 'structural forms of injustice that permeate the entire society yield only grudgingly to change'. Reducing or eliminating such inequalities are difficult to achieve. 'Symbolic and discursive changes' do not auto-matically lead to 'further practical changes', or indeed as Breitenbach (2006: 20) argues 'might end up being a substitute for them'. There has clearly been a change in the profile of equality issues in Scotland since devolution; however, their accounts demonstrate that changes in policy and practice have not been sufficient in addressing their needs in the schools they attended.

The girls' accounts serve to disrupt the myth or anecdote that *all* Gypsy/Traveller girls do not attend school beyond age twelve (Anon. Academic 1 2013, Personal communication). It is unsurprising that their educational experiences vary and are not homogenous. There are many shared experiences, but there is no single narrative. In fact, the girls revealed several reasons why there were stories of success in attainment and achievement and enjoyment in school. Positive experiences with Traveller and non-Traveller peers, school staff who demonstrate support and fair expectations without bias, and consistent attendance in school with little or no interruption, proved collectively instrumental in generating such optimism about their school experiences.

Most of the girls prefer flexible educational provision that incorporates and respects Traveller lifestyle, culture, values and ways of thinking—a more holistic process which incorporates family and community. All the girls place great value on the learning experienced at home and some reject the idea that only learning within formal school settings is valuable. There are also significant silences, contradictions and tensions that emerged in the findings.

It was not possible to identify firm evidence of inequalities brought about by poverty or class, as the girls did not reveal their socio-economic standard of living, and neither did I feel comfortable breaching their privacy. However, as with other adolescents, it was no surprise that their limited ability to challenge adult systems of power, especially in the face of discrimination, exposed their vulnerable position as young people. The evidence suggests that those who try, risk being labelled emotionally difficult or deviant by staff within the system.

References

Ahmed, S. (2004) Declarations of whiteness: The non-performativity of anti-racism. *Borderlands E-journal*, 3(2). Available at: http://borderlands. net.au/vol3no2_2004/ahmed_declarations.htm. Accessed 7 April 2016.

Ahmed, S. (2012) *On being included: Racism and diversity in institutional life*. Durham, NC: Duke University Press.

Allan, J. (2003) Daring to think otherwise? Educational policymaking in the Scottish Parliament. *Journal of Education Policy*, 18(3), pp. 289–301.

Anon. Academic 1. (2013) Personal communication. Conversation and notes, 18 April.

Anon. Quality Improvement Officer Inclusion. (2014) Personal communication. Telephone interview, 16 September.

Anon. Teacher 1. (2014) Personal communication. Interview and notes, 30 April.

Anon. Teacher 6. (2014) Personal communication. Interview and notes, 5 December.

Arshad, R., Almeida Diniz, F., Kelly, E., O'Hara, P., Sharp, S., and Syed, R. (2005) *Minority Ethnic Pupils' Experiences of School in Scotland (MEPESS)*. Edinburgh: Scottish Executive.

Back, L. (2007) *The art of listening*. New York: Berg Publishers.

Bancroft, A., Lloyd, M., and Morran, R. (1996) *The right to roam: Travellers in Scotland 1995/96*. Dunfermline: Save the Children in Scotland.

Bartlett, S., and Burton, D. (2007) *Introduction to education studies*, 2nd ed. London: Sage.

Basit, T. N. (1997) 'I want more freedom, but not too much': British Muslim girls and the dynamism of family values. *Gender and Education*, 9(4), pp. 425–440.

Belton, B. A. (2013) 'Weak power': Community and identity. *Ethnic and Racial Studies*, 36(2), pp. 282–297.

Benokraitis, N. V. E. (1997) *Subtle sexism: Current practice and prospects for change*. Thousand Oaks: Sage.

Bhopal, K. (2018) *White privilege: The myth of a post-racial society*. Bristol: Policy Press.

Bilge, S. (2014) Whitening intersectionality. *Racism and Sociology*, 5, p. 175.

Boler, M. (1999) *Feeling power: Emotions and education*. London: Psychology Press.

Breitenbach, E. (2006) Developments in gender equality policies in Scotland since Devolution. *Scottish Affairs*, 56, pp. 10–21.

Cemlyn, S., Greenfields, M., Burnett, S., Matthews, Z., and Whitwell, C. (2009) *Inequalities experienced by Gypsy and Traveller communities: A review*. Research Report 12. Manchester: Equality and Human Rights Commission. Available at: https://dera.ioe.ac.uk/11129/1/12inequalities_experienced_by_gypsy_and_traveller_communities_a_review.pdf.

Clark, C. (2006) Defining ethnicity in a cultural and socio-legal context: The case of Scottish Gypsy-Travellers. *Scottish Affairs*, 54, pp. 39–67.

Coll, C. G., Lamberty, G., Jenkins, R., McAdoo, H. P., Crnic, K., Wasik, B. H., and Garcia, H. V. (1996) An integrative model for the study of developmental competencies in minority children. *Child Development*, 67(5), pp. 1891–1914.

Collins, P. H. (1994) Shifting the centre: Race, class, and feminist theorizing about motherhood. In: Glenn, E. N., Chang, G., and Forcey, L. R. (eds.) *Mothering: Ideology, experience, and agency*. New York: Routledge, pp. 45–65.

Collins. P. H. (2000) *Black feminist thought. Knowledge, consciousness and the politics of empowerment*. London: Routledge.

Crenshaw, K. (1991) Mapping the margins: Intersectionality, identity politics, and violence against women of color. *Stanford Law Review*, 43(6), pp. 1241–1299.

Cullen, M. A., Johnstone, M., Lloyd, G., and Munn, P. (1996) *Exclusion from school and alternatives*. Three reports to the Scottish Office. Edinburgh: Moray House.

Education (Scotland) Act. (1980) Available at: https://www.legislation.gov.uk/ukpga/1980/44/contents. Accessed 25 July 2013.

Education Scotland. (2015) About inclusion and equalities. Available at: http://www.educationscotland.gov.uk/inclusionandequalities/about/index.asp. Accessed 25 February 2016.

Education (Additional Support for Learning (Scotland) Act. (2004) Available at: http://www.legislation.gov.uk/asp/2004/4/contents. Accessed 20 July 2013.

Education (Additional Support for Learning) (Scotland) Act. (2009) Available at: http://www.legislation.gov.uk/asp/2009/7/contents. Accessed 20 July 2013.

EHRC. (2015a) Developing successful site provision for Scotland's Gypsy/Traveller Communities. Available at: https://www.equalityhumanrights.com/sites/default/files/successful_site_provision_scotland.pdf. Accessed 21 April 2015.

EHRC. (2015b) Prejudiced-based bullying in Scottish schools: A research report. Available at: https://www.equalityhumanrights.com/en/publication-download/prejudice-based-bullying-scottish-schools-research-report. Accessed 30 April 2016.

Essed, P. (1991) *Understanding everyday racism: An interdisciplinary theory* (Vol. 2). London: Sage.

Farris, S. R., and de Jong, S. (2014) Discontinuous intersections: Second-generation immigrant girls in transition from school to work. *Ethnic and Racial Studies*, 37(9), pp. 1505–1525.

Ferguson, K. (2003) Silence: A politics. *Contemporary Political Theory*, 2(1), pp. 49–65.

Freire, P. (1998) *Pedagogy of freedom: Ethics, democracy, and civic courage.* Lanham: Rowman & Littlefield.

Gewirtz, S. (2006) Towards a contextualized analysis of social justice in education. *Educational Philosophy and Theory*, 38(1), pp. 69–81.

Hall, S. (1991) The local and the global. In: King, A. D. (ed.) *Culture, globalization and the world system.* London: Macmillan, pp. 19–40.

Hancock, A. M. (2007) When multiplication doesn't equal quick addition: Examining intersectionality as a research paradigm. *Perspectives on Politics*, 5(1), pp. 63–79.

Hartup, W. W., and Stevens, N. (1997) Friendships and adaptation in the life course. *Psychological Bulletin*, 121(3), pp. 355.

Heaslip, V. A. (2015) *Experience of vulnerability from a Gypsy/Travelling perspective: A phenomenological study.* Unpublished PhD thesis, Bournemouth: Bournemouth University.

hooks, B. (1994) Teaching to transgress: Education as the practice of freedom. *Journal of Engineering Education*, 1, pp. 126–138.

hooks, B. (2015) *Feminist theory: From margin to center.* London: Routledge.

Jordan, E. (2000) Outside the mainstream: Social exclusion in mobile families from home-school partnerships. *Scottish School Board Association,* Dumfries: Millennium Books.

Jordan, E., and Padfield, P. (2003a) *"Are these really for us?" Laptops for teachers of pupils educated in outwith school settings.* Edinburgh: School of Education, University of Edinburgh.

Jordan, E., and Padfield, P. (2003b) Education at the margins: Outsiders and the mainstream. In: Bryce, T. G. K., and Humes, W. M. (eds.) *Scottish education: Second edition post devolution.* Edinburgh: Edinburgh University Press, pp. 836–841.

Knowles, G., and Lander, V. (2011) *Diversity, equality and achievement in education.* London: Sage.

Ladd, G. W., Kochenderfer, B. J., and Coleman, C. C. (1996) Friendship quality as a predictor of young children's early school adjustment. *Child Development*, 67(3), pp. 1103–1118.

Ladson-Billings, G. (1996) Silences as weapons: Challenges of a Black professor teaching White students. *Theory Into Practice*, 35(2), pp. 79–85.

Ladson-Billings, G. (2009). *The dreamkeepers: Successful teachers of African American children*. San Francisco: Wiley.

Lee, K. W., and Warren, W. G. (1991) Alternative education: Lessons from gypsy thought and practice. *British Journal of Educational Studies*, 39(3), pp. 311–324.

Lloyd, G. (2005) *Problem girls: Understanding and supporting troubled and troublesome girls and young women*. London: Psychology Press.

Lloyd, G., and Norris, C. (1998) From difference to deviance: The exclusion of Gypsy-Traveller children from school in Scotland. *International Journal of Inclusive Education*, 2(4), pp. 359–369.

Lloyd, G., and McCluskey, G. (2008) Education and Gypsies/Travellers: 'Contradictions and significant silences'. *International Journal of Inclusive Education*, 12(4), pp. 331–345.

Lloyd, G., Stead, J., Jordan, E., and Norris, C. (1999) Teachers and Gypsy Travellers. *Scottish Educational Review*, 31(1), pp. 48–65.

Lorde, A. (2007) *Sister outsider: Essays and speeches*. Berkeley: Crossing Press.

Mandela, N. (2004) *Long walk to freedom: The autobiography of Nelson Mandela*. London: Abacus.

MECOPP. (2012) *Hidden carers, unheard voices*. Edinburgh: Minority Ethnic Carers of People Project. Available at: http://www.mecopp.org.uk/files/documents/annual_reports/hidden_carers___unheard_voices_report.pdf. Accessed 21 November 2012.

Mirza, H. S. (2008) *Race, gender and educational desire*. London: Institute of Education, University of London.

Mirza, H. S. (2009) Plotting a history: Black and postcolonial feminisms in 'new times'. *Race Ethnicity and Education*, 12(1), pp. 1–10.

Mirza, H. S. (2013) 'A second skin': Embodied intersectionality, transnationalism and narratives of identity and belonging among Muslim women in Britain. *Women's Studies International Forum*, 36(February), pp. 5–15.

Mirza, H. S. (2015) Harvesting our collective intelligence: Black British feminism in post-race times. *Women's Studies International Forum*, 51, pp. 1–9.

Mirza, H., Ali, S., Phoenix, A., and Ringrose, J. (2010) Intersectionality, Black British feminism and resistance in education: A roundtable discussion. *Gender and Education*, 22(6), pp. 647–661.

Nieto-Gomez, A. (1997) Sexism in the movimiento. In: Garcia, A. (ed.). *Chicana feminist thought: The basic historical writings*. New York: Routledge, pp. 97–100.

Okely, J. (1979) Trading stereotypes. In: Wallman, S. (ed.) *Ethnicity at work*. London: Palgrave, pp. 16–34.

Padfield, P. (2008) Education at the margins: Learners outside mainstream schooling. In: Bryce, T. G. K., and Humes, W. M. (eds.) *Scottish education: Beyond devolution*, 3rd ed. Edinburgh: Edinburgh University Press, pp. 777–782.

Picower, B. (2009) The unexamined whiteness of teaching: How White teachers maintain and enact dominant racial ideologies. *Race Ethnicity and Education*, 12(2), pp. 197–215.

Pring, R. (2004) *Philosophy of educational research*, 2nd ed. London: Continuum.

Pring, R. (2007) The common school. *Journal of Philosophy of Education*, 41(4), pp. 503–522.

Save the Children Scotland. (2005) *Having our say*. Available at: http://www.gypsy-Traveller.org/your-family/young-people/educational-reports-and-resources. Accessed November 2012.

Scottish Centre for Social Research. (2010) *Scottish social attitudes survey 2010*. Available at: http://www.scotland.gov.uk/Resource/Doc/355763/0120175.pdf. Accessed 7 November 2012.

Sleeter, C. E. (2001) Preparing teachers for culturally diverse schools research and the overwhelming presence of whiteness. *Journal of Teacher Education*, 52(2), pp. 94–106.

Smith, J. (2002) *Jessie's journey: Autobiography of a Traveller girl* (Vol. 1). Edinburgh: Birlinn Limited.

Solorzano, D. G., and Yosso, T. J. (2001) From racial stereotyping and deficit discourse toward a critical race theory in teacher education. *Multicultural Education*, 9(1), pp. 2.

Spivak, G. (1988) Can the subaltern speak? In: Nelson, C., and Grossberg, L. (eds.) *Marxism and the interpretation of culture*. Urbana and Chicago: University of Illinois Press, pp. 271–316.

Spivak, G. C. (1995) Teaching for the times. In: Pieterse, J. N., and Parekh, B. (eds.) *The decolonization of imagination: Culture, knowledge and power.* London and New Jersey: Zed, pp. 177–202.

Sue, D. W., Capodilupo, C. M., Torino, G. C., Bucceri, J. M., Holder, A., Nadal, K. L., and Esquilin, M. (2007) Racial microaggressions in everyday life: Implications for clinical practice. *American Psychologist*, 62(4), p. 271.

The Scottish Executive. (2006) *Report of the Gypsies and travellers strategic group*. Available at: http://www.gov.scot/Topics/People/Equality/gypsiestravellers/strategy. Accessed 24 February 2013.

The Scottish Government. (2015) *Gypsy/Travellers in Scotland: A comprehensive analysis of the 2011 census*. Available at: http://www.gov.scot/Publications/2015/12/5103. Accessed 4 January 2016.

Trepagnier, B. (2006) *Silent racism: How well meaning White people perpetuate the racial divide*. Boulder: Paradigm Publishing.

University of Edinburgh. (2016). Available at: https://www.ed.ac.uk/equality-diversity/about/equality-diversity. Accessed 14 January 2016.

Winch, C. (2002) The economic aims of education. *Journal of Philosophy of Education*, 36(1), pp. 101–117.

Winch, C., and Gingell, J. (2008) *Philosophy of education: The key concepts*. London: Routledge.

Wright, G. (1986) School processes: An ethnographic study. In: Eggleston, J., Dunn, D., and Anjali, A. *Education for some: The educational and vocational experiences of 15–18 year old members of ethnic minority groups*. Stoke on Trent: Trentham.

6

'Honour Thy Father and Mother': Love, Freedom and Control at Home

Based on the typology of intersecting systems of oppression (Collins 2000), the previous chapter discussed the structural and institutional inequalities experienced by the girls in various educational settings. I addressed the main research question: *How do Gypsy and Traveller girls frame their educational experiences?* In doing so, I explored the girls' own definitions and understandings of education and learning, and their positive experiences in school. The chapter uncovered their perceptions of the challenges and obstacles they faced in the schools they attended. The main findings exposed inherent, continuing structural impediments within the education system that mostly impacted negatively on the girls' lives. What is more, the girls' narratives disclosed the inadequacy of existing policies on inclusion, diversity, equality, and the performance cultures within these agendas. The rhetoric and discourse does not seem to have translated into creating more fulfilling spaces of learning at school for most of these girls.

This chapter examines the girls' views and reflections regarding family values, expectations and culture that influence their educational experiences because it is important to understand how experiences at home impact on experiences at school. This chapter focuses on the

© The Author(s) 2019   **203**
G. Marcus, *Gypsy and Traveller Girls*, Studies in Childhood and Youth,
https://doi.org/10.1007/978-3-030-03703-1_6

'hegemonic domain of power' reflected in family and community ideology and culture that potentially functions as challenges and barriers to their educational experiences (Collins 2000: 277). Beneficial familial and cultural influences are discussed, but the girls own accounts reveal how these can be limiting. Their narratives are interlaced with personal stories of joy, obligation, and frustration, and of belonging to family and community structures that they all ultimately care for and respect. Their descriptions paint a multifarious and complex portrait of their lives. None of the questions in my interview schedule directly addressed how family and community might impact on the girls' educational experiences, but these themes emerged from our discussions and the girls' narratives.

As there is no existing literature specific to the experiences of Scottish Gypsy and Traveller girls within their family environment, I have sought out relevant literature in England as signalled in the literature review. Okely's (1983: 201–214) chapter on Gypsy women in England, although dated, nevertheless was useful for contextualising my data, as does Heaslip's (2015) more recent work. Douglas and Wildavsky (1982), Douglas (2003) and hooks (2015) also provide instrumental concepts that assisted my analysis and discussion of some of these findings. In addition, literature on the experiences of girls from other backgrounds provide useful comparisons, which help to de-pathologise the matrix of power relations that surround women in general (Basit 1997; Dwyer 2000; Talbani and Hasanali 2000; Walkerdine et al. 2001; Archer 2002; Emejulu 2013; Farris and De Jong 2014).

These studies help to situate the experiences of Gypsy and Traveller girls within a broader context of shared gendered experiences of exclusion and agency across different communities. It prevents any one group from being essentialised or exoticised and sustains the idea that many girls experience gender discrimination and pressures to conform irrespective of their cultural backgrounds, albeit in different ways and to varying degrees. Whether the emphasis is on gender equality or on the needs of women, 'we are dealing with issues that concern all women' (Stambler, cited in hooks 2015: 7). However, Okely (1983: 48) reminds us that 'the single carefully chosen example offers generality through its very specificity'. Mirza (2015: 4) echoes this idea and stresses the importance of giving attention to 'situated localised accounts of "marginalised lives". Therefore, whilst operating within the context of racialisation and marginalisation, this study highlights aspects of the Gypsy and Traveller girls' experiences that are specific to their context and that other groups may not be going through.

This chapter is divided into four sections. The first part features the girls' perceptions of the cultural norms and expectations that influence their lives. Their accounts are sub-divided into the girls' descriptions of the structure of Gypsy and Traveller family life and family values, their views of freedom, control and honour within family settings, and the gendered expectations that are part of their family dynamics that impact on individual identity. Juxtaposed against this cultural backdrop, in the next section, the girls' interpretations of family expectations of education and school are explored. This section examines the reasons the girls give for their families' decision not to enrol their daughters in secondary school. As in the last chapter, the evidence suggests the girls' educational and domestic experiences vary and are not homogenous. There are some common patterns of experiences, but there is no single narrative. The challenges and barriers family and cultural traditions pose on the girls' educational experiences then follow. As was done previously, the girls' views are discussed in light of the literature highlighted above and my analysis, using an intersectional approach throughout the chapter. Where appropriate, I have included the opinions and comments derived from the focus group discussion held with members of Article 12 and interviews with stakeholders.

Cultural Norms and Expectations

In discussing their educational experiences, the girls talked at length about their families' influence on their lives. In Chapter 2, I referred to deeply embedded stereotypical ideas about Gypsy and Traveller communities held by Scottish society in general—namely the persistent perception that Gypsies and Travellers are not gainfully employed; their children do not go to school; their women are morally wayward; their girls get married very young; they are all poor; and they all live in caravans. Dwyer's (2000: 480) study on the diasporic identities of young British South Asian women also reflected similar prejudiced assumptions held about Asian girls. Dwyer's (2000: 480) participants voiced their irritation that 'people often made assumptions that "we're all the same"'. Like the Asian women in Dwyer's (2000: 480) study who were constructed by dominant discourses as 'passive victims of oppressive cultures', some studies, as noted in the Chapter 5, found teachers held stereotyped assumptions about Gypsy and Traveller girls, which then influenced the level of support they were given in schools (Lloyd and McCluskey 2008). These misunderstandings were found in Basit's (1997) research on British Muslim girls and the work of Farris and de Jong (2014) on second-generation immigrant girls in Europe. Contrary to these essentialised assumptions, all the girls interviewed, whether from a Muslim, South Asian, immigrant or Gypsy and Traveller background, reveal a complicated picture of family dynamics and culture.

The following section analyses the dynamics of Gypsy and Traveller family life and the role family values play in shaping their identities. What aspects the girls consider to be some of the defining characteristics of their culture are presented, and the importance of family relationships in their lives, and their understanding of what their families expect of them as young women. These perceptions have a considerable impact on how they then rationalise or frame their educational experiences. Whilst there were clear patterns of shared thinking, some ideas diverged from the common narrative. Most of the girls held views that were in line with their parents and extended families, but a few questioned certain traditions and voiced concern about inequalities and limitations faced by women in particular.

Gypsy and Traveller Families—Love and Care

Each of the girls had a strong sense of belonging to family and culture. All of them related how proud they were to be Travellers and how important family and culture were to them. This attitude in itself is perhaps not atypical, as Basit (1997: 425) acknowledges 'most commentators recognise that family is still highly valued in all classes and ethnic groups in Britain'. Nevertheless, she makes a crucial point that some ethnic groups 'stress family relationships and recognise obligations to kin, beyond the nuclear family, more than others' (Basit 1997: 425). Group solidarity is vital for political and economic survival where kinship is a major ingredient.

When asked if they would prefer to be someone else because of the discrimination they have faced in schools and in the wider community, all the girls declared they would not. 'I wouldn't change it. I like my life!' (Cara). May, who does not identify herself as a Traveller, said she was proud to be 'Gypsy', despite her 'suffering' in school. In Traveller culture, respect for parents and elders, the need to follow unwritten established rules within the family and community, controlled limits in relations between the sexes, honour and modesty, are greatly valued, as they are, for example, in other cultures (Basit 1997; Dwyer 2000; Archer 2002). None of the girls said they were unhappy with their family life or their parents. On the contrary, they spoke about their parents, siblings, and in some cases their grandparents with much fondness, love and respect. 'It's our mother and father and we give them respect, they brought us into this world so why not' (Kilda). Dana exclaimed, 'Family is everything!' Vaila described her close relationship with her grandfather in particular and enjoys listening to his stories from the past—'It's quite amazing how everything back then was so different to how it is today'. This is also of course a form of education, captured in oral history.

Table 6.1 shows that four out of the 13 girls I interviewed lived within an extended family structure—parents, grandparents, cousins, aunts and uncles—proof of kinship as core to Gypsies and Travellers. Six lived with their parents and siblings and reported having close relatives nearby whom they saw frequently. Cara and Dana lived with their mother, who is divorced, and with their grandmother. Ailsa is the only one who lives with a mother who is a single parent, which is not the norm in Gypsy and Traveller culture. Of the 13 interviewees, the largest family had nine children and the smallest family had three. The girls, except Vaila and Sandray who are the youngest in their families, take turns caring for their siblings and elderly grandparents. One other girl, who was the youngest in her family, considered herself a 'young carer' to

Table 6.1 Parental care and reasons for non-attendance (extended = parents and grandparents)

			Reasons for Non-Attendance								
Name	Age	Type of parental care	Bullying	No support from staff	Family fed up; say no more school	Cannot cope with school work	Basic lit & numeracy enough	Not allowed to attend secondary school	Home & sibling care a priority	Ill health	Travelling a priority
May	12	Extended	✓	✓	✓	✓	✓	✓	✓		✓
Cara	12	Single parent Grandparents	✓	✓	✓	✓	✓	✓	✓		✓
Ailsa	13	Single parent	✓	✓	✓	✓	✓	✓	✓		✓
Islay	13	Both parents	✓	✓	✓	✓	✓	✓	✓		✓
Dana	13	Single parent Grandparents	✓	✓	✓	✓	✓	✓	✓		✓
Fara	13	Both parents	✓	✓	✓			Fara chose not to go	✓		✓
Skye	15	Both parents									
Vaila	15	Extended a						✓	Youngest		
Shona	16	Both parents	✓	✓	✓	✓	✓		✓		✓
Iona	16	Both parents	✓	✓	✓			Iona chose not to go	✓		✓
Kilda	18	Both parents	✓	✓	✓	✓			✓	✓	✓
Rona	19	Extended a									
Sandray	22	Both parents							Youngest		
Total: 13			9	9	9	7	6	8	11	1	7

ᵃExtended = Both parents and grandparents

an older sibling. Extended family kinships are the norm in Gypsy and Traveller culture and form networks of support. All the girls demonstrated strong and confident relationships within their family structures.

Most of the girls reported they had lived in a range of accommodation and that this was quite common. Iona and Fara, for example, said they moved to a house during the winter months because it was less stressful and warmer than a trailer. May, who has attended 12 primary schools, explained the mechanics of travelling:

> *May*: I've lived in trailers, caravans, cottages and houses.
> *GM*: Okay so you've lived in all sorts of different types of…which is your favourite? Is there a difference?
> *May*: Yeah a lot! I'd probably say uh…a house because it's better because you're settled but like you're settled in and you don't need to keep moving on and on. All the stress, you don't need to shift.
> *GM*: And why do you shift, what sorts of reasons would your parents give for shifting?

May: Because there's a lot of reasons. My dad uh…well he wouldn't want…he gets fed up if the area around him… its hard…we've all got to move on then and when…it's hard to find work then we move on, and stuff like that.

GM: Okay…so basically your dad decides when you all move on.

Islay talked about living in different types of housing—'Sometimes we go to council camps or just like camps, sometimes we're on the road [side] when we don't have a house in the wintertime'. Scottish Travellers and Gypsies, like Scandinavian groups for example, traditionally spend winters in barns or other housing because of extremes of climate. Islay n explained in detail what it feels like to have to keep moving and some of the problems she and her family have faced:

> Normally we won't be there for long, we'll be there for two days just until we find a camp where we can shift to. I just hate it in the winter when the taps either freeze up or you need to go to the toilet and [laughter] and you've got nowhere to go! The winters are hard in the trailer. Yeah its cold, you're all shoved in one little place. Yeah well I can remember one time being in this one camp where one year we would freeze to the ground, like the…the jack wheels would be frozen like to the slabs and then the taps would freeze up, there would be no water, and it would be bad. We would have to go down to the…either a shop and we'd buy packs or crates of bottles of water and sometimes we would get these big like…can you remember what you would get, the big blue tubs and they were just filled with water? So we'd use it to boil the kettle and that. We would have electricity or if we pulled on to a council camp we would have a generator.

Sisters Fara and Iona talked about how living in a trailer can be difficult for teachers to understand. They described how they were late for school one day because a tree crashed into their trailer during a storm when they were asleep. They felt lucky to escape unharmed, but said they were scolded for being late and their teacher did not believe their story. With no heating for days, their mother had to eventually rent a house to live in for the rest of the winter, because their father was away working. The girls explained there are other difficulties. Even though they own the land they live on, their parents are unable to get planning permission for electricity and are currently in dispute with the planners in their local authority. They have to use several generators. Their closest neighbours living a mile away have complained to the authority of the noise from the generators. I witnessed the distance between each household and I was surprised that the neighbours could hear the rumble of generators. The girls' accounts reveal that living in trailers may be part of Gypsy and Traveller tradition, but doing so has its own struggles. Of the girls who lived in trailers only two reported they would invite non-Traveller peers home to visit. These challenges are unique to Gypsies and Travellers who live in trailers. Girls who live in other types of accommodation do not experience these specific problems.

The choice of accommodation is sometimes significant in that it is linked to the fear of being identified as a Gypsy and Traveller. Other minority groups who are visibly recognisable as being different from the dominant majority or not White do not seem to experience this phenomenon. Two Traveller women I spoke to on separate occasions explained they have lived in a house for years and have never told their neighbours about their ethnicity out of fear (Anon. Traveller woman 2015 , Personal communication; MECOPP 2013, Personal communication). One admitted when she travels she rents a trailer to avoid visibly owning one. Another Traveller woman, speaking at a Gypsy and Traveller awareness-raising event, revealed how living in a council house has affected her mental state. She felt claustrophobic, disconnected from her heritage and lamented the loss of freedom she experienced when she lived in a trailer and had a more outdoor lifestyle (MECOPP 2013, Personal communication). Despite the difficulties living in a trailer can present, especially in the face of winter and hostile neighbours, some Gypsies and Travellers still prefer it to settling in bricks and mortar. The Traveller woman explained that living in a trailer represents the freedom to travel at will, which for some Gypsies and Travellers is a major part of their cultural identity—'It's part of my heart, mind and soul' (MECOPP 2013, Personal communication).

The girls talked about how important travelling or 'shifting' was in their culture. Most of the girls said their families travel whenever they want, but few only travel in the summer, following the school academic calendar. The girls reported they travel mainly to see other members of their family and for their father to find work. At no point did any of the girls cite travelling as having a negative impact on their education. Yet as was stressed in Chapter 5, many teachers who were interviewed, and much of the literature on the educational needs of Gypsy and Traveller pupils, view their travelling lifestyle as a hindrance to learning and a problem to be managed. On the contrary, all the girls revealed how much they learn when they travel, as referenced in the previous chapter. The way in which a Gypsy and Traveller family's need or compunction to travel influences the decisions they make about their daughter's education is explored when family views of education, school and reasons for non-attendance as explained by the girls I interviewed are highlighted later in this chapter.

Freedom, Control and Honour

For a culture that prizes freedom of movement, nearly all the girls revealed that their individual movement was restricted. In other words, because they are girls they were not allowed to leave their homes unaccompanied. To be seen 'loitering' in shops or walking down the street was a cultural taboo. Shona who is 16 years old remarked 'never…never go too far from home because you might get lost!' As girls or young women, their physical space was confined to their home and community. Dana explained being at the youth centre makes her happy because being at home 'all day' can be difficult:

> We are really happy here because like when I'm at home I don't get nowhere, and I have to sit on the site, like we're in the trailer all day but then you come here you're actually somebody, and like you're talking to somebody.

Perhaps her constricted physical space limits her emotional and mental space. She is 'actually somebody' when she is at the school. Despite this confinement, she understands her parents have these arrangements for her protection. According to her, a girl's reputation 'is everything!' She repeated this phrase three times.

It's everything! It's everything! Yeah because if you get…like say your reputation gets like scandalised that's your whole family scandalised. And
family is everything! (Dana)

She goes on to explain in detail the delicate situation that girls in her
culture are in:

Because if I'm sitting here and I'm talking to a load of non- Travellers, say
there was a load of boys, and then say one of them out there seen me…
what are you doing talking to the country boys? Yeah! They wouldn't like
it! Your mammy and daddy won't like it and then none of your family
would like it because as soon as something's said about you then it's auto-
matically oh her sisters must be like that…and then her cousins must be
like that and her mother…(Dana)

If she was seen talking to a 'country boy' (non-Traveller boy), her marriage prospects would be damaged, and her family's honour destroyed.
The term 'country person' is a vital boundary maker between Gypsies
and Travellers and non-Travellers. None of them are permitted to be in
the company of Traveller boys and non-Traveller boys, unless accompanied by a family member. As Okely (1983: 203, 206) explained, a
Gypsy and Traveller girl cannot be seen or be alone with another boy
or man. My data echoes aspects of Okely's fieldwork. For example,
according to Dana, she never leaves home unaccompanied by a family member. As stated previously, she is transported by taxi to attend
classes in literacy and numeracy at the youth centre twice a week with
other Gypsy and Traveller children. She explained she only experiences
freedom when she is allowed out with her Traveller peers to buy lunch
down the high street. The other girls at the youth centre described the
same situation and mentioned how much they appreciated the sense of
fun and freedom that comes from being at the youth centre.

The girls' experiences point to the power of patriarchal control in
their lives and in their communities. Indeed, hegemonic patriarchy
parading under the cloak of protection for daughters, sisters and wives,
and in its multiple guises as preserving honour, reputation, safety,
occurs in many cultures (Basit 1997: 431; Emejulu 2013).

Some of the girls I interviewed spoke of a degree of fear, suspicion and slight confusion about non-Travellers whom they refer to as 'them', as this exchange suggests:

> *Islay*: I don't know my mammy and daddy say that we're not allowed to pal about with them because they know too much.
> *GM*: They know too much?
> *Islay*: Uh huh.
> *GM*: Of what?
> *Islay*: I don't know!

Islay said she knew it was for her protection, to keep herself separated from non-Traveller girls and boys. I asked Dana how she felt about 'having to sit around [in the trailer] because you are no allowed to go off'. She replied that she understood her family were trying to protect her, but 'sometimes it's like aggravating because we're not allowed to do nothing but other times it's like…it's for your own good, for your own benefit'. Like Islay, Dana could not explain how it might be for her benefit only that if she was not protected, 'other people' might think she did not belong to anybody: 'why is she standing there by herself, why has she not got somebody [to look after her]?'

Vaila, Skye, Rona and Sandray reported they had more freedom. They did not have to be accompanied by siblings or cousins. Rona and Sandray have non-Traveller boyfriends, and Vaila said even if her parents objected; she would still go out with a boy who was not a Traveller. Sandray pointed out that her father could not object if she were to go out with a non-Traveller because he married one, 'he's contradicting himself.' She claimed that her father believed he 'created' a Gypsy wife and here she gives an account of his words:

> She's good as a Gypsy and she knows all the traditions, she knows everything, so…it does'nae matter if she's not got Gypsy blood; she's still a Gypsy in my eyes because she's my wife.

Even here a woman who is not from a Gypsy and Traveller community is accepted only because the Gypsy and Traveller man has worked hard to transform her into one, to 'socialise' her into a proper Gypsy (Okely 1983: 211).

Skye, Iona and Fara said they were not keen on getting married. Consequently, whether or not they would be allowed to date a non-Traveller boy was not a concern for them. Vaila believed that things are changing, and for women too:

> Lot of today people stay by camps or stay on sites now, they don't actually stay like…pull in anywhere and back then it was the horse and wagons and they used to pull in and then by the camp fires, but the women was not allowed to go anywhere. They had to be at home so obviously we get a lot more freedom now.

She does recognise that a few Travellers are still traditional in their ways. She revealed she has been criticised by Traveller friends and members of her extended family for attending college, but admitted she did not care, even if they ostracised her, she was not ashamed. Her courage in the face of critical opposition is reflected in her description:

> So, they'll down you for being what you are because obviously whatever you do in a Traveller culture you're going to be talked about for it and it's going to be on your name because whatever you do…everything you do makes your name. I don't care what other people say! You can't win either way! Just give them something to talk about!

As a bearer of culture, a Gypsy and Traveller girl's honour needs to be protected because her actions and interactions are seen to impact on her family's honour (Okely 1983: 206; Anthias and Yuval-Davis 1996; Emejulu 2013). Such expectations necessitate constraints on her autonomy and identities (Emejulu 2013: 54), and this dominant patriarchy appears to be borne out by the findings in my research.

As bearers of seed, the line to the next generation has to be maintained and preserved by young women, and the right kind of young Gypsy and Traveller men. Kilda explained that 'you can't just…go out with a boy straightaway and not know him, we get to know a boy then when we like him enough we bring him to our dad. You know what

I mean it goes like that because you cannae just...pick anybody at all'. Shona, her sister, agreed, 'that would be scandalised...that would be my name scandalised'. Sandray referred to the courting ritual as a 'dance'. A young woman needs to be clean and pure, she should be kept safe from contamination, in order that the community might view her as a suitable catch. This finding again echoes Judith Okely's (1983) discussion on 'Gypsy Women' 'and the ideal behaviours expected of her by the Gypsies themselves'. Gypsy ideas surrounding female cleanliness, pollution and honour reflect the girls' accounts of the need for sobriety. Women are crucial for the preservation of Gypsy lineage. If left unguarded or misused, a young man could damage a girl's reputation when she is not escorted for protection. If there are no witnesses, she is open to risk and defamation:

> And it's like you could be clean and decent but that's your name done with, you know what I mean, no other boy would want you. That's the way it goes in our family. The word spreads. (Kilda)

Shona emphasises the imperative need for protection of one's reputation and honour even at the expense of one's freedom: 'just girls...just us girls...because that's how we work. Protecting...like...in our eyes, we've got to protect ourselves'. She adds that 'it's okay for like travelling boys to go to secondary school because they're boys. Going to school is not a problem for Travelling boys. For girls, it's not a place for us'. The girls in Article 12 confirmed that this was the case. One member said if there had been boys in their working group they would definitely not have been allowed to participate, especially when they were required to stay overnight away from home. 'It's just a thing with morals and decency. To keep your distance, girls are with girls, boys are with boys and staying overnight...if there were boys here and we wanted to stay overnight that would be completely wrong' (Member of Focus Group).

As highlighted earlier, my study does not consider the experiences of boys in Gypsy and Traveller culture, nor did it produce data that would allow a comparison with girls' experiences. What does emerge from findings and the language used by the girls, is that boys are perceived to have more freedom. Skye and Rona believed, for example, that Gypsies and Travellers can be 'sexist'. Kilda claimed that, in Gypsy and Traveller culture, if a boy walked into a caravan, as a girl, she would be expected to leave: 'we could never sit in the same caravan, we've got to get up and walk out and the oldest [girl] has got to come in and make that boy a sandwich and a juice or whatever, give him it and walk back out again'.

This phenomenon is not just confined to the socialisation of girls in Gypsy and Traveller culture. Talbani and Hasanali's (2000: 625) study of the gender role socialisation of adolescent females in South Asian immigrant culture found that the participants identified three key areas—'the differential treatment of boys and girls at home, girls are given less decision-making power, [and] there is more control over their intermingling with the opposite sex'.

We have come to expect that a few young people rebel against parental control and may even leave home early. In contrast the girls I interviewed, like the girls in Talbani and Hasanali's study, seem to accept that these different rules are part of their culture and are for their own protection. To the outsider it could be perceived as a form of discrimination, or even oppression, but the girls are comfortable with idea that different standards of behaviour are expected of them. The difference in standards arises out of 'unwritten rules that dictates how one behaves and interacts with elders, people of the opposite sex, and different age groups' (Talbani and Hasanali 2000: 625).

As Okely (1983) argues in her study, a Gypsy and Traveller girl's contact with the outside world, even in a school, poses a threat to her honour, and her reputation needs to be managed by the family, particularly the father. May disclosed her father would have to make the decision whether to allow her to attend the youth centre for more than just the two days—'It would depend on my dad'. Some of the girls said their fathers decide when, how often and where they 'shift'. Kilda explained her father plays a protective role in the family. It is his job to ensure that his daughters are kept away from certain types of boys and that 'he doesn't believe in having one [a boyfriend] until we're 18!' Her father believes that:

If you're 18 years old you've got enough sense by then to have a boyfriend...because boys at 17 can have a girlfriend at 15 but they're just children so that's not right…the Irish do that…they are allowed, but us Scotch we're different. Our dad says 18.

He has strict rules of behaviour for his daughters too, until they get married:

> We're not allowed to drink, we're not allowed to smoke, we're not allowed to do all that bad stuff, we're allowed to drink when we're married because at the end of the day you're married, you've got your own life, he's not responsible anymore like. (Kilda)

Of the 13 girls I interviewed only three girls said they had boyfriends, and all three were over 16 years of age. There seems to be less pressure to conform to the general expectation in mainstream culture, for example, for adolescent girls to have a boyfriend. A girl in a Gypsy and Traveller community must be a virgin till married, faithful to her father and then husband (Okely 1983: 214). This same expectation exists in many British Muslim and South Asian families. The strict requirement to be 'pure' also means that there is less freedom to explore relations with the opposite sex, and consequently less pressure to have such relations.

Most of the girls seem to accept that having relationships with boys was not permitted and rationalised their situation dispassionately. None complained and there did not seem to be any tension or conflict around these rules. Kilda is clear in her mind about her father's vital role in her life and understands that as a woman she should not need to work—'our father protects us and provides for us, you know? Our father does all that and provides for us'. The girls in the focus group discussion confirmed that Gypsy and Traveller fathers, as the sole breadwinners, are the main decision-makers and protectors in the family. However, one girl in the group revealed she had more freedom because her single mother brought her up. She said her mother encouraged her to attend school and have a career if she wanted to:

> We love her like more because she was both, she was mum and dad. She's so understanding with you. Aye like we were allowed to do things that maybe they were'nae allowed to do because of their dads, like we were allowed to go to the pictures. (Member of Focus Group)

The others agreed that life is easier for Gypsy and Traveller girls when their mothers are in charge and in control because 'mothers are more understanding' (Focus Group). The girls all reported their fathers were reluctant at first to allow them to participate in Article 12.

> Well my mother was really up for it, but father's side was really like strict with you, did'nae want you to go away because we would have to stay at overnight meetings and things. So, he was kind of edgy on it at first, but my mother was really up for it and like she felt it was a really good opportunity for us. She had an understanding like whereas if I wanted to do something I would do it kind of behind daddy's back, because mammy let you do it, daddy would'nae.

Gypsy and Traveller mothers tend to be solely responsible for the care of their home and children. As part of that duty, they have a special responsibility to train their daughters in housework and childcare so that they will be good daughters and wives who bring honour to their family and husband (Okely 1983: 203). Like most mothers, regardless of ethnicity, class and culture, Gypsy and Traveller mothers too have to maintain homeostasis and work to ensure that their daughters continue to maintain longstanding traditional divisions of labour within family structures. As in many other communities, there remain both undisguised and subtle restrictions on the activities that girls and women may pursue (Okely 1983: 204). For women certain ideals continue to be highly valued—virginity, monogamy, abstinence, and controlled sexuality (Okely 1983: 214). Gypsy and Traveller women, albeit like many other women, bear their community's cultural traditions, norms, and values. For these women and girls, deviations from the norm are perceived as a powerful threat to the existence of that family or community group and could bring shame to the family name. The notion of shame is also interwoven with issues of safety and protection so that they are not 'scandalised' (Dana). However, the overriding concern is the maintenance of the patriarchal order in family and community, which is inextricably tethered to the girls' honour and reputation.

The findings suggest that there is a strong construction of femininity in Gypsy and Traveller girls, which is related to the more dominant construction of masculinity. Female identity is crafted and controlled by family and community norms and expectations. It seems that there is little freedom to explore, expand and fulfil their identities as girls. Basit (1997: 436) argues that the notion of freedom is polemic and is interpreted differently by different people depending on their aspirations, perceptions and biases'. The girls' lack of freedom could be interpreted as their parents' wish to protect and 'nurture'.

The parents in Basit's (1997: 436) study reveal that 'they do not believe that [their daughters] are old enough to be autonomous and thus able to make rational decisions without parental guidance'. This was similar to my experience as a young Indian daughter. From a young age I was socialised to accept that my parents' rules and restrictions were for my own good, to the extent that I could rationalise it as being largely positive. I then perpetuated these restrictive, but protective nurturing practices, when I parented my own daughters here in Britain. Looking back, I always felt safe and secure within my family and as I grew older, began to negotiate more freedoms, but within the confines of deeply embedded family honour. The Gypsy and Traveller girls all spoke of respect for their parents and elders, as was noted earlier in this chapter, but this is also the case in other families (Basit 1997; Dwyer 2000; Talbani and Hasanali 2000). Being respectful and behaving respectfully as a daughter was linked to family honour. A disrespectful daughter could cast a poor light on their parenting skills and bring shame to parents. This in turn affects her reputation and marriage prospects, which again has a detrimental effect on a family's standing in the community.

As with Basit's (1997: 436) Muslim parents, what was never questioned or constrained in my family, was my freedom to attend school, get an education, and fulfil my potential. Unlike the experiences of many of the Gypsy and Traveller girls I interviewed, education for girls (and boys) was highly prized, firmly encouraged and was seen as bringing respect and honour to the family as a whole. There are specific ways in which girls and women across race and class experience the influence of patriarchy and the inequalities that can stem from it.

The next chapter reveals how the constraints on identity and femininity limit choices with regard to their ambitions and aspirations, but that this is not atypical as girls from other communities experience such constraints too.

Gendered Expectations

In our conversations, most of the girls highlight the role they have to play in their family because of their gender. We are 'cleaners and married and cook the food' and believed their destiny would be to marry between the ages of 16 and 21. Shona rationalised that it is all part of her culture:

> I learn…I learn like how…how we're going to finish growing up right, because uh…we're going to…we plan on growing up…we're planning on growing up and probably marrying into the same kind of people, because that's what happens and then…And then we go wherever our husband takes us.

A girl has to be subordinate to her father's order and then subsequently to her husband's orders (Okely 1983). Many were wary and worried about getting married too young. Shona was ambivalent as she protested, 'I still have a lot of child in me', and explained, 'most [Traveller] girls now marry at like 16, 17'. Her older sister, Kilda, accepted the status quo like some of the others I spoke to. Only a few of the girls were critical of early marriage and what they perceived as fixed gender roles and expectations.

Kilda was quick to add that 'we don't get our marriage arranged for us', but that she would have a choice in the matter. Ailsa knew that she would be able to choose her own husband. It was important that the prospective Gypsy and Traveller suitor asks permission from the father. According to Kilda, if a father decides that the suitor is trustworthy and 'can look after his girl and he's a nice enough boy, not bad to his girl then fair enough he can have permission…this is a rule for everybody, every Traveller'. These traditions hold great value in Gypsy and Traveller culture. Rona said her family have always encouraged her to mingle with non-Travellers and would not object if she married someone from another culture. One of her sisters is married to a non-Traveller. Her parents would rather they married a 'good non-Traveller', than a 'bad Traveller' from a rival family. As mentioned above, Rona herself has a non-Traveller boyfriend. Dwyer's (2000: 480) findings revealed that her South Asian women participants resisted the idea that 'all Asian girls have arranged marriages' and were annoyed by the stereotyped idea that they were powerless and lacked agency. The girls' explanations about having choice in who they marry, and even having the option to marry a non-Traveller was perhaps an attempt to resist myths that they were completely controlled by their parents.

The girls highlighted there was a strong expectation that they would marry a Traveller boy. I asked the girls why a Traveller boy was deemed better than a non-Traveller boy. Sandray explained clearly the difference between a Traveller boy and a non-Traveller boy:

> See if a Travelling boy asks you out he'll mean it. He'll not just…you know…ask you out and then just go at it does'nae matter! He will stick to…he'll ask you out…see Travelling girls don't say yes easily so they'll ask you out for months and months until eventually the girl goes right okay I'll go out with you! Whereas a non-Traveller boy is not like that. He doesn't intend to marry her.

She believed she would get more respect from her community if she was going out with a Traveller boy and her family would be more reassured, but she recognises the underlying prejudice and attempts to negotiate her way through the dilemma:

> I know that's so not right because you know…you can't differentiate between two people you know? So…but they know that a Travelling boy will marry you and take care of you, and look after you, whereas non-Travellers might not because they're not brought up like Travellers, that's how I'm saying that. I'm not saying they're bad, I'm not saying…I'm just saying they're different the way they are you know?

Skye said she thought most families are 'not keen on Travellers marrying non-Travellers…. That's like making people more racist… like Travellers say Oh My God! They are so racist towards us. It's a two-way thing. We are racist towards them!' Rona agreed with her and as the girls point out, the Other can be demonized on both sides. There are misperceptions, fears, prejudices, and racist attitudes in Traveller populations as well as in settled. A general reluctance to associate, befriend and even intermarry fuels these rifts and exacerbates misunderstandings. All the girls perceive there to be an expectation that Gypsies and Travellers cannot marry outside their community—a kind of protective segregation. Intermarriage is uncommon: only one girl, Sandray had a Gypsy father and a non-Traveller mother. The situation demonstrates the intricacies of power relations between two seemingly opposing sides, and the spaces in which these relations are enacted. Communities are segregated by values, traditions, friendships, and marriage. Again, marrying within one's race, ethnic or religious community is common across many cultures.

Gypsy and Traveller girls, as mentioned earlier, are expected to bear children. The more children a woman produces the better she is regarded (Okely 1983). The men were breadwinners and went to work; the women were carers and stayed at home. Men trained their sons and received support from them, and women trained their daughters and received support in turn; 'it's just the way we are like the boys go with their daddy and the girls go with their mammy' (Dana). Their family structures represent powerful models and patterns of existing that have lasted for generations (Okely 1983). The girls are expected to be hardworking and involved in many domestic (unpaid) duties—cooking, cleaning, and child rearing. It would seem difficult for the girls as young people to question embedded constructions of heteropatriarchy, but most accepted that there were different gender roles and expectations.

May, the Gypsy girl, said she plans to marry by 17, 'I wouldn't get a job I'd probably just stay home and cook, and clean, and do that'. When asked if there would be anything else in her life to look forward to she said 'No!', and Islay explains that 'We wouldn't be able to do both [career and marriage] …because like our community girls are just brought up to be that way'. She thinks that she would not get a job anyway 'once people knew [she] were a Traveller'.

GM: So, your main aim really at the end is to have…to be married, and to continue like your mum and dad…like your mum being married and having children?
Islay: Yeah and then you die!

Fara and her sister Iona both remarked they did not like doing chores, as is evidenced in this lively exchange:

> *Iona*: Well we don't enjoy cleaning! [Laughter]
> *GM*: Yeah, I was going to ask that because neither does my daughter! [Laughter]
> *Iona*: I like things looking neat and tidy, but I wouldn't clean.
> *Fara*: But it's a chore to us. It's just a chore.
> *GM*: That's normal!
> *Iona*: See like that window there it's not got many smudges on it, so I would leave it but if I couldn't see through it I would maybe wash it.
> *GM*: You should see my windows!
> *Iona*: I would maybe wash it if it was…like if you couldn't see through it.
> *GM*: So, you help mum a lot then?
> *Fara*: Aye!
> *GM*: Yeah and you obviously help with looking after the little ones?
> *Fara*: Sometimes!
> *Iona*: I'll need to do that now because they've disappeared! [Laughter]

Some of these accounts suggest that Gypsy and Traveller girls are destined to just get married and have children. I told the focus group that some stakeholders I met said all Gypsies and Travellers girls want to do is to get married and have children, and I asked them if they thought this was true. Like the Muslim girls in Basit's (1997) study who objected to such stereotyped prejudices, the girls from Article 12 were angry and said this was not entirely true. At this point, all tried to speak at once and it was difficult to register all their comments. But one member of the group said she felt 'it's like sickening, it makes me feel a bit sick to think that's what people think, we're just there to reproduce and stay'.

The girls stressed the importance of fighting these 'stereotypes' because 'the stereotype is that we're just bad. To show that there is good in us as well the same as everybody else. I just think it's about time that Gypsies had a voice so that's why I joined [Article 12] to make a difference!' (Member of Focus Group). However, with the girls' accounts and the admission from the focus group that their fathers have more control than their mothers over their lives, there is sufficient evidence that at times the male figure in Gypsy and Traveller society, especially in the shape of fatherhood, is supreme. His values define the nature of his family, their activities, rules of behaviour for sons and daughters. As in many cultures, and especially with the advent of industrialisation and capitalisation, men are defined and seen as naturally stronger, protective, logical decision-makers, and able to economically provide for others in the family (Nieto-Gomez 1997: 97; Davis 1983: 227). Women are defined as naturally dependant, childlike, and in need of protection and authority, first from their father, then from their husband. The women's primary functions, as wife and mother are to make others feel secure and cared for 'since her primary abilities are to conceive, procreate and nurture' (Nieto-Gomez 1997: 97).

As I pointed out earlier, many of the girls accept the traditional practices that define the roles that men and women in their society play. It seems to make sense to them and they readily play their part. The binary roles maintain balance, security within a clear family structure. It could be argued that the system works to a certain extent. hooks (2015: 5) defines being oppressed as the absence of choice. If members of the group are happy to accept the rules and arrangements in the culture, and do not feel oppressed, then one could suggest that the system itself is not unfair or oppressive from their point of view. The girls have the choice, however inadequate, to rebel against their parents' wishes; but they perhaps choose not to because they have a vested interest in belonging to the group. They have been socialised to understand expectations in their culture, as we all are, but have elected to comply because they value their families and traditions, as many of us do.

It might be premature to dismiss the girls' family life and cultural traditions as sexist, where the male is cast as superior and suppresses the female inferior, eventhough some of the girls use the term. hooks (2015: 5) explains that 'sexism has not meant an absolute lack of choices. They may know they are being discriminated against based on sex, but they do not equate this with oppression'. There is a danger in imposing simplistic paternalistic judgements based on the value systems of the culturally dominant group in Scottish society, which dictates that all children should be in school and that girls and boys ought to be treated equally. The expectations of many of the Gypsy and Traveller girls I interviewed vary from this prescribed 'ideal'.

There is not one way to manage or understand events. Given their age, limited lived experience and education, the girls may not, as hooks (2015: 94), argues 'understand the forms of power they could exercise...They need political education for critical consciousness to show them ways to exercise the limited powers they possess'.

Yet, the girls' narratives present a level of complexity that makes it difficult to be entirely critical of their families' values and way of life, and to judge their way of life with unwavering moral certainty. People have a right to live as they wish as long as they are not being harmed or harming others. Nevertheless, I recall Sandray's comment on whether a Gypsy and Traveller girl would know any better if not exposed to other influences. Most of the girls are adolescents, still in their formative years; arguably too young to understand or object to how they are being culturally conditioned. This is of course not atypical for a child or young person. Just as they seem afraid to question or oppose their teachers in school, the girls might be equally unsure about criticising their cultural traditions at home. Reflecting on Spivak (1988) I question if subaltern women can truly speak up about oppressive cultural practices and wonder how possible it is for the girls to voice their concerns.

There are exceptions, and some voiced their criticism of what they perceive to be unfair and unequal practices within their culture. As this chapter demonstrates, Sandray, Vaila, Rona, Skye, Iona and Fara, each in their own way have attempted to resist the patriarchal discourses that dictate their everyday existence and future. The girls endeavour to negotiate their roles within their families, push existing gendered boundaries and create new, or different identities for themselves. Some of the young British South Asian Muslim women in Dwyer's (2000: 481) study also demonstrate 'negotiations and reworking of gender identities', and in their case, within the multiple contexts of religion, ethnicity and national identity and diaspora, as their title suggests.

The next chapter builds on these findings about the strategies that the girls employ to manage, negotiate and reconcile 'public aspirations and private obligations' (Emejulu 2013: 53). In the main, my findings suggest that certain identities are foreclosed to the girls. Their experiences and understandings make it challenging for most to countenance imagining a different future than what has been mapped out for them, and this has considerable impact on their education and reasons for not attending school.

Family Views of Education, School and Reasons for Non-Attendance

In Scotland, it is illegal and a criminal offence for a young person aged five to 16 years to have no access to education. According to the Head of Education Law, Ian Nesbit this principle is apparently usually enforced through a caution or fine and a recommendation made to The Children's Panel to monitor and ensure proper access and attendance (Nisbet 2014a, Personal communication).

Some of the girls attempt to address why, in their view, Gypsy and Traveller families do not tend to send their daughters to secondary school. All of the girls whom I met attended primary school, and many attended multiple schools at this stage (see Table 5.1). In Chapter 5, I discussed the challenges and barriers experienced by most of the girls in the primary schools they attended, and I argued that race discrimination and possible gendered disadvantage within the school structure, were reasons for interruptions and non-attendance. Families can be reluctant to send their daughters to school in the face of such difficulties and where there is no positive support.

What is more, the girls' accounts contradict evidence that primary schools are seen as safer than secondary schools. As was discussed in the literature review, there is a range of data that supports this (Bancroft et al. 1996; Lloyd and Padfield 1996; Jordan and Padfield 2004; Cemlyn et al. 2009). Although, the situation is perhaps more nuanced. Scottish Government statistical evidence suggests that Gypsy and Traveller families are more likely to enrol their children in primary school, but it is not necessarily the case that this is due to the perception that these schools are benign spaces of learning. As stated earlier, there is growing evidence (Bancroft et al. 1996; McKinney 2001; Lloyd and McCluskey 2008; Cemlyn et al. 2009) that Gypsy and Traveller parents do value the basic education offered at the primary stage. One could argue that it is not that primary schools are necessarily safer, but that families are willing to accept the possible risk of bullying and lack of support from staff, in exchange for some opportunity for their children to learn to read and write.

> *Ailsa*: Um…well my parents were afraid of racism because its worse in secondary school and learning bad habits such as smoking and drinking.
> *GM*: So…I can understand why your parents want to protect you but… but they want you to come here, they're happy for you to come here [the youth centre]?
> *Ailsa*: Yeah because they want me to get a good education… also because other Travellers go here as well, and they've probably been through the exact same thing [negative experiences in primary school].

This attitude makes sense in the light of the utilitarian approach to getting an education referred to by some of the girls in the last chapter, and the fact that some parents allow their daughters to attend the youth centre two days a week. Some mentioned that their mothers were especially supportive of the beauty course on offer at the centre. Although this encouragement could be perceived as social conditioning of girls into 'soft' types of work, from the mothers' view, the girls were learning a relevant practical skill that could be sustained alongside their daughters' future duties as homemakers:

> *GM*: Okay and I hear they're going to be having beautician courses here — excited?
> *Cara*: Beautician!
> *Both*: Yes! (Laughter)
> *GM*: I wouldn't mind taking that…and you're already so fantastic at putting yourself together, your make-up, hair, both of you, did you learn to do that yourselves? Would you like the beautician course, Islay?
> *Islay*: Yeah! I would and run my own business!

The staff at the youth centre mentioned the possibility of inviting the girls' mothers to join in the course too. Staff, parents and pupils were all excited at the prospect, but I was hesitant to accept that this was quality education. A beauty course may entice girls to attend school and gain parents' approval, but I wondered if this was an example of teachers 'reinforcing paths', as was found in Farris and de Jong's (2014) study of second-generation immigration girls in Europe. Flexibility in the education system is important but not at the expense of quality of provision.

I was particularly perplexed by Islay's disclosure that she was not allowed to do science at school. She was at a secondary school for a very short period but left. Below is her account of what happened to her:

> *Islay*: I **wasn't allowed to do** all the classes, like I **wasn't allowed to do** um…science.
> *GM*: Why?
> *Islay*: I **don't know** I just **wasn't allowed to do** it.
> *GM*: Did you ask?
> *Islay*: What?
> *GM*: Did you ask whether you could do science?
> *Islay*: Uh…no, no my mummy and daddy…it was my mother that went into the school and said I want Islay to be **taken out** of science! Um… so I didn't get to do the science thing but…I wasn't bothered because I **didn't like** science!
> *GM*: Okay so you didn't get to do science, what subjects did you do then when you were there?
> *Islay*: I did maths, I did um…English, I did um…there was like Geography, just the normal classes. I **didn't always get to do** RME, like Religious and Moral Education I don't know why but I just **never got to do** that sometimes. Um…but when **I didn't** I was being **made to sit** in a room by myself so…
> *GM*: Why? That's very unusual why would you be…why would you be asked to sit on your own? What would you be doing?
> *Islay*: You **did nothing** you just sat in the room, when I **wasn't doing** like science or RME they brought me into the room where the high school office was and there was like a **detention** room. Like [Stewart], my brother [Stewart], when he was in detention that's where he went but you sit there, and **you don't do nothing.**

Islay's account is heavily negative. Her choice of words, emphasised in bold italic, shows she was almost a non-person, her presence as a person negated. She is misrecognised. She 'wasn't allowed to', 'did nothing', 'never got to do', and she didn't know why. Her confusion is in my view apparent. She is not aware of what is happening and why. She does not seem able or willing to voice her questions and she seems to have no choice in the matter. I sensed her lack of control and agency in this situation. She did not like detention, but neither could she do anything about it. Her account resonates with the UNCRC's (2016) findings on the use of 'isolation rooms' to exclude or control behaviour, with little or no justification for its use.

Only one good thing occurred in her view, she did not like Science and was glad she was taken out of class. Islay explained she was soon taken out of school altogether as she recalls, possibly within several weeks of starting. She recalled that the best thing about school was lunchtime—'The only good thing about it was lunchtime, you could go down the street, and that was it!'

Vaila disclosed that when she left primary school her parents did not let her attend secondary, even though she was doing well in school. If she had a chance to attend secondary school she would have. When I asked her why they prevented her from going, this was her explanation:

> At the time I wanted to, but my mother just said no. I don't know any other Traveller who goes to high school, so she goes…if you go she goes obviously you're going to start picking up a few more bad habits she goes, because we're not allowed to smoke or drink or nothing. She goes if you start like hanging around with pals and things and going out late she goes obviously it is going to happen. I said but it depends on the friends you pick! But she just didn't want me going.

Community perceptions clearly matter to Vaila's parents and there is perhaps pressure to conform to the norm, however that norm is defined by dominant patriarchal power structures and attitudes within communities (Basit 1997; Talbani and Hasanali 2000; Walkerdine et al. 2001). Vaila compared her experience to her grandmother's opportunity to attend secondary school, but 'her parents pulled her out', even though like Vaila she was enjoying school and doing well in her studies. Vaila believes her grandmother 'should have been able to stay because it is an education and it would have helped her along the way'. She reasoned that her parents were concerned about what family and friends would say about Vaila going to secondary school, because nobody else in the family had gone. Two years later, her parents changed their mind and offered her a chance to attend her local further education college. Vaila disclosed she had 'no idea' why they changed their mind.

Shona who only attends lessons from time to time in a local authority mobile unit or portacabin based on her Traveller site, declared:

> I paid more attention because I knew...I knew that after I came out of primary school I wasn't going back to school, so I paid more attention you know? I made sure I did my very best but I'm not too sure if I did my very best on my reading but I'm actually picking it up like really good now, still a bit tricky, but I'll catch up to them.

According to the Scottish Government, the overall number of Gypsy and Traveller girls attending both primary and secondary school has been increasing slightly since 2011. Yet, the number of Gypsy and Traveller girls in primary school is always higher than in secondary. In 2015, for example, 400 girls who self-identified as White Gypsy and Traveller attended primary school, but the figure dropped to 126 in secondary. In addition to the negative experiences in primary cited in the earlier chapter, here I include some other explanations offered by the girls.

Table 6.1 shows the family circumstances of each girl and the reasons for not attending school, particularly at the secondary stage. In the last chapter, I discussed the positive experiences of four girls—Skye, Rona, Vaila and Sandray—who attended school consistently and with minimal interruption. The dark shaded cells show these girls offer no reasons for non-attendance, although they do suggest reasons why other Gypsy and Traveller girls who do not attend school.

Only two reasons are a direct result of challenges and barriers faced at school—bullying and lack of support from staff. The other reasons stem from cultural norms and expectations, lifestyle choices and family decisions that conflict with the education system as a whole. The conflict is exacerbated by their daughters' negative experiences at primary school.

Just as there is no consistent direct correlation between a participant's family composition, the type of home she lives in and her socio-economic circumstance (see Table 6.1), neither could I find a direct co-relation between a participant's family composition and her attendance or non-attendance at school (see Table 6.1). In other words, whether a girl lived with one parent, both parents or within an extended family environment seemed to have no bearing on the nature of her attendance at school. It is clear from the data that certain cultural norms and expectations, as perceived by the girls, do have an impact on their educational experiences.

The study by Save The Children (Bancroft et al. 1996) revealed girls possibly stayed on longer in school, with boys having to work from the age of 12. The study found that gendered division of labour was adhered to rigidly (Bancroft et al. 1996). Only four girls—the ones who had positive experiences in school—criticised some of these traditions as having a negative impact on the educational, and life, experiences of the daughters of Gypsy and Traveller communities in Scotland. Rona clarified, 'I have heard for myself from like a Traveller mum... [If her daughter goes to school her] daughter will have boyfriends, start smokin', drinkin', sleep around with boys ... you'll be classed as like a little whore basically'. Skye interjected:

> But it's not like that at all...It's more like a fear sort of... but it's ridiculous! It's like you have to send your kids to high school or they're not going to have much of a future... they (Traveller girls) depend on the man. The man will bring in all the money all the time.

Skye and Rona stated strongly that from their view, most Gypsy and Traveller girls are not allowed to go to school because there is no need for them to be financially independent:

> *Skye*: They have like no choice in anything and that really sucks!
> *Rona*: I'm going to make sure my kids are in school.

Skye: You're surrounded by other Travellers [at the mobile school] and maybe if you pick the wrong thing to do...maybe if like the boy picked something that wasn't...manly enough.
Rona: I've kind of noticed that as well.
Skye: He'd be sort of picked on by the rest of the Travellers as well...
Rona: Like a girl becoming a mechanic!
Skye: Travellers are quite sexist.

Skye's view that Gypsy and Traveller girls 'have no choice in anything' and her description of Travellers as 'quite sexist', reflects hooks (2015: 5) argument that it is the absence of choice that is the seed of oppression. A Traveller woman giving a talk about her life at an awareness raising event in Edinburgh said that she was thrilled when she got her first bank card because it symbolised some independence. She said not all women have bank cards and that some chose not to.

The bank card is my independence – it's something that naebody could take. That is something I gained myself. It is a very new thing to Travelling People, women in particular, because men have always been the head of the family (Rose). (MECOPP et al. 2014: 121)

In defiance of this lack of choice and suggestion of oppression, Skye and Rona stressed the importance of learning more than just basic literacy and numeracy. Skye said she would like to go as far as she can and 'maybe even attend university'. Unlike the other research participants, they not only valued and argued for pursuing what they called a 'good education', but critically evaluated their community's traditional views about the role of education in Traveller women's lives. Both were proud to be Scottish Travellers but expressed their disapproval of what they labelled as 'racism' and 'sexism' within their communities.

Rona, Skye, Vaila and Sandray all said their families tended not to travel during the school term and were more 'settled'. In an interview with Skye's mother in September 2014, she explained she and her husband decided to stop travelling so that Skye, her youngest child, could have a consistent education in school. She recognised that Skye was 'very bright' and 'deserved a better chance' to reach her full potential and be able to stand up for herself and her culture. McKinney (2001: 21–23), Jordan and Padfield (2004), and Lloyd and McCluskey (2008) report a growing trend for some Gypsy and Traveller families to settle in one area, travelling only during school holidays, in order that their children can receive a better, uninterrupted education in school. According to these studies, increasing numbers of Gypsy and Traveller parents think basic literacy and numeracy are important for their children. Attendance at primary school is seen as positive, useful, less threatening and more safe than secondary. According to some girls, their parents have actively encouraged them to continue their education beyond primary, perhaps indicating aspirations that actually fit with their daughters' interests and potentials as individuals.

Most of the Gypsy and Traveller girls, often considered by their parents and communities to be young women at 12 years, left mainstream school because their parents did not want them to be 'contaminated' by non-Traveller boys, drinking, drugs, sex education, and what Gypsy and Traveller parents perceive as the morally corrupting lifestyle of the settled community. Ailsa said her parents would not want her to be influenced by what they think might happen to her at secondary school, and that is one reason why she is not allowed to attend. Islay claimed that her parents thought her few weeks in secondary school was 'changing' her. 'I didn't want to be like them but like I was coming back from school and I wouldn't do my cleaning up no more' (Islay). Cara was not sure about why she was not allowed to attend secondary school.

> I don't know um...I think my mummy and my daddy and my granddad they don't believe in putting us to high school. I don't know because like...like we get bullied in high school, it's like different from primary school. Primary school is like...I don't know it's different, I think it's different.

Three members of the focus group had some experience of secondary school. They explained they had a choice as to whether they wanted to attend secondary school, but left by the age of 15 years:

GM: Why not, why didn't you want to go to school anymore?

F1: Because the school you did'nae want to get up in the morning, it was just the normal reasons, I did'nae want to go to school! I was like I don't need to go so I'm taking that opportunity, so I got a choice, it was either stay home and clean up, help look after things at home or go to school. I was like well I'm staying home, I can sleep all day, I can do this, I can do that.

F2: It was my choice as well.

GM: Yeah so you chose not to go to school.

F3: I chose to go to school at first but then I chose to take myself out of it.

Another member of the focus group admitted that at first, she 'chose' not to attend secondary, but 'I got so bored sitting about' she returned to school. According to the group, apart from the bullying and inter- rupted learning as a result of travelling, there was no incentive for them, and no pressure on them to attend school. They could choose not to go, and their parents did not encourage them to attend. One Traveller mother I met said she did not want her daughters to touch textbooks touched by non-Traveller children because it is unhygienic, and this was the reason why they did not attend school (Anon. Traveller mother 1 2014, Personal communication). In her view, she was protecting her children. Vaila explained her view:

> I think that it's because the way their parents have got them like…ob- viously non-Traveller parents will say don't mix with Travellers they might have like…bad habits and things and they're saying to their… the Travellers are saying to their children don't mix with non-Travellers because they've got different rules and bad things obviously we don't want to pick up on. I hear that a lot where people say we don't want to mix with them because they're different to us and the other group also say the same thing so everyone's in their own little corner and nobody wants to mix. I don't think it's very fair because at the end of the day everyone is the same we've just got different…live different lifestyles.

The Gypsy and Traveller parents I spoke to were not only concerned about their daughters' exposure to other cultures, but also their safety and purity, which ought to be preserved to protect family honour (Anon. Traveller mother 1 2014, Personal communication; Anon. Traveller mother 2 2014, Personal communication). I discovered that issues of safety, cleanliness and contamination were emerging reasons for non-attendance in mainstream school after 12 years of age. Mixed sex secondary schools, they state, are dangerous places for their daughters. 'We do not go to secondary school because we're not really allowed to mix with country people' (Dana). Although the girls do not mention sex education as a reason for non-attendance, it is taboo to discuss sex, and this is a major reason why Gypsy and Traveller girls are not in secondary school (Bancroft et al. 1996). As mentioned earlier, this contrasts with parents from other minority ethnic groups who encourage attendance and accomplishment in school, whilst maintaining their culture and values (Mirza 1992; Basit 1997).

The girls' accounts may be understood in terms of the powerful themes of pollution, shame and risk which are inextricably tied to the image and role of the Gypsy and Traveller woman (Okely 1983). I am reminded of Douglas' (1982) argument that risks in a community are a 'collective construct' and are based on fear. Risks are 'cultural', 'hidden', 'selected', and the assessment of that risk is 'biased' (Douglas and Wildavsky 1982). However irrational it may seem to staff in schools or to the majority population, a Gypsy and Traveller girl is deemed to be at risk and then poses a risk to her family, if she attends secondary school and mixes with non-Travellers. Okely argues that a Gypsy woman can be perceived as weak and oppressed, but she is feared as well and thus ascribed the power to do much good for her community or much harm. The Gypsy women in Okely's study led a contained lifestyle and seem vulnerable, but she explains they also have the power to disrupt. However, most of the girls I met do not hold such power because of their age and youth. Their subordinate position as girls and as young people places them at the lowest rung of the hierarchical structure within their families.

Although, in contrast, Skye and Rona considered themselves to be 'different' from the norm as the following conversation suggests. The girls looked critically at some of the behaviour and traditions within their community.

Rona: They [TravellerGypsy and Travellers girls] don't have any friends.
Skye: Their friends are like just their cousins yeah.
Rona: They don't really get out much either.
Skye: No but that's not the question.
Rona: Yeah what stops them?
Skye: What stops them yeah like…no yeah, it's just like the gender stereotypes, they're meant to stay at home with the children and that's what their goal is. There's like nothing passed that.

Her last statement reminded me of May's declaration that she had nothing else to look forward to beyond marriage and childrearing. Islay's pragmatic summation at aged 13 years, echoed in my mind; 'and then you die', suggesting a tragic sense of finality and perhaps sadness about their situation in life. The girls accept that this is just the way of their culture and reiterate they are happy. I question what other options might be open to them and begin to understand their predicament and rationale for managing it—'Because like our community girls are just brought up to be that way' (Islay). As mentioned earlier, Cara emphasises that she wouldn't change it because she likes her life. As a young person, it must be difficult to criticise, and question decisions made on her behalf within the power of heteropatriarchal family structures. Perhaps, because of their youth these young women do not seem to grasp that the 'enervating domestic obligations of women in general provide flagrant evidence of the power of sexism' (Davis 1983: 238).

The girls said they would not be allowed to attend the youth centre for more than the two allocated days, because they have no choice but to complete their chores for the week. Recall May's earlier assertion that it would be up to her father to decide if she could do more days in school. School would interfere with housework:

Cara: Whatever your parents say you've got to do it because if you don't do it then…say you wanted a top up for your phone they wouldn't give it you until you did all your chores.
Islay: Yeah. Yeah. Um… I've got to do it. If I don't clean up I don't get to go away at the weekends with my friends.

The self-image of Gypsy and Traveller girls is intertwined with their gender, femininity, roles as women and family expectations, and these collectively influence their ability to access formal secondary education. British Muslim, South Asian and white working class and middle-class girls in some studies do not report restricted access to education, but experience significant gender disadvantages in different ways (Basit 1997; Dwyer 2000; Talbani and Hasanali 2000; Walkerdine et al. 2001; Emejulu 2013).

The voices below reveal the tension between divergent elements in the lives of the Gypsy and Traveller girls I interviewed:

The first point uncovers the tension between childhood and rushed adulthood:

Skye: Yeah, I know you're meant to finish school when you're 12.

Rona: A lot of Traveller girls when they finish…when they come out of school like usually they come out of primary school…

Skye: That's them! 12! And that's them all grown up apparently! You're still a child. I think I am a child! We are still children! I'm quite childish for my age and I'm still a child, leave me alone!

The second area exposes the tension between differences in age and experience, alongside ideas influenced by members of the family seen as role models:

Rona: I think the mother and father kind of put that into their head as well and plus they see it from what their mother and father act like and they think oh well that's the way I should be.

GM: So that's their role models?

Rona: Yeah!

Skye: They don't see anything wrong with like their mother and father's relationship because…it depends on what type of family [you are in].

The third issue illustrates some of the distinctions in her view between how men and women are treated in Gypsy and Traveller culture:

There's like no gender equality among Travellers, they're just like the women and men have to…they have like no choice in anything and that really sucks because like I won't…when I grow up I want to have my own job and everything and I don't want to have to live off… like… a man… Yeah, it's ridiculous! (Skye)

Both Rona and Skye acknowledged that they are who they are because their families have allowed them to be so. Even though Skye and Rona feel able to criticise cultural traditions, family still matters to them too, as is revealed in this account of a mother's dilemma:

> My mother is still kind of like…she has sort of the old traditions in her because of the way she was brought up. But she's trying to keep me as open as possible, but I can tell that she would rather me be like…she'd rather I'd have a boyfriend right now and she'd rather I'd be talking about marriage and stuff. I think my mum still has some of those beliefs but she's trying…she doesn't force anything upon me. (Skye)

Such dilemmas are, of course, not confined to Gypsy and Traveller mothers with teenage girls. Basit (1997: 433) found that 'the parents of [British Muslim girls] in the present study neither wanted to be too permissive, nor too oppressive as regards control of their [girls]'. One mother in the study spoke of the dangers of granting 'too much freedom' and another advised that 'there should be a middle course' (Basit 1997: 433).

bell hooks (1981) argues, as many other feminists do, that minority women are worst affected as they are often doubly oppressed because of their race and gender. Just as there are stubborn perceptions in Western consciousness about female minorities (Groot 2013; Spivak 1988), there exist stereotyped perceptions of the life ambitions and aspirations of young Gypsy and Traveller women. Gypsies and Travellers in Scotland include semi-nomadic minorities whose identities clash with the majority population not just because of their race, ethnicity, cultural traditions, but also over age and gender. These differences and conflicts are interrelated and reflect the 'intersection' of multiple forms of discrimination and oppression (Knudsen 2006).

A minority ethnic female who leads a semi-nomadic lifestyle and who is additionally inhibited by economic circumstances is positioned at the crux of this intersection. One should not necessarily assume that all minority ethnic women are vulnerable or feel vulnerable and in need of protection. Vulnerability can generate, in the case of some of the girls I met, a formidable spirit of resilience and determination to succeed beyond the realms of marriage and childrearing. In this respect, Skye and Rona have challenged my own stereotyped perceptions of Traveller women.

The Moray House School of Education Ethics Form (2012: 4) implies that research participants from minority ethnic communities constitute a vulnerable group, but I question the assumption that all research participants from minority ethnic communities are necessarily 'vulnerable', and ask if they should all be treated as such from the outset. Conversations with the girls demonstrate that the situation is more complex. Some of these young women were confident and ebullient, and held strong views about gender equality, marriage, school, their family, their identity and racism. Heaslip's (2015) study on the nature of vulnerability within the Gypsy and Traveller community maintains that her participants reported problems with identity, split identity and having to conform to live a particular way of life. Interestingly, none of the girls in my study complained of feeling vulnerable within their community. They all demonstrated a strong sense of family and cultural identity, but as the next chapter will reveal, some found it hard to cope with contrasting values in Gypsy and Traveller and non-Traveller societies.

Challenges and Barriers

Whilst academic literature (Kenrick and Clark 1999; Clark 2001; Clark and Greenfields 2006), and reports from the Equal Opportunities Committee (EOC) and Amnesty International (2010, 2012a, b, 2013) often point to the 'single issue' of racism experienced by Scottish Gypsies and Travellers, interviews with the girls I met suggest a more diversified interplay of multiple issues. Audre Lorde (2007: 138) contends that 'there is no such thing as a single-issue struggle because we do not live single-issue lives'. One of the most striking findings is the liminality of their positioning, betwixt and between intersections of space, race, gender, culture and intergenerational tensions.

Some of these young women seemed doubly oppressed by systemic institutional inequities and fixed gender expectations from within their culture and families, whilst others express strong views and aspirations about their future roles as women, which may challenge stereotyped perceptions. All are governed by their family and locality, and the physical, social and emotional spaces they inhabit. Their varied experiences illustrate that 'there are many kinds of power, used and unused, acknowledged or otherwise' (Lorde 2007: 53). Their multiple voices reflect multiple realities influenced by long-standing institutional, structural, political, and cultural agendas. The girls are caught within these structures and what Sandray below refers to as a bubble, which emphasises the complexity of the situation:

> *Sandray*: You can't just stay in that bubble and think oh I'm going to get married, and I'm going to have weans, and I'm not going to talk to non-Travellers. I couldn't do that you know? Do you understand what I mean?
>
> *GM*: I do! I do! And I agree with you, it is…it is difficult.
>
> *Sandray*: Very very difficult and complex!
>
> *GM*: It's…it's also very messy but then I think life is messy, isn't it?
>
> *Sandray*: Yeah! I agree.
>
> *GM*: So, I think that it's…I think that Traveller girls I don't know about boys because I've not spoken to any boys, that Traveller girls I think, Gypsy or Traveller girls, are caught potentially, if they begin to think about it. What do you think?
>
> *Sandray*: Yeah! Yeah! Definitely! Girls don't think! You just do what you're told kind of thing! It's such a shame!

The findings in this chapter reveal multiple challenges and powerful barriers the girls face, whether they perceive them to be so. They encountered racist bullying in schools from their peers. They are affected negatively because of the lack of support from staff in schools and could be disadvantaged because of their gender. And, there are cultural factors that indicate gender discrimination at home, influenced by intergenerational conflict between the young and the power of the older generation who are keen to preserve traditions and a way of life. What has been more difficult to determine is the role that class and poverty play in reinforcing the more overt inequalities experienced by the girls I interviewed. Just as their space to learn safely is compromised by the institutional structures of the school, their space to thrive and reach their full potential have arguably been compromised by cultural norms, expectations and taboos. What emerges from the interviews is a feeling on their part that most of the girls sense they exist to perform the fixed gender roles expected of them.

I am in no doubt that the girls' families do not seek to undermine their daughters' sense of self or ambition. On the contrary, as many of the girls acknowledge, their parents' aim is to protect. The girls' narratives demonstrate that strict gender expectations and cultural taboos can hamper the physical, emotional and mental space to flourish as a human being. Some of the girls appear content to accept that this pre-determined condition is part of who they are as Gypsies and Travellers, but others have not.

> *GM*: And because we...I think the world is changing rapidly, um...politically, socially, economically, things...people are moving, people are travelling, cultures are being...are mixed up.
>
> *Sandray*: I'm going to just stick up for what I believe in and like...I know it's their children, and I know it's what they want, they want them to be brought up in a Gypsy/Traveller community. Things are changing; things are changing so when she reaches 12 and she's going to high school, and she's getting home schooled she could change. Like the mother could change and think oh actually it's not so bad.

As has been shown, the girls have fixed roles and responsibilities within their family and communities. Those girls who make changes to these fixed roles do so only with family permission and support, or risk being ostracised because, as they have been told, family shame and family honour is largely a woman's responsibility to bear. In this regard, there are potential similarities with other traditional cultures in the Indian, Pakistani or Muslim communities in the UK, as I have demonstrated elsewhere in this chapter. Their experiences are not unique, but nevertheless reflect gendered expectations, and disadvantage and discrimination on multiple levels. Rona and Skye confirm that they are aware of similarities between their culture and other minority groups mentioned above.

It could be argued that in electing for the girls to not attend school and exclude themselves from the system, their parents, and at times the girls themselves, exercise choice in how they are educated. The education system is used and accessed to a certain extent in primary school and rejected when it is no longer deemed safe, 'fit for purpose', or when it is perceived as conflicting with long-standing cultural practices. When issues of safety and cleanliness become a dominant source of concern, Gypsy and Traveller parents withdraw their daughters from school. In contrast, it has been found that British Muslim and South Asian parents manifestly encourage their children to obey and respect their teachers and the rules in school, as Basit (1997: 434) maintains, 'Muslim parents play an important role in shaping their daughters' ethnic identity and educational outlook, albeit within the limits set by their culture and religion'.

What is questionable is if the girls are suitably provided with alternative quality provision or left with little or no formal secondary education as a consequence. According to the law, parents' right to choose how their child is educated takes precedence, until that child is 16 years. In the case of many of these girls, it might be too late or complicated for them to exercise their own right to choose to be educated in a formal setting. Again, one is reminded of hooks (2015: 5) assertion that the absence of choice can be oppressive, but the restriction of choices can be equally discriminatory. I am not concerned with the morality or efficacy of the choice, I am not passing judgment as to the wisdom of choices made, rather it is the lack or control of choice that seems unjust.

Sandray was the only girl who contacted me directly when hearing from others about my research. She said she wanted to speak to me about her experiences as a Gypsy and Traveller girl living in Scotland, as she wanted people to understand. Sandray explained in detail her passion for ensuring that the next generation of girls in her family have the best opportunity to succeed:

> I feel like it's such a shame because Traveller girls are missing out on so much…so much and I felt like I was so glad see when I found out like all this. I've completely changed as a person and see when I found out that there was so much out there and so much to learn I was like wow like…

like I was shocked! Because you go from this wee tiny community to this massive world and it's like your head explodes because there is so much to learn. And education is just...the best. I cannae express how good it is for me personally. And that's what I want for my nieces because...and I will...I'll push until they get what they deserve because they deserve to have a proper education, they deserve to choose what they want to do instead of getting told they're getting married at 16. I believe that and I'm strongly going to put up a fight you know? And they're smart girls but...they're 4 and 5 and 8 and they are talking about getting married! It's crazy, you know!

In the next chapter, I discuss Sandray's ambitions in greater detail, especially the music and lyrics she composes that reflect her strong views.

As in the earlier chapter, the girls' narratives show that their experiences are not homogeneous. Most of the girls accept and feel obliged to carry on family and cultural expectations, but a few are critical of what they interpret as sexism. Some girls reported positive encounters with non-Traveller peers and school staff, success in attainment and achievement where there has been positive attitudes and support from family for continuous attendance in school, more open attitudes to mixing with non-Travellers and trust of mainstream education. Good relations and understanding between family and school are vital for positive educational experiences to exist. I found that some of these girls are beginning to contest these binding spaces of long held values and traditions, imagining a world in which they have greater agency and choice. Some girls are content and have chosen to accept that this is just part of who they are as Gypsies and Travellers, perhaps because it is perceived there are no alternatives. I question how informed such choices to follow existing cultural practices are.

As a researcher, it is difficult to observe inaction or silent acquiescence with precision. It is challenging to analyse power that is not noticed by those who are seemingly disempowered by it. The potential for their identities to flourish beyond the roles of dutiful daughter, wife and mother are restricted, and according to Skye and Rona 'sexist' and oppressive. As Alexander suggests, '"culture" becomes a site for struggle over meaning, constructed through the relations of power, in which identities are created, negotiated and contested as part of an ongoing search for control' (1996, cited in Archer 2001: 98).

In the main, the girls' only role models are their parents and relatives. Exposure to other ways of being is not within their lived experience, further limiting their choices and aspirations. Unlike, the British Muslim and South Asian girls who have been 'socialised to hold certain occupations in high esteem' and who have career-oriented members of their family (Basit 1997: 240), many of the Gypsy and Traveller girls have been socialised to the contrary. However, Archer (2002) argues '"choice" can be differently constructed and valued across 'race' and gender'. Class also determines how choice is framed, and how much parental guidance is provided (Reay and Ball 1998). As is evidenced in the accounts of some of the girls I interviewed, family values and support can make a positive difference to educational experiences in school and their lives in general. One of the most striking findings was the genuinely strong sense of family, community and belonging, as the girls declared how much they respected and valued their families and their culture.

Taken collectively, the evidence suggests that most of the girls seem to be caught betwixt and between structural inequalities in school and within their family and community structures. Just as lack of support from school staff act as barriers to learning, lack of approval for education beyond 12 years, and lack of encouragement from families, can impede motivation to succeed in school and disable the girls' power to make individual choices in life and lifestyle. Institutional and everyday racism (within the school structure), gender discrimination (at school, and within family and community structures), arguably act jointly to compromise the girls' potential to lead fulfilling lives. Collins (2000: 284) asserts that 'school curricula, community cultures and family histories have long been social locations for manufacturing ideologies needed to maintain oppression…and shape [individual] consciousness'. Gypsy and Traveller girls or women, like many other minorities here in Britain, suffer racial and gender discrimination.

Through the critical application of intersectional analysis, the girls I interviewed revealed their situated experiences of domination and control from sometimes overwhelming patriarchal systems. Racial discrimination in school and in the community, gendered discrimination in school and at home within their culture, everyday and institutionalised systems of exclusion and silencing. Their stories and identities obliterated, erased from historical and current texts; their voices unheard, they are infantilised by their teachers and their families, but for very different reasons. Their youth places them at a disadvantage when faced with such powerful influences from school and home.

Such inequalities can be enervating and, in the main, the girls lack options and the freedom to make choices. I have shown that the girls' experiences are not entirely unique, although there are subtle differences between their narratives and the narratives of minoritised girls or white working class or middles class girls who were interviewed in a range of studies highlighted in this chapter. The collection of similar yet varied narratives and dilemmas in fact demonstrate the range and complexity of the patriarchy in racialised, gendered experiences and discrimination.

References

Amnesty International (AIUK). (2010, 7 June) Letter written by J. Watson to Aberdeen City Council Chief Executive.

Amnesty International (AIUK). (2012a) *On the margins.* Available at: http://www.amnesty.org.uk/sites/default/files/amnesty_international_on_the_margins_2012.pdf. Accessed 8 May 2013.

Amnesty International (AIUK). (2012b) *Caught in the headlines.* Available at: http://www.amnesty.org.uk/sites/default/files/amnesty_international_caught_in_the_headlines_2012.pdf. Accessed 8 May 2013.

Amnesty International (AIUK). (2013) *Scottish Gypsy Travellers, Amnesty International UK.* Available at: http://www.amnesty.org.uk/content.asp?CategoryID=12418. Accessed 8 May 2013.

Anon. Traveller mother 1. (2014, 10 June) Personal communication. Conversation and notes.

Anon. Traveller mother 2. (2014, 6 September) Personal communication. Interview and notes.

Anon. Traveller woman. (2015) Personal communication. Telephone interview and notes, 15 August, 6 October.

Anthias, F., and Yuval-Davis, N. (1996) *Racialized boundaries: Race, nation, gender, colour, and class and the anti-racist struggle.* London: Routledge.

Archer, L. (2001) 'Muslim brothers, black lads, traditional Asians': British Muslim young men's constructions of race, religion and masculinity. *Feminism and Psychology*, 11(1), pp. 79–105.

Archer, L. (2002) Change, culture and tradition: British Muslim pupils talk about Muslim girls' post-16 'choices'. *Race, Ethnicity and Education*, 5(4), pp. 359–376.

Bancroft, A., Lloyd, M., and Morran, R. (1996) *The Right to Roam: Travellers in Scotland 1995/96*. Dunfermline: Save the Children in Scotland.

Basit, T. N. (1997) 'I want more freedom, but not too much': British Muslim girls and the dynamism of family values. *Gender and education*, 9(4), pp. 425–440.

Cemlyn, S., Greenfields, M., Burnett, S., Matthews, Z., and Whitwell, C. (2009) *Inequalities experienced by Gypsy and Traveller communities: A review*. Research Report 12. Manchester: Equality and Human Rights Commission. Available at: https://dera.ioe.ac.uk/11129/1/12inequalities_experienced_by_gypsy_and_traveller_communities_a_review.pdf.

Clark, C. (2001) *'Invisible lives': The Gypsies and Travellers of Britain*. Unpublished PhD thesis, Edinburgh: University of Edinburgh.

Clark, C., and Greenfields, M. (2006) *Here to stay: The Gypsies and Travellers of Britain*. Hatfield: University of Herfordshire Press.

Collins, P. H. (2000) *Black feminist thought. Knowledge, consciousness and the politics of empowerment*. London: Routledge.

Davis, A. (1983) *Women, race and class*. New York: Vintage.

Douglas, M. (2003) *Purity and danger: An analysis of concepts of pollution and taboo*. London: Routledge.

Douglas, M., and Wildavsky, A. (1982) How can we know the risks we face? why risk selection is a social process. *Risk Analysis*, 2(2), pp. 49–58.

Dwyer, C. (2000). Negotiating diasporic identities: Young British South Asian Muslim Women. *Women's Studies International Forum*, 23(4), pp. 475–486.

Emejulu, A. (2013) Being and belonging in Scotland: Exploring the intersection of ethnicity, gender and national identity among Scottish Pakistani groups. *Scottish Affairs*, 84(1), pp. 41–64.

Farris, S. R., and de Jong, S. (2014) Discontinuous intersections: Second-generation immigrant girls in transition from school to work. *Ethnic and Racial Studies*, 37(9), pp. 1505–1525.

Groot, N. (2013) So you think you know Muslim women? Campaigning against stereotypes in the Netherlands Open Society Foundations (OSF). Available at: http://www.opensocietyfoundations.org/voices/so-you-think-you-k...ium=emailandutm_content=image_link=andutm_campaign= europe_A_031413. Accessed 8 March 2013.

Heaslip, V. A. (2015) *Experience of vulnerability from a Gypsy/Travelling perspective: A phenomenological study.* Unpublished PhD thesis, Bournemouth: Bournemouth University.

hooks, b. (1981) *Ain't I a woman: Black women and feminism.* Boston: South End Press.

hooks, b. (2015) *Feminist theory: From margin to center.* London: Routledge.

Jordan, E., and Padfield, P. (2004) *Issues in school enrolment, attendance, attainment and support for learning for Gypsy/Travellers and school-aged children and young people based in Scottish local authority sites.* Edinburgh: Moray House School of Education, The University of Edinburgh.

Kenrick, D., and Clark, C. (1999) *Moving on: The Gypsies and Travellers of Britain.* Hatfield: University of Hertfordshire Press.

Knudsen, S. V. (2006) Intersectionality – A theoretical inspiration in the analysis of minority cultures and identities in textbooks. In: Bruillard, E., Aamotsbakken, B., Knudsen, S., and Horsley, M. (eds.) *Caught in the web or lost in the textbook.* Eighth International Conference on Learning and Educational Media, IARTEM, pp. 61–76.

Lloyd, G., and McCluskey, G. (2008) Education and Gypsies/Travellers: 'contradictions and significant silences'. *International Journal of Inclusive Education*, 12 (4), pp. 331–345.

Lloyd, G., and Padfield, P. (1996) Reintegration into mainstream? 'Gi'e us peace!'. *British Journal of Special Education*, 23(4), pp. 180–186.

Lorde, A. (2007) *Sister outsider: Essays and speeches.* Berkeley: Crossing Press.

McKinney, R. (2001) *Different lessons: Scottish Gypsy/Travellers and the future of education.* Scottish Travellers Consortium.

MECOPP. (2013, May 28) Personal communication. Awareness raising event, notes and materials from seminar.

MECOPP, Lloyd, M., and Ross, P. (2014) *Moving minds.* Edinburgh: MECOPP.

Mirza, H. S. (1992) *Young, female and black.* London: Routledge.

Mirza, H. S. (2015) Harvesting our collective intelligence: Black British feminism in post-race times. *Women's Studies International Forum*, 51, pp. 1–9.

Moray House School of Education. (2012) Moray House School of Education Student Application Form. Available at: http://atate.org/mscel/assignments/ Dissertation-Ethics-Form-Tate.pdf. Accessed 5 January 2013.

Nieto-Gomez, A. (1997) Sexism in the movimiento. In: Garcia, A. (ed.) *Chicana feminist thought: The basic historical writings.* New York: Routledge, pp. 97–100.

Nisbet, I. (2014a, May 21) Personal communication. Head of Education Law, Govan Law Centre, Lecture, TENET seminar.

Okely, J. (1983) *The Traveller-Gypsies.* Cambridge: Cambridge University Press.

Reay, D., and Ball, S. J. (1998) 'Making their minds up': Family dynamics of school choice. *British Educational Research Journal,* 24(4), pp. 431–448.

Spivak, G. (1988) Can the subaltern speak? In: Nelson, C., and Grossberg, L. (eds.) *Marxism and the interpretation of culture.* Urbana and Chicago: University of Illinois Press, pp. 271–316.

Talbani, A., and Hasanali, P. (2000) Adolescent females between tradition and modernity: Gender role socialization in South Asian immigrant culture. *Journal of Adolescence,* 23(5), pp. 615–627.

UNCRC. (2016) *Concluding observations on the fifth periodic report of the United Kingdom of Great Britain and Northern Ireland.* Available at: http://www.crae.org.uk/media/93148/UK-concluding-observations-2016.pdf. Accessed 14 January 2017.

Walkerdine, V., Lucey, H., and Melody, J. (2001) *Growing up girl: Psycho-social explorations of gender and class.* London: Palgrave Macmillan.

7

Power in Agency: Ambitions, Aspirations and Success

Best things for weans is education. They need that to work. Years ago, they just faced the fields. If they don't have an education they are lost. My wee lass is convinced she is going to visit planets. Weans are far more advanced than I was. (Isabella MacGregor, Traveller woman, HOTT 2017)

In the previous two chapters, the girls' accounts revealed incidences of racial and gender discrimination in school and gender discrimination at home. Some girls expressed constrains by family and cultural obligations, whilst others saw the need to negotiate new boundaries and imagine other identities and roles beyond daughter, wife and mother. Most seemed to be caught between the interplay of these structural and cultural influences. With a few exceptions, neither school nor home presented them with an alternative range of opportunities to thrive and further maximise their potential. As shown in Chapter 6, the girls' experiences of gender inequalities are by no means unique (Basit 1996, 1997; Dwyer 2000; Walkerdine et al. 2001; Archer 2002; Breitenbach 2006; Emejulu 2013). Their problems are ones that girls and women, regardless of race, ethnicity, class, age and sexuality face in general—living within patriarchal family structures that dictate how we ought to

© The Author(s) 2019
G. Marcus, *Gypsy and Traveller Girls*, Studies in Childhood and Youth,
https://doi.org/10.1007/978-3-030-03703-1_7

be. However, by raising awareness of the 'situated localised accounts' of their 'lived lives' this study highlights aspects of the Gypsy and Traveller girls' experiences that other groups may not encounter, but help 'to reveal the ways of "being and becoming" a gendered, sexed, raced and classed subject of materialist discourse' (Mirza 2015: 4).

As noted in Chapters 5 and 6, Collins (2000) argues that individuals have agency and their identities, experiences and worldview play systemic roles. I reiterate that there are no studies that have attempted to explore the ambitions of Gypsy and Traveller girls in Scotland. This chapter attempts to address this gap and provides a space to demonstrate their agency—centering their individual accounts of success, aspirations and identity. It focuses on emancipation—the girls imagining their future and daring to 'dream big'. Some of these young people might not be able to actualise those dreams, but it is still valuable to elicit and analyse these views (Hutchings 1997). I thus seek to address the final research questions: *What are the girls' life ambitions and aspirations? Where there is perceived success, what explanations do the participants offer?*

During our discussions, the girls were asked:

- What are you good at?
- What does success or being successful mean to you?
- If you had a magic wand, what would you like to do in the future when you grow up?
- Do you think you will get there? Why or why not?

These questions were asked as a direct response to a statement made by one stakeholder in particular that, 'Gypsy and Traveller girls, are only interested in marriage and having babies, so there is no point as the girls have no ambitions or aspirations... you won't get any data, you are wasting your time' (Anon. Academic 1 2013, Personal communication). Structural, hegemonic and interpersonal spheres of domination can interact with individual and group agency to construct systems of power and oppression (Collins 2000: 276). This chapter explores the complex ways in which the young people's individual identity intersects with their identities as learners and their family and cultural identity, which ultimately affect how they perceive their future.

First, I highlight their individual definitions of the word 'success' and their understanding of what it is to be a successful person. The next part explores their aspirations, and I argue that the term 'success' is too subjective and personal to be defined for the purpose of this study, but instead is left open for consideration by the girls. In a narrow sense, it could be taken to mean 'academic success', but by including achievements in other areas that have either impacted on their educational experiences or vice versa, they could equally define it in a broader sense. Success can be seen to emphasise individual achievement, and not necessarily be inclusive of one's family and community, or even abandoning these ties if necessary. Finally, building on previous chapters, I discuss silences, tensions and contradictions in their discourse.

Definitions of Success

In discussing the girls' educational experiences, most spoke of negative and harmful encounters at school. As many seemed to have shunned formal education and not experienced much success in academic attainment or achievements in school, I was curious to discover how they defined success. I had expected them to talk about achieving wealth and living in relative comfort, and for some to still cite having good academic results, but I was surprised by what they articulated.

When asked about what it means to be successful, Skye spoke of 'achieving [her] dream' but has 'no ten-year plan'. Rona said she hoped she would 'just stay [herself] and not try to hide… not change'. The following discussion took place:

Rona: Yeah I think that would be success for me like just…grow old gracefully, like not try to be older…I don't know I can't think.
Skye: I think another way of success to me would…just being happy with my own life. I think to be successful you've got to be happy.
Rona: Yeah I think for success I'd probably just like surround myself with…
Skye: Things that make you happy?
Rona: Yeah like…my family have a lot to do with my happiness…

GM: You're a TravellerGypsy and Travellers and I get the feeling that you're very proud of being a Traveller?
Skye: I don't know…I hope I'm a good person so…I don't know…I would hate it if anybody described me as…narrow-minded or…I don't know I just…I really just want to be open about my thoughts.

Again, like Skye and Rona, Vaila said happiness was an important element of being or feeling successful, but her family was a crucial part of that happiness.

I see success as just being happy, and then like having a job, being happy doing it, being happy with all your family, all your family and things, I'd rather be…. if you're going to be married you're better being…you'd be better being like happy and poor than being rich and miserable.

Sandray, the oldest of the girls I interviewed, asserted, after some discussion, that success to her was about:

Doing something that's true to you and you know…not what everybody…as I say not what everybody else wants you to do and as long as you're doing what you want to do and you're not…restricted in any way that's what I call success, because I feel like a lot of these Travellers are'nae getting…they are'nae getting the education and the opportunities as other people are getting because they're restricted and because they're… they've been brought up differently.

When asked what they thought success meant, the girls at the youth centre in particular struggled to explain. I then asked if they could tell me what they thought they were good at, and apart from Ailsa, the girls struggled to give examples. Islay, aged only 13, said that there was 'nothing much really' that she was good at. If you recall, she is the same girl who admitted there was going to be nothing more to her life after marriage and bearing children, declaring 'and then you die'. When encouraged to think about it more, they still could not give any examples of talents or activities of which they were proud. I recalled their description of their life as consisting mainly of household duties and 'sitting around' the trailer and being confined to the Traveller site. They did say that the highlight of their life at the present time was to go to lunch with their friends at the youth centre, which they attend two days a week. They did not mention having extracurricular activities. As if to brush off my persistent questioning, they mentioned enjoying Maths and that they were quite good at it. Their inability or reluctance to talk about success or to explain what they were good at reminded me of my conversation with Sandray, who was critical of her community and the way it treated girls:

> The more knowledge I gained throughout my own life the more I was open to embrace like whatever was flung at me because you know as I say Travellers and Gypsies right, they're very limited in their knowledge of the world. And like books and things like that, and like languages, and places, they're very limited because they don't know a lot. And the girls you don't know if they're happy or if they're not happy because it's their first ever boyfriend and they don't know any better. And I don't believe like sleeping around is a good thing, I'm not like that at all, but you should at least like experience going out with different people, and maybe even travelling for a bit, like travelling the world for a bit and getting an insight to life rather than staying in your home town and marrying somebody from your home town and passing that on. I just want them to get an education like definitely!

Her explanation highlighted a lack of knowledge and experience amongst girls in her community, restricted choice and outlook. I told her about some of the girls I had met who had expressed career aspirations beyond marriage and child rearing. She conceded, 'that's true and that's what happens with Travellers as well, however, I feel like because it's getting more a modern age I feel like the girls also get a wee bit of a say now. Slowly things are changing'.

Ailsa was the only girl at the youth centre who readily talked about her love of art, knitting and dressmaking:

> *Ailsa*: Uh…I've always loved drawing and painting and stuff, I also like…I make clothes as well.
> *GM*: So you might just combine it with fashion design?
> *Ailsa*: Yeah.

GM: With your artistic talents that's wonderful. So the top that you're
  wearing at the moment is beautiful, did you choose that for yourself?
Ailsa: Yeah
GM: So do you go out and buy the material for sewing and knitting?
Ailsa: I go out and buy material and I make them too
GM: And your mum and dad they encourage this?
Ailsa: Uh…no I've just always liked doing it.

In contrast, the two sisters, Iona and Fara, were distinctive in their
response. Despite periods of interrupted learning, having attended 13
schools, and currently no longer enrolled in any school through their
own choice; they were passionate about their ambition to pursue their
interests in horses, animal welfare and art. Sixteen-year-old Iona spends
most of her time with her horse at the local livery and her parents
actively encourage her zeal and what seems more than just a hobby. The
series of exchanges below reveals Iona's interest in and love of horses,
which is consistent and central to Gypsy and Traveller culture, trades
and lifestyle, as Williamson (1994) details with joy in his book *The
Horsieman: Memories of a Traveller*. The love, regard and care of horses
play a major role in Traveller life. To Iona, success lies with her horses.

Iona: All I ever go on about is my horse by the way! Because she's my life
  and I love show jumping.
GM: And you clearly know everything there is to know about looking
  after your horse? [Laughter]
Iona: If there's any books or anything on the Internet I've read it and seen
  it and watched it!
GM: That's wonderful!
Iona: And I'd love to do competitions but I've never been to one.
GM: So you really understand the behaviour of the horses that you're
  with?
Iona: Aye I love natural horsemanship.
GM: How do you think you got that? Where did you learn that from?
  Did you read that information somewhere or did you…just from
  watching them all the time?
Iona: Well…I've worked with them (horses) for a few years now and —
  I'm not the best and I'm not…I would'nae call myself good but I love

what I do. I like bitless riding it's just…it's like a bridle but…or a rubber bit I use and I put syrup on it so the horse can taste it.
GM: So it really excites you?
Iona: It really excites me. I get all butterflies in my stomach because I wonder what will I learn today?

Fara admitted she was afraid of horses and spends most of her time at the youth centre drawing, painting, knitting, and crochet. Her mother brought out some of her pieces to show me and together we talked at length about some of Fara's work and the effort she put into her creativity. Her sister interjected into our conversation and proudly declared Fara is 'very creative'.

Fara: I dinnae think I'm good at them but I'd like to be like…if somebody ken was professional at it…I'd like for them to say that I'm good at it.
GM: Yeah okay so you don't think you're good at it you're just doing it? You wouldn't say yourself that you're good at it?
Fara: Aye!
GM: Why not?
Fara: Just because like there's always somebody better than you.
GM: I know but that doesn't mean you're not good right? So you're very humble. [Laughter]

When asked what success meant to them, Iona explained that for her it would entail 'achieving something like work wise, if I got…I'd love to be a trainer for…you know like a personal trainer or even just working at a riding school'. Fara did not explain what success meant but gave an example of what it would look like to her:

Like in 20 years time I'd love to be famous…I'd love to have one of my paintings or something that I did in a gallery, or…somebody buying things that I do and just to be able to know that I can actually do something for others to enjoy.

I enjoyed my time with Fara, Iona and their family. Spending a whole morning in their trailer and walking around their land, I observed closeness, lots of laughter and strong sense of camaraderie amongst them. Highly independent and spirited young women, they decided to design and follow an informal curriculum that suited their needs and interests. Learning at home was safer than learning in school. Neither mentioned socialising with their peers—Travellers or otherwise—and I assumed that such interactions may be limited to family members and cousins. They were articulate and passionate about their own interests and, at times, I forgot that they had both left school by the age of 12. With their parents' support, they have been allowed and encouraged to pursue a range of skills and interests outwith the formal school curriculum.

These vignettes demonstrate that there is a range of interpretations of success—from not being able to define or highlight moments of achievement in their lives to girls who have a clearer sense of how they would determine if they were successful women. As noted earlier, none of the girls discussed success in terms of achieving wealth, nor academic attainment as a marker of accomplishment. In Gypsy and Traveller culture, it is usually presumed that wealth must be distributed among kin. Individual capitalist accumulation is not usually valued, let alone allowed to remain.

While there is no literature on the educational aspirations of Gypsy and Traveller girls to draw upon, evidence from studies conducted with other minority ethnic girls provides useful comparisons. As highlighted in Chapter 6, some British Muslim, South Asian and Scottish Pakistani girls suggested that in their lives there is a clear trajectory, supported by their parents and focused on educational attainment and career success. Such accomplishments were not only highly prized, but also seen as bringing honour to the family. For the girls from working class backgrounds, their middle-class aspirations provided a bridge to a better life and higher status, not just for them, but for their families (Basit 1996, 1997; Dwyer 2000; Archer 2002; Emejulu 2013). Basit (1997: 437) for example maintained that 'they wish to improve and advance through routes of education and careers, but not to the detriment of their ethnic identity of origin'. They 'constructed inequalities of racism/sexism as shaping and constraining choices' in the workplace (Archer 2002: 373).

Some of the Gypsy and Traveller girls report having fears that they would be racially discriminated against when trying to secure a job. Sandray, Vaila and Rona in particular grappled with whether they ought to declare their ethnic identity:

> You don't really want to be singled out, but it's stupid that they're hiding it, like not all people like judge you... I think if you try and hide it as well people are more determined to pick on you because of it, because if you're ashamed then they have a reason to, because if you stay open and honest with everyone you're not going to be a victim are you? There's nothing to hold against you. (Skye)

And Vaila explained:

> *GM*: You're going to say that you're a Traveller and what happens if you don't get a job?
> *Vaila*: Then I'm going to have to keep trying, keep trying but I don't see the point in hiding what I am so... I don't know like if I went for a job I wouldn't come out with it straightaway like I'm a Traveller I would leave it be until if someone did ask.

To hide their ethnicity and pass as White Scottish might secure them a job, but hiding their identity would be a betrayal of their parents, family, culture and heritage. All the girls declared that they would not deny who they were, especially if asked, and even if it meant loss of employment or discrimination at work. Although I did meet several girls at university who did not wish to take part in the study because they did not want to reveal or discuss their Gypsy or Traveller heritage.

Walkerdine et al. (2001) offer insight into the complexities involved when girls try to realise their aspirations, and reveals that class inequalities continue to hamper White girls in different ways. The study found that socio-economic forces in a patriarchal world continue to burden middle class girls' achievements as they struggle to either balance a career with household and childrearing duties, or choose one at the expense of the other. Limits are also set on the dreams of working class girls, who lack the social capital to transcend their situations should they wish to do so. In a seemingly post-sexist world, Walkerdine et al. (2001) problematise the phenomenon of 'girl power' where young women are led to believe they are able to 'have it all'. They question to what extent girls and women are able to forge a 'feminine future' within predominantly patriarchal systems (Walkerdine et al. 2001).

Inequalities that arise from ethnicity, cultural norms, values and gendered expectations and class conspire to restrict girls' lives and ambitions in a variety of ways (Walkerdine et al. 2001; Archer 2002; Emejulu 2013). Herein lies the complexity of freedom and choice in the lived aspirations of minority ethnic girls who wish to realise their dreams. But they are not alone, as White middle class and working class girls also experience such challenges. Hegemonic patriarchy and powerful masculinity in families and communities, across race and class affect women from a range of ethnic backgrounds in different ways (Basit 1997; Dwyer 2000; Talbani and Hasanali 2000; Walkerdine et al. 2001; Archer 2002; Emejulu 2013; Farris and de Jong 2014).

Aspirations and Ambitions

Given that most of the girls interviewed did not attach high value to education and educational attainment, I was curious to discover what alternative aspirations and ambitions they harboured, what they hoped to achieve and what they dreamt of doing in the future. I asked them, 'What would you like to do in the future, when you grow up?' Table 7.1 summarises their choices.

As the table shows, 11 girls aspired to being married and having children, and out of those, six did not see themselves combining marriage with a career, and two in particular said they were not sure if it was possible to do so. Many of these girls seem to be able to anticipate the pressures of maintaining traditional roles of wife and mother, and pursuing a career. Their reservations subtly reflect the continuing constraints of socio-economic forces that limit young women's career aspirations, when faced with societal expectations that it is still largely their

Table 7.1 Career and marriage aspirations of the 13 research participants

Name of participant	Age	No of primary schools attended	Marriage between 16 and 18 years	Job only	Job and marriage	Unsure if marriage and job can be combined
Skye	16	1			✓	
Rona	19	1			✓	
May	12	12	✓			
Ailsa	13	4			✓	✓
Islay	13	8	✓			
Cara	12	5	✓			
Dana	13	5	✓			
Shona	16	2	✓			
Kilda	18	2	✓			
Vaila	15	3			✓	✓
Iona	16	13		✓		
Fara	13	13		✓		
Sandray	22	1			✓	
Total	13		6	2	5	2

role to perform unpaid domestic labour in the home (Davis 1983: 225; Walkerdine et al. 2001).

Only two girls, Iona and Fara, said they were not interested in getting married or having children. The last two chapters revealed that apart from these two exceptions, all the girls who had left mainstream education by 12 years of age did not see the need to attend school because they were destined to be homemakers and carers. Most acknowledged that even if they had aspirations to pursue a career, they knew it was expected that they would marry and have children, unless they had their family's approval to do otherwise. Their silent acceptance of the status quo was a reflection of their respect for their parents, but also propagates the community's traditions and existence. To challenge that status quo might mean being ostracised and viewed as a threat to the community, as some of the girls reveal below. The next section details their ideas about marriage and the kind of jobs they dreamed of doing.

For sisters Shona and Kilda, learning to drive was their current ambition and example of success—as they emphasised clearly (Fig. 7.1).

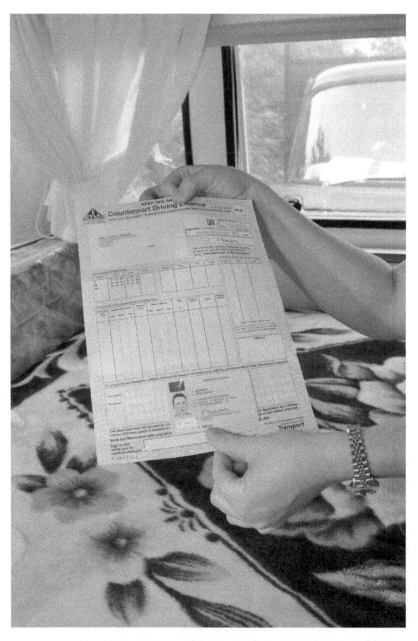

Fig. 7.1 Freedom (*Source* Courtesy of MECOPP/©Peter E. Ross)

When I got my driving licence, aw it was like a ticket to freedom. The world was my oyster when I got this (Jolene). (MECOPP et al. 2014: 126)

Other than that, the sisters wanted to get married and knew that was what was expected of them both. Kilda said she was happy with her life and her parents' expectations for her:

Yeah I'm happy with what I've got yeah…it's the way I was brought up you know what I mean? I'm happy doing it yeah. We couldn't see ourselves living any different.

I noted her seemingly uncomplicated acceptance of life, and her contentment. I was equally struck by Shona's idea of success. 'Well my mother and father brought up nine children… They have brung up nine, my mum's got three boys and six girls so that's a lot.' Her ambition is to be just like her parents, as they are her principal role models. For her, being a success is managing her home and family, just like her parents, and being a 'close big sister' to her siblings. In Chapter 5, it was clear from the evidence of their accounts that teachers too were not inspirational role models. Of those girls who had some experience of secondary school, none mentioned getting career advice from their teachers. Other studies of minority ethnic girls affirm this phenomenon (Basit 1996, 1997; Archer 2002). Basit (1996: 232) also argues that 'the development of career choices is a complex process, with [many] not choos[ing] occupations in a meaningful sense'. Given the lack of alternative role models and poor support and guidance, the low aspirations the girls had for themselves is perhaps not surprising. Basit (1996: 232) contends that young people 'simply take what is available within narrowly-spaced, horizontal social-class barriers'. That appears to be what might be happening with the girls in my study.

The extended conversation below demonstrated the sisters' determination to adhere to long held values and traditional expectations:

Kilda: That's pretty much our job like we cook and clean that's a job to us but to us that's like normal life, because that's what you're going to have to do when you get married, you're going to have to cook and clean for your husband. [Laughter]

Shona: Yeah like…like we pick up everything from our mothers, how to cook, how to clean, how to cook and clean, and like babysit, and I love brothers and sisters! Yeah I love spending my time with them and I don't think I'll be getting married at 18 because I think I'll be staying at home a lot longer yeah

Kilda: You could be doing worser things at my age do you know what I mean?

GM: Absolutely.

Kilda: To be honest I feel proud of myself because at the end of the day I've got…I've never had a boyfriend so if I've never had a boyfriend no boy can talk behind my back, I've helped and I've done my bit do you know what I mean so if I get married I've done my bit at home. I've done my bit you know and one of my other sisters will take over from that because that's what happens.

Kilda: Yeah it's the way I was brought up you know what I mean? I'm happy doing it yeah. We couldn't see ourselves living any different.

GM: Yeah it's just your…it's part of your blood?

Kilda: Yeah it is part of our blood. Part of who we are! We don't put ourselves down for anybody,

GM: And you're happy with what you've got?

Kilda: Yeah I'm happy with what I've got yeah!

Kilda stressed that it was vital to marry a boy who could look after her well.

That's just the way they work, it's like you'd rather a rich boy or…not a rich boy but at the end of the day it doesn't matter if you marry rich yes or no as long as…at the end of the day as long as that boy can look after you know what I mean? As long as he can look after you, as long as you've got a roof over your head and clothes on your back.

Her expectations seemed basic to me, almost at the point of embracing mere survival. It is her father's responsibility in particular to judge the trustworthiness of the prospective groom, but it is important to make the right choice because if the chosen husband was not good enough and the marriage failed, 'we don't look for another husband because that's not the way…we've had our husband that's that! We'd never look for another husband again do you know what I mean?' (Kilda). Also, the boy would not be at fault but 'it's not…the boy…there would be nobody talking about the boy, it would be everybody talking about us…the girl and her family'. What was clear from this conversation was that should her marriage fail because the boy was not a good enough husband, it would be deemed her fault, and she would not be able to re-marry and neither would she be allowed to work or have a career. This perception that boys and girls are treated differently in Gypsy and Traveller culture, and indeed in some other minority ethnic cultures, was discussed in the previous chapter. What was also apparent was her limited knowledge of the alternative choices for her life that might be open to her.

Islay, Cara and Dana mentioned that they would like to have a job before getting married, but said they recognised that they would have to eventually give it up. They would have liked to become hairdressers or beauticians as this could fit well with their lifestyle and traditions — self-employment, owning their own business, working with women as clients, whilst being mobile for all or parts of the year. This phenomenon is relative new compared with the seasonal farm work, fortune-telling and selling of goods, that Traveller women would have done in the past.

However, marriage and career were still seen as mutually exclusive. In this rapid exchange, Islay and Cara explained:

Islay: I don't think we can do both.
Cara: No!
Islay: We wouldn't be able to do both. Because like our community girls are just brought up to be -
Cara: Like cleaners and -
Islay: Cleaners and married and cook the food. And look after the family. We wouldn't be able to do both.

Even though Islay said she would have no choice but to get married, she asserted that she would like to be a 'boss' and own a beautician business. She smiled when she said it and acknowledged that this dream is unlikely to be fulfilled. Similarly, May stated that she would just get married. She seemed determined that this was what she wanted, to be married and to have children. Below is an account of her clipped answers to my questions:

> *GM*: What would you like to be when you grow up? What would you like…what do you see yourself doing?
> *May*: Probably…well I wouldn't get a job I'd probably just stay home and cook, and clean, and do that.
> *GM*: So you would be married, and how many children would you like to have?
> *May*: Don't know!
> *GM*: Okay! And do you see yourself getting married, what age do you see yourself getting married by?
> *May*: 17, 19!
> *GM*: Would there be anything else?
> *May*: No!

Dana said because she was not good at reading and writing, and labelled a dyslexic, she believed she could not get a job or have a career. 'I always felt uncomfortable, like always, not clever enough'. When she started at the youth centre, her teacher discovered that she was not actually dyslexic and she was happy about that. She also said that given the chance she would like to go to college. The following exchange reveals contradictory statements of marriage, and when to marry, some confusion on her choices, a lack of advice and guidance on career options and on how to become a beautician:

> *GM*: So we were talking about what you would like to do. What's your dream?
> *Dana*: Like I want to take the course and then like…because there's supposed to be a good university…like no. What do you call it? A college or something? To be a beautician.
> *GM*: Yeah a college!
> *Dana*: A college where I stay and I want to go on and try and finish the course proper but…you never know.
> *GM*: So if you keep coming to this youth centre you could get better…. good grades and then you could go to this college because you'll need

to have a few of the grades to go to college to be a beautician. What are you going to do after that?

Dana: Like…I dunno…then probably it's time to get married because I'll be like 18-19.

GM: Okay do you see yourself getting married at that age?

Dana: Well…some people look at it if you don't get married at that age there's something wrong with you but I don't want to get married at that age.

GM: Okay! Is it your choice?

Dana: Yeah it's your choice but other…

GM: Again people will judge you if you're not?

Dana: Yeah like if you're not married before you're 20, 21, 22, 23 it's like there's something wrong with her, she must be scandalised and that's it.

GM: So that's a lot of pressure on you?

Dana: Hmm! But I probably won't get married.

GM: Why won't you get married?

Dana: I will get married when it's time to get married. My mummy and daddy got married when my mummy was 17, my daddy was 21.

GM: Yeah when you feel you're ready?

Dana: When I feel like I'm ready.

Dana's parents are her principal role models but they are divorced and she lives with her mother and grandmother. I asked her what advice she might give to a Traveller girl:

GM: If you had a chance to give advice to a young girl just like you, a Traveller girl, what would you say to her about her education?

Dana: I'd say to try and come to one of these [the youth centre] and make something of your life.

GM: And get married?

Dana: Yeah but not when you're 16, 17, 18 you're still a child, still in your teens.

What seems clear from these exchanges is that some of the girls believed that getting married and having children, doing housework and being a housewife is all that is ultimately available to them. Low expectations from parents and teachers, and the fear of interacting with non-Travellers and facing racial discrimination perhaps explain their restricted aspirations for themselves. Their accounts indicate that their choices are restricted by gendered and racialised boundaries. Again, the girls' experiences in my study are not unique but given that other minority ethnic girls are over-performing in education and have high aspirations for themselves speaks to the need for more research on this topic (Emejulu 2013; The Scottish Parliament 2016).

Ailsa was the only girl from the youth centre who said she could possibly combine her dream to be an artist or fashion designer with marriage. She thought she would probably get the support from her parents to do so. I deduced that her parents' separation and her mother's limited income may possibly be the reason for her desire to empower herself with a degree of financial security.

> *Ailsa*: Uh…yeah my mummy told me that she would want me to do something with my life first before I get married. And I told her that's what I wanted to do.
> *GM*: What's your plan?
> *Ailsa*: My plan is to go to college.
> *GM*: I mean do you think that um…your family might stop you from achieving your dream? Are your mum and dad happy for you to be an artist?
> *Ailsa*: No my family want me to achieve my dream. Being a Traveller I think that might stop me from getting my dream achieved.
> *GM*: Because you're a Traveller you think people might stop you from achieving your dream if they find out you're a Traveller?
> *Ailsa*: Yes I do. But… no… everyone wants to get a good job but they end up getting married but um…no it isn't true… But I wouldn't get married at a young age. Yeah I don't want to get married at a young age. We're allowed to choose our own husband.

Knowing that she and her family lived in difficult economic circumstances, possibly struggling to make ends meet, it is all the more admirable just how positive this young girl is about life and what she would like to achieve for herself. I sensed that there was a longing to be accepted and to be liked by everyone, to be appreciated for who she was and for her ethnicity as a Traveller. I sensed a sad acceptance, yet shock at how some people have treated her, and that being discriminated against because of her ethnicity would prevent her from achieving her aspirations.

Iona and Fara were not keen on marriage, not even at the age of 20 or 21. I asked their mother how she felt about it and she did not dispute their ideas. Both girls said they were not sure about having children. Iona is desperate to get a job. She declared, 'I've got bigger ambitions in my life!' Here again is a rapid exchange between the girls and I:

> *GM*: Yeah so you…would you like to get married?
> *Iona*: No!
> *GM*: Okay why not?
> *Fara*: Ask the other one that question?
> *GM*: Why not?
> *Fara*: Just because like say other travelling lassies they get married too young and they waste their life that's the way I see it.
> *GM*: So it's not marrying its marrying too young?
> *Fara*: Aye.
> *Iona*: If I was ever going to marry I'd probably be in my 30s or my 20s. I would'nae leave but I would maybe have my own place next to them [her parents] but I dinnae plan on ever getting married.
> *GM*: Why not?
> *Iona*: Because I've got bigger ambitions in my life!
> *GM*: I get it, the two of you are not thinking of marriage, certainly not at a young age, you'd rather get out there and do things with your life, you've got your horses that you're passionate about and you've got your artistic stuff that you love doing. Right. Mum how do you feel about the fact that your girls don't want to get married?
> *Iona*: Do you know what she told us when we were younger, wait until you're 16 and you'll want a boyfriend, it's still not happening. [Laughter]
> *GM*: I know they're a bother aren't they?
> *Iona*: I'd rather my horse! I don't want children! My family is going to be horses, and dogs, and cats, and…guinea pigs! [Laughter]

For Iona, having a successful career in horsemanship is her dream. As highlighted earlier, she is making a concerted effort to teach herself and hopes to be formally trained at the local livery. Her passionate enthusiasm for learning, her dedication, was obvious in her description of the work she does with horses.

> Just…the way I work with them, like what I do when I first meet a horse is I don't jump on its back and go, I'll go in the pen and let it loose and just watch that horse for 20 minutes. If its focused on you it'll have one ear locked on you and be looking at you and walking around you, circling you.

Iona then adds that it is actually difficult for her to predict what she might do: 'I dinnae really know because you could think you're going to have the best life in the world but something bad can happen and it's going to end up going downhill'.

Vaila is at college and is currently pursuing two courses—professional cookery and hairdressing. She tells me that she has also taken on extra classes in Mathematics because she thinks this will help her career and help her run her business.

> *GM*: Uh huh so actually you're someone who might end up doing either, either the hairdressing or even the cooking?
>
> *Vaila*: Yeah because I thought that if I went to college to do two different courses at least then I'd have a qualification each so I'd always be able to choose. Um…if I was to get married and then had stopped working you know I'd probably enjoy it at first just…but then I think I probably would end up wanting to start working again until like two years down the line if I ended up having like children I would want to stay at home.

She struck me as having clear ideas about what she wanted to do with her life and was actively pursuing her dreams. Vaila won an award for her effort and grade in one of her courses and was recognised for it in an official ceremony. No one from her family attended the ceremony, and this could be to avoid revealing her ethnicity in public, or that her family might have felt uncomfortable in that formal setting. She is worried about her future opportunities in the workplace because she is a Traveller:

> *GM*: And do you think when Travellers who are getting as you say a better education, better jobs do you think that they are…that it's easier for them to get jobs now and -
> *Vaila*: I think so!
> *GM*: And are they saying that they are Travellers or are they maybe not saying that?
> *Vaila*: No they're not saying that.
> *GM*: And why do you think they're not saying that?
> *Vaila*: Because my sister went to get a job and as soon as she said that she was a Traveller they were like okay we'll arrange another interview for you to come back and things and then…we'll phone you but they never did and I think that's something to do with her being a Traveller.

I asked Vaila if her parents would insist that she get married and if so whether she would obey their request:

> *Vaila*: See I don't know because like my family have always supported everything I've done so far.
> *GM*: Right so that's nice so…so you know that they would respect your choice even if they think maybe it's not what they would choose for themselves?
> *Vaila*: They'd probably advise me not to do it but they would say…I'm asking you not to do it but if you really want to you can go ahead and do it. And if I really wanted to…if it meant a lot to me I would.

At 22 years old Sandray was the oldest young woman I interviewed. She did well at school, has recently finished a music course at college, plays two instruments, sings, writes her own songs, teaches music to young children, and plans to go to university.

GM: You're following your dream?

Sandray: My dream! So...and it's led me to...I'm doing teaching now. I'm teaching kids to sing, and I'm going to be starting a band soon so I'm writing my own songs.

Music-making is of course core to some Gypsy and Traveller traditions including songs and ballads aby women. She was an impressive young woman. She has a non-Traveller boyfriend whom I also met, does not plan to get married soon but does think that it is possible to combine a career and family life:

I really want to get like a music career, I'd really love to get a music career and just do that for the rest of my life. And I do plan on getting married, but just not right this minute. I want my career first and I do want children and I want to get married. Every girl wants that you know?

She said her parents 'did'nae mind if you know...if I was to get married or not. They were'nae like totally fussed that you have to get married kind of thing'. Her older sister is not married and has a career. She admitted that until she went to college she led a sheltered life and her parents were strict with her. The process of emancipation began earlier, 'I think I found my niche in secondary, I found like music and people were 'nae really too bothered as much as they were in primary that I was a Gypsy'. She expressed her passion for music and being a musician, but that she had to learn about other people and other ways of doing and living:

But I only started to find out like other people's views...because obviously I'd been brought up with my own views and my family's traditions I started to embrace like other people's ways of living. And I thought that's not right, or that's wrong, but then obviously as you get older you start to accept people for who they are and you start to accept other people's ways of seeing things... but because I knew about like other things like the world, and I was getting an education it just opened my mind up a bit more and it made me more easy going rather than strict. Able to make decisions for myself.

Sandray contacted me to be interviewed. Like the girls in Article 12 she cares passionately about her community and is aware of the changes that need to be made especially for girls:

> Gypsies....Travellers don't have sex before marriage. They don't do that. So...the only escapism is if they marry their boyfriend they'll be able to do that. And I feel like that's...one of the reasons why they get married is to have sex and to get a life like that. And...you know...yeah like I feel like that's one of the reasons why they want to get married and the other reason is they don't know any better. They don't know, like...some of my cousins have married their first ever boyfriend. They don't know any better... you don't know if they're happy.

Sandray thinks that Gypsy and Traveller girls should be true to themselves and she has written a song about it:

> Don't wait around and you know waiting for it to happen, just going out and doing it for yourself and thinking...one of the lyrics says it's not too late to break the chain. So I feel like I've kind of broken the chain because I've broken tradition and I've broken like my views on life. Like not broken them but like I broke free.

Rona and Skye, Vaila, and Sandray explained how much they valued formal education as a means to get a job. They wanted to pursue a career, and gain financial and social independence from men. Vaila said, 'a lot of Travellers nowadays are actually getting jobs and getting better education'. However, she recognised that this may not be easy. She admitted she would 'try and keep work until I got married and after you're married it's going to change because you're going to have to be a stay at home wife'. Sandray, as she explained above, believed that it was important to have choice in life, to break free of tradition and to have the freedom to be true to yourself. The lyrics to her song are powerful:

> So basically be true to yourself and if you want to go to school, or if you want to go to college, or if you want to go to university you do it! If you

want to learn a new subject you do it! And don't let anybody bully you or put you off.

Her impassioned words reveal that Gypsy and Traveller girls (as do girls in general) need better support at home and at school. The implication is that some or many may be trapped by cultural expectations at home and low expectations in school as the girls' accounts in Chapters 5 and 6 demonstrate; and that they may lack the advice and support to aspire differently to reach their full potential. They may seem happy and may even insist that they are genuinely so, but as Sandray highlighted, they may not actually know any better.

The girls from Article 12 have made it their mission to have 'a chance to change opinions'. They believe that:

> Traveller girls need more opportunities, like to get to see life, like we have, get to learn that they can do stuff and they don't need to get married and like… but half of them is terrified of the outside world and how they're going to be treated to actually do anything.

One of the focus group was married, but the others were still single. All were above the age of 16. One member of the group said she had only contemplated getting married before, but since her work with Article 12 other opportunities for work have opened up to her. Another said she wanted to study English at university because she wrote good stories, 'and the teacher says they were really good in primary school, and I was really good at English in high school' (Member of Focus group). A third member of the group revealed:

> Uh…well since I've been 13 I've had the same ambition and one day I will get it, I'd love to be a Gypsy Traveller Liaison Officer. I would have loved somebody that was a Traveller to come and understand my problems and help us when we're in camps. So I think there should be more Travellers that knows the problem, understands it and knows how to help. I mean like my mother felt…like she kept saying to me aye do that, because she wanted me to have something with my life, not just get married, and that's the end of it.

The girls are articulate and ambitious ambassadors for Article 12 and Gypsy/Travelling communities in Scotland. Their friendship and sisterhood is key to their empowerment as young women, with one member describing how important they were to each other: 'Well with all of us together. Our relationship has been key in the trust with parents, it's been key to get through all those challenges and barriers we faced together'. The girls are looking for formal accreditation for the work that they have done, not just at local level but also throughout Scotland and in Europe:

> We are a massive project that so many people are aware of now, not just at the UK level but European level that we have been asked to be part of this wider European project that will support us through recognising the credit, the work that we do. Either through um…work paths or an academic path… better equipped to be more… to challenge that structural inequality that all of us have faced.

At the end of our discussion one member summed up their work: 'If this generation can make a change, the next generation can enjoy it'. Whilst Rona, Skye, Vaila, and Sandray seemed to already enjoy such changes—and Iona and Fara were content with their choices and passion for horses and art—I could not help but wonder about the restricted opportunities available to the rest of the girls. They seemed accepting that marriage and child rearing, cooking and cleaning were what their families expected of them and that it was part of their tradition. Sandray's warning about whether they knew any better kept echoing in my mind. Their loyalty and love for their families perhaps subsume their potential.

Even so, the girls who are reaching beyond marriage and childbearing seemed to only be aspiring to feminised options in the arts and crafts or in vocational pursuits. As highlighted in Chapters 4 and 5, none of them have mentioned aspiring to professional career paths. A few— Rona, Skye, Vaila, Sandray—alluded to having good grades in school, and yet seemed to have excluded themselves from what could be perceived as higher status options. Their choices reveal commonly accepted gendered occupational roles. There might be a case for inferring that girls from Gypsy and Traveller backgrounds, like other young girls, identify as having lower self-esteem, that they are not likely to succeed in certain fields of work, or do not aspire to these because it may not fit in with traditions and family expectations. It was unacceptable in my view for a young person not to be able to talk about at least one thing they were good at and Islay's answer 'Nothing much really', is an indication of how badly she has been served by structural and cultural systems that surround her. In many of the cases, their families shape who they are, who they can be and how far they are allowed to dream.

In Chapter 2, I discussed Heaslip's (2015) findings that reveal her participants—male and female—who come from a range of backgrounds, ages, and housing, felt vulnerable both outwith and within their communities. Using Heaslip's findings in Chapter 5, I argued that some aspects of exposure to the outside community threatened the girls: being an outsider, negative perceptions of themselves from their non-Traveller peers and teachers, feeling that they had to conform to the majority non-Traveller values, feeling discriminated against and persecuted and threatened, and at times feeling powerless, especially when faced with racist bullying in the playground and non-supportive school staff. However, conversations about family relations showed that the girls betrayed no feelings of vulnerability within the Gypsy and Traveller community itself. A few were critical of the community's attitude to girls and women, and called for there to be greater freedom of choice. Only one girl, Sandray, said at times she felt confused about who she was. Mixing with both non-Traveller and Traveller peers caused her to question her sense of identity, but even then, she felt this was part of a positive process of growing up.

The findings in this chapter indicate that some of the girls may actually be vulnerable, even if they do not think they are. Their vulnerability stems from their youth, their lack of choice, their lack of agency, lack of information on the sorts of subjects they could pursue at school and the fields of work open to them. The school system, via the efforts of teachers and support staff, reinforces certain paths and does not offer the range of possibilities. There seems to be a lack of encouragement. Similarly, at home parents and their community reinforce traditional paths and expectations, and there is a lamentable lack of opportunities for these girls. From a black feminist viewpoint, the girls' narratives at times suggest that they can be infantilised and it perhaps suits schools, families and communities to keep them, and to certain extent all women, feeling vulnerable and in need of protection, disempowering them in the process.

Silences, Tensions and Contradictions

As in Chapter 6, the girls' silent acceptance of the status quo was a reflection of their respect for their parents, but also propagates the community's traditions and existence. To challenge the status quo might result in them being ostracised.

They did not talk about their financial circumstances being prohibitive of their future aspirations. Class and wealth were not discussed and were not even cited as measures of success. What was not entirely visible was their lack of choice because of their social class or economic circumstances of their families. Matters to do with sex or sexuality in the context of family life, for example, were not discussed, and I would not have expected them to do so with a researcher, although there is a growing movement amongst Roma LGBT communities to highlight the challenges they face (Romani Arts 2018). Silence and conformity were part of, perhaps even, complicit in the hegemonic patriarchy in family and community.

Sandray did talk about the lack of sexual opportunity before marriage, and that she believed a reason why Gypsy and Traveller girls get married young was so they could have sexual relations. She believed it was important to have several partners before settling down. Her views contrast powerfully with Gypsy and Traveller values and the sexual taboos within the communities.

Again, most were silent on the matter of facing pressure to marry young and have children. In talking about their career aspirations, Rona, Skye and Sandray directly acknowledged this pressure to conform existed in their communities. Similarly, I was not sure if these silences existed because the girls were largely unaware, or because the silences represent paths of least resistance, or if they might have felt awkward criticising their families. Most did not complain that they had to conform to live a particular way of life—they seemed to just accept it. Some were ambivalent about why they wanted to get married, and when they intended to achieve their goal. They were trying to negotiate when they thought it would be reasonable to be married and what their parents might expect of them. Shona, for example, declared she would be expected to get married by 18, but that she still felt she was a child.

Ailsa faced the same conundrum. She was unsure or conflicted in her opinion that her parents would support her career choice to become an artist. Although four girls—Rona, Skye, Vaila, and Sandray—remarked upon the vulnerable position of Gypsy and Traveller girls, they stated that they were different and were not in that position. The strong desire for most of the girls to quietly conform, to belong and take refuge in the safety of the community (Belton 2013) was again evident.

Most did not seem able or empowered to negotiate a more balanced perspective of their own identity and the identity they gain from family and cultural heritage—how to be true to oneself, as Sandray mentioned—and yet be loyal to the group. The family and community loyalty that they demonstrate reinforces Okely's argument (1975) that identity and a sense of belonging is not a one-way process, as it requires both social and self-ascription. If one is to judge these practices as sexist, then it is not just men that oppress women. In discussing their aspirations and ambitions, most of the girls' acceptance or silence and loyalty reinforce the idea that both men and women cooperate to maintain powerful norms that control and preserve the Gypsy and Traveller way of life. Unsurprisingly, these discussions reveal that both men and women have a vested interest in the preservation of their communities' culture and 'ethnic inheritance' (Okely 1983: 207). Equally, the fact that some of them are willing to criticise and question the status quo suggests that they represent a voice of change, which in turn reveals that cultures, communities and identities can be challenged and are not fixed constructs. I am reminded of Deleuze and Guattari's (1977, 1987) and Grosz's (1994) assertions that culture and community values are not only powerful, but rhizomatic and volatile. Gypsy and Traveller societies are of course not immune to change. Like other minority groups, they have had to change in relation to the dominant society with whom they are economically and politically interdependent. The girls from Article 12 are working to bring about change in the way their communities are perceived and treated, and they are trying to change the way their communities perceive the role of women. They have become positive role models. Discussions on success and ambition show that Rona, Skye, Sandray, and to a certain extent Vaila, may not just represent anomalies, but hint at a generation that is reinventing or reinterpreting long established attitudes and beliefs.

The girls' narratives show that their experiences are not homogenous. This chapter reveals that most aspire for a career, but also believe that their dream career cannot be fulfilled. The majority expect to follow tradition and get married soon after 16 years of age. The evidence shows that strict gender expectations and cultural taboos can restrict the physical, emotional and mental space to flourish as a Gypsy and Traveller girl. However, I stress that this is not unique. All girls and women, regardless of race, ethnicity, class, age and sexuality experience varying degrees of gender oppression, some of which is overt and others hidden. Discussion on their aspirations and success reinforce findings in previous chapters that some of the girls are beginning to challenge the binding spaces of long held values and traditions, reimagining a world in which they have greater agency and choice. I am equally aware that the choices they have made, beyond marriage and childrearing, are vocational and not professional. Some girls are content and have chosen to accept that this is just part of who they are as Gypsies and Travellers. I question how informed their choice to follow existing cultural practices is and wonder if they are actually compelled to do so through family and cultural pressure. This is not clear to me.

This chapter has endeavoured to present findings and analysis that demonstrate the Gypsy and Traveller girls' complex and agentic ways. Notions of freedom and choice are not fixed constructs, but my research provides further evidence that these ideas are contested, context-bound, restricted and at times negotiated. The girls' assertions of choice were bounded by both gendered and racialised relations. Their youth places them in a vulnerable position as the pressure to respect their elders and conform to cultural norms prevail in their mindset.

As in Chapters 5 and 6, the evidence here reinforces findings that most of the girls seem to be caught betwixt and between structural inequalities in school and within their family and community structures. In the main, they seem to lack choices and the freedom to make choices. Issues of 'space' or lack of 'space' to thrive physically, mentally and emotionally seem apparent. As some of the girls attest, and as is further exemplified by the participants from Article 12, family values and support do make a positive difference to their educational experiences in school and their lives in general. The girls' definitions of success vary, but none define it in terms of wealth or academic success, reinforcing the idea that interpretations of success are not universal, but cross-cultural. One of the most striking findings was the genuinely strong sense of family, community and belonging. Arguably, family and other bonds across all cultures can suppress girls' identities as individuals. hooks (2015: 5) reminds us that 'being oppressed means the absence of choices'. In the main, from their narratives, the possibility of expanding their gender roles and identities appear completely closed to many of them. Back (2007: 22) advises that 'sociological attention is reflective, contestable, uncomfortable, partisan and fraught', and after listening to the girls, I felt that I needed more time to think about the implications of what they were saying, and I am reluctant to make firm conclusions.

The findings suggest that for a few girls, even their attempts to imagine and invent different identities and aspirations are constrained by structural and hegemonic forces they might not be aware of. The girls' lived experiences provide a snapshot of the challenge of realising what Walkerdine et al. (2001) refer to as a 'feminine future'. Consequently, family and cultural expectations can subsume aspirations, or occasionally become boundaries to be tested and sensitively negotiated, and at times individual pursuits are placed on par with the interests of community. For all the girls, commitment to family and community is in marked opposition to the neoliberal tendency to feel accountable to primarily one self. For them the pursuit of individual ambition is not paramount and the evaluation of their success in those terms is not in the narrative of their lived experiences. bell hooks (1981) argues, as many other Black feminists continue to do, that minority women must negotiate a complex terrain because of the inequalities that arise from the intersecting inequalities of race, class and gender. The situation is inherently more complex.

References

Anon. Academic 1. (2013, April 18) Personal communication. Conversation and notes.

Archer, L. (2002) Change, culture and tradition: British Muslim pupils talk about Muslim girls' post-16 'choices'. *Race, Ethnicity and Education*, 5(4), pp. 359–376.

Back, L. (2007) *The art of listening*. Oxford: Berg.

Basit, T. N. (1996) 'I'd hate to be just a housewife': Career aspirations of British Muslim girls. *British Journal of Guidance and Counselling*, 24(2), pp. 227–242.

Basit, T. N. (1997) 'I want more freedom, but not too much': British Muslim girls and the dynamism of family values. *Gender and Education*, 9(4), pp. 425–440.

Belton, B. A. (2013) 'Weak power': Community and identity. *Ethnic and Racial Studies*, 36(2), pp. 282–297.

Breitenbach, E. (2006) Developments in gender equality policies in Scotland since Devolution. *Scottish Affairs*, 56, pp. 10–21.

Collins, P. H. (2000) *Black feminist thought. Knowledge, consciousness and the politics of empowerment*. London: Routledge.

Davis, A. (1983) *Women, race and class*. New York: Vintage.

Deleuze, G., and Guattari, F. (1977) *Rhizom* (Vol. 67). Berlin: Merve.

Deleuze, G., and Guattari, F. (1987) *A thousand plateaus: Capitalism and schizophrenia*. London: The Athlone Press, pp. 3–25.

Dwyer, C. (2000) Negotiating diasporic identities: Young British South Asian Muslim women. *Women's Studies International Forum*, 23(4), pp. 475–486.

Emejulu, A. (2013) Being and Belonging in Scotland: Exploring the intersection of ethnicity, gender and national identity among Scottish Pakistani Groups. *Scottish Affairs*, 84(1), pp. 41–64.

Farris, S. R., and de Jong, S. (2014) Discontinuous intersections: Second-generation immigrant girls in transition from school to work. *Ethnic and Racial Studies*, 37(9), pp. 1505–1525.

Grosz, E. A. (1994) *Volatile bodies: Toward a corporeal feminism*. Bloomington: Indiana University Press.

Heaslip, V. A. (2015) *Experience of vulnerability from a Gypsy/Travelling perspective: A phenomenological study*. Unpublished PhD thesis, Bournemouth: Bournemouth University.

hooks, B. (1981) *Ain't I a woman: Black women and feminism*. Boston: South End Press.

hooks, B. (2015) *Feminist theory: From margin to center*. London: Routledge.

HOTT. (2017) *A sense of identity. An exhibition in celebration of Scotland's Travelling community*. Available at: www.heartofthetravellers.scot. Accessed 12 June 2018.

Hutchings, M. (1997) *Children's constructions of work*. London: University of North London.

MECOPP, Lloyd, M., and Ross, P. (2014) *Moving minds*. Edinburgh: MECOPP.

Mirza, H. S. (2015) Harvesting our collective intelligence: Black British feminism in post-race times. *Women's Studies International Forum*, 51, pp. 1–9.

Okely, J. (1975) Gypsies travelling in Southern England. In: Rehfisch, F. (ed.) *Gypsies, Tinkers and other Travellers*. London: Academic Press, pp. 55–66.

Okely, J. (1983) *The Traveller-Gypsies*. Cambridge: Cambridge University Press.

Romani Cultural and Arts Company. (2018) *LGBT*. Available at: http://www.romaniarts.co.uk/tag/lgbt/. Accessed 20 August 2018.

Talbani, A., and Hasanali, P. (2000) Adolescent females between tradition and modernity: Gender role socialization in South Asian immigrant culture. *Journal of Adolescence*, 23(5), pp. 615–627.

The Scottish Parliament. (2016) 1st Report, 2016 (Session 4): Removing Barriers: Race, ethnicity and employment. Available at: http://www.parliament.scot/parliamentarybusiness/CurrentCommittees/96080.aspx. Accessed 6 May 2016.

Walkerdine, V., Lucey, H., and Melody, J. (2001) *Growing up girl: Psycho-social explorations of gender and class*. London: Palgrave Macmillan.

Williamson, D. (1994) *The Horsieman: Memories of a Traveller 1928–1958*. Edinburgh: Canongate Press.

8

Conclusion: The Power of Inequality

For the first time the gendered voices of Gypsy and Traveller girls about their racialised, classed, and generational experiences of discrimination, have been in focus, which no prior studies have comprehensively addressed. I have sought to present how Gypsy and Traveller girls in Scotland frame their educational experiences, and to utilize relevant studies and theoretical tools for contextualizing those perceptions. The research examines explanations offered by 17 girls on the perceived challenges and barriers they have encountered in school and at home, particularly in view of their life ambitions and aspirations. Where there is perceived success, their definition of what that represents is identified. The girls' stories are juxtaposed with the general problems encountered by Gypsies and Travellers in Scotland and reveal a complex narrative. This research primarily addresses a gap in the literature in which Gypsy and Traveller girls' experiences are both misrecognised and erased through non-representation. In addition, accounts of Scottish Gypsy and Traveller life reflect an authored gender imbalance in being largely written by men.

This book advances the use of participants' voices that are traditionally marginalised. To ensure accuracy, the interviews conducted for

© The Author(s) 2019
G. Marcus, *Gypsy and Traveller Girls*, Studies in Childhood and Youth,
https://doi.org/10.1007/978-3-030-03703-1_8

this study were recorded and transcribed ad verbatim. These are used throughout the main chapters and provide a reflection of the girls' culture, language, identity, thoughts and emotions. Due to the sample size, this research makes no claims though of generalisability. Instead, the study serves as a vignette of a community closed to outsiders and establishes a basis for future research in this area. In its critical framing of the girls' interviews as primary sources, the book offers space for their voices to be heard, and in so doing underscores their potential for agency in the private spaces of home and the public spaces of formal education. The external view of Gypsy and Traveller girls predicated on the notion that they do not value education and only aspire to a traditional gendered role as wife and mother is contested by the girls' accounts of their lives.

The book demonstrates that although the girls' exclusion and subordination based on class were not overtly visible in the collected data, their youth placed them at a disadvantage when they challenged and accepted deeply embedded discrimination in institutional and hegemonic structures, and the pressure to conform to long held cultural values and expectations within their homes. In this regard, Collins' (2000: 276) discussion of a 'matrix of domination' has provided a useful interpretive tool for analysing the girls' narratives. By adopting an intersectional approach to theorizing the original research, I critically examine the multiple interlocking inequalities that affect the girls' lived experiences. Matsuda's encouragement to 'ask the other question', 'sensitized' my enquiry to acknowledge not just one type of bias but a range of inequalities—race, gender, patriarchy, class, age (Matsuda, cited in Crenshaw 1991: 1245). As noted in Chapter 4, this heuristic tool has helped to identify instances of within-group diversity and 'the limitations of groups within categories to self-identify in a personally relevant or empowering way' (Hancock 2007: 75). Placing the evidence within an intersectional framework, locates common themes that characterise the experiences of the Gypsy and Traveller girls and the ways in which their experiences differ.

Chapters 2 and 3 have offered a critical overview of the context for the book and outlined the background historical setting in which to consider the main themes presented in the literature on Gypsies and

Travellers in the UK and in Scotland in particular. Reference is made to the limited literature on Gypsy and Traveller women in Scotland and the UK, and their educational experiences in Scottish schools. I provide an account of the main groups of Gypsies and Travellers in Scotland and their ethnic and cultural identities. This literature review indicates the clear gaps in published research to date and sets the basis for the argument that Gypsies and Travellers are a racialised minority who are 'normatively absent yet pathologically present' in the Scottish imagination (Mirza 2015: 3). The 'complex machinery of hegemony' pervades the lives of Gypsy and Traveller girls and women.

In Chapter 5, I explored how the girls frame their educational experiences, the forms of educational establishments they have access to, and clarified the Scottish legal context for school enrolment and attendance. The girls' own definitions and understandings of education and learning are foregrounded, prior to revealing their positive experiences and the challenges and obstacles they face. Their narratives demonstrate that although their experiences are not homogenous, the racism and bullying by peers, lack of respect and insufficient support and understanding from school staff, pressure from their families not to attend, together with fear and absence of trust account for why most of the girls cite negative experiences at school. These factors were mentioned as discouraging them from attending mainstream educational facilities.

The evidence exposes the influence of 'levelling down' of the curriculum (Lloyd et al. 1999; Lloyd 2005; Farris and de Jong 2014), a lack of alternative role models and meaningful career guidance, and an indication of gendered discrimination by school staff. These experiences appear to have had an enduring impact on most of the girls in developing collective perceptions of educational spaces as unsafe and risky. Gypsy and Traveller youth continue to be marginalised and excluded in schools (Bhopal and Myers 2016; Bhopal 2018).

The girls' accounts also suggest that through self-exclusion from mainstream education and electing to stay hidden and silent, they and their families exert a measure of control and safety leading to protective segregation. In the few narratives indicating success in attainment and enjoyment of school, some of the girls affirm that consistent attendance with little or no interruption, and positive school experiences with

Traveller and non-Traveller peers and school staff who demonstrated support without overt bias, proved germane to optimistic appraisals of their educational experiences. Some schools clearly endeavour to understand and include Gypsy and Traveller families, and their children's educational needs are met, but others have a long way to go. As discussed, most of the girls prefer flexible educational provision that incorporate their Traveller lifestyle, culture and values. All the girls attach chief value to the learning they experience at home from their parents, extended family and community, and this is a fundamental conclusion at the heart of my findings.

In Chapter 6, I examined the girls' perceptions of how family values, expectations and culture influenced their educational experiences. Hegemonic inequalities reflected in family and community culture can function as challenges and barriers to the girls' educational experiences. The positive influences of family and culture are highlighted, though the girls' accounts also reveal the extent to which some of these were limiting and at times obstructive. The girls' perceptions of Gypsy and Traveller family structure, their understanding of concepts of freedom, honour, choice, love, and the gendered expectations within their culture are discussed. The chapter provides a backdrop for evaluating the girls' interpretations of family expectations for formal education and reasons given for not enrolling them in secondary school. Their narratives often reveal evidence of stringent gendered assumptions and restrictive cultural taboos designed in part to protect the girls' 'honour'.

Many of the girls appear to be caught in a classic liminal state, betwixt and between institutional inequalities in school and within their family and community structures. They lack options and the freedom to make what one might deem informed choices. Their primary role models are parents and relatives. Exposure to other ways of being is limited within their lived experience, which further serves to restrict choices and aspirations. Most of the girls accept and feel obliged to adhere to family and cultural expectations, but a few were critical of what they interpret as sexism. This subset of girls explained that their families enjoyed good relations and understanding with school staff and that their educational experiences were largely unproblematic.

By comparing their experiences with those of other girls, I show how the girls' experiences are not unique. Evidence suggests that despite differences, in some fundamental ways the Gypsy and Traveller girls encounter similar challenges to those from British Muslim, South Asian and Scottish Pakistani ethnicity in the UK, white working-class girls, and many second-generation immigrant girls in Europe. Although facing racialised and gendered discrimination in school, the general community and in the workplace, the above studies have shown that regular school attendance and educational attainment were highly prized and encouraged by parents, within the boundaries of their own culture and religious values. The varied narratives and dilemmas indicated in the girls' interviews, juxtaposed with the experience of other minority ethnic girls, confirm the range and complexity of gendered experiences and gendered discrimination. Drawing on Archer (2002), notions of 'choice' can be differently constructed and valued across race and gender. Freedom is another contested concept in the context of restrictive parenting that can also be viewed as protective parenting (Basit 1997; Archer 2002: 370). Just as educators need to make an effort to understand the social world of the girls they teach, minority ethnic families 'also need to understand why the notion of freedom is sacrosanct to the majority group' (Basit 1997: 437).

Each of the girls in my study has according to their own circumstances accepted and rationalised certain if not all the constraints on them, however some of them attempt to negotiate new boundaries and imagine alternative futures for themselves. One of the most striking findings was the strong sense of family, community and belonging expressed by the girls, as they underscore the degree to which they respect and value their families and the distinctiveness of their cultural identity. The issue of respect, though, potentially serves to constrain their gendered identities and possibilities for their future.

The third aspect of the primary research question, as addressed in Chapter 7, applies Collins' (2000) positioning of the forms of agency individuals pursue. I focus on its application to interpersonal matters relating to the girls' accounts of success, identity and aspirations. Their personal definition of the word 'success' and their understanding of what it is to be a successful person are considered. Their aspirations are explored against the background of their experiences in school and at home, as first detailed in Chapters 5 and 6. Chapter 7 demonstrates how their goals resonate alongside the tension negotiated between the love and respect for their families, and the cultural restrictions at home and at school. Most of the girls aspire to a career and believe that their dream career cannot be fulfilled. Many of those interviewed expect to follow tradition and get married soon after reaching 16 years of age. Discussion around their aspirations and notions of success reinforced findings in previous chapters that some of the girls are beginning to challenge the binding spaces of long held values and traditions, imagining circumstances in which they have greater agency. Others appear content to accept that this condition is just part of who they are as Gypsies and Travellers. At times, I am sceptical of how much access to information they had for such choices to be made, or wonder if my own bias and circumstances prevent me from valuing their decision to accept their situation as being sufficient within itself in the name of family and community, putting aside the sole pursuit of their individual aspirations.

Chapter 7 builds on findings and analysis that demonstrate the Gypsy and Traveller girls' perceptions of education and envisaging future goals in relation to received cultural practices, reflects complex and agentic responses. The evidence affirms that notions of freedom and choice are not fixed constructs, as these ideas are contested, context-bound, restricted and at times negotiated. In her recent book *The Cost of Living* Levy (2018: 35) says that 'Freedom is never free. Anyone who has struggled to be free knows how much it costs'. The girls' assertions of choice are bounded by both gendered and racialised relations. Their youth also places them in a vulnerable position, as the pressure prevails to respect their elders and conform to cultural norms. The evidence shows that for a few of the girls, their efforts to imagine and invent alternative identities and aspirations were constrained by structural and hegemonic forces they might be unaware of. The girls' lived experiences present portraits of the persistent debates around what Walkerdine et al. (2001) refer to as a 'feminine future'.

The complexities of addressing the educational needs of minority ethnic communities, especially those of Gypsy and Traveller girls, continues to pose challenges for schools and parents. Much more needs to be done in schools to acknowledge the intersecting inequalities that affect pupils' educational and lived experiences. Simply by having legislation and policy documents stating that race and gender discrimination should be addressed and that inclusion is vital, does not make it so (Ahmed 2012). Such on-going discourse reflects an apathetic lack of practical action in some classrooms across the country, serving rather as a tick box exercise that engenders sluggish progress at grassroots level. There needs to be a more coherent approach within and across schools which also incorporates 'a strong leadership ethos in which schools must have leaders who take issues of social justice and equity seriously in their quest to ensure that all children feel valued and accepted' (Bhopal 2018: 41). Effective leaders in schools should look beyond the myopic focus on class-related poverty to include other searing social inequalities like gender, race and age discrimination. Evidence also suggests that teachers in Scotland continue to lack confidence in identifying and handling discrimination, and that more sustained and meaningful training needs to be prioritized (EHRC 2015). Otherwise, the status quo maintains and reinforces institution-induced inequalities, and the patriarchy within institutional racism and gender discrimination. It restricts mechanisms for the voices and counter-narratives of Gypsy and Traveller girls to be heard, whilst allowing White privilege to continue unchecked in our schools.

Areas for Future Research

As scholarly research on the lives of Gypsies and Travellers in Scotland is limited, there are numerous possibilities for future research, several of which might be useful to identify here. In the first instance, there would be a benefit of conducting further interviews with Gypsy and Traveller girls, especially those who have attended school uninterrupted, those who attend independent schools, and those who are in higher education, in order to discern factors that distinguish them from the norm. In similar vein to Walkerdine's et al. (2001) long-term study on the experiences of white working class and middle-class girls, it would also be pertinent in a longitudinal study to reflect on the positive experiences of girls such as Rona, Skye, Vaila and Sandray—to further analyse the factors that contribute to their views and impact on their future lived experience. It would be of interest to establish with greater certainty, as indicated in Chapter 5 and in the Farris and de Jong (2014) study on second-generation immigrant girls in Europe, whether Gypsy and Traveller girls are disadvantaged or discriminated against in school because of their gender, and not only because of their race.

Further research into the employment prospects of Gypsy and Traveller girls after leaving school would be relevant to better assess how their educational experiences affect employment prospects. Do they receive appropriate career guidance in school, and if so how effective is it? The research could respond to Farris and de Jong's (2014: 1515) queries relevant to whether the girls are 'disproportionally unemployed, work in precarious jobs, experience longer waiting times before obtaining their first job, are overqualified for their jobs, or are forced to become self-employed due to lack of access to the mainstream labour market'. Following the assertion by Carbado et al. (2013: 304) that 'there is potentially always another set of concerns to which [intersectionality as a theory] can be directed, other places to which the theory might be moved, and other structures of power it can be deployed to examine', then a comparative study of the educational experiences of girls and boys from Gypsy and Traveller communities could provide new insights.

As discussed, most of the girls I interviewed reported negative experiences in school. At policy level, I would advocate further analysis of the reports, recommendations and guidelines at national and local authority level relating to the educational experiences of Gypsies and Travellers. As Ahmed (2012: 6) infers, how is the language in these documents framed and what have they achieved? How widely are they circulated and adhered to in schools? At the level of school leadership, research into how effectively management teams implement and audit their equality duty, especially regarding Gypsy and Traveller pupils, could present insights into institutional attitudes on diversity in general and race and gender in particular.

Recent studies on Gypsy/Roma/Travelling communities in Europe (Szira 2015; Fernandez 2016) suggest that where there has been relative success in integration and education, communities have been engaged in dialogic participation and respectful partnership in solving problems and creating programmes for change. Therefore, another possible future area for research would be to gather and explore examples in Scotland of dialogic cooperation and conciliatory practices that acknowledge and respect Gypsy and Traveller culture and knowledge as valuable contributions to the education process. While Cemlyn et al. (2009) found that where there were instances of good practice in schools these were not being widely shared. Any research that highlights or investigates teamwork with Gypsy and Traveller communities is of value:

> Developing work with Travellers: recognition of Travellers as a minority ethnic/cultural group; inclusion of Travellers in equality policy and practice; training for workers; changes to referral systems; development of community support services; specialist posts; support to, and outreach work in partnership with, voluntary agencies; interagency initiatives; and, crucially, consultation with Travellers'. (Cemlyn et al. 2009: 349)

It would be of interest to conduct a research project which looks at the impact of cultural factors on Gypsy and Traveller boys in primary and secondary education, and how attainment shapes their career prospects, and potentially to undertake a comparative study of boys' and girls' experiences.

Problematising Gypsy and Traveller communities in the Academy, in policy documents and guidelines, should cease (Surdu 2016; Matache 2017). The conscious or dysconcious devaluation of the image, traditions and way of life (mobile or otherwise), and being classed as a dangerous race, needs to be disrupted and actively discouraged. Misperceptions continue to go unchallenged and well-intentioned practices can alienate and cause harm. Learning about Gypsies and Travellers from Gypsies and Travellers would be the ideal scenario, to counter decades of research done on them by the 'whiteness' within the social sciences (Smith, Personal Communication 2014; Matache 2017).

Recommendations and Reassessment

During the focus group discussion, the girls from Article 12 proposed three recommendations that in their view would help Gypsy and Traveller pupils in Scotland. Their expressed views on what they think might be of systemic use to delivering a more equitable and expansive educational experience are included here.

Firstly, they believe it is important that staff in schools are trained to understand diversity and Gypsy and Traveller culture in particular because of the general lack of understanding within society about their lifestyle and traditions. One member of the group said:

> *F1*: You see I think that's the main thing that they need, if they want to learn…to learn anything about Travellers, to work with them in any way, they need to understand our way of life, and they need to experience it as I say. Like they'd have to come out and see it for themselves. Not just their own opinion, and as you said they need to be like not judgmental, just to understand us, to give us that wee bit of a challenge to experience education fully.

Stereotypes need to be challenged and staff re-educated to consider who Gypsies and Travellers are, rather than basing their ideas on prejudiced judgements to engender a social model approach as opposed to deficit model approach:

> *F2*: I think personally I feel as soon as I meet somebody they think oh Gypsy, as you said thick, cannae read, cannae write, going to steal everything, going to wreck everything, going to do this, going to do that, cannae do nothing normal, cannae do anything proper. This doesn't help us and the weans in school.
> *F1*: Can I suggest one thing? That it becomes mandatory in all primary and high schools that there's awareness raising about Gypsy

and Traveller culture and its part of your social awareness as it is with every...the other ethnicities and that you...that it becomes a module within the curriculum.

Gypsy and Traveller history and culture should be introduced and celebrated in the school curriculum as part of Scotland's heritage.

Secondly, the Article 12 interviewees affirmed that building trust is a major factor for improving relations between Gypsy and Traveller families, communities and schools. 'Trust needs to be built before anything can happen—even just a little bit of trust can go a long way to help' (Focus Group). Basit (1996: 240) argues that 'effective home-school liaison is crucial not only for ethnic-minority families, but also for those indigenous parents who do not come into school'. Schools will have anti-racist and anti-bullying policies in place because they are required to do so by law. But the evidence and girls' accounts confirm that simply having these policies on a shelf does not protect the rights of some groups. It is illegal for schools to discriminate against someone because of their race. Schools therefore have a moral and legal duty to build trust, foster and promote social inclusion and social justice for the education of all children.

Thirdly, the girls saw advantages in setting up a state school exclusively for Gypsies and Travellers. Positive affirmative action may be necessary, though they recognise this initiative might serve to segregate them further from their peers in mainstream education in an effort to enhance attainment. Previous attempts to provide segregated education were not successful and served to drive further divisions between Gypsy and Traveller communities and the settled population. However, they stressed that Gypsy and Traveller pupils should not be forced to attend such schools:

F1: That's where there's a fine line, not getting a school where they need to go but the option, if they would prefer this school—
F3: Or even like a class inside the normal school.
F4: I think they're concerned as well that the standard of education wouldn't be as good as mainstream and still the opportunities wouldn't be as good therefore.
F2: I think it would be brilliant! If standards were as good as mainstream.

F1: If people were to accept one another then that's like your ultimate goal, you're integrated not assimilated, and that you are getting the same standard of education as everyone else. The problem I have with current segregated education for Travellers is that it's rubbish! The standard of education is terrible! So I would have choice, I'd make it more accessible and I'd make it more…a fancy word I'd make it more culturally sensitive.

The participants recognised that 'Traveller girls need more opportunities to get to see life, like we have, get to learn that they can do stuff and they don't need to get married' (Member of Focus Group). In their work with Article 12, raising awareness of Gypsy and Traveller culture, they see themselves as role models for other Gypsy and Traveller girls. Basit (1996: 240) also affirms that successful role models who share their experiences can be helpful in persuading young women and their parents to visualise alternative paths in life. Though families may need to provide their girls with these 'advancements':

If there are more opportunities like say working for instance, if they felt safe, and they thought they were'nae going to go out and get harassed and traumatised by all this abusive racist to go out and get a job, or go out and do things, maybe they would do it. (Member of Focus Group)

Many Gypsy and Traveller parents do not believe their daughters are safe in schools, and are afraid to complain when there is a problem. When they do raise concerns the situation can get worse for their children, who are not viewed as 'victims', but as the deviant problem (Lloyd and Norris 1998; Lloyd 2005). Consequently, parents withdraw their daughters from school, perhaps choosing alternative forms of education or perhaps not. This then impacts on the future of these young women and so they can be caught betwixt and between forces beyond their control.

I spoke with the girls from Article 12 in February 2015 and a year later in June 2016, the strategic solutions they offered to facilitate: access to education and to fix the deficit in choice and opportunity is powerfully reflected in the UNCRC's findings and proposals:

The Committee recommends that the State party:

22 (c) Strengthen its awareness-raising and other preventive activities against discrimination and stigmatization and, if necessary, take temporary special measures for the benefit of children in vulnerable situations. (2016: 5)

73.(b) Use the disciplinary measure of permanent or temporary exclusion as a means of last resort only, forbid and abolish the practice of "informal" exclusions and further reduce the number of exclusions by working closely with social workers and educational psychologists in school and using mediation and restorative justice;

  (c) Ensure that children have the right to appeal against their exclusion and are provided with legal advice, assistance and, where appropriate, representation for those without means;
  (d) Abolish the use of isolation rooms;
  (g) Make children's rights education mandatory.

75. With reference to its general comment No. 17 (2013) on the right of the child to rest, leisure, play, recreational activities, cultural life and the arts, the Committee:

  (a) Strengthen its efforts to guarantee the right of the child to rest and leisure and to engage in play and recreational activities appropriate to the age of the child, including by adopting and implementing play and leisure policies with sufficient and sustainable resources (UNCRC 2016: 18–19).

Article 12 have since responded with their own written appraisal based on the report, summarising what needs to be done for young Gypsies and Travellers over a range of issues, including accommodation, mental and sexual health, family environment, administration of juvenile justice, employment, and of course, discrimination and education.

My research challenges stereotyped assumptions about the educational and lived experiences of Gypsy and Traveller girls in Scotland, while acknowledging Anthias' (2013: 13) advisement on investigating perceived inequalities of women within their own communities and within their own families. She argues that there are limits to how much public institutions can do to predict and prevent combinations of intersecting inequalities within the private space of home and close-knit communities. However, by seeking to understand the influence of the dominant discourses that focus on the Gypsy and Traveller as a "problematic" and elusive Other, I question the shared myths and assumptions on which their identity is predicated.

According to the most recent Scottish Social Attitudes Survey report, negative attitudes remain stubbornly entrenched, in particular for Gypsy/Travellers (Scottish Centre for Social Research 2016). 31% were unhappy about a close relative marrying or forming a long-term relationship with a Gypsy Traveller and 34% said that a Gypsy or Traveller would be an unsuitable primary school teacher. These prejudices are persistently exacerbated by negative media portrayals. Article 12 has conducted a four-year media audit focussing on online media in Scotland. In 2015, findings revealed the press interest in the Gypsy and Traveller community in Scotland was still high, showing no signs of decreasing.

> The number of articles published continues to be disproportionate to the population size of Gypsy and Travellers living in Scotland. 78% of articles were focused on sites, up a further 12% from 62% last year [this includes unauthorised encampments, official sites, plans for new official sites and so on]; 49% discussed the Gypsy/Traveller community in general, up from 38% last year; 23% of articles contained negative stereotyping, a decrease of 1% since last year; and 14% focused on crime, an increase of 2% since last year...In 2015, only 1% of audited articles were classed as positive. This means that an overwhelming majority of articles are still portraying the Gypsy/Traveller community in a negative and misleading light. (Article 12 2018)

With regard to everyday educational practice, policy makers, teachers and schools need to stimulate efforts to respect, understand, include and work collaboratively with those of us who are different and not considered part of the dominant mainstream because of race, ethnicity, or gender. They need to seriously challenge existing policies and practices to disrupt on-going patterns of 'non-performativities' (Ahmed 2004), and quicken the glacial progress being made in anti-racist discrimination and gender discrimination in schools.

According to my analysis, rather than providing a safe, progressive environment for inclusiveness that nurtures all pupils, regardless of ethnicity and gender, schools as institutions are inculcated in an oppressive process that devalue and restrict these young women's agency and aspiration. Schools ought to be safe spaces for all children and young people to grow, make friendships, heal and focus ahead to their futures. The role of education to empower and generate hope is crucial. The accounts of the girls I interviewed are an embarrassing indictment of our schools. With the few exceptions of those girls in this study who strive to break the mould and challenge the status quo, most seem trapped by and even accepting of fixed racialised and gendered roles. In addition, as the girls' narratives indicate, problems they encounter also lie within the power structures of their families and communities.

The original proposal for this research project stated openly that there is 'a lack of understanding' about the Gypsy and Traveller community (McCluskey and Riddell 2011). In my view, this statement seriously understates the gravity of the problems faced by Gypsies and Travellers and the girls from these communities in particular, and does not reflect 'the matrix of domination' (Collins 2000: 276) that surrounds their lives.

Much more needs to be done than just improve understanding. It is imperative that we counter the systems of patriarchy that continue to hold a pervasive influence on the situated and lived experiences of not only Gypsy and Traveller girls, but other racialised and marginalised girls and women. Just as patriarchy is not homogenous or limited in its focus, so too are the experiences of girls and women not homogenous. There is no single thread or narrative, yet the Gypsy and Traveller girls' voices highlight the importance of counter-storytelling; the importance of naming and claiming of experience, not keeping silent in the hope that the silence offers a shield of protection.

Matache (2017) rightly asserts: 'We are facing a stringent need to shift the frameworks of thought and [Gypsy/Roma/Traveller] scholarly production from [their] vulnerability, to white privileges; from participation and achievement gaps to opportunity gaps'. Likewise, Surdu

(2016) argues 'knowledge production on Roma is neither objective nor disinterested but rather is co-produced by political and academic actors driven by organizational interests with rather narrow disciplinary research traditions, as well as by political manifestos'. This book is an attempt to decolonise existing ways of thinking and doing, offering a different framework of knowledge and thought on Gypsy and Traveller communities. It presents possibilities to celebrate Gypsy and Traveller strengths and aspirations.

For the first time, the principles of intersectional methodology are applied to expose the multidimensional social inequalities that are inherent within the structures of our institutions, communities, and families, in which Gypsy and Traveller youth can be trapped. Girls and women in Gypsy and Traveller communities in Scotland experience marginalization, racial discrimination and sexism. They are romanticised, hypersexualised and exploited in the media. Everyday silencing, erasure of identities and colonised manipulation of their histories—individual or collective, disqualifies their voices. Intersectionality explores the challenges of breaking down fixed identities, single narratives, binaries and established categories. In doing so, the book exposes and explores tensions and contradictions between settled and Traveller communities, and within Gypsy and Traveller groups themselves.

Further projects should be built on the principles of effective local, national and transnational participation and direct engagement of communities that suffer racist discrimination deemed acceptable for centuries (Coxhead 2007). Projects should promote strong collaboration beyond academia and with networks of families, community activists/workers, human rights practitioners, in the enactment of evidenced-based research and policy, into genuine practice (Ahmed 2004).

It is important to stare out the patriarchal gaze by calling out not only the symbolic and cultural violent oppressions of racism and sexism, but crucially the everyday, subtle microaggressions we face that take a toll on individual and collective spirit. The girls' accounts demonstrate that concepts of identity, belonging, and home are complex, heterogeneous, intertwined—yet fluid and dynamic. Their voices 'decolonise' the stereotyped image and discourses of Gypsy and Traveller girls and women. Their narratives counter the persistent portrayal by dominant systems of oppression that they are all victims, figures with no agency, no choice, no voice, fragile individuals (Cressy 2018). Their discussions also reveal ongoing tensions and contradictions both within themselves as individuals, and with their teachers, friends, families and communities.

Patriarchy and its enormously complex structures exists in all human institutions—the home, workplace, governments, the law, military, church, culture, media. It affects us all as hooks (2010: 170) reminds us that 'patriarchy has no gender'. Recognising it, naming it and recognising it for what it is, form the first steps towards envisioning alternative structures and systems of existence. Individuals, be they men or women, that perpetrate the worst of its ills are signs and symptoms, not the ailment itself. And within patriarchy, the oppression of women is multifaceted and affects us in different ways. Despite our individual differences and circumstances *as women*, and because of them, much work remains to be done to collectively connect, to give space and pride to our lived experiences, to disrupt the 'white patriarchal gaze' that pervades what Collins (2000: 276) so powerfully described as 'the matrix of domination' and the power of inequality to disrupt and destroy lives.

References

Ahmed, S. (2004) Declarations of whiteness: The non-performativity of anti-racism. *Borderlands E-Journal*, 3(2). Available at: http://borderlands. net.au/vol3no2_2004/ahmed_declarations.htm. Accessed 7 April 2016.

Ahmed, S. (2012) *On being included: Racism and diversity in institutional life.* Durham, NC: Duke University Press.

Anthias, F. (2013) Intersectional what? Social divisions, intersectionality and levels of analysis. *Ethnicities*, 13(1), pp. 3–19.

Archer, L. (2002) Change, culture and tradition: British Muslim pupils talk about Muslim girls' post-16 'choices'. *Race, Ethnicity and Education*, 5(4), pp. 359–376.

Article 12. (2018) Resources and publications: 2015—4th report: Discrimination and on-line media. Available at: http://www.article12.org/gypsytravellers/. Accessed 25 March 2018.

Basit, T. N. (1996) 'I'd hate to be just a housewife': Career aspirations of British Muslim girls. *British Journal of Guidance and Counselling*, 24(2), pp. 227–242.

Basit, T. N. (1997) 'I want more freedom, but not too much': British Muslim girls and the dynamism of family values. *Gender and Education*, 9(4), pp. 425–440.

Bhopal, K. (2018) *White privilege: The myth of a post-racial society*. Bristol: Policy Press.

Bhopal, K., and Myers, M. (2016) Marginal groups in marginal times: Gypsy and Traveller parents and home education in England, UK. *British Educational Research Journal*, 42(1), pp. 5–20.

Carbado, D. W., Crenshaw, K. W., Mays, V. M., and Tomlinson, B. (2013) Intersectionality. *Du Bois Review: Social Science Research on Race*, 10(2), pp. 303–312.

Cemlyn, S., Greenfields, M., Burnett, S., Matthews, Z., and Whitwell, C. (2009) *Inequalities experienced by Gypsy and Traveller communities: A review*. Research Report 12. Manchester: Equality and Human Rights Commission. Available at: https://dera.ioe.ac.uk/11129/1/12inequalities_experienced_by_gypsy_and_traveller_communities_a_review.pdf.

Collins. P. H. (2000) *Black feminist thought. Knowledge, consciousness and the politics of empowerment*. London: Routledge.

Coxhead, J. (2007) *The last bastion of racism: Gypsies, Travellers and policing*. Stoke on Trent: Trentham Books.

Crenshaw, K. (1991) Mapping the margins: Identity politics, intersectionality, and violence against women. *Stanford Law Review*, 43(6), pp. 1241–1299.

Cressy, D. (2018) *Gypsies: An English history*. Oxford: Oxford University Press.

EHRC. (2015) Prejudiced-based bullying in Scottish schools: A research report. Available at: https://www.equalityhumanrights.com/en/publication-download/prejudice-based-bullying-scottish-schools-research-report. Accessed 30 April 2016.

Farris, S. R., and de Jong, S. (2014) Discontinuous intersections: Second-generation immigrant girls in transition from school to work. *Ethnic and Racial Studies*, 37(9), pp. 1505–1525.

Fernandez, C. (2016) *Two milestones put Romani cultural discourse in the hands of Roma themselves*. Open Society Foundations. Available at: https://www.opensocietyfoundations.org/voices/two-milestones-put-romani-cultural-discourse-hands-roma-themselves? Accessed 20 January 2016.

Hancock, A. M. (2007) When multiplication doesn't equal quick addition: Examining intersectionality as a research paradigm. *Perspectives on Politics*, 5(1), pp. 63–79.

hooks, b. (2010) *Teaching critical thinking: Practical wisdom*. New York: Routledge.

Levy, D. (2018) *The cost of living*. London: Penguin Books.

Lloyd, G. (2005) *'Problem' girls: Understanding and supporting troubled and troublesome girls and young women*. London: Psychology Press.

Lloyd, G., and Norris, C. (1998) From difference to deviance: The exclusion of Gypsy-Traveller children from school in Scotland. *International Journal of Inclusive Education*, 2(4), pp. 359–369.

Lloyd, G., Stead, J., Jordan, E., and Norris, C. (1999) Teachers and Gypsy Travellers. *Scottish Educational Review*, 31(1), pp. 48–65.

Matache, M. (2017) The legacy of Gypsy studies in modern Roma scholarship. Available at: https://fxb.harvard.edu/the-legacy-of-gypsy-studies-in-modern-romani-scholarship/. Accessed 23 August 2017.

McCormick, A. (1907) *The Tinkler-Gypsies*. Dumfries: J. Maxwell and Son.

McCluskey, G., and Riddell, S. (2011) Improving our understanding of Gypsy/Travellers in Scotland. Research Proposal, CREID, Moray House School of Education, University of Edinburgh.

Mirza, H. S. (2015) Harvesting our collective intelligence: Black British feminism in post-race times. *Women's Studies International Forum*, 51, pp. 1–9.

Scottish Centre for Social Research. (2016) Scottish social attitudes survey 2015. Available at: http://www.ssa.natcen.ac.uk/read-the-reports/scottish-social-attitudes-2015/attitudes-to-discrimination-positive-action.aspx. Accessed 7 March 2017.

Smith, J. (2014) Personal communication. Traveller writer and storyteller, recorded interview, 14 May.

Surdu, M. (2016) *Those who count*. Budapest: Central European University Press.

Szira, J. (2015) *What the "Roma decade" really achieved*. Open Society Foundations. Available at: https://www.opensocietyfoundations.org/voices/what-roma-decade-really-achieved? Accessed 1 October 2015.

UNCRC. (2016) Concluding observations on the fifth periodic report of the United Kingdom of Great Britain and Northern Ireland: Committee on the Rights of the Child. Available at: http://www.ohchr.org/EN/NewsEvents/Pages/DisplayNews.aspx?NewsID=19952&LangID=E. Accessed 2 March 2017.

Walkerdine, V., Lucey, H., and Melody, J. (2001) *Growing up girl: Psycho-social explorations of gender and class*. London: Palgrave Macmillan.

Appendices

Appendix A: List of Primary Sources and Profiles of Gypsy and Traveller Girls

Interviews undertaken by the author with the Gypsy and Traveller girls who participated in this study. To protect their identity, the informants have been given pseudonyms.

Ailsa (2014) Recorded Interview, 18 June.
Cara (2014) Recorded Interview, 18 June.
Dana (2014) Recorded Interview, 18 June.
Fara (2014) Recorded Interview, 27 October.
Iona (2014) Recorded Interview, 27 October.
Islay (2014) Recorded Interview, 18 June.
Kilda (2014) Recorded Interview, 29 October.
May (2014) Recorded Interview, 17 September.
Rona (2014) Recorded Interview, 26 May.
Sandray (2014) Recorded Interview, 29 August.
Shona (2014) Recorded Interview, 29 October.
Skye (2014) Recorded Interview, 26 May.
Vaila (2014) Recorded Interview, 12 November.

© The Editor(s) (if applicable) and The Author(s) 2019
G. Marcus, *Gypsy and Traveller Girls*, Studies in Childhood and Youth,
https://doi.org/10.1007/978-3-030-03703-1

In addition, four further Gypsy and Traveller girls who are members of the non-governmental organisation, Article 12, were interviewed as a focus group:

Article 12 (2015) Recorded focus group discussion, Glasgow, 26 February.

May (12)

Of all the research participants, May is the only one who self-identifies as an English Gypsy. She is 12 years old and moved to Scotland when she was eight with her parents and siblings. She is the third youngest in a family of eight, the oldest is 22 years and the youngest is seven. Five of her siblings are married including her recently wed 17-year-old brother. May said, 'I've lived in trailers, caravans, and houses, but now I live in a bungalow', which she prefers. However, she is only there for part of the week. She lives with her cousins in a different town so she can attend a youth centre dedicated solely to the education of Travellers. Her cousin attends the centre too. His family recommended it as 'a safe place to go to learn'. May said she has been in 12 primary schools, almost one or two a year. Four of those schools were in England, and the majority were in Scotland. May believed her experiences in school were 'probably worse' in Scotland then in England. With tears in her eyes, May explained the hurtful and negative impact bullying, exclusions and the ensuing interruptions have had on her life and her education. She said she was happy in the two-day youth centre where her teachers are 'kind and helpful'. She feels safe when she is only with Traveller pupils. May was the only one who believed passionately that her people should live separately and be educated separately from non-Travellers.

Ailsa (13)

Ailsa is 13 years old and described herself as a Scottish Traveller. She has five siblings and she is the oldest in her family. She lives with her mother and her siblings in a council flat that provided as emergency accommodation. Her teachers have informed me that her parents separated, but during the interview, she mentioned both her parents, and so I would not have known that her parents are no longer together. Ailsa does not have a room of her own and sleeps on a sofa in her living room. Ailsa has attended three different schools since the age of five. She is now 'allowed to' attend her fourth 'school' by her parent, 2 days a week. A council run bus service transports her back and forth. Ailsa is soft-spoken and quietly confident. She comes across as a gentle person. She rarely spoke excitedly during our conversations. During class time, amongst her peers, she was calm, and hardworking, respectful of her teachers. She spoke of her love for drawing, painting, knitting bags and making clothes. She did enjoy aspects of primary school and others were generally 'nice' to her but her experiences in school she reported got worse as she got older and progressed through school. Ailsa's responses tend to be brief, at times monosyllabic. Mostly one word or very brief responses (one sentence or less). Unlike the other participants, there were a lot of pauses and hesitancies ('Um, 'am not sure', 'I don't know'). Ailsa does speak passionately when talking about the injustices she has suffered—racist abuse, attacks, conflicts in school involving either herself or her siblings and cousins. She explained her fear of being ostracised by non-Traveller peers has impeded her chances for fuller holistic education at a secondary school. Despite these negative experiences, Alisa proudly declared she would not change who she is and values what she learns when she travels with her family.

Islay (13) and Cara (12)

I interviewed Islay and Cara together at the same youth centre that Ailsa attends. They asked to be together so they would be more comfortable. Islay is a 13-year-old Scottish Traveller and Cara is 12. Islay is the more forward and confident of the two. Both girls do not attend their local secondary school because their parents and grandparents did not permit it. They are at the youth centre two days a week because they are with their 'own kind'. The two-day routine also fits in with their other responsibilities and chores at home, so neither could consider attending school five days a week. Their parents would not permit such a commitment.

Cara informed me that she is 'comfortable' at the youth centre and Islay confirmed that she could be herself there. They both said they felt safe and they are not judged for who they are. They also do not like getting up early in the morning to get to school. Islay has been to eight primary schools.

Cara has been to five primary schools, 'because we travel around... we shift around all the time'. She explained, in a soft lyrical Irish accent, that she has stayed on the same council run Traveller site in Scotland all her life except when she and her family 'shift down to England mostly, we go to England mostly...because granddad just likes going there. He loves England for some reason'. Both girls tell stories of their largely negative encounters in each of the schools they have attended, citing many examples of bullying by other pupils, lack of understanding, respect and support from teachers. Islay and Cara are the only research participants who do not distinguish between the terms 'Traveller' and 'Gypsy'. Unlike others, they did not seem to be aware of the negative connotations in the term 'Gypsy' and seemed quite comfortable acknowledging that that is who they are. Both girls also identified their religion, making a further distinction, in their view, between Catholics and Christians. When I suggested that 'some people have a problem with difference', both retorted emphatically that they 'do not want to blend in or change'. Islay said, 'I think most people think to blend in is good but...I prefer to be different'. Cara agreed. Their parents would not allow them to 'pal about with [non-Travellers] because they know too much'. However, the girls could not explain how non-Traveller pupils might 'know too much' or what it is that the 'gadjo pupils' might know that makes them unsafe with which to fraternise. Their protected innocence shines through and it is clear how sheltered they are from the culture of settled communities. They do not mention words like 'drugs', 'alcohol' or 'sex', and it is apparent that these influences are not in their sphere of knowledge or experience. Islay and Cara are not sure exactly what about 'know too much' they should fear, only that they should fear such knowledge. Like all the other research participants, Islay and Cara are proud of their ethnicity and heritage. They love travelling to new places, meeting 'new people', going to Appleby Fair; but it is sobering to hear details of the harmonious disorder in which they live. Islay acknowledged that the travelling lifestyle could be challenging. Yet they talk fondly of their lifestyle and customs. Both girls dream of being beauticians, possibly run their own business and 'do make-up for Travellers'. They also accepted that they would have to get married and have children, just like their parents. Their dreams may not actually be fulfilled. Islay said, 'I guess I have no choice... [but to get married]...yeah and then you die! But still both are adamant that they would not change the status quo because on the whole they like their life.

Dana (13)

I spoke with Dana who is 13 years old and is Cara's older sister. Like her sister, she has been to five primary schools and said they 'just like moving... it's part of our lifestyle', but she also revealed her parents are divorced and 'now every year we shift [to also see] my daddy'. He lives far away on the other side of the country, she told me. She and her two sisters live with their mother and grandma on a council run Traveller site. Her father has re-married and has a new family, whom she considers part of her own. 'I have three sisters now and I am the oldest'. Her sister Cara does not mention any of this to me during the interview. When asked about her ethnicity, Dana initially described herself as a 'Traveller', but went on to explain that she has a mixed heritage. 'I'm a Traveller, but we're half breeds... half Irish half Scottish'. When asked how she felt about her mixed ethnicity, she said it doesn't bother her because 'that's the way God made you, in it?' Like her sister, Cara, she mentioned her religious affiliation without prompting from me. She volunteered that they are Catholic and 'We do go to church but we believe that you can be religious in your own home that's the way we look at it'.

Dana is shy and quietly spoken. She has a strong Irish accent and I am struck by her choice of words, like 'half breed', and what to me sounded like rather traditional turns of phrase, something I might expect from a much older person. She does not use words like 'cool', 'awesome' or 'fab', for instance. Unlike the other research participants, she rarely used the pronoun 'I'. All her statements were consistently in the third person—'we', 'you', and 'us'—throughout the interview.

She referred to non-Travellers as 'country people' and non-Traveller boys as 'country boys', whom she quickly added she must avoid at all costs. We talked about why she was not in secondary school. 'No, it's just the way we are like the boys go with their daddy and the girls go with their mummy'. I asked her what she does at home on the three weekdays that she is not at school, and she replied, 'Just like...just clean up and you sit around, cleaning up and helping mummy'. However, she praised her current teachers highly and she talked at length about their dedication and kindness, emphasising how different they were to the many teachers she had encountered in the primary schools she had attended. She revealed she did not enjoy being in primary school because the teachers were not supportive and there was a fair amount of bullying especially in the playground. She likes the centre for Travellers because 'we're separate from everybody else anyways!' She also explained she did not feel good being at any of the schools she was in and believed she was not clever. She particularly enjoys socialising with her Traveller friends and she knows it is safe for her to do so. She appreciates being able to walk to the shops with them to get her own lunch two days a week. The only disadvantage was to get up early in the morning. Dana said she is very happy being a Traveller and that she 'wouldn't change it for the world' because she just loves being a Traveller. Like, Cara and Islay, Dana acknowledged that travelling is not always easy and she disclosed that 'in Aberdeen there was a lot of bother!' It is difficult to find work she explained, and non-Travellers are told not to hire Travellers. She and her family prefer going down to England. She has many relatives who live there and she said she feels safer, although there can be trouble there too.

Her dream is to try to go to college; although she was unsure as to what course she would take. However, she clarified that it would probably not happen because she is destined to be married and have children by 18 or 19 years. She explained even though it is 'your choice', there is pressure from the community, because they might think 'there's something wrong with her, she must be scandalised and that's it'. However, later in a defiant tone she asserted, 'I will get married when it's time to get married...when I feel like I'm ready'. To get married at 18 is too soon because she reasoned, 'you're still a child, still in your teens'.

Iona (16) and Fara (13)

Iona and Fara are two sisters whom I interviewed in their trailer, situated on their privately-owned site. Their mother was present, added explanations and comments occasionally, but did not at any point contradict what her daughters said. Of all the research participants, Iona and Fara are the only two who have not received any kind of formal education since they left primary school. Iona is 16 years old and Fara is 13 years old. They have been in '13 different schools' and 'no matter where we were, we were always in a school', but neither has been enrolled in a secondary school because they said they have 'had enough'. They revealed they are not 'home tutored' and they do not attend any mobile unit for Travellers.

They revealed detailed instances of bullying, racist name-calling, unsupportive and unkind teachers, and unfair punishments. When asked if they felt unsafe in school because of these experiences they reported they did sometimes. Fara disclosed that she has been in some trouble at school, and explained she does not 'mind them [pupils] speaking about me but it's when they speak about my family... I don't like it...it boils my blood.' She was not excluded but was 'separated', 'put into another room for the day... because they thought I was up to nae good'. Iona, on the other hand, said she never fought back because 'if you're going to fight back with that person you're just as bad as them...if you can stoop to their level then you're just the same person'. They both acknowledged that there were benefits to being in school. However, the girls think that school is not the only place to learn as we can all learn from what is around us. Fara spends her time knitting, crocheting, drawing and pursuing other creative activities. Her mother brought out her folio to show me. She explained Iona is also a 'talented drawer, both like their gran'. Her pride is clear to see. Iona said she loves to spend time with her horses and demonstrates her knowledge and passion as she articulates how she cares for her animals.

The girls were a great double act, as they supported each other's ideas, finished each other's sentences and they both have a wonderful sense of humour. When asked what other activities or responsibilities they have at home, both chimed in unison they don't like cleaning. Their mother agreed with a smile, 'but it's a chore to them... it's just a chore'. They do help around the house and they help look after their two little siblings, but they add with a smile, only 'sometimes'. Fara does not want to get married too young and Iona is not interested at all, because she does not want to leave home. She explained she is 'a really active outgoing person', desperate to work and have a career with horses. I observed a healthy, positive rapport and respect between the girls and their mother. The latter was visibly proud of her children and supportive of their ideas and identity. She nodded her head in approval several times during our conversation.

I was given a tour of their home, the site and the countryside beyond, before leaving. They all acknowledged that they are happy living on their own land because life on the road was dangerous and unpleasant for them. They are struggling to get planning permission for proper electricity supply. In recent years, in the winter months they have had to rent a house in the nearby village so that the family have greater comfort and warmth. The generators on the site are not powerful enough to protect them in harsh winter conditions and they have been left without heating or cooking facilities in the past. Also, their nearest non-Traveller neighbours, who live about half a mile away, have complained to the council about the sound of the generators.

Their father is often away for work and the mother explains that it is challenging for her to manage the family and the site during the winter especially as there is greater likelihood of bad weather and breakdowns. The trailers are not insulated. One year the winds were so strong, a tree crashed through the side of the trailer in the middle of the night. The children were late for school the next morning and were scolded for telling lies when they explained about the tree and why they were delayed. The family still experience daily prejudice but they accept that this is part of their reality and as Fara in her youthful wisdom has come to accept, 'life is not perfect'.

Skye (15)

Skye is 15 years old and described herself as a Scottish Traveller. She is the youngest in a family of seven children. She lives with her entire family in two permanent trailers on a council-run site. Skye is still at school and enjoys being there. Unlike most of the other research participants, her family have remained in one place to enable her to receive an uninterrupted education. Skye said she has had only positive experiences at the nursery, primary and secondary schools she attended. She also said she has

ambitions to carry on until she completes sixth year studies. Skye is adamant to get a job; have a career and plans to gain the qualifications she
needs to do so. When I met first met her she was in an all-black ensemble,
with a striking red-tie, her jet-black hair, cut short and swept back with
gel, tastefully made up with a Goth look. Of all the 12 girls I interviewed,
Skye was the only one who seemed to consciously make a statement
rejecting the overtly feminine image, projected by and expected of most
Traveller girls. Her positive outlook and happiness was infectious and did
not reflect the hardships experienced by her family. Skye is a young carer
for her sister who is registered disabled. The family continues to encounter many challenges, with various local government departments in
health, planning, housing, social services and the law, in trying to secure
better provision for Skye's sister. Skye's mother took her local council to
court for racial discrimination and won her case.

Vaila (15)

Vaila is a 15-year-old Scottish Traveller who is currently attending a course
at a further education college. She lives with her four groups of relatives
on a private site owned by her grandfather…' so it's just family on our
site. She explained her father does not deal in scrap metal. She has been
to three primary schools because her family travelled. After her primary
school education was complete, even though she was doing well, her parents decided that she should not go to secondary school. The usual reasons were cited—fear of bullying, lack of trust of staff, the possibility of
exposure to non-Traveller customs and undesirable habits like drinking,
drug taking, and contact with non-Traveller boys.

Vaila said her parents did not attend school, but talked proudly about
her grandmother who did well in school, and like her was not allowed to
attend secondary school for very long. Unlike all the other participants,
Vaila has no responsibility caring for younger siblings, as she is the youngest of three sisters. She explained at the age of 14 her parents realised
that she did not have enough to do at home. She was bored and they
might be restricting her potential to do well in a career of her choosing. She convinced them to permit her to attend a professional cookery course, and with the support of the local education officer, she was
accepted, along with her older sister who was also permitted to attend.
Vaila said she enjoyed the course, had no problems attending, did well
and won a prize for her commitment. Unlike her sister who went on to
get married, Vaila then enrolled in a beauty course at the same college.
She won first prize for doing excellent work and was named best student
of the year. She was awarded this prize at a formal prize giving ceremony

that her parents did not attend. The education officer explained the family may not have felt comfortable in that formal non-Traveller setting and was not sure how to interpret their daughter's success. The education officer believed it was unfortunate that Vaila's success and the prize-giving event went unmarked and was seemingly not applauded by the family. Vaila is looking for an apprenticeship that will eventually lead to a permanent job. Vaila said she would like to get married and have children, 'but not too young because a lot of the girls get married at 16 or 17 but I think that's too young because you've got to live your life a little yet'.

Shona (16) and Kilda (18)

Shona and Kilda are two sisters who live with their extended family on a council run Traveller site. Their trailer was cold, damp and sparse, devoid of many of the modern conveniences one might expect in a home. Apart from the inbuilt sofas, a small kitchen and two beds, there was nothing else in the trailer. Poverty was a living reality for Shona and her family, and their teacher told me that the family 'struggles'. Kilda walked in, confidently introduced herself and offered to look after the toddlers so that Shona and I could speak uninterrupted. There seemed to be no other adult around, although, according to one teacher I spoke to, this is unusual. The teacher on site told me that in the past there were relatives and extended family around, but some have recently left to live on a better refurbished site and others happen to be travelling. Both girls seemed to love and care for their toddler siblings. Their parents have had nine children. Two girls are now married; one boy is in prison and the rest still live with their parents. Their mother is often away looking after her own parents. Kilda, who is 18, is the oldest girl on the site and has taken over the rearing of the children since her older sisters married and left. Having so many younger siblings to look after has a considerable impact on the educational experiences of these girls. Their time and energy is focused on their family responsibilities, leaving little occasion to attend school or study. Their teacher explained they crave the social interaction they have with staff at the school and enjoy attending when they can do so. They especially appreciate discussing the articles and images they come across in a range of reading materials used for literacy lessons. Magazines like *Heat* and *Take a Break* are particular favourites because they present a glimpse into the world beyond the Traveller site—fashion, celebrities, and music—the sort of topics that interest most teenage girls. They do not have a computer and I did not see a television in either of the trailers I was in. Kilda tells me that she left formal schooling at five when she was diagnosed with a serious illness, and she never went back. She can read and write only a little. Shona on the other hand said she enjoyed school and attending lessons at the mobile unit 'whenever she can'. Her favourite subject is Mathematics and she believes that she is good at it, wishing she could do more. The girls explained their duties at home, the expectation that they would be married soon and that having a career is just not possible. The girls are fully responsible for maintaining the home, looking after the younger children, cooking and cleaning. Their father works and their mother must look after their grandparents who live on another site. Their main ambition at the moment is to learn how to drive as this skill gives them the freedom to meet their friends and cousins, away from the site. Of all the girls, I met I thought Shona and Kilda seemed to be the most vulnerable, lacking the opportunity to make independent choices for their own lives.

Rona (19)

At 19 years of age, Rona is the second oldest research participant who took part in the study. Like Skye, she lives on a council run Traveller site with her family. She attended her local nursery, primary and secondary school. Rona chose to go to the main school in the local area because she 'liked being around people [non-Travellers]'. Like Skye, she too is a young carer. This common experience brought them together several years ago. They have remained firm friends ever since. I interviewed them together over coffee and lunch in a small rural hotel. My abiding memory of them was their insistence that they were never bullied in school, had never encountered any racism, and that they were both very unlike other Traveller girls, declaring that they are 'unique'.

At 16 years old, Rona left school and travelled to Australia with her non-Traveller boyfriend, to live and work. Her family were not happy about the situation but according to Rona, they accepted it eventually. Rona said her family have always encouraged her to mingle with non-Travellers and would not object if she married someone from another culture. One of her sisters is married to a non-Traveller. Her parents would rather they married a 'good non-Traveller', than a 'bad Traveller' from a rival family. Rona is currently looking for a job at a beauty salon and would like to open her own business. She said she would never deny her ethnicity to a prospective employer.

Sandray (22)

Sandray is the oldest research participant. She is the most qualified of the participants, having completed a diploma in music at a further education college and she plans to go to university. She sings, plays the guitar, piano and drums. She is the only participant from a mixed heritage. Her father is a Gypsy and her mother is a non-Traveller. She is also the only participant who lives in a house, which her parents own. Her family only travelled during the school holidays, which enabled Sandray and her siblings to attend school uninterrupted from primary to secondary. Sandray left school after sixth year. She has two siblings. Her brother is married to a Traveller and her sister, who is older to her and in her 30's, has chosen to remain unmarried and has a career. She said she had a strict upbringing and her father restricted her contact with non-Travellers, even though he was married to a non-Traveller. Sandray pointed out the contradictions in her father's attitudes, and she said she quietly defied his wishes, with her mother's support. Sandray's boyfriend is a non-Traveller and her family have accepted him. She explains that she is torn between two cultures and between two lives, 'because I had Traveller pals and I had non-Traveller pals and when I was with my travelling pals I would act like a Traveller, which was 'nae really me because I was 'nae really… I spoke the Cant which I didn't do with my non-Traveller pals because they didn't understand me'. She admitted she was 'very confused in her teenage years', but the more education she received, the more she 'questioned both the worlds'. Eventhough her Travelling friends looked down on her for going to college and not getting married, her parents are very proud of her accomplishments in music. Sandray believes that there is 'tension all the time' between being and acting like a Traveller and being and acting like a non-Traveller. However, living on a house, away from the Travelling community on a Traveller site, enabled her to manage those tensions. Her parents, and particularly her mother, Sandray think were able to support Sandray's education and career aspirations, unencumbered by the 'gossip and expectations' of the community…I feel like because it's getting more a modern age I feel like the girls also get a wee bit of a say now…slowly'. However, Sandray reports that she has never heard of a Traveller girl combining marriage with a career. She either does one or the other. She registers her strong views about the importance of choice and the importance of an education for the girls and women in her community. At the end of our conversation, she sings me a song she composed, advising girls that 'it's not too late to break the chain, don't be afraid, just take a chance on your dreams, it's not as hard as it seems'.

Appendix B: Examples of Stakeholder Questions

List of Stakeholders (Formal Interviews)

Academic 1	Interview and notes	15 May 2014
Academic 2	Interview and notes	25 August 2014
Charity Liaison Officer	Recorded interview	10 September 2014
Gypsy/Traveller Liaison Officer 2	Telephone interview and notes	16 June 2014
Head of charity 1	Recorded interview	8 April 2014
Head of charity 2	Recorded interview	10 September 2014
Health worker	Interview and notes	10 June 2014
Member of staff SCCYP	Recorded interview	1 October 2014
Planning Advisor 1	Recorded interview	8 October 2014
Quality Improvement Officer Inclusion	Telephone interview and notes	16 September 2014
Teacher 1	Interview and notes	30 April 2014
Teacher 5	Recorded interview	12 November 2014
Teacher 6 (2014)	Interview and notes	5 December 2014
Traveller woman	Telephone interview and notes	15 August and 6 October 2015
Nisbet, I.	Head of Education Law, Govan Law Centre, recorded interview	2 September 2014
Oswald, C.	Head of Policy (Scotland) Equality and Human Rights Commission, Email interview	9 November 2014
Jess Smith	Traveller writer and storyteller, recorded interview	14 May 2014

Appendix C: Scottish Census 2011 Household Questionnaire (HO) p. 13, Question No. 15 on Ethnicity

(New category included—A. White Gypsy/Traveller).

Person 2 - Individual questions continued

12 How do you usually travel to your main place of work or study (including school)?

♦ Tick one box only.

♦ Tick the box for the longest part, by distance, of your usual journey to work or study.

- [ ] Driving a car or van
- [ ] Passenger in a car or van
- [ ] On foot
- [ ] Bus, minibus or coach
- [ ] Train
- [ ] Underground, subway, metro, light rail or tram
- [ ] Taxi
- [ ] Bicycle
- [ ] Motorcycle, scooter or moped
- [ ] Other

13 What religion, religious denomination or body do you belong to?

♦ This question is voluntary.

- [ ] None
- [ ] Church of Scotland
- [ ] Roman Catholic
- [ ] Other Christian, please write in below
- [ ] Muslim
- [ ] Buddhist
- [ ] Sikh
- [ ] Jewish
- [ ] Hindu
- [ ] Another religion or body, please write in

14 What do you feel is your national identity?

♦ Tick ALL that apply.

- [ ] Scottish
- [ ] English
- [ ] Welsh
- [ ] Northern Irish
- [ ] British
- [ ] Other, please write in

15 What is your ethnic group?

♦ Choose ONE section from A to F, then tick ONE box which best describes your ethnic group or background.

A White

- [ ] Scottish
- [ ] Other British
- [ ] Irish
- [ ] Gypsy / Traveller
- [ ] Polish
- [ ] Other white ethnic group, please write in

B Mixed or multiple ethnic groups

- [ ] Any mixed or multiple ethnic groups, please write in

C Asian, Asian Scottish or Asian British

- [ ] Pakistani, Pakistani Scottish or Pakistani British
- [ ] Indian, Indian Scottish or Indian British
- [ ] Bangladeshi, Bangladeshi Scottish or Bangladeshi British
- [ ] Chinese, Chinese Scottish or Chinese British
- [ ] Other, please write in

D African

- [ ] African, African Scottish or African British
- [ ] Other, please write in

E Caribbean or Black

- [ ] Caribbean, Caribbean Scottish or Caribbean British
- [ ] Black, Black Scottish or Black British
- [ ] Other, please write in

F Other ethnic group

- [ ] Arab, Arab Scottish or Arab British
- [ ] Other, please write in

Further Reading

Acton, T. (1994) Modernisation, moral panics and the Gypsies. *Sociology Review*, 4(1), pp. 24–28.

Acton, T. A. (ed.) (2000) *Scholarship and the Gypsy Struggle: Commitment in Romani Studies: A Collection of Papers and Poems to Celebrate Donald Kenrick's Seventieth Year*. Hatfield: University of Hertfordshire Press.

Acton, T. (2004) Modernity, culture and 'Gypsies': Is there a meta-scientific method for understanding the representation of 'Gypsies'? And do Dutch really exist?' In: Saul, N., and Tebbutt, S. (eds.) *The role of the Romanies. Images and counter-images of 'Gypsies'/Romanies in European cultures*. Liverpool: Liverpool University Press.

Acton, T. (2007) Here to stay: The Gypsies and Travellers of Great Britain. *Ethnic and Racial Studies*, 30(2), pp. 1170–1171.

Ahmed, S. (2012) *On being included: Racism and diversity in institutional life*. Durham, NC: Duke University Press.

Allen, D. (2000) Gypsies and planning policy. In: Acton, T. (ed.) *Scholarship and the Gypsy struggle: Commitment in Romani studies*. Hatfield: University of Hertfordshire Press.

Alt, B., and Folts, S. (1996) *Weeping violins: The Gypsy tragedy in Europe*. Kirksville: Thomas Jefferson University Press.

© The Editor(s) (if applicable) and The Author(s) 2019
G. Marcus, *Gypsy and Traveller Girls*, Studies in Childhood and Youth,
https://doi.org/10.1007/978-3-030-03703-1

Anderson, R. (2003) The history of Scottish education pre-1980. In: Bryce, T. G. K., and Humes, W. M. (eds.) *Scottish education: Post-devolution*, 2nd ed. Edinburgh: Edinburgh University Press, pp. 219–228.

Anon. Academic 1. (2014, May 15) Personal communication. Discussion, interview and notes.

Anthias, F. (2013) Intersectional what? Social divisions, intersectionality and levels of analysis. *Ethnicities*, 13(1), pp. 3–19.

Archer, L. (2002) Change, culture and tradition: British Muslim pupils talk about Muslim girls' post-16 'choices'. *Race, Ethnicity and Education*, 5(4), pp. 359–376.

Askins, K. (2009) 'That's just what I do': Placing emotion in academic activism. *Emotion, Space and Society*, 2(1), pp. 4–13.

Back, L., and Solomos, J. (eds.). (2009) *Theories of race and racism: A reader*, 2nd ed. Abingdon: Routledge.

Bancroft, A., Lloyd, M., and Morran, R. (1996) *The Right to Roam: Travellers in Scotland 1995/96*. Dunfermline: Save the Children in Scotland.

Basit, T. N. (1997) 'I want more freedom, but not too much': British Muslim girls and the dynamism of family values. *Gender and Education*, 9(4), pp. 425–440.

Bauman, Z. (1989) *Modernity and the Holocaust*. Ithaca: Cornell University Press.

Bauman, Z. (2001) *Community*. Cambridge: Polity Press.

Behlmer, G. K. (1985) The Gypsy problem in Victorian England. *Victorian Studies*, 28(2), pp. 231–253.

Bell, E. J., Riding, M. H., Collier, P. W., Wilson, N. C., and Reid, D. (1983) Susceptibility of itinerants ("travelling people") in Scotland to poliomyelitis. *Bulletin of the World Health Organization*, 61(5), p. 839.

BERA. (2011) Revised ethical guidelines for educational research [Online]. Available at: https://www.bera.ac.uk/wp-content/uploads/2014/02. Accessed 5 January 2014.

Berlant, L. (1997) *The Queen of America Goes to Washington City: Essays on Sex and Citizenship*. Durham and London: Duke University Press.

Binns, D. (1984) *Children's literature and the role of the Gypsy*. Manchester: Self-Published.

Borrow, G. (ed.) (1843, 1991) *Lavengro*. London: Constable.

Breitenbach, E. (2006) Developments in gender equality policies in Scotland since Devolution. *Scottish Affairs*, 56, pp. 10–21.

Brockie, W. (1884) *The Gypsies of yetholm: Historical, traditional, philological and humorous*. Kelso: J. and J. H. Rutherford.

Causey, V. E., Thomas, C. D., and Armento, B. J. (2000) Cultural diversity is basically a foreign term to me: The challenges of diversity for preservice teacher education. *Teaching and Teacher Education*, 16(1), pp. 33–45.

Cemlyn, S., Greenfields, M., Burnett, S., Matthews, Z., and Whitwell, C. (2009) *Inequalities experienced by Gypsy and Traveller communities: A review*. Research Report 12. Manchester: Equality and Human Rights Commission. Available at: https://dera.ioe.ac.uk/11129/1/12inequalities_experienced_by_gypsy_and_traveller_communities_a_review.pdf.

Chambers, W. (1886) *Exploits and anecdotes of the Scottish Gypsies: With traits of their origin, character, and manners*. Edinburgh: W. Brown.

Cho, S., Williams, K., and McCall, L. (2013) Towards a field of intersectionality studies: Theory, applications and praxis. *Signs*, 38(4), pp. 785–810.

Clark, C., and Campbell, E. (2000) "Gypsy invasion": A critical analysis of newspaper reaction to Czech and Slovak Romani asylum-seekers in Britain, 1997. *Romani Studies (Continuing Journal of the Gypsy Lore Society)*, 10(1), pp. 23–47.

Clark, C., and Taylor, B. (2014) Is nomadism the 'problem'? The social construction of Gypsies and Travellers as perpetrators of 'anti-social' behaviour in Britain. In: Pickard, S. (ed.) *Anti-social behaviour in Britain: Victorian and contemporary perspectives*. Basingstoke: Palgrave Macmillan, pp. 166–178.

Clarke, B. (1998) The Irish travelling community—Outcasts of the celtic tiger? Dilemmas for social work. *Social Work in Europe*, 5, pp. 28–34.

Clavell-Bate, R. (2012) Elective home education: Supporting access to education for children and young people within the Gypsy, Roma and Traveller community. In: J. Visser, H. Daniels, and T. Cole (eds.) *Transforming troubled lives: Strategies and interventions for children with social, emotional and behavioural difficulties*. Bradford: Emerald Group Publishing, p.175–191.

Clebert, J. P. (1961) *The Gypsies*. Harmondsworth: Penguin Books.

Cochran-Smith, M., and Lytle, S. L. (2009) *Inquiry as stance: Practitioner research for the next generation*. New York: Teachers College Press.

Cohen, S. (1985) *Visions of social control: Crime, punishment and classification*. Cambridge: Polity Press.

Collins, P. H. (1994) Shifting the centre: Race, class, and feminist theorizing about motherhood. In: Glenn, E. N., Chang, G., and Forcey, L. R. (eds.) *Mothering: Ideology, experience, and agency*. New York: Routledge, pp. 45–65.

Coxhead, J. (2007) *The last bastion of racism: Gypsies, Travellers and policing*. Stoke on Trent: Trentham Books.

Crenshaw, K. (1991) Mapping the margins: Intersectionality, identity politics, and violence against women of color. *Stanford Law Review*, 43(6), pp. 1241–1299.

Cresswell, J. W. (2007) *Qualitative inquiry and research design: Choose among five approaches.* London: Sage.

Crouch, S. (1996) Race is over. *New York Times.* Available at: http://www. nytimes.com/1996/09/29/magazine/race-i-over.html. Accessed 8 March 2015.

Davis, J., Hill, L., Tisdall, K., Cairns, L., and McCausland, S. (2014) *Social justice, the common weal and children and young people in Scotland.* Jimmy Reid Foundation. Edinburgh: University of Edinburgh.

Dawson, R. (2005) *The 1895 Scottish Traveller Report.* Derbyshire: Dawson and Rackley.

Dearling, A. (1998) *No boundaries: New Travellers on the road outside of England.* Lyme Regis: Enabler Publications.

Dearling, A. (1999) 'Get a life' or 'got a life': New Travellers as a problem or a solution? *Qual-Net*, 1(1), pp. 4–7.

Deleuze, G., and Guattari, F. (1977) *Rhizom* (Vol. 67). Berlin: Merve Verlag.

Derrington, C. (2007) Fight, flight and playing white: An examination of coping strategies adopted by Gypsy Traveller Adolescents in English secondary schools. *International Journal of Educational Research*, 46(6), pp. 357–367.

Deuchar, R., and Bhopal, K. (2017) *Young people and social control: Problems and prospects from the margins.* Basingstoke: Palgrave Macmillan.

Devine, T. M. (1999) *The Scottish nation, 1700–2000.* London: Penguin Books.

Devine, T. M. (ed.) (2000) *Scotland's shame?: Bigotry and sectarianism in modern Scotland.* Edinburgh: Mainstream Publishing Company.

Dodds, N. (1966) *Gypsies, Didikois and other Travellers.* London: Johnson Publications.

Doughty, L. (2014) *Fires in the dark.* London: Faber & Faber.

Douglas, M. (2003) *Purity and danger: An analysis of concepts of pollution and taboo.* London: Routledge.

Douglas, M., and Wildavsky, A. (1982) How can we know the risks we face? why risk selection is a social process. *Risk Analysis*, 2(2), pp. 49–58.

Duffee, D. (1980) *Explaining criminal justice: Community theory and criminal justice reform.* Cambridge, MA: Oelgeschlager, Gunn and Hain.

Duffy, R., and Tomlinson, A. (2009) *Education on the Hoof.* Paper presented to First Centre for Education for Social Justice Seminar at Bishop Grosseteste University College Lincoln (19 January).

European Commission. (2015) *Report on the implementation of the EU Framework for National Roma Integration Strategies: Communication from the Commission to the European Parliament, The Council, The European Economic and Social Committee and the Committee of the Regions.* Available at: https://eurlex.europa.eu/legal-content/EN/TXT/PDF/?uri=CELEX:52015DC0299&qid=1546026375643&from=EN.

Fan, C., and Karnilowicz, W. (1997) Measurement of definitions of success among Chinese and Australian girls. *Journal of Cross-Cultural Psychology*, 28(5), pp. 589–599.

Feder, G. (1990) The politics of Traveller health research. *Critical Public Health*, 1(3), pp. 10–14.

Forrester, B. (1985) *The Travellers' handbook*. London: Interchange Books.

Gadamer, H. G. (1976) *Philosophical hermeneutics*. Berkeley: University of California Press.

Grönfors, M. (1982) From scientific social science to responsible research: The lesson of the Finnish Gypsies. *Acta Sociologica*, 25(3), pp. 249–257.

Grzanka, P. (2014) *Intersectionality: A foundations and frontiers reader*. Boulder: Westview Press.

Haraway, D. (1988) Situated knowledges: The science question in feminism and the privilege of partial perspective. *Feminist Studies*, 14(3), pp. 575–599.

hooks, B. (1981) *Ain't I a woman: Black women and feminism*. Boston: South End Press.

hooks, B. (1994) Teaching to Transgress: Education as the Practice of Freedom. *Journal of Engineering Education*, 1, pp. 126–138.

hooks, B. (2003) *Teaching community: A pedagogy of hope* (Vol. 36). London: Psychology Press.

hooks, B. (2015) *Feminist theory: From margin to center*. London: Routledge.

James, Z. (2007) Policing marginal spaces: Controlling Gypsies and Travellers. *Criminology & Criminal Justice*, 7(4), pp. 367–389.

Jarman, E., and Jarman, A. O. H. (1991) *The Welsh Gypsies: Children of Abram Wood*. Cardiff: University of Wales Press.

Jordan, E. (2000) Outside the mainstream: Social exclusion in mobile families from home-school partnerships. *Scottish School Board Association*, Dumfries: Millennium Books.

Kaplan, A. (2005) *The anarchy of empire in the making of US culture*. Cambridge: Harvard University Press.

Kaplan, E. A. (1997) *Looking for the other: Feminism, film, and the imperial gaze*. New York: Routledge.

Kiddle, C. (1981) Gypsy women and the land. *Heresies*, 4(1), pp. 26–30.

Ladson-Billings, G. (1996) Silences as weapons: Challenges of a Black professor teaching White students. *Theory Into Practice*, 35(2), pp. 79–85.

Ladson-Billings, G. (2009) *The dreamkeepers: Successful teachers of African American children*. San Francisco: Wiley.

Lee, K. W., and Warren, W. G. (1991) Alternative education: Lessons from gypsy thought and practice. *British Journal of Educational Studies*, 39(3), pp. 311–324.

Lewis, A. (1992) Group child interviews as a research tool. *British Educational Research Journal*, 18(4), pp. 413–421.

Liégeois, J.-P. (1986) *Gypsies: An illustrated history*. London: Al-Saaqi.

Liégeois, J.-P. (1994) *Roma, Gypsies, Travellers*. Strasbourg: The Council of Europe.

Lloyd, G. (2005) *Problem girls: Understanding and supporting troubled and troublesome girls and young women*. London: Psychology Press.

Lloyd, G., and McCluskey, G. (2008) Education and Gypsies/Travellers: 'Contradictions and significant silences'. *International Journal of Inclusive Education*, 12(4), pp. 331–345.

Lloyd, G., and Norris, C. (1998) From difference to deviance: The exclusion of Gypsy-Traveller children from school in Scotland. *International Journal of Inclusive Education*, 2(4), pp. 359–369.

Lloyd, G., and Stead, J. (2001) 'The boys and girls not calling me names and the teachers to believe me'. Name calling and the experiences of travellers in school. *Children and Society*, 15(5), pp. 361–374.

Lloyd, G., Stead, J., Jordan, E., and Norris, C. (1999) Teachers and Gypsy Travellers. *Scottish Educational Review*, 31(1), pp. 48–65.

Mackenzie, A. (1883 [2012]) *The History of the Highland clearances*, Lenox, MA: Hard Press Publishing.

Mandla vs. Dowell-Lee [1983] UKHL 7, (1983) 2 AC 548.

McKinney, R. (2003) Views from the margins: Gypsy/Travellers and the ethnicity debate in the new Scotland. *Scottish Affairs*, 42 (Winter), pp. 13–31.

MECOPP, Lloyd, M., and Ross, P. (eds.) (2014) *Moving Minds: Gypsy/Travellers in Scotland*. Edinburgh: MECOPP.

Mekdjian, S. (2015) Mapping mobile borders: Critical cartographies of borders based on migration experiences. In: Szary, A. A., and Giraut, F. (eds.) *Borderities and the politics of contemporary mobile borders*. London: Palgrave Macmillan, pp. 204–223.

Mies, M. (1983) Towards a methodology for feminist research. In: Bowles, G., and Klein, R. (eds.) *Theories of women's studies*. London: Routledge and Kegan Paul, pp. 117–139.

Mirza, H. S., and Gunaratnam, Y. (2014) 'The branch on which I sit': Reflections on black British feminism. *Feminist Review*, 108(1), pp. 125–133.

Moray House School of Education. (2012) Moray House School of Education Student Application Form. Available at: http://atate.org/mscel/assignments/Dissertation-Ethics-Form-Tate.pdf. Accessed 5 January 2013.

Myers, M., and Bhopal, K. (2009) Gypsy, Roma and Traveller children in schools: Understandings of community and safety. *British Journal of Educational Studies*, 57(4), pp. 417–434.

Myers, M., and Bhopal, K. (2018) *Home schooling and home education: Race, class and inequality*. London: Routledge.

National Association of Teachers of Travellers (NATT). (2015) Gypsy Roma Traveller history month: Myths and truths. Available at: http://grthm.natt.org.uk/myths-and-truths.php. Accessed 3 September 2014.

Nisbet, I. (2014a, 21 May) Personal communication. Head of Education Law, Govan Law Centre, Lecture, TENET Seminar.

Nisbet, I. (2014b, 2 September) Personal communication. Head of Education Law, Govan Law Centre, Recorded Interview.

O'Hanlon, C., and Holmes, P. (2004) *The education of Gypsy and Traveller children: Towards inclusion and educational achievement*. Stoke on Trent: Trentham Books.

Parry, G., Van Cleemput, P., Peters, J., and Moore, J. et al. (2004) *The Health Status of Gypsies and Travellers in England*. Sheffield: University of Sheffield.

Pillow, W. (2003) Confession, catharsis, or cure? Rethinking the uses of reflexivity as methodological power in qualitative research. *International Journal of Qualitative Studies in Education*, 16(2), pp. 175–196.

Razack, S. (ed.). (2002) *Race, space, and the law: Unmapping a White Settler Society*. Toronto: Between the Lines.

Reay, D., and Ball, S. J. (1998) 'Making their minds up': Family dynamics of school choice. *British Educational Research Journal*, 24(4), pp. 431–448.

Ridge, M., and Yin-Har Lau, A. (2011) Addressing the impact of social exclusion on mental health in Gypsy, Roma, and Traveller communities. *Mental Health and Social Inclusion*, 15(3), pp. 129–137.

Reid, S. (2008) *Never to return*. Edinburgh: Black and White Publishing.

Samantrai, R. (2002) *AlterNatives: Black feminism in the postimperial nation*. Stanford: Stanford University Press.

Save the Children Scotland. (2005) *Having our say*. Available at: http://www. gypsy-Traveller.org/your-family/young-people/educational-reports-and-re-sources. Accessed November 2012.

Scottish Centre for Social Research. (2015) Scottish Social Attitudes Survey 2015 [Online]. Available at: https://www.gov.scot/publications/scottish-so-cial-attitudes-2015-attitudes-discrimination-positive-action/. Accessed 10 October 2016.

Scottish Executive. (2007) Advisory Committee on Scotland's Travelling People's. Appendix C Advisory Committee Recommendations 1971–1999. Publication date November 21, 2000. Available at: https://www2.gov.scot/Publications/2007/05/22093426/16. Accessed 24 February 2013.

Seagrave, J. (1996) Defining community policing. *American Journal of Police*, 15(2), pp. 1–22.

Sennett, R. (2003) *Research in a world of inequality*. London: W. W. Norton.

Sime, D., and Fox, R. (2014) Home abroad: Eastern European children's fam-ily and peer relationships after migration. *Childhood*, 22(3), pp. 377–393.

Sinclair, P. (1993) Casting out the outcasts. *Geographical Magazine*, March, pp. 14–18.

Smith, J. (2002) *Jessie's journey: Autobiography of a Traveller girl* (Vol. 1). Edinburgh: Birlinn Ltd.

Smith, J. (2006) *Bruar's rest*. Edinburgh: Mercat Press.

Smith, J. (2008) *Tales from the tent*. Edinburgh: Birlinn Ltd.

Smith, J. (2012a) *Way of the wanderers: The story of Travellers in Scotland*. Edinburgh: Birlinn Ltd.

Smith, J. (2012b) *Tears for a Tinker: Jessie's journey concludes* (Vol. 3). Edinburgh: Birlinn Ltd.

Smith, J. (2013) *Sookin' Berries*. Edinburgh: Birlinn Ltd.

Stewart, M. (1992) Gypsies at the horse-fair: A non-market model of trade. In: Dilley, R. (ed.) *Contesting markets*. Edinburgh: Edinburgh University Press.

Stewart, M. (1997) *The time of the Gypsies*. Oxford: Westview Press.

Stewart, M. (2012) *Gypsy 'menace'*. London: Hurst and Company.

Stewart, S. (2006) *Queen among the heather: The life of Belle Stewart*. Edinburgh: Birlinn Ltd.

Stewart, S. (2008) *Pilgrims of the mist: The stories of Scotland's Travelling people*. Edinburgh: Birlinn Ltd.

Surdu, M. (2016) *Those who count: Expert practices of Roma classification*. Budapest: Central European University Press.

Taylor, Charles. (1994) The politics of recognition. In Goldberg D. T. (ed.) *Multiculturalism: A Critical Reader*. Oxford: Blackwell, pp. 75–106.

The Encyclopaedia Britannica. (1954) *Gypsy*, p. 852.

The Encyclopaedia Britannica. (1974) *Slang in European Languages*, pp. 852–853f.

Thompson, T. W. (1928) Gleanings from constables' accounts and other sources. *Romani Studies*, 7(1), pp. 30–48.

Tobler, C. A. (2012) *Breathing it in: The musical identity of the Scottish Travellers*. Unpublished PhD thesis, Baltimore: University of Maryland Press.

Tong, D. (1998) *Gypsies: An interdisciplinary reader*. London: Taylor & Francis.

Turner, R. (2000) Gypsies and politics in Britain. *The Political Quarterly*, 71(1), pp. 68–77.

UNCRC. (2016) *Concluding observations on the fifth periodic report of the United Kingdom of Great Britain and Northern Ireland*. Available at: http://www.crae.org.uk/media/93148/UK-concluding-observations-2016.pdf. Accessed 14 January 2017.

Vavrus, M. (2012) Diversity: A contested concept. In: Banks, J. (ed.) *Encyclopedia of diversity in education volume 2*. Los Angeles: Sage, pp. 667–676.

Virdee, S. (1997) Racial harassment. In: Modood, T. et al. (ed.) *Ethnic minorities in Britain: Diversity and disadvantage*. London: Policy Studies Institute.

Walkerdine, V., Lucey, H., and Melody, J. (2001) *Growing up girl: Psycho-social explorations of gender and class*. London: Palgrave Macmillan.

Williamson, D. (1994) *The Horsieman: Memories of a Traveller 1928–1958*. Edinburgh: Canongate Press.

Whyte, B. (2000) *Red rowans and wild honey*. Edinburgh: Birlinn Ltd.

Whyte, B. (2001) *The yellow on the broom: The early days of a Traveller woman*. Edinburgh: Birlinn Publishers.

Whyte, D. (2001) *Scottish Gypsies and other Travellers: A short history*. Alfreton: Robert Dawson.

Yoors, J. (1967) *The Gypsies*. London: Allen & Unwin.

Young, M. (1999) *Unwanted journey. Why Central European Roma are fleeing to the UK*. London: Refugee Council.

Index

© The Editor(s) (if applicable) and The Author(s) 2019
G. Marcus, *Gypsy and Traveller Girls*, Studies in Childhood and Youth,
https://Doi.org/10.1007/978-3-030-03703-1

N

Nacken 8
naïve egalitarianism 81
New Age Travellers 16, 18
Nomad 7, 28, 31, 35, 43, 52, 53,
    115, 238
Nomadism 7, 31, 35, 36, 45, 46, 87
Non-attendance 87, 88, 117, 164,
    175, 187, 195, 211, 226, 230,
    231, 235
Non-performativity 92, 95
Non-Travellers 30, 35, 36, 88, 94,
    153, 154, 165, 166, 212, 213,
    220, 221, 234, 235, 240, 243,
    266, 302, 304, 305, 310, 311

O

Oppression 10, 16, 38, 43, 55, 59–61,
    108–117, 119, 168, 184, 203,
    216, 224, 225, 232, 235, 238,
    239, 244, 250, 277, 278, 297
Organisation for Economic
    Cooperation and Development
    (OECD) 6
Othering 29, 92, 114

P

Pakistani 241, 256, 285
Partial perspectives 131
Passivity 12, 122–124, 183, 206
Patriarchy 4, 10, 37, 49, 59–61, 91,
    92, 117, 184, 195, 212, 214,
    218, 219, 225, 229, 244, 245,
    249, 257, 258, 275, 282, 287,
    295–297
Pigmentary privilege 116

Pike 33, 34
Pikey 33, 158, 159
Planning 20, 45, 54, 122, 123, 210,
    220, 307, 308, 312
Play 112, 115, 138, 147, 160, 174,
    178, 187, 206, 220, 224, 240,
    242, 250, 254, 293
Politics 41, 92, 108, 109, 112, 120,
    131
Porajmos 34, 48
Power 4, 12, 38, 40, 45, 55, 59, 60,
    80, 92, 107, 108, 110–116,
    124, 126, 127, 130, 131, 138,
    164, 185, 194–196, 204, 212,
    216, 222, 225, 229, 235, 236,
    240, 243, 244, 250, 258, 288,
    295, 297
Pseudonym 129

R

Race 2, 8, 10–14, 16, 33, 35, 37, 41,
    60, 61, 80–83, 89, 109–112,
    114–117, 119, 127, 161, 184,
    185, 188, 194, 219, 222, 226,
    238, 239, 244, 249, 250, 258,
    277, 279, 282, 285, 287–289,
    291, 294
Race equality 8, 83, 94
Race Equality Statement 8
Race Relations Act (1976, 2000) 12,
    16
Racial discrimination 5, 83, 162,
    182, 184, 190, 191, 244, 266,
    296, 308
Racism 10–15, 29, 50, 77, 81, 83,
    86, 88, 93, 95, 109, 110, 116,
    117, 123, 127, 128, 131, 138,

Lightning Source UK Ltd.
Milton Keynes UK
UKHW021125110719
345940UK00002B/170/P